MW01055339

Expressionism in Philosophy: Spinoza

Translated by Martin Joughin

Expressionism in Philosophy: Spinoza

Gilles Deleuze

ZONE BOOKS · NEW YORK

1992

© 1990 Urzone, Inc.

ZONE BOOKS

1226 Prospect Avenue

Brooklyn, NY 11218

First Paperback Edition
Fifth Printing 2013

Originally published in France as *Spinoza et le problème de
l'expression* © 1968 Les Editions de Minuit.

Printed in the United States of America.

Distributed by The MIT Press,
Cambridge, Massachusetts, and London, England

Library of Congress Cataloging-in-Publication Data

Deleuze, Gilles
    [Spinoza et le problème de l'expression. English.]
    Expressionism in philosophy: Spinoza / Gilles Deleuze;
translated by Martin Joughin.
        p.   cm.
    Includes bibliographical references and index.
    ISBN 978-0-942299-51-9 (pbk.)
    1. Spinoza, Benedictus de, 1632–1677—Contributions
in concept of expression. 2. Expression. I. Title.

B3999.E9D4513 1990
199'.492—dc19
                                88-20607

Contents

Translator's Preface

"We discover new ways of folding...but we are always folding, unfolding, refolding": so ends *Le Pli*, Deleuze's latest book, on Leibniz, his first major historical study of a philosopher since the present book was published twenty years before. Here the main text closes: "It is hard, in the end, to say which is more important: the differences between Leibniz and Spinoza in their evaluation of expression; or their common reliance on this concept in founding a Postcartesian philosophy." Spinoza and Leibniz: two different expressions of "expressionism in philosophy," an expressionism characterized in this book as a system of *implicatio* and *explicatio*, enfolding and unfolding, implication and explication, implying and explaining, involving and evolving, enveloping and developing. Two systems of universal folding: Spinoza's unfolded from the bare "simplicity" of an Infinity into which all things are ultimately folded up, as into a universal map that folds back into a single point; while Leibniz starts from the infinite points in that map, each of which enfolds within its infinitely "complex" identity all its relations with all other such points, the unfolding of all these infinite relations being the evolution of a Leibnizian Universe.

We are always involved in things and their implications and

5

developments, always ourselves developing in our bodily "enve-lope," always explaining and implying. In Spinoza's Latin the distinctions between these various ways of being enfolded in a universal "complication" or complexity of things are borne by the different contexts, mental, physical, and so on, in which *implicare,* *explicare,* and their derivatives are used. An English translator must often identify the implicit or explicit context of a particular use of one of these words and choose between, say, "imply," "impli-cate," "enfold" – or "explain," "explicate," "unfold" – while Deleuze can retain in the French *impliquer* and *expliquer* several of the multiple senses of the Latin. The English language has developed differently from the French language. It has integrated Latin and Germanic roots, where French has unfolded directly from Latin. And this double system of English roots has allowed a splitting of senses in the language of "folding" itself, so that a Germanic vocabulary of "folds" must often be used in external, physical, contexts, and one can only talk of a universal "folding" of thoughts and things metaphorically. But what then becomes, in English translation, of Deleuze's attempt to organize Spinoza's Universe of internal Thought and external Extension in terms of an "unfolding" of which the distinction of "inner" and "outer" sides of things (ideas and bodies) is precisely the initial fold?

The problem does not end with folding itself, but becomes more complex as the discussion extends to a general dynamics of Spin-oza's system. Thus while the Latin *comprehendere* and the French *comprendre* cover both the "mental" sense of understanding (con-taining or comprehending in thought) and the "physical" sense of comprising, including (containing, "properly speaking"), an English translator must either stretch his language beyond break-ing point in an attempt to find some term (say, "comprehend") to cover both "sides" of the Latin or French word (everywhere substituting it, then, for "understand," "include," "comprise"), or simply ask the reader to try to constantly bear in mind that both sorts of containment are always to be understood as corresponding to a single "term" of the exposition, a term whose single grammar or expressive logic must be understood as organizing the relations of the two English "sides" of the term throughout the book.

Then consider the Latin couple *involvere* and *evolvere*: an order of continuous "turning" inward and outward, involution and evolution, rather than the elementary order of folds. The French *envelopper* covers both abstract and physical senses of "involving" and "enveloping" or (once more) "enfolding." (Just to complicate matters further, the "envelope" which is the human body, later identified by Deleuze as the primary "fold" of internal subjective space in external visible space, is linked in French to that order of folding by the fact that *pli* and *enveloppe* are two names for the "envelope" in which we enfold things we send through the postal system.)

Is this all a case of a seductive metaphor being finally neutralized in English, once the implicit divergences of the "mental" and "physical" grammars of folding in Latin and French are at last made explicit? The metaphorical use of the language of "folding" would then amount (in a familiar analysis) to a partial transposition or translation of the logic of some term ("fold," say) from its true or proper linguistic context (all the sentences in which it can properly occur, with all their implications and explications) into some only partly or superficially similar "analogous" context. English might then be said to have developed in accordance with the Scholastic project of systematically distinguishing between the multiple senses of "equivocal" words, in order to construct a complete logic of true (as opposed to specious) implications

7

and explications – with the "technical" or formal use of words like "mode" (for example) properly distinguished from the imprecise informal use of the Latin *modus* or French *mode*, informally rendered in English as "manner," "way."

Deleuze's reconstruction of Spinoza's system as a logic of *expression* is diametrically opposed to such a conception of "equivocation." Curley does not list (the "equivocal," "informal") *exprimere* as a "systematic" term in his glossary, and most commentators, as Deleuze notes in his Introduction, have also passed over this term in their reconstructions of the "logic" of the system. Deleuze's use of a disregarded term as the principal axis of his reconstruction of a philosophical or literary system had already characterized his earlier studies of Nietzsche and Proust (and has analogies with, say, Barthes' contemporary reading of Racine "in terms of" solar imagery, which so scandalized the Old Criticism). Indeed the language of "folding," and an insistence upon the "metaphorical" multiplicity of sense as *prior* to any projected unitary logical syntax, had already been applied in the 1964 reading of Proust. And in the *Logic of Sense* that followed the present study of Spinoza we find Deleuze inverting the traditional figures of metaphorical use as a partial transposition or translation of a given logic or grammar from its true context to some partly similar context, and of metaphor or analogy "breaking down" at some point where the logic of the two contexts diverges. Words are there considered as "multiplicities" of sense, with no stable "home" context, no primary identity: as transferrable among multiple contexts to produce various patterns of relations between things as their essentially incomplete grammars or logics unfold in interaction with those of other words. Already in *Difference and Repetition*, published jointly with the present book, it was precisely

8

the "breakdown" of the traditional logic of identity that organized fundamental "divergences" or radical differences as the prime dimensionality or structure of unfolding experience.

Deleuze's thought evolved from his first book (on Hume, 1953) down to the present work in a series of historical studies (on Nietzsche, Kant, Proust, Bergson and Sacher-Masoch). In each of these the development of a "philosophy" is traced from some version of an initial situation where some term in our experience diverges from its apparent relations with some other terms, breaking out of that "space" of relations and provoking a reflection in which we consider reorientations or reinscriptions of this and other terms within a "virtual" matrix of possible unfoldings of these terms and their relations in time. As reflection confronts wider and wider systems of relations it proceeds toward the inscription of all experience within the unchanging figure of unfolding Time itself – that is, in Eternity. Such a "philosophy" comes full-circle when the "subject," as that term in our experience which is the locus of orientation of the space of present appearances within the virtual matrix of all unfolding in time, "orients" its own practical activity of interpretation, evaluation or orientation of the terms of experience within this universal matrix it has itself unfolded.

This figure of a practical and empirical "philosophy," unfolded through the sequence of earlier studies, here finds a systematic and symmetric exposition in terms of "folding" itself, as a system of universal "expression." But Spinoza sets out this system "beginning with Infinity," beginning from the bare or otherwise indeterminate form of predication, attribution or determination itself. In *Difference and Repetition* Deleuze sought to present the universal "folding" of experience beginning rather with the finite terms of the initial situation of reflection – beginning, so to speak, with the plurality of finite modes rather than the abstract unity of substance. But the form of his presentation there (as, together with this study, one of two theses submitted in order to become eligible for a professorial chair in the old French university system) was organized by what he has since called the abstract textual code of the History of Philosophy: it was institutionally abstracted from that dramatic interplay of discursive text and external context already implicit in the insistence here on the radical "expressive" parallelism of internal Thought and external Extension, as articulated in the rhetorical orientation of Spinoza's logic in the "practical" apparatus of the scholia (and reflected in Spinoza's own dramatic embedding of biblical text in historical context in the *Theologico-Political Treatise*). This book and the companion thesis may thus be seen to prepare the transition from an abstract treatment of historical schemes of experience into the "dramatization" of reflection first manifested in the general scenography of *Capitalism and Schizophrenia*, as Deleuze's logic is embedded in the rhetorical apparatus of Guattari's critique of the coupled repression (rather than expression) of inner and outer worlds. A second series of Deleuzian reflections unfolds from this "scenography" of History toward its universal dramatic frame, moving from a discursive confrontation with the visual space of a Bacon painting, and with a visual space-time articulated in the kinetics or kinematics of twentieth-century experience, through the Foucauldian figure of the radical "folding" of inner in outer worlds that articulates the dynamic of Western subjectivity, to a new coordination of the "internal" logical or psychological folding of experience with the correlative external space of visible relations (Deleuze once more finding in Leibniz, as he had in *Difference and Repetition*, a primary model for the inversion of the relations of infinite Substance and finite modes).

This second series of reflections will, it seems, once more conclude with Spinoza. Deleuze, discussing with the translator the place of *Expressionism in Philosophy* in his development, writes:

"What interested me most in Spinoza wasn't his Substance, but the composition of finite modes. I consider this one of the most original aspects of my book. That is: the hope of making substance turn on finite modes, or at least of seeing in substance a *plane of immanence* in which finite modes operate, already appears in this book. What I needed was both (1) the expressive character of particular individuals, and (2) an immanence of being. Leibniz, in a way, goes still further than Spinoza on the first point. But on the second, Spinoza stands alone. One finds it only in him. This is why I consider myself a Spinozist, rather than a Leibnizian, although I owe a lot to Leibniz. In the book I'm writing at the moment, *What is Philosophy?*, I try to return to this problem of absolute immanence, and to say why Spinoza is for me the 'prince' of philosophers."

Expressivist traditions in Proport, religion

INTRODUCTION /3-22

The Role and Importance

of Expression

absolute ∞ consisting of
∞ of attributes
Each attribute expresses an eternal and ∞ essence
expresses the essence of substance
being or reality
substantial
existence
eternity

The idea of expression appears in the first Part of the *Ethics* as
early as the sixth Definition: "By God I understand a being abso- ∞ *w/∞∞*
lutely infinite, that is, a substance consisting of an infinity of attributes, of which each one *expresses* an eternal and infinite essence."
The idea goes on to develop increasing importance. It is taken
up again in various contexts. Thus Spinoza says that each attribute expresses *a certain* infinite and eternal *essence*, an essence
corresponding to that particular kind of attribute. Or: each attribute expresses the *essence* of substance, its being or reality. Or *emanat*ⁿ
again: each attribute expresses the infinity and necessity of substantial *existence*, that is, expresses eternity.[1] He also shows how
to pass from each of these formulations to the others. Thus each
attribute expresses an essence, insofar as it expresses in one form[a]
the essence of substance; and since the essence of substance necessarily involves existence, it belongs to each attribute to express,
together with God's essence, his eternal existence.[2] At the same
time the idea of expression contains within it all the difficulties
relating to the unity of substance and the diversity of its attributes. The expressive nature of attributes thus appears as one of
the basic themes of the first Part of the *Ethics*.

Modes are, in their turn, expressive: "Whatever exists ex-

Substance
attributes
modes (modus)

presses the nature or essence of God in a certain and determinate way" (that is, in a certain mode).[3,b] So we must identify a second level of expression: an expression, as it were, of expression itself. Substance first expresses itself in its attributes, each attribute expressing an essence. But then attributes express themselves in their turn: they express themselves in their subordinate modes, each such mode expressing a modification of the attribute. As we will see, the first level of expression must be understood as the very constitution, a genealogy almost, of the essence of substance. The second must be understood as the very production of particular things. Thus God produces an infinity of things because his essence is infinite; but having an infinity of attributes, he necessarily produces these things in an infinity of modes, each of which must be referred to an attribute to which it belongs.[4] Expression is not of itself production, but becomes such on its second level, as attributes in their turn express themselves. Conversely, expression as production is grounded in a prior expression. God expresses himself in himself "before" expressing himself in his effects: expresses himself by in himself constituting *natura naturans*, before expressing himself through producing within himself *natura naturata*.

The range of the notion of expression is not merely ontological; its implications are also epistemological.[c] This is hardly surprising, for ideas are modes of Thought: "Singular thoughts, or this or that thought, are modes which express God's nature in a certain and determinate way."[5] So knowledge becomes a sort of expression. The knowledge of things bears the same relation to the knowledge of God as the things themselves to God: "Since without God nothing can exist or be conceived, it is evident that all natural phenomena *involve and express* the conception of God as far as their essence and perfection extend, so that we have greater and more perfect knowledge of God in proportion to our

14

knowledge of natural phenomena."[6] The idea of God is expressed in all our ideas as their source and their cause, so that ideas as a whole exactly reproduce the order of Nature as a whole. And ideas, in turn, express the essence, nature or perfection of their objects: a thing's definition or idea is said to express the thing's nature as it is in itself. Ideas are all the more perfect, the more reality or perfection they express in their object; ideas which the mind forms "absolutely" thus express infinity.[7] The mind conceives things *sub specie aeternitatis*[d] through having an idea that expresses the body's essence from this point of view.[8] Spinoza's conception of the adequacy of ideas seems always to involve this expressive character. From the *Short Treatise* onward he was seeking a conception of knowledge that would account for it, not as some operation on an object that remained outside it, but as a reflection, an expression, of an object in the mind. This requirement persists in the *Ethics*, albeit understood in a new way. In neither case can it suffice to say that truth is simply present in ideas. We must go on to ask what it is that is present in a true idea. What expresses itself in a true idea? What does it express? If Spinoza advances beyond the Cartesian conception of clarity and distinctness to form his theory of adequacy, he does so, once again, in terms of this problem of expression.

The word "express" has various synonyms. The Dutch text of the *Short Treatise* does employ *uytdrukken* and *uytbeelden* (to express), but shows a preference for *vertoonen* (at once to manifest and to demonstrate): a thinking being *expresses* itself in an infinity of ideas corresponding to an infinity of objects; but the idea of the body directly *manifests* God; and attributes *manifest themselves* in themselves.[9] In the *Correction of the Understanding* attributes manifest (*ostendunt*) God's essence.[10] But such synonyms are less significant than the correlates that accompany and further specify the idea of expression: *explicare* and *involvere*. Thus definition is said not only to express the nature of what is defined, but to *involve* and *explicate* it.[11] Attributes not only express the essence of substance: here they explicate it, there they involve it.[12] Modes involve the concept of God as well as expressing it, so the ideas that correspond to them involve, in their turn, God's eternal essence.[13]

To explicate is to evolve, to involve is to implicate. Yet the two terms are not opposites: they simply mark two aspects of expression. Expression is on the one hand an explication, an unfolding of what expresses itself,[e] the One manifesting itself in the Many (substance manifesting itself in its attributes, and these attributes manifesting themselves in their modes). Its multiple expression, on the other hand, involves Unity. The One remains involved in what expresses it, imprinted in what unfolds it, immanent in whatever manifests it: expression is in this respect an involvement. There is no conflict between the two terms, except in one specific case which we will deal with later, in the context of finite modes and their passions.[14] Expression in general involves and implicates what it expresses, while also explicating and evolving it.

Implication and explication, involution and evolution[f]: terms inherited from a long philosophical tradition, always subject to the charge of pantheism. Precisely because the two concepts are not opposed to one another, they imply a principle of synthesis: *complicatio*. In Neoplatonism *complication* often means at once the inherence of multiplicity in the One, and of the One in the Many. God is Nature taken "complicatively"; and this Nature both explicates and implicates, involves and evolves God. God "complicates" everything, but all things explain and involve him. The interplay of these notions, each contained in the other, constitutes expression, and amounts to one of the characteristic figures of Christian and Jewish Neoplatonism as it evolved through the

Middle Ages and Renaissance. Thus expression has been taken to be a basic category of Renaissance thought.[15] In Spinoza, Nature at once comprises and contains everything, while being explicated and implicated in each thing. Attributes involve and explicate substance, which in turn comprises all attributes. Modes involve and explicate the attribute on which they depend, while the attribute in turn contains the essences of all its modes. We must ask how Spinoza fits into an expressionist tradition, to what extent his position derives from it, and how he transforms it.

The question takes on added importance from the fact that Leibniz also took expression as one of his basic concepts. In Leibniz as in Spinoza expression has theological, ontological and epistemological dimensions. It organizes their theories of God, of creatures and of knowledge. Independently of one another the two philosophers seem to rely on the idea of expression in order to overcome difficulties in Cartesianism, to restore a Philosophy of Nature, and even to incorporate Cartesian results in systems thoroughly hostile to Descartes's vision of the world. To the extent that one may speak of the Anticartesianism of Leibniz and Spinoza, such Anticartesianism is grounded in the idea of expression.

If the idea of expression is so important, at once for an understanding of Spinoza's system, for determining its relation to that of Leibniz, and as bearing on the origin and development of the two systems, then why have the most respected commentators taken so little, if any, account of this notion in Spinoza's philosophy? Some completely ignore it. Others give it a certain indirect significance, seeing in it another name for some deeper principle. Thus expression is taken to be synonymous with "emanation": an approach that may already be found in Leibniz's criticism that Spinoza understood expression in cabalistic terms, reducing it to a sort of emanation.[16] Or expression is taken as another word for *explication*. Postkantian philosophers would seem to have been well placed to recognize the presence in Spinozism of that genetic movement of self-development for which they sought anticipations everywhere. But the term "explication" confirmed their view that Spinoza had been no more able to conceive a true evolution of substance, than to think through the transition from infinite to finite. Spinoza's substance seemed to them lifeless, his expression intellectual and abstract, his attributes "attributed" to substance by an understanding that was itself "explicative."[17] Even Schelling, developing his philosophy of manifestation (*Offenbarung*), claimed to be following Boehme, rather than Spinoza: it was in Boehme, rather than in Spinoza or even Leibniz, that he found the idea of expression (*Ausdruck*).

But one cannot reduce expression to the mere explication of understanding without falling into anachronism. For explication, far from amounting to the operation of an understanding that remains outside its object, amounts primarily to the object's own evolution, its very life. The traditional couple of *explicatio* and *complicatio* historically reflects a vitalism never far from pantheism. Rather than expression being comprehensible in terms of explication, explication in Spinoza as in his forerunners seems to me to depend on some idea of expression. If attributes must in principle be referred to an understanding that perceives or comprehends them, this is primarily because they express the essence of substance, and infinite essence cannot be expressed without being "objectively" manifest in divine understanding. It is expression that underlies the relation of understanding between thought and object, rather than the reverse. As for emanation, one does of course find traces of this, as of participation, in Spinoza. The theory of expression and explication was after all developed, in the Renaissance as in the Middle Ages, by authors steeped in Neoplatonism. Yet its goal, and its result, was to thoroughly transform such Neoplatonism, to open it up to quite new lines of development, far removed from those of emanation, even where the two themes were both present. I would further claim that emanation hardly helps us understand the idea of expression, but that the idea of expression explains how Neoplatonism developed to the point where its very nature changed, explains, in particular, how emanative causes tended more and more to become immanent ones.

Some recent commentators have directly considered the idea of expression in Spinoza. Kaufmann sees in it a guiding thread through the "Spinozist labyrinth," but he insists upon the mystical and aesthetic character of the notion in general, independently of the use made of it by Spinoza.[18] Darbon, from a different viewpoint, devotes a fine passage to expression, but finally judges it incomprehensible: "To explain the unity of substance, Spinoza tells us only that each attribute expresses its essence. The explanation, far from being any help, raises a host of difficulties. In the first place, *what is expressed* ought to be different from what expresses itself. . . ." And Darbon concludes that "Each attribute expresses the eternal and infinite essence of God; again we cannot distinguish between *what is expressed* and *what it expresses*. One sees how difficult a task the commentator faces, and how the question of the relations between Spinozist substance and attributes could have given rise to so many divergent interpretations."[19]

One can, though, explain this difficulty: The idea of expression is neither defined nor deduced by Spinoza, nor could it be. It appears as early as the sixth Definition, but is there no more defined than it serves to define anything. It defines neither substance nor attribute, since these are already defined (Definitions 3 and 4). Nor God, who might equally well be defined without reference to expression. Thus in the *Short Treatise* and in his correspondence Spinoza often calls God a substance consisting of an infinity of attributes, each of which is infinite.[20] So the idea of expression seems to emerge only as determining the relation into which attribute, substance and essence enter, once God for his part is defined as a substance consisting of an infinity of attributes that are themselves infinite. Expression does not relate to substance or attributes in general, in the abstract. When substance is absolutely infinite, when it has an infinity of attributes, then, and only then, are its attributes said to express its essence, for only then does substance express itself in its attributes. It would be wrong to invoke Definitions 3 and 4 in order to deduce directly from them the relation between substance and attribute in God, because God himself "transforms" their relation, rendering it absolute. *Definitions 3 and 4 are merely nominal, the sixth Definition alone is a real one*, with real consequences for substance, attribute and essence. But what is this "transformation of relations"? We will better understand it if we consider why expression is no more deduced than it is defined.

To Tschirnhaus, worried about the famous sixteenth Proposition of Part One of the *Ethics*, Spinoza concedes the important point that there is a fundamental difference between philosophical demonstration and mathematical proof.[21] From a definition a mathematician can normally deduce only a single property of the object defined; to know several properties he must introduce new points of view and relate "the thing defined to other objects." Geometrical method is thus doubly limited, by the externality of its viewpoints and the distributive character of the properties it investigates. This was just Hegel's point as, thinking of Spinoza, he insisted that geometrical method was unable to frame the organic movement or self-development that is alone appropriate to the Absolute. Consider for example the proof that the sum of the angles of a triangle is equal to two right angles, where one begins by extending the base of the triangle. The base is

20

hardly like some plant that grows by itself: it takes a mathematician to extend it, just as it is the mathematician who considers
from a new point of view the side of the triangle to which he
draws a line parallel, and so on. We cannot imagine that Spinoza
was unaware of such objections, for they are just those made by
Tschirnhaus.

Spinoza's reply may at first seem disappointing: he says that
when the geometrical method is applied to real entities, and *a
fortiori*, when applied to absolute Being, then we are able to
deduce several properties at once. One might well think that
Spinoza is taking for granted just what is in question. But we are
disappointed only to the extent that we confuse two very different problems of method. Spinoza asks: Is there not some way that
various properties deduced independently might be taken together, and various points of view extrinsic to a given definition
brought within what is defined? Now, in the *Correction of the
Understanding*, Spinoza had shown that geometrical figures may
be defined genetically, or by a proximate cause.[22] A circle is not
only the locus of points equally distant from a fixed point called
the center, but also the figure described by the moving endpoint
of any line whose other endpoint is fixed. Similarly, a sphere is
a figure described by the rotation of any semicircle about its
axis. Of course such causes are in geometry fictitious: *fingo ad
libitum*. As Hegel would say — and Spinoza would agree — a semicircle doesn't rotate by itself. But if such causes are fictitious or
imaginary, it is because their only reality comes by inference from
their supposed effects. They are seen as heuristic devices, as con-
trived, as fictions, because the figures to which they relate are
things of reason. It is nonetheless true that properties that are
deduced independently by the mathematician, take on a collective being through these causes, by means of these fictions.[23]
When we come to the Absolute, however, there is no longer any

fiction: cause is no longer inferred from effect. In taking Absolute Infinity as a cause, we are not postulating, as for a rotating semicircle, something that lies outside its concept. It involves no fiction to consider modes in their infinite variety as properties jointly deduced from the definition of substance, and attributes as points of view internal to the substance on which they are so many views. So that if philosophy is amenable to mathematical treatment, this is because mathematics finds its usual limitations overcome in philosophy. No problem is posed by the application of geometrical method to the Absolute; rather does it there find the natural way to overcome the difficulties that beset it, while applied to things of reason.

Attributes are like points of view on substance; but in the absolute limit these points of view are no longer external, and substance contains within itself the infinity of its points of view upon itself. Its modes are deduced from substance as properties are deduced from a thing's definition; but in the absolute limit, these properties take on an infinite collective being. It is no longer a matter of finite understanding deducing properties singly, reflecting on its object and explicating it by relating it to other objects. It is now the object that expresses itself, the thing itself that explicates itself. All its properties then jointly "fall within an infinite understanding." So that there is no question of deducing Expression: rather is it expression that embeds deduction in the Absolute, renders proof the *direct manifestation* of absolutely infinite substance. One cannot understand attributes without proof, which is the manifestation of the invisible, and the view within which falls what thus manifests itself. Thus demonstrations, says Spinoza, are the eyes through which the mind sees.[24,g]

22

PART ONE

The expressive nature of attributes

The Triads of Substance

substance
attribute
essence

Numerical and Real Distinction

Expression presents us with a triad. In it we must distinguish substance, attributes and essence. Substance expresses itself, attributes are expressions, and essence is expressed. The idea of expression remains unintelligible while we see only two of the terms whose relations it presents. We confuse substance and attribute, attribute and essence, essence and substance, as long as we fail to take into account the presence of a third term linking each pair. Substance and attribute are distinct, but only insofar as each attribute expresses a certain essence. Attribute and essence are distinct, but only insofar as every essence is expressed as an essence of substance, rather than of attribute. The originality of the concept of expression shows itself here: essence, insofar as it has existence, has no existence outside the attribute in which it is expressed; and yet, as essence, it relates only to substance. An essence is expressed by each attribute, but this as an essence of substance itself. Infinite essences are distinguished through the attributes in which they find expression, but are identified in the substance to which they relate. We everywhere confront the necessity of distinguishing three terms: substance which expresses itself, the attribute which expresses, and the essence which is expressed. It is through attributes that essence is distinguished from substance, but through essence that substance is itself distinguished from attributes: a triad each of whose terms serves as a middle term relating the two others, in three syllogisms.

Expression is inherent in substance, insofar as substance is absolutely infinite; in its attributes, insofar as they constitute an infinity; in essence, insofar as each essence in an attribute is infinite. Thus infinity has a nature. Merleau-Ponty has well brought out what seems to us now the most difficult thing to understand in the philosophies of the seventeenth century: the idea of a positive infinity as the "secret of grand Rationalism" – "an innocent way of setting out in one's thinking from infinity," which finds its most perfect embodiment in Spinozism.[1] Innocence does not of course exclude the "labor of the concept." Spinoza needed all the resources of a novel conceptual frame to bring out the power and the actuality of positive infinity. If the idea of expression provided this, it did so by introducing into infinity various distinctions corresponding to the three terms, substance, attribute and essence. What is the character of distinction within infinity? What sort of distinction can one introduce into what is absolute, into the nature of God? Such is the first problem posed by the idea of expression, and it dominates Part One of the *Ethics*.

28 - 34

At the very beginning of the *Ethics* Spinoza asks how two things, in the most general sense of the word, can be distinguished, and then how two substances, in the precise sense of that word, must be distinguished. The first question leads into the second, and the answer to the second question seems unequivocal: if two "things" in general differ either by the attributes of their substance, or by its modes, then two substances cannot differ in mode, but only in attribute. So that there cannot be two or more substances of the same attribute.[2] There is no question that

28

bodily substance

shape   motion

Mental substance

affirmation   memory

Spinoza is here setting out from a Cartesian framework, but what must be most carefully considered is just what he takes over from Descartes, what he discards and, above all, what he takes over from Descartes in order to turn it against him.

The principle that there are only substances and modes, modes being in something else, and substance in itself, may be found quite explicitly in Descartes.[3] And if modes always presuppose a substance, and are sufficient to give us knowledge of it, they do so through a primary attribute which they imply, and which constitutes the essence of the substance itself. Thus two or more substances are distinguished and distinctly known through their primary attributes.[4] From this Descartes deduces that we can conceive a real distinction between two substances, a modal distinction between a substance and a mode that presupposes it (without in turn being presupposed by it) and a distinction of reason between a substance and the attribute without which we could have no distinct knowledge of the substance.[5] Exclusion, unilateral implication and abstraction correspond to these as criteria applicable to corresponding ideas, or rather as the elementary data of representation[a] which allow us to define and recognize these varieties of distinction. The characterization and application of these kinds of distinction play a crucial part in the elaboration of the Cartesian system. Descartes no doubt drew on the earlier efforts made by Suarez to bring order into this complicated area,[6] but his own use of the three distinctions seems, in its very richness, to introduce many further ambiguities.

An initial ambiguity, admitted by Descartes, concerns the distinction of reason, modal distinction and the relation between them. The ambiguity comes out in the use of the words "mode," "attribute" and "quality" themselves. Any given attribute is a quality, in that it qualifies a substance as this or that, but also a mode, in that it diversifies it.[7] How do primary attributes appear

for

Conceptual and ???

in this light? I cannot separate a substance from such an attribute except by abstraction; but as long as I do not make it something subsisting by itself, I can also distinguish such an attribute from the substance, by considering it just as the substance's property of changing (of having, that is to say, various different shapes or different thoughts). Thus Descartes says that extension and thought may be distinctly conceived in two ways: "insofar as one constitutes the nature of body, and the other that of the soul"; and also through distinguishing each from their substance, by taking them simply as "modes" or "dependents."[8] Now, if in the first case attributes distinguish the substances that they qualify, then it surely appears, in the second case, that modes distinguish substances with the same attribute. Thus different shapes may be referred to this or that body, really distinct from any other; and different thoughts to really distinct souls. An attribute constitutes the essence of the substance it qualifies, but this doesn't prevent it from also constituting the essence of the modes which it links to substances sharing the same attribute. This dual aspect generates major difficulties in the Cartesian system.[9] Let it suffice here to note the conclusion that *there exist substances sharing the same attribute. In other words, there are numerical distinctions that are at the same time real or substantial.*

A second difficulty concerns real distinction considered alone. It is, no less than the other forms, a datum of representation. Two things are really distinct if one can conceive one of them clearly and distinctly while excluding everything belonging to the concept of the other. So that Descartes explains the criterion of real distinction to Arnauld as the completeness of the *idea* alone. He can quite rightly claim never to have confused things conceived as really distinct with really distinct things; and yet the passage from one to the other does appear to him to be perfectly legitimate – the question is, where to make this passage. In the prog-

ress of the *Meditations* we need only proceed as far as a divine
Creator to see that he would be singularly lacking in truthfulness
if he were to create things differing from the clear and distinct
ideas he gives us of them. Real distinction does not contain
within it the ground of things differing, but this ground is fur-
nished by the external and transcendent divine causality that creates substances conformably to our manner of conceiving them
as possible. Here again, all sorts of difficulties develop in relation to the idea of creation. The primary ambiguity attaches to
the definition of substance: "A thing that can exist by itself."[10] Is
there not a contradiction in presenting existing-by-itself as itself
being simply a possibility? Here we may note a second conclusion: God as creator effects our passage from substances conceived
as really distinct to really distinct substances. *Real distinction*,
whether between substances with different attributes, or those
with the same attribute, *brings with it a division of things, that is,
a corresponding numerical distinction*.

The opening of the *Ethics* is organized around these two Cartesian conclusions. Where lies the error, Spinoza asks, in supposing several substances sharing the same attribute? He refutes the
error in two ways, using a favorite style of argument: first through
a *reductio ad absurdum*, and then through a more complex proof.
If there were several substances with the same attribute, they
would have to be distinguished by their modes, which is absurd,
since substance is in its very nature anterior to its modes, none
of which it implies (this is the short way, taken at I.5). The positive demonstration comes further on, in a scholium to Proposition 8: two substances with the same attribute would be only
numerically distinct – and the character of numerical distinction
is such as to exclude the possibility of making of it a real or substantial distinction.

According to the Scholium, a distinction would not be numer-

31

ical if the things distinguished did not have the same concept or definition; but in that case the things would not be distinct, were there not an external cause, beside the definition, which determined that they exist in such a number. So that two or more numerically distinct things presuppose something outside their concept. Thus substances could only be numerically distinct through the operation of some external causality that could produce them. But only by holding conjointly a number of confused ideas can we claim that substances are produced. We say they have a cause, but that we do not know how this cause operates; we imagine that we have a true idea of these substances, since they are conceived in themselves, but we are unsure of the truth of this idea, because we do not know, from the substances themselves, whether they exist. This amounts to a criticism of the odd Cartesian formula "what *can* exist by itself." External causality does make sense, but only in relation to the existence of finite modes: every existing mode may be referred to another, precisely because it *cannot* exist by itself. To apply such causality to substance is to make it operate outside the terms that legitimate and define it — to propose its operation in a sort of void, and quite indeterminately. In short, external causality and numerical distinction share the same fate of applying to modes, and to modes alone.

The argument of Scholium 8 has, then, the following form: (1) Numerical distinction requires an external cause to which it may be referred; (2) But a substance cannot be referred to an external cause, because of the contradiction implied in such a use of causal principles; (3) So two or more substances cannot be distinguished *in numero*, and there cannot be two substances with the same attribute. The structure of the argument here differs from that of the first eight proofs, which runs: (1) Two or more substances cannot share the same attribute, for they would then

32

have to be distinguished by their modes, which is absurd; (2) So that a substance cannot have a cause external to it, for to be produced or limited by another substance it would have to share the same nature or the same attribute; (3) So that there cannot be numerical distinction in any substance, of whatever attribute, and "Every substance must be infinite."[11]

On the one hand, one deduces from the nature of numerical distinction that it is inapplicable to substance; on the other, one deduces from the nature of substance its infinity, and thus the impossibility of applying to it numerical distinctions. In either case, numerical distinction can never distinguish substances, but only modes that involve the same attribute. For number expresses in its own way the character of existing modes: the composite nature of their parts, their limitation by other things of the same nature, their determination from outside themselves. Number thus goes on *ad infinitum*. But the question is, can it ever reach infinity itself? Or, as Spinoza puts it: even in the case of modes, is it from the multitude of parts that we infer their infinity?[12] When we make of numerical distinction a real or substantial distinction, we carry it to infinity, if only to ensure the convertibility that then becomes necessary between the attribute as such and the infinity of finite parts which we distinguish in it. Great absurdities then follow: "If an infinite quantity is measured by parts equal to a foot, it will consist of an infinitely many such parts, as it will also, if it is measured by parts equal to an inch. And therefore, one infinite number will be twelve times greater than another."[13] The absurdity does not, as Descartes thought, lie in hypostatizing extension as an attribute, but rather in conceiving it as measurable and composed of finite parts into which one supposes it convertible. Physics here intervenes to support the principles of logic: the absence of a vacuum in nature means simply that division into parts is not real distinction. Numerical

33

distinction is division, but division takes place only in modes, only modes are divisible.[14]

34·37

✓ *There cannot be several substances with the same attribute.* From which one may infer: from the viewpoint of relation, that one substance is not produced by another; from the viewpoint of modality, that it belongs to the nature of substance to exist; and from the viewpoint of quality, that any substance is necessarily infinite.[15] But all these results are, so to speak, involved in the argument relating to numerical distinction, and it is the latter that brings us back around to our starting point: "There exists only one substance of the same attribute."[16] Then, from Proposition 9 on, Spinoza's objective seems to shift. It is no longer a question of demonstrating that there is only one substance for each attribute, but that there is only one substance for all attributes. The passage from one theme to the next seems difficult to grasp. For, in this new perspective, what implication should be assigned to the first eight propositions? The problem is clarified if we see that the passage from one theme to the other may be effected by what is called in logic the conversion of a negative universal. Numerical distinction is never real; then conversely, real distinction is never numerical. Spinoza's argument now becomes: attributes are really distinct; but real distinction is never numerical; so there is only one substance for all attributes.

Spinoza says that attributes are "conceived to be really distinct."[17] One should not see in this formulation a weakened sense of real distinction. Spinoza is neither suggesting that attributes are other than we conceive them, nor that they are just conceptions we have of substance. Nor indeed should we think that he is making a purely hypothetical or polemical use of real distinc-

34

tion.[18] Real distinction, in the strictest sense, is always a datum of representation. Two things are really distinct when they are so *conceived* – that is, "one without the aid of the other," in such a way that we *conceive* one while denying everything belonging to the *concept* of the other. In this respect there is no disagreement whatever with Descartes: Spinoza accepts both his criterion and his definition. The only thing at issue is whether real distinction thus understood is, or is not, attended by a real division among things. For Descartes, only the assumption of a divine creator sustained such association. According to Spinoza, one can only make division correspond to a real distinction by making of the latter at least a potential numerical distinction, that is, by confusing it with modal distinction. But real distinction cannot be numerical or modal.

When Spinoza is asked how he comes to the idea of a single substance for all attributes, he points out that he has put forward two arguments: the more reality a being has, the more attributes must be ascribed to it; and the more attributes we ascribe to a being, the more we must accord it existence.[19] But no such argument would suffice were it not supported by the analysis of real distinction. Only that analysis, in fact, shows it to be *possible* to ascribe all attributes to one being, and so to pass from the infinity of each attribute to the absoluteness of a being that possesses them all. And this passage, being possible, or implying no contradiction, is then seen to be necessary, as in the proof of God's existence. Furthermore, it is the same argument over real distinction which shows that *all* the attributes amount to an infinity. For we cannot pass through just three or four attributes without bringing back into the absolute the same numerical distinction which we have just excluded from infinity.[20]

If substance were to be divided according to its attributes, it would have to be taken as a genus, and the attributes as specific

35

differences. Substance would be posited as a genus which would tell us nothing in particular about anything. It would differ from its attributes, as a genus from its differentia, and the attributes would be distinct from corresponding substances, as specific differences are distinct from the species themselves. Thus, by making of the real distinction between attributes a numerical distinction between substances, one carries over mere *distinctions of reason* into substantial reality. There can be no necessity of existence in a substance of the same "species" as an attribute – a specific difference determines only the possible existence of objects corresponding to it within the genus. So substance is once more reduced to the mere possibility of existence, with attributes being nothing but an *indication*, a *sign*, of such possible existence. The first critique to which Spinoza subjects the notion of sign in the *Ethics* appears precisely in relation to real distinction.[21] Real distinction between attributes is no more the "sign" of a diversity of substances than each attribute is the specific character of some substance that corresponds, or might correspond, to it. Substance is not a genus, nor are attributes differentia, nor are qualified substances species.[22] Spinoza condemns equally a thinking that proceeds by genus and differentia, and a thinking that proceeds by signs.

Régis, in a book in which he defends Descartes against Spinoza, invokes the existence of two sorts of attributes: "specific" ones which distinguish substances of different species, and "numerical" ones which distinguish substances of the same species.[23] But this is just what Spinoza objects to in Cartesianism: according to him, attributes are never specific or numerical. It seems we may sum up Spinoza's thesis thus: (1) In positing several substances with the same attribute we make of numerical distinction a real distinction, but this is to confuse real and modal distinctions, treating modes as substances; and (2) in positing as many substances

36

as there are different attributes we make of real distinction a numerical distinction, confusing real distinction not only with modal distinction, but with distinctions of reason as well.

In this context *it appears difficult to consider the first eight propositions as having only a hypothetical sense*. Some proceed as though Spinoza began by arguing on the basis of a hypothesis that he didn't accept, as if setting out from a hypothesis that he intended to refute. But this misses the categorical sense of the first eight propositions. There are not several substances of the same attribute, and numerical distinction is not real: we are not here confronting a provisional hypothesis, valid up to the point where we discover absolutely infinite substance, but have before us, rather, a development that leads us inevitably to posit such a substance. And the categorical sense of the initial propositions is not merely negative. As Spinoza says, "there exists only one substance of a certain nature." The identification of an attribute as belonging to an infinitely perfect substance is, in the *Ethics* as in the *Short Treatise*, no provisional hypothesis, but should be interpreted positively from the viewpoint of *quality*. There is one substance per attribute from the viewpoint of quality, but one single substance for all attributes from the viewpoint of *quantity*. What is the sense of this purely qualitative multiplicity? The obscure formulation reflects the difficulties of a finite understanding rising to the comprehension of absolutely infinite substance, and is justified by the new status of real distinction. It means: substances as qualified are qualitatively, but not quantitatively, distinct – or to put it better, they are "formally," "quidditatively," and not "ontologically" distinct.

37 - 39

One of the sources of Spinoza's Anticartesianism is to be found in the theory of distinctions. In the *Metaphysical Thoughts* he sets out the Cartesian conception: "There are three kinds of distinction between things, real, modal, and of reason." And he seems to give his approval: "For the rest, we pay no attention to the hodgepodge of Peripatetic distinctions."[24] But what counts is not so much the list of accepted distinctions, but their meaning and precise application. In this respect Spinoza retains nothing Cartesian. The new status of real distinction is fundamental: as purely qualitative, quidditative or formal, real distinction excludes any division. Yet isn't this just one of those apparently discredited Peripatetic distinctions returning under a Cartesian name? That real distinction is not and cannot be numerical appears to me to be one of the principal themes of the *Ethics*. This thoroughly upsets the other distinctions. Not only is real distinction no longer referred to numerically distinguished *possible* substances, but modal distinction, in its turn, is no longer referred to accidents as *contingent* determinations. In Descartes a certain contingency of modes echoes the simple possibility of substances. It's all very well for Descartes to insist that accidents are not real, but substantial reality still has accidents. To be produced, modes require something other than the substance to which they relate – either another substance that impresses them in the first, or God who creates the first along with all that depends on it. Spinoza's view is quite different: there is no more a contingency of modes in relation to substance than a possibility of substance in relation to attributes. Everything is necessary, either from its essence or from its cause: Necessity is the only affection of Being, the only modality. And the distinction of reason is, in turn, thereby transformed. We will see that there is no Cartesian axiom (Nothing has no properties, and so on) that does not take on a new meaning, hostile to Cartesianism, on the basis of the new theory of distinctions. The theory has as its fundamental principle the qualitative status of real distinc-

38

tion. Detached from all numerical distinction, real distinction is carried into the absolute, and becomes capable of expressing difference within Being, so bringing about the restructuring of other distinctions.

CHAPTER TWO

41 -51

Attribute as Expression

41~44

Spinoza doesn't say that attributes exist of themselves, nor that they are conceived in such a way that existence follows or results from their essence. Nor again does he say that an attribute is in itself and conceived through itself, like substance.[1] The status of the attributes is sketched in the highly complex formulations of the *Short Treatise*. So complex, indeed, that various hypotheses are open to the reader: to assume various different dates of composition; to recognize the undeniably imperfect state of the manuscripts; or even to advert to the still hesitant state of Spinoza's thought. Such arguments are, however, only relevant once we admit that the formulations of the *Short Treatise* are together inconsistent, and inconsistent, furthermore, with the later matter of the *Ethics*. But this does not seem to be the case. The relevant passages of the *Short Treatise* are not so much supplanted by the *Ethics* as transformed – and this through a more systematic use of the idea of expression. So that, conversely, they may serve to clarify the conceptual component of Spinoza's thought that is informed by this idea of expression.

These passages say, in turn: (1) "Existence belongs to the essence of the attributes,[a] so that outside them[a] there is no essence or being"; (2) "We understand them only in their essence, and not

in their existence, i.e. [we do not understand] that their essence
necessarily belongs to their existence"; "you do not conceive of
them[b] as existing by themselves"; (3) They exist "formally" and
"in act"; "we prove *a priori* that they exist."[2]

According to the first formulation, essence as essence has no
existence outside the attributes that constitute it. So that essence
distinguishes itself *in* the attributes in which it has existence. It
always exists in a genus – in as many genera as there are attributes. Each attribute, then, becomes the existence of an eternal
and infinite essence, a "particular essence."[3] Spinoza can thus say
that it belongs to the essence of attributes to exist, but to exist,
precisely, in the attributes. Or even: "The existence of the attributes does not differ from their essence."[4] The idea of expression, in the *Ethics*, adapts this initial step: the essence of substance
has no existence outside the attributes that express it, so that
each attribute expresses a certain eternal and infinite essence.
What is expressed has no existence outside its expressions; each
expression is, as it were, the existence of what is expressed. (This
is the same principle one finds in Leibniz, however different the
context: each monad is an expression of the world, but the world
therein expressed has no existence outside the monads that
express it.)

How can one say that the attributes express not only a certain
essence, but the essence of substance? This essence is expressed
as the essence of substance, and not that of an attribute. Essences
are thus distinct in the attributes in which they have their existence, but amount only to one single essence of substance. The
rule of convertibility states that every essence is the essence of
something. Essences are really distinct from the viewpoint of the
attributes, but essence is single from the viewpoint of the object
with which it is convertible. Attributes are not attributed to
corresponding substances of the same genus or species as them-

42

selves; rather do they attribute their essence to *something else*, which thus remains the same for all attributes. So that Spinoza can go so far as to say: "If no existence follows from any substance's essence if it is conceived separately, it follows that it is not something singular, but must be something that is an attribute of another, viz. the one, unique, universal being.... So no real substance can be conceived in itself; instead it must belong to *something else*."[5] All existing essences are thus expressed by the attributes in which they have existence, but this as the essence of something else – that is, of one and the same thing for all attributes. We can then ask: What is it that exists through itself, in such a way that its existence follows from its essence? This is clearly substance, the correlate of essence, rather than the attribute in which essence has existence solely as essence. The existence of essence should not be confused with the existence of its correlate. All existing essences relate or are attributable to substance, and this inasmuch as substance is the only being whose existence necessarily follows from its essence. Substance is priv- ileged to exist through itself: *it is not the attribute* that exists through itself, but that to which the essence of each attribute relates, in such a way that existence necessarily follows from the essence thus constituted. So Spinoza may perfectly consistently say of the attributes: "We conceive them only in their essence, and not in their existence; we do not conceive them in such a way that their existence follows from their essence." This second sort of formulation does not contradict the previous one, but rather gives a measure of the deepening of a question, or a change in perspective on it.

What is expressed has no existence outside its expression, but is expressed as the essence of what expresses itself. Once again we face the necessity of distinguishing three terms: substance which expresses itself, attributes which are its expressions,

43

and the essence which is expressed. Yet if attributes do indeed express the essence of substance, how is it that they do not also express the existence that necessarily follows from it? These same attributes to which an existence in themselves is refused have nonetheless, as attributes, an actual and necessary existence. Furthermore, in demonstrating that something is an attribute, we demonstrate, *a priori*, its existence. So the diverse formulations of the *Short Treatise* should be interpreted as relating in turn to the *existence of essence*, the *existence of substance* and the *existence of the attribute itself*. And it is the idea of expression that, in the *Ethics*, combines these three moments and gives them a systematic form.

44-49

The problem of divine attributes had always been closely related to that of divine names. How could we name God, had we not some sort of knowledge of him? But how could we know him, unless he made himself known in some way, revealing and expressing himself? It is a God who speaks, the divine Word, who seals the alliance of attributes and names. Names are attributes, insofar as attributes are expressions. True, the whole question is then that of knowing what they express: the very nature of God as it is in itself, or only the actions of God as Creator, or even just extrinsic divine qualities, relative to creatures? Spinoza does not fail to bring in this traditional problem. He is too good a grammarian to overlook the connection between names and attributes. In the *Theologico-Political Treatise* he asks under what names, or by which attributes, God reveals himself in Scripture: asks what it is for God to speak, what expressive character should be seen in the voice of God. And when he wants to illustrate what he personally understands by an attribute, he thinks of the example of proper names: "By Israel I understand the third patriarch;

I understand the same by Jacob, the name which was given him because he had seized his brother's heel."[6] The relation of Spinozism to the theory of naming must be considered in two aspects. How does Spinoza fit in this tradition? But above all how does he renew it? One may already foresee that he renews it doubly: by an alternative conception of names or attributes, and by an alternative determination of what an attribute is.

Attributes are for Spinoza dynamic and active forms. And here at once we have what seems essential: attributes are no longer attributed, but are in some sense "attributive." Each attribute expresses an essence, and attributes it to substance. All the attributed essences coalesce in the substance of which they are the essence. As long as we conceive the attribute as something attributed, we thereby conceive a substance of the same species or genus; such a substance then has in itself only a possible existence, since it is dependent on the goodwill of a transcendent God to give it an existence conforming to the attribute through which we know it. On the other hand, as soon as we posit the attribute as "attributive" we conceive it as attributing its essence to something that remains identical for all attributes, that is, to necessarily existing substance. The attribute refers his essence to an immanent God who is the principle and the result of a metaphysical necessity. Attributes are thus truly *Words* in Spinoza, with expressive value: they are dynamic, no longer attributed to varying substances, but attributing something to a unique substance.

But what do they attribute, what do they express? Each attribute attributes an infinite essence, that is, an unlimited quality. And these qualities are substantial, because they all qualify an identical substance possessing all the attributes. So there are two ways of identifying what is an attribute: either one looks, *a priori*, for qualities conceived as unlimited, or, setting out from what is limited, one looks, *a posteriori*, for qualities that may be taken to infinity, which are as it were "involved" in the limits of the finite – from this or that thought we deduce Thought as an infinite attribute of God, from this or that body we deduce Extension as an infinite attribute.[7]

The latter, *a posteriori*, method, should be studied closely, for it presents the problem of the involvement of infinity in its entirety. It amounts to giving us a knowledge of the divine attributes which begins from that of "creatures." But its way is not through abstraction or analogy. Attributes are not abstracted from particular things, still less transferred to God analogically. *Attributes are reached directly as forms of being common to creatures and to God, common to modes and to substance.* One can easily enough see the supposed danger of such a method: anthropomorphism and, more generally, the confusion of finite and infinite. An analogical method sets out explicitly to avoid anthropomorphism: according to Aquinas, qualities attributed to God imply no community of form between divine substance and creatures, but only an analogy, a "congruence" of proportion or proportionality. In some cases God formally possesses a perfection that remains extrinsic for creatures, in some cases he eminently possesses a perfection that is formally congruent with that perfection in creatures. The significance of Spinozism may here be judged by the way in which it inverts the problem. Whenever we proceed by analogy we borrow from creatures certain characteristics in order to attribute them to God either equivocally or eminently. Thus God has Will, Understanding, Goodness, Wisdom and so on, but has them equivocally or eminently.[8] Analogy cannot do without equivocation or eminence, and hence contains a subtle anthropomorphism, just as dangerous as the naive variety. It is obvious that a triangle, could it speak, would say that God was eminently triangular. The analogical method denies that there are forms common to God and to creatures but, far from escaping the mis-

46

take it denounces, it constantly confuses the essences of creatures with the essence of God. In some cases it does away with the essence of particular things, reducing their qualities to determinations that can belong intrinsically only to God, in some cases it does away with the essence of God, lending to him eminently what creatures possess formally. Spinoza, on the other hand, insists on the identity of form between creatures and God, while permitting no confusion of essence.

Attributes constitute the essence of substance, but in no sense constitute the essence of modes or of creatures. *Yet they are forms common to both*, since creatures imply them both in their own essence and in their existence. Whence the importance of the rule of convertibility: the essence is not only that without which a thing can neither be nor be conceived, but is conversely that which cannot be nor be conceived outside the thing. It is in accordance with this rule that attributes are indeed the essence of substance, but are in no sense that of modes, such as man: they can very easily be conceived outside their modes.[9] It remains that modes involve or imply them, and *imply them precisely in the form belonging to them insofar as they constitute the essence of God*. Which amounts to saying that attributes in their turn contain or comprehend the essences of modes, and this formally, not eminently. *Attributes are thus forms common to God, whose essence they constitute, and to modes or creatures which imply them essentially*. The same forms may be asserted of God and of creatures, even though God and creatures differ in both essence and existence. The difference consists precisely in this, that modes are only comprehended under these forms, while God, on the other hand, is convertible with them. But such a difference does not impinge on the formal reason of the attribute taken as such.

Spinoza is very conscious of his originality here. On the grounds that creatures differ from God both in essence and existence, it

47

was claimed that God had nothing in common with creatures formally. But in fact quite the reverse is the case: the same attributes are predicated of God who explicates himself in them, and of modes which imply them – imply them in the same form in which they are congruent with God. Furthermore, as long as one refuses community of form, one is condemned to confuse the essences of creatures and God through analogy. As soon as one posits community of form, one has the means of distinguishing them. Spinoza can thus pride himself not only on having reduced to the status of creatures things that had previously been considered as attributes of God, but on having at the same time raised to the status of divine attributes things that had before him been considered as creatures.[10] As a rule Spinoza sees no contradiction between the assertion of a community of form and the positing of a distinction of essences. In adjacent passages he says: (1) If things have nothing in common, one cannot be the cause of the other; (2) If a thing is cause of both the essence and existence of another, then it must differ from it both in the ground of its essence, and in that of its existence.[11] The matter of reconciling these two passages does not seem to me to raise any particular problem in Spinozism. Spinoza is himself taken aback that his correspondents should be taken aback, and reminds them that he has every ground for saying both that creatures differ from God in essence and existence, *and* that God has something in common with creatures formally.[12]

Spinoza's method is neither abstract nor analogical. It is a formal method based on community, working with common notions. And the whole of Spinoza's theory of common notions finds its principle precisely in this status of the attribute. If one is to give a name to this method, as to the underlying theory, it is easy to recognize here the great tradition of univocity. I believe that *Spinoza's philosophy remains in part unintelligible if one does not*

48

see in it a constant struggle against the three notions of equivocation, eminence and analogy. The attributes are, according to Spinoza, univocal forms of being which do not change their nature in changing their "subject" – that is, when predicated of infinite being and finite beings, substance and modes, God and creatures. I believe it takes nothing away from Spinoza's originality to place him in a perspective that may already be found in Duns Scotus. The analysis of how Spinoza for his part interprets the notion of univocity, how he understands it in an altogether different way from Duns Scotus, must be postponed until later. It will suffice for the moment to bring together the primary determinations of the attribute. Attributes are infinite forms of being, unlimited, ultimate, irreducible formal reasons; these forms are common to God whose essence they constitute, and to modes which in their own essence imply them. Attributes are Words expressing unlimited qualities; these qualities are as it were involved in the limits of the finite. Attributes are expressions of God; these expressions of God are univocal, constituting the very nature of God as *natura naturans*, and involved in the nature of things or *natura naturata* which, in a certain way, re-expresses them in its turn.

49 - 51

Spinoza is able on this basis to distinguish attributes and *propria*. His starting point is Aristotelian: a *proprium* is what belongs to a thing, but can never explain what it is. Thus the *propria* of God are just "adjectives" which give us no substantial knowledge; God would not be God without them, but is not God through them.[13] Spinoza could, in accordance with a long tradition, give to these *propria* the name of attribute; but there would then still be, according to him, a difference of nature between two sorts of attribute. But what does Spinoza mean, when he adds that the *propria* of God are only "modes which may be attributed to him"?[14] Mode should not here be taken in the particular sense often given to it by Spinoza, but in the more general scholastic sense of a "modality of essence." Infinite, perfect, immutable, eternal are *propria* that may be predicated of all attributes. Omniscient, omnipresent are *propria* predicated of a particular attribute (Thought, Extension). All attributes express the essence of substance; each attribute expresses an essence of substance. But *propria* express nothing: "Through these *propria* we can know neither what the being to which these belong is, nor what attributes it has."[15] They do not constitute the nature of substance, but are predicated of what constitutes that nature. So they do not form the essence of Being, but only a modality of that essence as already formed. Infinite is the *proprium* of substance, that is, the modality of each of the attributes that constitute its essence. Omniscient is the *proprium* of thinking substance, that is, the infinite modality of that attribute, Thought, which expresses an essence of substance. *Propria* are not properly speaking attributes, precisely because they are not *expressive*. Rather are they like "impressed notions," like characters imprinted, either in all attributes, or in some one or other of them. The opposition of attribute and *proprium* turns then on two points. Attributes are Words expressing substantial essences or qualities, while *propria* are only adjectives indicating a modality of those essences or qualities. God's attributes are common forms, common to substance which is their converse, and to modes which imply them without being convertible with them, while God's *propria* are truly proper to God, not being predicable of modes, but only of attributes.

A second category of *propria* relate to God as cause, insofar as he acts or produces something: not as infinite, perfect, eternal, immutable, but as cause of all things, predestination, providence.[16] Now, since God produces things within his attributes, these *propria* are subject to the same principle as the previous ones. Some are predicable of all attributes, others of one or other of them. The second sort of *propria* are still adjectival, but instead of indicating modalities, these indicate relations – God's relations to his creatures or to his productions. Finally, a third category embraces *propria* that do not even belong to God: God as *summum bonum*, as compassionate, as just and charitable.[17] Here it is primarily the *Theologico-Political Treatise* that clarifies the matter. The treatise speaks of divine justice and charity as "attributes which a certain manner of life will enable men to imitate."[18] These *propria* do not belong to God as cause; it is no longer a question of some relation of God to his creatures, but of extrinsic determinations which indicate only the way in which creatures imagine God. It is true that these denominations have extremely variable senses and values: they go so far as to give God eminence in all kinds of things – a divine mouth and eyes, moral qualities and sublime passions, mountains and heavens. But, even if we restrict ourselves to justice and charity, we arrive at nothing of God's nature, nor of his operations as Cause. Adam, Abraham and Moses were ignorant not only of the true divine attributes, but also of most of the *propria* of the first and second sort.[19] God revealed himself to them under extrinsic denominations which served them as warnings, commandments, rules and models of life. More than ever, it must be said that this third kind of *proprium* is in no way expressive. They are not divine expressions, but notions impressed in the imagination to make us obey and serve a God of whose nature we are ignorant.

CHAPTER THREE

Attributes and Divine Names

According to a long tradition, divine names relate to manifestations of God. Conversely, divine manifestations are a speech
through which God makes himself known by some name or other.
So that it amounts to the same thing to ask whether the names
that designate God are affirmations[a] or negations, or whether the
qualities that manifest him and the attributes that belong to him
are positive or negative. The concept of expression, at once
speech and manifestation, light and sound, seems to have a logic
of its own which favors both alternatives. Sometimes one may
emphasize positivity, that is, the immanence of what is expressed
in expression, sometimes "negativity," that is, the transcendence
of what expresses itself in relation to all expressions. What conceals also expresses, but what expresses still conceals. Thus it is
all a question of emphasis in the problem of divine names, or the
attributes of God. That theology that is called negative admits
that affirmations are able to designate God as cause, subject to
rules of immanence which lead from what is nearest to what
is farthest from him. But God as substance or essence can be
defined only negatively, according to rules of transcendence
whereby one denies in their turn names that are farthest from
him, then those that are nearest. And then suprasubstantial and

superessential deity stands splendidly as far from all negation as from all affirmation. Negative theology thus combines the negative method with the affirmative, and claims to go beyond both. How would one know what must be denied of God as essence, if one didn't first of all know what one should affirm of him as cause? Negative theology can therefore only be defined by its dynamics: one goes beyond affirmations in negations, and beyond both affirmations and negations in a shadowy eminence.

A theology of more positive ambitions, such as that of Saint Thomas, relies on analogy to ground new affirmative rules. Positive qualities do not merely indicate God as a cause, but belong to him substantially, as long as they are treated analogically. That God is good doesn't mean that God is not evil, nor that he is the cause of goodness; the truth is rather that what we call goodness in creatures "preexists" in God in a higher modality that accords with divine substance. Here once more, it is a dynamic that defines the new method. This dynamic, in its turn, maintains the force of the negative and the eminent, but comprehends it within analogy: one proceeds from a prior negation to a positive attribute, the attribute then applying to God *formaliter eminenter*.[1]

Both Arab and Jewish philosophy came up against the same problem. How could names apply not only to God as cause, but to the essence of God? Must they be taken negatively, denied according to certain rules? Must they be affirmed, according to other rules? If, though, we adopt the Spinozist viewpoint, both approaches appear equally false, because the problem to which they relate is itself an altogether false one.

Spinoza's tripartite division of *propria* obviously reproduces a traditional classification of divine attributes: (1) symbolic denominations, forms and figures, signs and rites, metonymies from the sensible to the divine; (2) attributes of action; (3) attributes of essence. Take an ordinary list of divine attributes: goodness, being, reason, life, intelligence, wisdom, virtue, beatitude, truth, eternity; or greatness, love, peace, unity, perfection. It might be asked whether these attributes belong to the essence of God, whether they must be understood as conditional affirmations, or as negations marking only the ablation of some privation. But according to Spinoza, such questions do not arise, because the greater part of these attributes are only *propria*. And the rest are beings of reason. They express nothing of the nature of God, either negatively or positively. *God is no more concealed in them than expressed by them. Propria* are neither negative nor affirmative; one might say, in Kantian style, that they are indefinite. When one confuses the divine nature with *propria*, one inevitably has an idea of God that is itself indefinite. One then oscillates between an eminent conception of negation and an analogical conception of affirmation. Each, through its dynamic, implies something of the other. One gets a false conception of negation by introducing analogy into what is affirmed. And an affirmation that is no longer univocal, no longer formally affirmed of its objects, is no longer an affirmation.

It is one of Spinoza's principal theses that the nature of God has never been defined, because it has always been confused with his "*propria*." This explains his attitude toward *theologians*. And philosophers have in their turn followed the path of theology: Descartes himself thought that the nature of God consisted in infinite perfection. Infinite perfection, though, is only a modality of that which constitutes the divine nature. Only attributes in the true sense of the word (Thought, Extension) are the constitutive elements of God, his constituent expressions, his affirmations, his positive and formal reasons, in a word, his nature. But one then asks precisely why these attributes, with no inherent tendency to concealment, should have been passed over, why God was denatured by a confusion with the *propria* which gave him an indefinite image. A reason must be found to explain why Spinoza's predecessors, in spite of all their ingenuity, confined themselves to properties and were unable to discover the nature of God.

Spinoza's answer is simple: they lacked a historical, critical and internal method capable of interpreting Scripture.[2] They didn't ask about the plan of the sacred texts. They took them as the Word of God, God's way of expressing himself. What the texts said of God all seemed to be something "expressed," and what they didn't say seemed inexpressible.[3] It was never asked "does religious revelation relate to the nature of God?," "is its end to make this nature known to us?," "is it amenable to the positive or negative treatments whose application is supposed to complete the determination of this nature?" Revelation concerns, in truth, only certain *propria*. It in no way sets out to make known to us the divine nature and its attributes. What we find in Scripture is of course heterogeneous: here we have specific ritual teachings, there universal moral teachings; sometimes we even find speculative teaching – the minimum of speculation required for moral teaching. But no attribute of God is ever revealed. Only varying "signs," extrinsic denominations that guarantee some divine commandment. At best, "*propria*" such as divine existence, unity, omniscience and omnipresence, which guarantee a moral teaching.[4] For the end of Scripture is to subject us to models of life, to make us obey, and ground our obedience. So it would be absurd to think that knowledge might be substituted for revelation: how could the divine nature, were it known, serve as a practical rule in daily life? And still more absurd to believe that revelation makes known to us something of the nature or essence of God. Yet this absurdity runs through all theology. *And thereby compromises philosophy as a whole.* Sometimes the *propria* of revelation are subjected to a special treatment that reconciles them with reason; sometimes, even, *propria* of reason are found, distinct from those of revelation. But this provides no way out of theology; one still relies on properties to express the nature of God. One fails to appreciate the difference of nature between them and true attributes. And God will always inevitably be eminent in relation to his *propria*. Once one ascribes to them an expressive value they do not have, one ascribes to divine substance an inexpressible nature which it does not have either.

Revelation and expression: never was the effort to distinguish two domains pushed further. Or to distinguish two heterogeneous relations: that of sign and signified, that of expression and expressed. *A sign always attaches to a proprium*; it always signifies a commandment; and it grounds our obedience. *Expression always relates to an attribute*; it expresses an essence, that is, a nature in the infinitive; it makes it known to us. So that the "Word of God" has two very different senses: an expressive Word, which has no need of words or signs, but only of God's essence and man's understanding; and an impressed, imperative Word, operating through sign and commandment.[b] The latter is not expressive, but strikes our imagination and inspires in us the required submission.[5] Should one say, at least, that commandments "express" the wishes of God? But that would in turn prejudge will as belonging to the nature of God, take a being of reason, an extrinsic determination, for a divine attribute. Any mixing of the two domains is fatal. Whenever one takes a sign for an expression, one sees mysteries everywhere, including, above all, Scripture itself. Like the Jews who think that everything, unconditionally, expresses God.[6] One then gets a mystical conception of expression: it seems no less to conceal than to reveal what it expresses. Enigmas, parables, symbols, analogies, metonymies come in this way to disturb the rational and positive order of pure expression. Truly, Scripture is indeed the Word of God, but as a command-

57

ing speech: imperative, it expresses nothing, because it makes known no divine attribute.

Spinoza's analysis does not merely mark the irreducibility of these domains. It proposes an explanation of signs which is a sort of genesis of an illusion. It is not, indeed, false to say that everything expresses God. The whole order of Nature is expressive. But it is a simple misunderstanding of natural law to grasp it as an imperative or commandment. When Spinoza comes to illustrate different kinds of knowledge with the famous example of proportional numbers, he shows that, on the lowest level, we do not understand the rule of proportionality: so we hold on to a sign that tells us what operation we *should* make on these numbers. Even technical rules take on a moral aspect when we make no sense of them and only cling to a sign. This is still more the case with laws of Nature. God reveals to Adam that ingesting the apple would have terrible consequences; but Adam, powerless to grasp the constitutive relations of things, imagines this law of Nature to be a moral law forbidding him to eat the fruit, and God himself to be a ruler who punishes him for having eaten it.[7] The sign is the very thing of prophecy; and prophets, after all, have strong imagination and weak understanding.[8] Expressions of God never enter the imagination, which grasps everything under the aspect of sign and commandment.

God expresses himself neither in signs, nor in *propria*. When we read in *Exodus* that God revealed himself to Abraham, Isaac and Jacob, not as Jehovah, but as *Shaddai* (sufficing for the needs of all), we should not see in this the mystery of the tetragrammaton, or the supereminence of God considered in his absolute nature. We should see rather that the revelation does not have the expression of this nature or essence as its object.[9] Natural knowledge, on the other hand, does imply the essence of God; implies it because it is a knowledge of the attributes that actu-

58

ally express this essence. God expresses himself in his attributes, and attributes express themselves in dependent modes: this is how the order of Nature manifests God. The only names expressive of God, the only divine expressions, are then the attributes: common forms predicable of substance and modes. If we know only two of these, it is just because we are constituted by a mode of Extension and a mode of Thought. These attributes do not, at least, require any revelation, but only the light of Nature. We know them as they are in God, in their being that is common to substance and modes. Spinoza insists on this point, citing a passage from Saint Paul which he makes almost a manifesto of univocity: "The invisible things of God from the creation of the world are clearly seen, being understood by the things that are made...."[10,c] The univocity of attributes merges with their expressivity: attributes are, indissolubly, expressive and univocal.

Attributes no more serve to deny anything than they are themselves denied of essence. Nor are they affirmed of God by analogy. An affirmation by analogy is worth no more than a negation by eminence (there is still something of eminence in the first case, and already some analogy in the second). It is true, says Spinoza, that one attribute is *denied* of another.[11] But in what sense? "If someone says that Extension is not limited by Extension, but by Thought, is that not the same as saying that Extension is infinite not absolutely, but only so far as it is Extension?"[12] So negation here implies no opposition or privation. Extension as such suffers from no limitation or imperfection resulting from its nature, and so in vain might we imagine a God who possessed Extension "eminently."[13] In what sense, conversely, is an attribute affirmed of substance? Spinoza often insists on the point that substances or attributes exist in Nature *formally*. Now, among the many senses of the word "formal" we must bear in mind the one in which it is opposed to "eminent" or "analogical." Substance

59

should never be thought of as comprehending its attributes eminently, nor should attributes, in their turn, be thought of as containing the essences of modes. Attributes are formally affirmed of substance; they are formally predicated of the substance whose essence they constitute, and of the modes whose essences they contain. Spinoza constantly reminds us of the affirmative character of the attributes that define substance, and of the need for any good definition to be itself affirmative.[14] Attributes are affirmations; but affirmation, in its essence, is always formal, actual, univocal: therein lies its expressivity.

Spinoza's philosophy is a philosophy of pure affirmation. Affirmation is the speculative principle on which hangs the whole of the *Ethics*. Here we may investigate how Spinoza comes upon, and uses, a Cartesian idea. For real distinction tended to give to the concept of affirmation a genuine logic. Indeed real distinction as used by Descartes sets us on the way toward a profound discovery: the terms distinguished each retain their respective positivity, instead of being defined by opposition, one to another. *Non opposita sed diversa* is the formula of the new logic.[15] Real distinction appeared to open up a new conception of the negative, free from opposition and privation, and a new conception of affirmation too, free from eminence and analogy. We have already seen why this conception does not lead Spinoza back into Cartesianism: Descartes still gives real distinction a numerical sense, a function of substantial division in Nature and among things. He conceives every quality as positive, all reality as perfection; but all is not reality in a qualified and distinguished substance, and not everything in a thing's nature is a perfection. Spinoza is thinking of Descartes, among others, when he writes: "To say that the nature of the thing required this limitation, and therefore it could not be otherwise, is to say nothing; for the nature of the thing cannot require anything unless it exists."[16]

For Descartes there are limitations "required" by a thing by virtue of its nature, ideas that have so little reality that one might almost say they came from nothing, natures that lack something. And through these everything that the logic of real distinction had been thought to throw out, privation, eminence, is reintroduced. We will see how *eminence, analogy, even a certain equivocation, remain almost as spontaneous categories of Cartesian thought.* In order to bring out the deepest consequences of real distinction conceived as a logic of affirmation, on the other hand, it was necessary to reach the idea of a single substance with all its attributes really distinct. And it was first of all necessary to avoid all confusion, not only of attributes with modes, but of attributes with *propria*.

Attributes are affirmations of God, *logoi* or true divine names. Let us return to the passage where Spinoza invokes the example of Israel, so named as patriarch, but called Jacob in relation to his brother.[17] It illustrates in this context the distinction of reason as it applies between substance and attribute: Israel is called Jacob (*Supplantor*) in relation to his brother, as a "plane" might be called "white" in relation to a man looking at it, and as a substance might be called this or that in relation to an understanding that "attributes" to it this or that essence. The passage certainly favors an intellectualist or even idealist interpretation of attributes. But a philosopher is always led to simplify his thought on some occasions, or to formulate it only in part. Spinoza doesn't fail to underline the ambiguity of the examples he cites. The attribute is not in truth just a manner of seeing or conceiving; its relation to the understanding is indeed fundamental, but is to be otherwise interpreted. It is because attributes are themselves *expressions* that they are necessarily referred to the understand-

61

ing as to the only capacity for perceiving what is *expressed*. It is because attributes explicate substance that they are, thereby, correlative with an understanding in which all explication is reproduced or "explicates" itself objectively. The problem thus becomes more definite: attributes are expressions, but how can different expressions refer to one and the same thing? How can different names have the same referent? "You want me to explain by an example how one and the same thing can be designated (*insigniri*) by two names."

The role of understanding amounts to its part in a logic of expression. Such a logic is the outcome of a long tradition, from the Stoics down through the Middle Ages. One distinguishes in an expression (say, a proposition) what it expresses and what it designates.[18] What is expressed is, so to speak, a sense that has no existence outside the expression; it must thus be referred to an understanding that grasps it objectively, that is, ideally. But it is predicated of the thing, and not of the expression itself; understanding relates it to the object designated, as the essence of that object. One can then conceive how names may be distinguished by their senses, while these different senses relate to the same designated object whose essence they constitute. There is a sort of transposition of this theory of sense[d] in Spinoza's conception of attributes. Each attribute is a distinct name or expression; what it expresses is so to speak its sense; but if it be true that what is expressed has no existence outside the attribute, it is nonetheless related to substance as to the object designated by all the attributes. Thus all expressed senses together form the "expressible" or the essence of substance, and the latter may in its turn be said to express itself in the attributes.

It is true that in assimilating substance to an object designated by different names, we do not resolve the essential problem — that of the difference between those names. Worse still, the difficulty is only increased, in that these names are univocal and positive, and so apply formally to what they designate: their respective senses seem to introduce into the unity of what is designated a necessarily actual multiplicity. In an analogical view this is not the case: names apply to God by analogy, their senses "preexist" in him in an eminent mode which ensures their inconceivable, inexpressible, unity. What, though, if divine names have the same sense as applied to God and as implied in creatures, the same, that is, in all uses, so that their distinction can no longer be grounded in created things, but must be grounded in this God they all designate? Duns Scotus, as is well known, raised this problem in the Middle Ages, and provided a profound solution. It was without doubt Scotus who pursued farther than any other the enterprise of a positive theology. He denounces at once the negative eminence of the Neoplatonists and the pseudoaffirmation of the Thomists, and sets against them the univocity of Being: *being is predicated in the same sense* of everything that is, whether infinite or finite, albeit not in the same "modality." But the point is that being does not change in nature, in changing modality – that is, when its concept is predicated of infinite being and of finite beings (so that, already in Scotus, univocity does not lead to any confusion of essences).[19] And the univocity of being itself leads to the univocity of divine attributes: the concept of an attribute that may be taken to infinity is itself common to God and creatures, as long as it be considered in its formal reason or its quiddity, for "infinity in no way abolishes the formal reason of that to which it is added."[20] But, formally and positively predicated of God, how can infinite attributes or divine names not introduce into God a plurality corresponding to their formal reasons, their distinct quiddities?

This is the problem to which Scotus applies one of his most original concepts, which complements that of univocity: the idea

63

of formal distinction.[21] It relates to the apprehension of distinct quiddities that nevertheless belong to the same subject. This must obviously be referred to an act of understanding. But the understanding isn't merely expressing an identical reality under two aspects that might exist separately in other subjects, or expressing an identical thing at different degrees of abstraction, or expressing something analogically in relation to some other realities. It objectively apprehends actually distinct forms which yet, as such, together make up a single identical subject.[e] Between animal and rational there is not merely a distinction of reason, like that between *homo* and *humanitas*; the thing itself must already be "structured according to the conceivable diversity of genus and species."[22] Formal distinction is definitely a real distinction, expressing as it does the different layers of reality that form or constitute a being. Thus it is called *formalis a parte rei* or *actualis ex natura rei*. But it is a minimally real distinction because the two really distinct quiddities are coordinate, together making a single being.[23] *Real and yet not numerical*, such is the status of formal distinction.[24] One must also recognize that in the order of finitude two quiddities such as animal and rational are connected only through the third term to which each is identical. But this is not the case in the infinite. Two attributes taken to infinity will still be formally distinct, while being ontologically identical. As Gilson puts it, "Because it is a modality of being (and not an attribute), infinity can be common to quidditatively irreducible formal reasons, conferring on them an identity of being, without canceling their distinction of form."[25] Thus two of God's attributes, Justice and Goodness for example, are divine names designating a God who is absolutely one, while they signify different quiddities. There are here as it were two orders, that of formal reason and that of being, with the plurality in one perfectly according with the simplicity of the other.

The attribution of such a status to formal reason finds a dedicated opponent in Suarez, who cannot see how formal reason is not to be reduced either to a distinction of reason or a modal distinction.[26] It says either too much or not enough: too much for a distinction of reason, but not enough for a real distinction. Descartes, when the question arises, is of the same view.[27] We still find in Descartes the same repugnance toward conceiving a real distinction between things which does not lie in different subjects, that is, which isn't attended by a division of being or a numerical distinction. The same is not true of Spinoza: in his conception of a nonnumerical real distinction, it is not hard to discern Scotus's formal distinction. Furthermore, with Spinoza formal distinction no longer presents a minimum of real distinction, but becomes real distinction itself, giving this an exclusive character.

1. Attributes are, for Spinoza, really distinct, or conceived as really distinct. They have irreducible formal reasons; each attribute expresses, as its formal reason or quiddity, an infinite essence. Thus attributes are distinguished "quidditatively," formally: they are indeed substances in a purely qualitative sense. 2. Each attributes its essence to substance, as to *something else*. Which is a way of saying that to the formal distinction between attributes there corresponds no division of being. Substance is not a genus, nor are attributes specific differences. So there are no substances of the *same* species as the attributes, no substance which is *the same thing* (*res*) as each attribute (*formalitas*). 3. This "other thing" is thus the *same for* all attributes. It is furthermore the *same as* all attributes. And the latter determination in no way contradicts the former one. All formally distinct attributes are referred by understanding to an ontologically single substance. But understanding only reproduces objectively the nature of the forms it apprehends. All formal essences form the essence

of an absolutely single substance. All qualified substances form only one substance from the point of view of quantity. So that attributes themselves have at once identity of being and distinction of formality. Ontologically one, formally diverse, such is their status.

Despite his allusion to the "hodgepodge of Peripatetic distinctions," Spinoza restores formal distinction, and even gives it a range it didn't have in Scotus. *It is formal distinction that provides an absolutely coherent concept of the unity of substance and the plurality of attributes, and gives real distinction a new logic.* One may then ask why Spinoza never uses the term, and speaks only of real distinction. The answer is that formal distinction is indeed a real distinction, and that it was to Spinoza's advantage to use a term that Descartes, by the use he had made of it, had in a sense neutralized theologically. So that the term "real distinction" allowed great audacity without stirring up old controversies which Spinoza doubtless considered pointless or even harmful. I don't believe that Spinoza's Cartesianism went any further than this. His whole theory of distinctions is profoundly Anticartesian.

To picture Spinoza as Scotist rather than Cartesian is to risk certain distortions. I intend it to mean only that Scotist theories were certainly known to Spinoza, and played a part, along with other themes, in forming his pantheism.[28] What then becomes of primary interest is the way Spinoza uses and transforms the notions of formal distinction and univocity. What in fact did Duns Scotus call an "attribute"? Justice, goodness, wisdom and so on – in brief, *propria*. He of course recognized that the divine essence could be conceived without these attributes; but he defined the essence of God by intrinsic perfections, understanding and will. Scotus was a "theologian" and, in this capacity, was still dealing with *propria* and beings of reason. Thus formal distinction does not with him have its full range, and is always at work on beings

66

of reason like genera and species, and faculties of the soul, or on *propria* such as the supposed attributes of God. Furthermore, univocity in Scotus seems compromised by a concern to avoid pantheism. For his theological, that is to say "creationist," perspective forced him to conceive univocal Being as a *neutralized, indifferent* concept. Indifferent as between finite and infinite, singular and universal, perfect and imperfect, created and uncreated.[29] For Spinoza, on the other hand, the concept of univocal Being is perfectly determinate, as what is predicated in one and the same sense of substance in itself, and of modes that are in something else. With Spinoza univocity becomes the object of a pure affirmation. The same thing, *formaliter*, constitutes the essence of substance and contains the essences of modes. Thus it is the idea of immanent cause that takes over, in Spinoza, from univocity, freeing it from the indifference and neutrality to which it had been confined by the theory of a divine creation. And it is in immanence that univocity finds its distinctly Spinozist formulation: God is said to be cause of all things *in the very sense* (*eo sensu*) that he is said to be cause of himself.

CHAPTER FOUR

The Absolute

Spinoza carefully shows how every (qualified) substance must be unlimited. The sum of the arguments of the *Short Treatise* and the *Ethics* may be presented thus: If a substance were limited, this would have to be either by itself, or by a substance of the same nature, or by God who had given it an imperfect nature.[1] But it could not be limited by itself, for "it would have had to change its whole essence."[a] Nor by another substance, for there would then be two substances with the same attribute. Nor by God, since God is in no way imperfect or limited, and so still less faced with things that would "require" or imply some limitation or other before being created. Spinoza indicates the importance of these themes, but this elliptically: "If we can prove that there can be no limited substance, every substance belonging to the divine being must be unlimited."[a] The transition appears to be as follows: if every substance is unlimited, we must recognize that each is in its genus or form infinitely perfect; there is thus *equality* between all forms or all genera of being; no form is inferior to any other, none is superior. This is the transition formulated explicitly by Spinoza in another passage: "There is no inequality at all in the attributes."[2]

Thus one cannot imagine that God might contain the reality

or perfection of an effect in a higher form than that involved in the effect, because no form is higher than any other. One may infer from this that all forms being equal (attributes), God cannot possess one without possessing the others; he cannot possess one that doubles, eminently, for another. All forms of being, as *infinitely perfect*, must without limitation belong to God as *absolutely infinite* Being.

This principle of equality of forms or attributes is but another aspect of the principle of univocity, and the principle of formal distinction. It is nonetheless a particular application of it: it forces us to pass from Infinite to Absolute, from infinitely perfect to absolutely infinite. Forms of being, all being perfect and unlimited, and so infinitely perfect, cannot constitute unequal substances calling for the infinitely perfect as for a distinct being playing the role of eminent and efficient cause. No more can they amount to substances equal among themselves; for equal substances cannot be such only numerically, they would have to have the same form, "they would necessarily have to limit one another, and consequently, would not be infinite."[3] Forms, equally unlimited, are thus attributes of a single substance that possesses them all, and possesses them actually. But it would then be a great mistake to think that infinite perfection is enough to define the "nature" of God. Infinite perfection is the modality of each attribute, that is to say, the "*proprium*" of God. But the nature of God consists in an infinity of attributes, that is to say, in absolute infinity.

One may already foresee the transformation to which Spinoza, countering Descartes, will subject the proofs of God's existence. For all the Cartesian proofs proceed from infinite perfection. And not only do they proceed from it, they move within the infinitely perfect, which they identify with God's nature. The proof *a posteriori*, in its first formulation, runs: "The idea I have of a being more perfect than my own, must necessarily have been set in me by a being who is indeed more perfect." The second formulation is: "From the simple fact that I exist, and have in me the idea of a supremely perfect being (that is, of God), God's existence is very obviously proven."[4] And the ontological or *a priori* proof is stated thus: "What we clearly and distinctly perceive to belong to the nature or essence, or to the unchanging and true form of some thing; that can be truly predicated or affirmed of this thing; but after having quite carefully inquired what God is, we clearly and distinctly conceive that it belongs to his true and unchanging nature that he exist; we can therefore truly affirm that he exists."[5] Now the inquiry to which Descartes alludes in the minor premise consists precisely in the determination of the "supremely perfect" as the form, essence or nature of God. Existence, being a perfection, belongs to this nature. Thanks to this major premise one can conclude that God does indeed exist.

Thus the ontological proof itself involves an identification of infinite perfection with the nature of God. For consider the second set of objections made against Descartes's *Meditations*. He is reproached for not having proved, in the minor premise, that the nature of God was possible, or implied no contradiction. It is argued against him that God exists *if he is possible* (Leibniz takes up the objection in some celebrated passages[6]). Descartes replies that the supposed difficulty in the minor premise is already resolved in the major premise. For the latter does not mean: What we clearly and distinctly conceive to belong to the nature of some thing can truly be said to belong to the nature of this thing. That would be a mere tautology. The major premise means: "What we clearly and distinctly conceive to belong to the nature of some thing, that can be truly predicated or affirmed *of this thing*." Now

71

this proposition guarantees the possibility of anything that we conceive clearly and distinctly. If some other criterion of possibility is required, a sort of sufficient reason on the side of the object, we confess our ignorance, and the powerlessness of understanding to reach such a reason.[7]

Descartes seems to sense the meaning of the objection, and yet not understand, or want to understand, it. He is criticized for not having proven the possibility of the nature of a being *of which "infinite perfection" can be only a proprium*. Such a proof is itself, perhaps, impossible: but in that case the ontological argument does not follow.[8] In any case, infinite perfection gives us no knowledge of the nature of the being to which it belongs. If Descartes thinks to have solved all the difficulties in the major premise, this is in the first place because he confuses the nature of God with a *proprium*: he then thinks that a clear and distinct conception of the *proprium* is enough to guarantee the possibility of the corresponding nature. Descartes does admittedly oppose the aspect under which God is presented in Scripture ("manners of speaking...which do indeed contain some truth, but only insofar as this is considered in relation to men") to the aspect under which God himself appears in the light of Nature.[9] But he is thereby only opposing *propria* of one sort to those of another. In relation to a being that has as a rational property that of being infinitely perfect, the question "Is such a being possible?" persists in its entirety. And if it be asked how Descartes is able, from his viewpoint, to identify *proprium* and divine nature, I reply that once more the reason is to be found in the way he invokes eminence and analogy. Descartes reminds us that "of the things which we conceive to be in God and in ourselves," none is *univocal*.[10] Now, it is just insofar as one admits a basic inequality between forms of being, that the infinitely perfect can come to designate a higher form which may be taken for the Nature of God.

Descartes defines God by giving a list of properties: "By the name God, I understand a substance infinite, eternal, unchanging, independent, omniscient, omnipotent...."[11] In their misty eminence these properties may, considered as a whole, appear like a simple nature.

In Leibniz, two themes are deeply related: infinite perfection does not suffice to constitute the nature of God, and a clear and distinct idea does not suffice to guarantee its own reality, that is to say, the possibility of its object. The two principles meet in the requirement of sufficient reason or real definition. Infinite and perfect are only distinctive marks; the clear and distinct knowledge that we have of them in no way tells us whether these characteristics are compatible; there might perhaps be a contradiction in *ens perfectissimum*, just as there is in "the greatest number" or "the greatest velocity." The essence of such a being is only conjectural, and so any definition of God by perfection alone remains nominal. Whence Leibniz's severe criticism: Descartes does not in general go any further than Hobbes, as there is no reason to trust the criteria of a psychological consciousness (clarity and distinctness) any better than simple combinations of words.[12] These same themes appear, in a wholly different context, to be shared by Spinoza. It is hardly surprising that there should be some basic common points in the Anticartesian reaction toward the end of the seventeenth century. According to Spinoza, infinite perfection is only a *proprium*. The property tells us nothing of the nature of the being to which it belongs, and does not suffice to prove that such a being involves no contradiction. Until a clear and distinct idea is grasped as "adequate" one may doubt its reality and the possibility of its object. Until one gives a real definition, bearing on the essence of a thing rather than on *propria*, one remains among the vagaries of what is merely conceived, without relation to the reality of the thing as it is out-

73

side our understanding.[13] Thus sufficient reason seems to impose its requirements in Spinoza as well as in Leibniz. Spinoza sets adequacy as sufficient reason of a clear and distinct idea, and absolute infinity as sufficient reason of infinite perfection. The ontological argument, in Spinoza, no longer bears on an indeterminate being that is supposed infinitely perfect, but rather on absolute infinity, determined as that which consists of an infinity of attributes. (Infinite perfection being only the mode of each of these attributes, the modality of essence expressed by each.)

If this claim is correct, however, one may well be surprised by the way that Spinoza proves *a priori* that the absolutely infinite, that is, a substance consisting of an infinity of attributes, necessarily exists.[14] An initial proof runs: If it did not exist, it would not be a substance, for every substance necessarily exists. A second: If absolutely infinite being did not exist, there would have to be a reason for this nonexistence; this reason would have to be internal, and so absolute infinity would have to imply a contradiction; "but it is absurd to affirm this of Being absolutely infinite and supremely perfect." These arguments clearly still advance via infinite perfection. The absolutely infinite (substance consisting of an infinity of attributes) necessarily exists, or it would not be a substance; or it would not be infinitely perfect. But the reader has a right to insist on a deeper proof, on which these are founded. It must be shown that a substance that exists necessarily has as its nature to consist of an infinity of attributes or, which comes to the same thing, that the infinitely perfect has as its reason or principle the absolutely infinite.

And Spinoza has indeed done precisely what the reader is entitled to require of him. The idea that Spinoza in the *Ethics* "installs" himself in God and "begins" with God is only an approximation of the truth and is, strictly speaking, inaccurate. What is more we will see that, according to Spinoza, it is altogether impossible to *set out* from the idea of God. The proof of God's existence appears in Proposition 11. But the first ten have shown that *numerical distinction not being real, any really distinct substance is unlimited and infinitely perfect; conversely, real distinction not being numerical, all infinitely perfect substances together make up an infinitely perfect substance of which they are the attributes; infinite perfection is thus the* proprium *of the absolutely infinite, and absolute infinity the nature or reason of the infinitely perfect.* Herein lies the importance of these opening proofs, which are in no sense hypothetical, and herein lies the importance of considering numerical and real distinctions. Only on this basis can Proposition 11 conclude: Absolutely infinite substance, implying no contradiction, necessarily exists; if it did not, it would not have infinite perfection as a property, nor indeed would it be a substance.

The opening scheme of the *Ethics* is thus as follows: 1. *Definitions 1–5*: Merely nominal definitions, needed in the mechanism of subsequent proofs; 2. *Definition 6*: The real definition of God, as absolutely infinite Being, that is, as "substance consisting of an infinity of attributes, each of which expresses an eternal and infinite essence." The definition takes up the terms "substance" and "attribute" and gives them the status of realities. But the reality of the definition itself does not mean that it immediately shows the possibility of its object. For a definition to be real, one need only be able to prove the possibility of the object as defined; this at once demonstrates the reality or truth of the definition; 3. *Propositions 1–8*: The first stage in the proof of the reality of the definition: numerical distinction not being real, every really distinct attribute is infinitely perfect, and every qualified substance is unique, necessary and infinite. This sequence obviously relies only upon the first five definitions; 4. *Propositions 9 and 10*: The second stage: as real distinction is not numerical, distinct attributes or qualified substances together form one and the same substance having all these qualifications, that is, all the attributes. This second sequence closes in the Scholium to Proposition 10, which establishes that an absolutely infinite substance implies no contradiction, so that Definition 6 is indeed a real one[15]; 5. *Proposition 11*: The absolutely infinite necessarily exists; otherwise it could not be a substance, and could not have as a property infinite perfection.

A confirmation[b] of this scheme is provided by examining the *Short Treatise*. For what is wrongly said of the *Ethics* applies well enough to the *Short Treatise*, which does indeed begin with God, installs itself in his existence. At the time of its composition Spinoza still believed that it was possible to set out from an idea of God. Thus the *a priori* argument receives an initial formulation that conforms entirely to Descartes's statement of it.[16] And so the argument, moving altogether within infinite perfection, gives us no way of knowing the nature of the corresponding being. As it stands at the head of the *Short Treatise*, the ontological argument serves no purpose whatever. So Spinoza adds a thoroughly obscure second proposition: "the existence of God is essence."[17] I believe that, taken literally, this formulation can no longer be understood from the viewpoint of infinite perfection, but only from that of absolute infinity. Indeed, for the existence of God to be essence, the same "attributes" that constitute his essence must also constitute his existence. Thus Spinoza adds an explanatory note, anticipating the development of the *Short Treatise*, by invoking here, already, the attributes of an absolutely infinite substance: "To the nature of a being that has infinite attributes, an 'attribute' belongs, which is Being."[18] The differences between the *Short Treatise* and the *Ethics* seem to be these: 1. The *Short Treatise* begins by showing "That God is," before any real definition of God. Thus, strictly speaking, it has available only the Cartesian proof, and is therefore forced to set alongside the orthodox statement of this proof an altogether different version which anticipates Chapter Two ("What God is"); 2. The *Ethics*, rather than setting beside one another two formulations, one proceeding from infinite perfection, the other from absolute infinity, presents a proof that still proceeds from infinite perfection, but that is entirely subordinated to the prior and well-grounded positing of absolute infinity. Then the second formulation of the *Short Treatise* is no longer needed, and no longer obscure and out of place: its equivalent is to be found in the *Ethics*, but no longer as a proof of God's existence, only of his immutability.[19]

Thus far there is no difference between Leibniz's requirements and Spinoza's: the same call for a real definition of God, for a nature or reason of the infinitely perfect. The same subordination of the ontological proof to a real definition of God, and to the demonstration that this definition is indeed a real one. Which makes Leibniz's account of things all the more surprising. We can here draw upon two texts. First, a note added to the manuscript "Quod ens perfectissimum existit," in which Leibniz speaks of his discussions with Spinoza in 1676: "When at the Hague I showed Spinoza this argument, which he thought solid. As he initially disagreed with it, I wrote it out and read him this sheet."[20] Then his notes on the *Ethics*: he complains of Spinoza's Definition 6 that it *is not* a real definition. It does not show the equivalence of the terms "absolutely infinite" and "consisting of an infinity of attributes"; it doesn't show the compatibility of the attributes among themselves; it doesn't show the possibility of the object defined.[21] Either Leibniz means that Definition 6 does not immediately show the possibility of what is defined – but Leibniz believes no more than Spinoza in the existence of such an intuition of God. Or he means that Spinoza has not noticed that the reality of the definition has to be proven – but such a criticism would completely misconstrue the general project of the *Ethics* and the sense of the first ten propositions. In fact, if one considers the formulations through which Leibniz himself proves the possibility of God, one does not at first sight perceive any difference between these and Spinoza's.

For Leibniz, God is possible because infinite perfection is the *proprium* of an "absolute Being" that includes in itself all "attributes," "all simple forms taken absolutely," all "natures which are susceptible of the highest degree," "all positive qualities expressing something without limitation."[22] How do these forms suffice to prove the possibility of God? Each is simple and irreducible, conceived in itself, *index sui*. Leibniz says that it is their very disparity that assures their compatibility (the impossibility of their contradiction), and their compatibility that assures the possibility of the Being to which they belong. Nothing in this sets Leibniz against Spinoza. Everything is literally common to them, including the use of the idea of expression, and including the thesis according to which expressive forms are "the fount of things." In this respect at least, Spinoza had nothing to learn from Leibniz. We are left to conclude that Leibniz did not report the conversation at the Hague accurately. Or that Spinoza listened, and spoke little, privately recognizing the coincidence of Leibniz's ideas with his own. Or perhaps a disagreement was revealed, but this over their respective ways of understanding infinite positive forms or qualities. For Leibniz conceives these as primary possibles in the divine understanding. Moreover, these prime possibles, "absolutely simple notions," lie outside our knowledge: we know that they are necessarily compatible, without knowing what they are. They appear anterior to, and above, any logical relation: knowledge reaches only to "relatively simple notions" which serve as terms of our thinking, and of which the best, perhaps, one can say is that they have a symbolic relation to the prime simples.[23] Leibniz hereby escapes the absolute necessity which he denounces as the danger of Spinozism: he stops "metaphysical" necessity getting out from God and communicating itself to creatures. He introduces a sort of finality, a maximal principle, into the ontological proof itself. After his meetings with Spinoza, Leibniz considers absolute necessity the enemy. Could not Spinoza conversely think, though, that in order to save creatures and creation, Leibniz was retaining all the perspectives of eminence, analogy and symbolism in general? Perhaps Leibniz only appears to advance beyond infinite perfection, only appears to arrive at a nature or reason.

Spinoza thinks that the definition of God as he gives it is a real definition. By a proof of the reality of the definition must be understood a veritable generation of the object defined. This is the sense of the first propositions of the *Ethics*: *they are not hypothetical, but genetic.* Because attributes are really distinct, irreducible one to the others, ultimate in their respective forms or in their kinds, because each is conceived through itself, they cannot contradict one another. They are necessarily compatible, and the substance they form is possible. "It is of the nature of a substance that each of its attributes be conceived through itself, since all the attributes it has have always been in it together, and one could not be produced by another, but each expresses the reality, or being of substance. So it is far from absurd to attribute many attributes to one substance."[24] In the attributes we reach prime and substantial elements, irreducible notions of unique substance. There appears here the idea of a logical constitution of substance, a "composition" in which there is nothing physical. The irreducibility of the attributes not only proves, but constitutes the nonimpossibility of God as unique substance with all attributes. There cannot be contradiction except between terms

79

of which one, at least, is not conceived through itself. And the compatibility of attributes is not grounded, for Spinoza, in a region of the divine understanding above logical relations themselves, but *in a logic proper to real distinction*. It is the nature of real distinction between attributes that excludes all division of substance; it is this nature of real distinction that preserves in distinct terms all their respective positivity, forbidding their definition through opposition one to another, and referring them all to the same indivisible substance. Spinoza seems to have gone further than any other along the path of this new logic: a logic of pure affirmation, of unlimited quality, and thus of the unconditioned totality that possesses all qualities; a logic, that is, of the absolute. Attributes should be understood as the elements of such a composition of the absolute.

Attributes as expressions are not simply "mirrors." Expressionist philosophy brings with it two traditional metaphors: that of a mirror which reflects or reflects upon an image, and that of a seed which "expresses" the tree as a whole. Attributes are one or the other of these, depending on the viewpoint taken. On the one hand, essence is reflected and multiplied in attributes, attributes are mirrors, each of which expresses in its kind the essence of substance: they relate necessarily to an understanding, as mirrors to an eye which sees in them an image. But what is expressed is at the same time involved in its expression, as a tree in its seed: the essence of substance is not so much reflected in the attributes as constituted by the attributes that express it; attributes are not so much mirrors as dynamic or genetic elements.

God's nature (*natura naturans*) is expressive. God expresses himself in the foundations of the world, which form his essence, before expressing himself in the world. And expression is not simply manifestation, but is also the constitution of God himself. Life, that is, expressivity, is carried into the absolute. There is a unity of the diverse in substance, and an actual diversity of the One in the attributes. Real distinction applies to the absolute, because it combines these two moments and relates each to the other. So it is not enough to say that Spinoza privileges *Ens necessarium* over *Ens perfectissimum*. What is actually most important is *Ens absolutum*. *Perfectissimum* is only a *proprium*, a *proprium* from which one sets out as the modality of each attribute. *Necessarium* is another *proprium*, at which one arrives as the modality of a substance having all attributes. But between these is discovered Nature or the absolute: the substance to which are referred Thought, Extension and so on, all the univocal forms of being. This is why Spinoza insists in his letters on the necessity of not losing sight of Definition 6, of constantly returning to it.[25] That definition alone presents us with a nature, the expressive nature of the absolute. To return to this definition is not just to keep it in mind, but to return to a definition that has meanwhile been proven to be real. And that proof is not a sort of operation performed by an understanding that remains outside substance; it amounts to the life of substance itself, the necessity of its *a priori* constitution.

"When I define God as the supremely perfect Being, since this definition does not express the efficient cause (for I conceive that an efficient cause can be internal as well as external) I shall not be able to discover all the properties of God from it; but when I define God as 'a Being, etc.' " (see *Ethics*, Part One, Definition 6).[26] Such is Spinoza's transformation of the proof *a priori*: he goes beyond infinite perfection to absolute infinity, in which he discovers sufficient Reason or Nature. *This step leads into a second triad of substance*: (1) All forms of being are equal and equally perfect, and there is no inequality of perfection between attributes; (2) Every form is thus unlimited, and each attribute

THE TRIADS OF SUBSTANCE

expresses an infinite essence; (3) All forms thus belong to one
and the same substance, and all attributes are equally affirmed,
without limitation, of an absolutely infinite substance. The first
triad was that of attribute–essence–substance. The second is:
perfect–infinite–absolute. The first was founded on a polemical
argument: real distinction cannot be numerical; and on a positive argument: real distinction is a formal distinction between
attributes affirmed of one and the same substance. The polemical argument for the second triad is: *propria* do not constitute a
nature; and the positive argument: everything in Nature is perfect. No "nature" lacks anything; all forms of being are affirmed[c]
without limitation, attributed to something absolute, since the
absolute is in its nature infinite in all its forms. The triad of the
absolute thus complements that of substance: it carries it forward,
leading us on to discover a third and last determination of God.

CHAPTER FIVE

Power

There is a theme that constantly recurs in all Leibniz's criticism of Descartes: he goes "too quickly." Descartes thought that it was enough in the order of being to consider the infinitely perfect, enough in the order of knowing to possess a clear and distinct idea, and enough, in order to pass from knowing to being, to examine quantities of reality or perfection. Descartes is always led, in his hurry, to confuse relative and absolute.[1] If we look once more for what is common in the Anticartesian reaction, we see that Spinoza, for his part, takes issue with Descartes's *facility*. Descartes's willingness to make philosophical use of "easy"[a] and "difficult" had already worried many of his contemporaries. When Spinoza comes up against the Cartesian use of the word "easy," he loses that professorial serenity with which he had promised to set forth the *Principles* differing in nothing by "the breadth of a fingernail"; here he even seems to show a kind of indignation.[2] He is not of course the first to denounce this facility, any more than Leibniz was the first to denounce rapidity. But the criticism takes on with Leibniz and Spinoza its most complete, its richest and its most effective form.

Descartes gives two statements of the *a posteriori* proof of God's existence: God exists because his idea is in us; and also because we ourselves, with our idea of him, exist. The first proof is based directly on the consideration of quantities of perfection or reality. A cause must have at least as much reality as its effect; the cause of an idea should have at least as much reality formally as the idea has objectively. But I have the idea of an infinitely perfect being (that is, an idea that contains "more objective reality than any other"[3]). The second proof is more complex, since it proceeds from an absurd hypothesis: Had I the power to create myself, it would be much easier for me to give myself properties of which I have an idea, and it would be no more difficult for me to preserve myself than to produce or create myself.[4] The principle in this case is: What can do more can do less. "What can do more, or the more difficult thing, can also do a lesser thing."[5] But if it is more difficult to create or preserve a substance than to create or preserve its properties, it is because the substance has more reality than the properties themselves. One may object that the substance is the same thing as its properties considered collectively. But "distributively" the attributes are like parts of a whole, and it is in this sense that they are easier to produce. One may in turn object that a (say, finite) substance cannot be compared with the (say, infinite) attributes of some other substance. But if I had the power to produce myself as a substance, the perfections of which I have an idea would be part of myself, so that it would indeed be easier for me to give myself them than to produce or preserve myself as a whole. It may be objected, finally, that a determinate cause, destined by nature to produce a certain effect, cannot "more easily" produce some other effect, be it even of a lesser quantity. But, from the viewpoint of a first cause, the quantities of reality corresponding to attributes and modes enter into relations of whole to part that allow the determination of greater and lesser, easier and more difficult.[6]

84

The same argument clearly lies at the heart of both proofs. Descartes either relates quantities of objective reality to quantities of formal reality, or he brings quantities of reality into the relations of whole and part. The entire proof *a posteriori*, at any rate, proceeds by examining quantities of reality or perfection considered simply as such. Spinoza, expounding Descartes, does not refrain from attacking the second proof; he again finds, or carries over, objections to the notion of "facility." And the manner in which he does this leads one to think that, if he were speaking for himself, he would have no greater sympathy for the first proof. One does in fact find many versions of an *a posteriori* proof of God's existence in Spinoza's work. I believe these all have something in common, some involving a criticism of the first Cartesian proof, the others of the second, *but all sharing the end of substituting an argument based on power for an argument based on quantities of reality*. It is as though Spinoza were always, in very diverse ways, proposing the same criticism: Descartes takes what is relative as absolute. In the *a priori* proof, Descartes confuses absolute with infinitely perfect, but infinitely perfect is only a relative term. In the *a posteriori* proof, Descartes takes quantity of reality or perfection as an absolute, but this is again only relative. Absolute infinity as nature and sufficient reason of infinite perfection; power as sufficient reason of the quantity of reality: these are the correlative transformations to which Spinoza submits the Cartesian proofs.

The *Short Treatise* contains no trace of the second Cartesian argument; but it preserves the first, in terms similar to those of Descartes[7]: "If there is an idea of God, the cause of [this idea] must exist formally and contain in itself whatever the idea has objectively. But there is an idea of God...." But the proof of this first proposition is thoroughly modified. We see syllogisms multiply, evidence of a state of Spinoza's thought, however indistinct, in which he is already trying to advance beyond the argument based on quantities of reality and substitute an argument based on power. His reasoning runs as follows: A finite understanding has not in itself the "capacity" to know infinity, nor indeed to know this rather than that; but it "can"[b] know something; there must then, formally, be an object that determines it as knowing this rather than that; and it "can" conceive infinity; so God must himself exist formally. In other words, Spinoza asks: Why must the cause of the idea of God contain formally all that this idea contains objectively? Which amounts to saying that Descartes's axiom does not satisfy him. The Cartesian axiom was: there must be "at least as much" formal reality in an idea's cause as there is objective reality in the idea itself. (Which guaranteed that there was not "more" in the case of an infinite quantity of objective reality.) But we sense that Spinoza is looking for a deeper reason. This section of the *Short Treatise* is already elaborating various elements that will play their part in an *axiom of powers*: understanding has no more power to know than its objects have to exist and act; the power of thinking and knowing cannot be greater than a necessarily correlative power of existing.

Is it really a question of an *axiom*? Another passage of the *Short Treatise*, certainly of later date, states: "There is no thing of which there is not an idea in the thinking thing, and no idea can exist unless the thing exists."[8] This principle is basic to all of Spinozism. Once proved it leads to the equality of two powers. The first part of the formula is, it is true, difficult to prove, if one does not assume the existence of God. But the second is easily proved. An idea that was not the idea of some existing thing would not be distinct at all, would not be the idea of this or that. Or, to give a better proof: To know is to know by the cause, so that nothing can be known without a cause of its being in existence or in essence. One may already infer from this argument that the power of thinking, in which all ideas participate, is not superior to a power of existing and acting in which all things participate. And this is what matters from the viewpoint of an *a posteriori* proof.

We have an idea of God; we must then assert an infinite power of thinking as corresponding to this idea; but the power of think-ing is no greater than the power of existing and acting; we must then assert an infinite power of existing as corresponding to the nature of God. The existence of God is not inferred directly from the idea of God; *we pass through the detour of powers* to find, in the power of thinking, the ground of the objective reality con-tained in the idea of God, and in the power of existing the ground of the formal reality of God himself. The *Short Treatise* seems to me to be already elaborating the elements of a proof of this kind. An explicit formulation is then given in the *Correction of the Understanding*.[9,c] But it is in a letter that Spinoza most clearly reveals what he was after from the *Short Treatise* on: the substitu-tion of an axiom of powers for the Cartesian axiom of quantities of reality, considered unclear. "The power of Thought to think about or to comprehend things, is not greater than the power of Nature to exist and to act. This is a clear and true axiom, accord-ing to which the existence of God follows very clearly and validly from the idea of him."[10]

We should however note that Spinoza comes rather late into the possession of his "axiom." Nor, furthermore, does he give it in the fullest form which would imply strict equality between the two powers. Further still, he presents as an axiom a proposition that he knows to be in part demonstrable. But there is a reason for all these ambiguities. The equality of powers is all the better demonstrable if one begins with an already existing God. So that as he advances to a more perfect formulation of this equality,

Spinoza ceases to use it to establish God's existence *a posteriori*; he reserves it for another use, another domain. The equality of powers will in fact play a fundamental role in Book Two of the *Ethics*; but that role is to be the decisive factor in the demonstration of parallelism, once God's existence is already proved.

One should not, therefore, be surprised that the *a posteriori* proof of the *Ethics* should differ in kind from that of the *Short Treatise* and the *Correction of the Understanding*. It is still based on power. But it no longer proceeds via the idea of God, or a corresponding power of thinking, to an infinite power of existing. It proceeds directly within existence, via the power of existing. The *Ethics* thus follows suggestions already proposed by Spinoza in the reworked version in the *Principles*. There Spinoza set out the first Cartesian proof without commentary or emendation, but the second proof was thoroughly reworked. Spinoza violently took issue with Descartes's use of the word "easy," and proposed a thoroughly different argument: 1. The more something has of reality or perfection, the more existence does it involve (possible existence corresponding to finite degrees of perfection, or necessary existence corresponding to infinite perfection); 2. Whatever has the *power* (*potentia* or *vis*) to preserve itself, requires no cause of its existence to "exist possibly," or even "necessarily." Whatever has the power to preserve itself thus exists necessarily; 3. I am imperfect, and so have no necessary existence, and have not the power to preserve myself; I am preserved by something else, something else that must necessarily have the power to preserve itself, and must therefore exist necessarily.[11]

In the *Short Treatise* there is no trace of Descartes's second argument; the first is retained but proved in an altogether different way. In the *Ethics*, on the other hand, there remains no trace of the first (because the argument from powers is now reserved for a better use). But one does find in the *Ethics* a version of the *a posteriori* proof which is related to Descartes's second argument, if only as an implicit criticism of it, and as its reworking. Spinoza attacks those who imagine that the more that belongs to a thing, the more difficult it is to produce.[12] But he goes farther than he had gone in the *Principles*. The exposition there left out what was most important: existence, whether possible or necessary, is itself power; *power is identical to essence itself*. It is just because essence is power that possible existence (in a thing's essence) is not the same as a "possibility." The *Ethics* presents, then, the following argument: (1) The capacity to exist (that is, the possible existence involved in the essence of a finite thing) is a power; (2) Now, a finite being already exists necessarily (by virtue of some external cause which determines its existence); (3) If absolutely infinite Being did not itself exist necessarily, it would have less power than finite beings, which is absurd; (4) But the necessary existence of the absolutely infinite cannot obtain by virtue of an external cause; so that it is through itself that the absolutely infinite being necessarily exists.[13] Thus based on the power of existing, the *a posteriori* proof leads to a new *a priori* proof: the more reality or perfection that belongs to the nature of some thing, the more power does it have, that is, the more forces tending to its existence (*virium... ut existat*); "God therefore has, of himself, an absolutely infinite power of existing. For that reason he exists absolutely."[14]

Spinoza's argument from power thus has two aspects, one relating to his criticism of Descartes's first proof, the other to criticism of the second. But we should look in each case, and especially in the second, which represents the definitive state of Spinoza's thought, for the implications of the argument. A power of existing is attributed to a finite being as identical to its essence. Of course a finite being exists not by its own essence or power, but by virtue of some external cause. It has nevertheless its own power of existing, even though this power necessarily only becomes effective under the action of external things. Yet another reason to ask: On what condition do we attribute to a finite being, which does not exist through itself, a *power of existing and acting* identical to its essence?[15] Spinoza's reply would appear to be as follows: We affirm this power of a finite being to the extent that we consider this being as part of a whole, as a mode of an attribute, a modification of a substance. This substance itself thus has an infinite power of existing, all the more power the more attributes it has. And the same reasoning applies to the power of thinking: we attribute to a distinct idea a power of knowing, but this to the extent that we consider this idea as part of a whole, as a mode of the attribute Thought, a modification of a thinking substance that itself has an infinite power of thinking.[16]

It now appears more clearly how the *a posteriori* proof of the *Ethics* leads to a proof *a priori*. One has only to recognize that God, having all attributes, fulfills, *a priori, all the conditions* for a power to be asserted of some thing: he thus has an "absolutely infinite" power of existence, *exists* "absolutely" and through himself. We furthermore see how God, having as one attribute Thought, also has an absolutely infinite power of thinking.[17] Attributes seem in all this to have an essentially dynamic role. Not that they are themselves powers. But, taken collectively, they are the conditions for the attribution to absolute substance of an absolutely infinite power of existing and acting, identical with its formal essence. Taken distributively they are the conditions for the attribution to finite beings of a power identical with their formal essence, insofar as that essence is contained in this or that attribute. On the other hand, the attribute of Thought is, taken in itself, the condition for assigning to absolute substance an absolutely infinite power of thinking, identical with its objective essence, and for the attribution to ideas of a power of knowing, identical with the objective essence that respectively defines them. It is in this sense that finite beings are conditioned, being necessarily modifications of substance or modes of an attribute. Substance is as it were the unconditioned totality, because it possesses or fulfills *a priori* the infinity of conditions. Attributes are conditions common to substance which possesses them collectively and to modes which imply them distributively. As Spinoza says, it is only by human attributes (goodness, justice, charity and so on) that God "communicates" to human creatures the perfections they possess.[18] It is, on the other hand, through his own attributes that God communicates to all creatures the power proper to each.

The *Political Treatise* presents an *a posteriori* proof akin to those given in the *Principles* and the *Ethics*. Finite beings do not exist and are not preserved by their own power, but are dependent for their existence and preservation on a being able to preserve itself and to exist through itself. Thus the power by which a finite being exists, is preserved, and acts, is the power of God himself.[19] One might imagine that such an argument tends in some respects to suppress any power proper to creatures. But this is not at all the case. All of Spinozism agrees in conferring on finite beings a power of existence, action and perseverance; and the very context of the proof in the *Political Treatise* emphasizes that things have their own power, identical with their essence and constitutive of their "right." Spinoza does not mean that a being that does not exist of itself has no power; he means that it has no power of its own except insofar as it is part of a whole, that is, part of the power of a being that does exist through itself. (The whole *a posteriori* proof rests on this argument from the conditioned to the unconditioned.) Spinoza says in the *Ethics*: man's power is "part of the infinite power of God."[20] But the part turns out to be irreducible, an original degree of power distinct from all others. We are a part of the power of God, but this just insofar as this power is "explicated" by our essence itself.[21] Participation is always thought of by Spinoza as a participation of powers. But the participation of powers never does away with the distinction of essences. Spinoza never confuses the essence of a mode with an essence of substance: my power remains my own essence, God's power remains his own essence, while my power is at the same time part of the power of God.[22]

How can this be so? How can a distinction of essences be reconciled with a participation of powers? If the power or essence of God can be "explicated" by a finite essence, this is because attributes are forms common to God whose essence they constitute, and finite things whose essences they contain. God's power divides and explicates itself in each attribute according to the essences comprised in that attribute. *Thus the part–whole relation tends to merge with the mode–attribute, modification–substance relation.* Finite things are parts of the divine power because they are modes of God's attributes. But the reduction of "creatures" to the status of modes, far from taking away their own power, shows rather how a part of their power properly belongs to them, along with their essence. The identity of power and essence is to be asserted equally (under the same conditions) of modes and substance. These conditions are the attributes, through which substance possesses an omnipotence identical to its essence. And thus modes, implicating these same attributes that constitute God's essence are said to "explicate" or "express" divine power.[23] Reducing things to modes of a single substance is not a way of making them mere appearances, phantoms, as Leibniz believed or pretended to believe, but is rather the only way, according to Spinoza, to make them "natural" beings, endowed with force or power.

The identity of power and essence means: a power is always an act or, at least, in action. A long theological tradition had asserted the identity of power and act, not only in God, but in Nature.[24] At the same time, a long tradition of materialism in physical theory asserted the actual character of all power in created things themselves: for the distinction of power and act, potentiality and actuality, was substituted the correlation of a power of acting and a power of being acted on or suffering action, both actual.[25] The two currents meet in Spinoza, one relating to the essence of substance, the other to the essence of modes. For in Spinozism all power bears with it a corresponding and inseparable capacity to be affected. And this capacity to be affected is always, necessarily, exercised. To *potentia* there corresponds an *aptitudo* or *potestas*; but there is no aptitude or capacity that remains ineffective, and so no power that is not actual.[26]

A mode's essence is a power; to it corresponds a certain capacity of the mode to be affected. But because the mode is a part of Nature, this capacity is always exercised, either in affections produced by external things (those affections called passive), or in affections explained by its own essence (called active). Thus the distinction between power and act, on the level of modes, disappears in favor of two equally actual powers, that of acting, and that of suffering action, which vary inversely one to the other, but whose sum is both constant and constantly effective. Thus Spinoza can sometimes present the power of modes as an invariant identical to their essence, since the capacity to be affected remains fixed, and sometimes as subject to variation, since the power of acting (or force of existing) "increases" and "diminishes" according to the proportion of active affections contributing to the exercise of this power at any moment.[27] It remains that a mode, in any case, has no power that is not actual: it is at each moment all that it can be, its power is its essence.

93

The essence of substance, at the other extreme, is also power. This absolutely infinite power of existence carries with it a capacity to be affected in an infinity of ways. But in this case the capacity to be affected can be exercised only by active affections. How could absolutely infinite substance have a power of suffering action, since this obviously presupposes a limitation of its power of action? Substance, being omnipotent in and through itself, is necessarily capable of an infinity of affections, and is the active cause of all affections of which it is capable. To say that the essence of God is power, is to say that God produces an infinity of things by virtue of the same power by which he exists. *He thus produces them by existing.* Cause of all things "in the same sense" as cause of himself, he produces all things in his attributes, since his attributes constitute at once his essence and his existence. It is not enough, then, to say that God's power is actual: it is necessarily active, it is act. God's essence cannot be his power without an infinity of things proceeding from it, and this precisely in the attributes that constitute it. So that modes are also the affections of God, but God never suffers the activity of his modes; his only affections are active.[28]

Every essence is the essence of some thing. One should therefore distinguish between essence as power, that of which it is the essence, and the corresponding capacity to be affected. That of which an essence is the essence is always a quantity of reality or perfection. But a thing has the greater reality or perfection, the greater the number of ways in which it can be affected: *the quantity of reality is always grounded in a power identical to an essence.* The *a posteriori* proof sets out from the power proper to finite beings: one seeks the condition of a finite being having a power, and rises from this to the unconditioned power of absolutely infinite substance. For the essence of a finite being is only a power in relation to a substance of which this being is a mode. But this

94

a posteriori approach only provides us with an access to a deeper *a priori* approach. The essence of absolutely infinite substance is omnipotence, since substance possesses *a priori* all the conditions for the attribution of power to some thing. But if it be true that modes, by virtue of their power, exist only in their relation to substance, then substance, by virtue of its power, exists only in its relation to modes: it has an absolutely infinite power of existence only by exercising in an infinity of things, in an infinity of ways or modes, the capacity to be affected corresponding to that power.

Spinoza hereby leads us to a final triad of substance. Setting out from the arguments from power, the discovery of this triad occupies the whole concluding section of Part One of the *Ethics*. It takes the following form: the essence of substance as an absolutely infinite power of existing; substance as *ens realissimum* existing of itself; a capacity to be affected in an *infinity of ways*, corresponding to this power, and necessarily exercised in affections of which substance is itself the active cause. This third triad takes its place alongside the previous two. It does not correspond, like the first, to the necessity of a substance with all attributes; nor, like the second, to the necessity that such a substance should exist absolutely. It corresponds rather to the necessity that this substance should produce an infinity of things. And it does not merely serve to allow our passage from substance to modes, but communicates itself to or applies to these. So that modes themselves present us with the following triad: a mode's essence as a power; an existing mode defined by its quantity of reality or perfection; the capacity to be affected in a *great number* of ways. Thus Part One of the *Ethics* may be seen as the unfolding of three triads, which all find in expression their principle: those of substance, of absolute and of power.

95

PART TWO

Parallelism and Immanence

Chapter Six

Expression in Parallelism

Why does God produce anything at all? The problem of a sufficient reason for the production of things does not disappear in
Spinozism, but rather gains in urgency. For God's nature is, as
natura naturans, in itself expressive. This expression is so natural, or essential, to God, that it does not merely reflect a ready-
made God, but forms a kind of unfolding of divinity, a logical and
genetic constitution of divine substance. Each attribute expresses
a formal essence; all formal essences are expressed as the absolute
essence of a single identical substance whose existence necessarily follows; this existence is thus itself expressed by the attributes.
These are the very moments of substance; expression is, in God,
his very life. So that one cannot say God produces the world, universe or *natura naturata*, *in order* to express himself. For not only
must the sufficient reason necessitate the result, ruling out any
argument from finality, but God expresses himself in himself, in
his own nature, in the attributes that constitute him. He has no
"need" to produce, lacking nothing. We must take literally a
metaphor used by Spinoza to show that the world he produces
adds nothing to God's essence: when a workman sculpts heads
and chests, and then joins a chest to a head, this addition adds
nothing to the essence of the head.[1] This maintains the same

essence, *the same expression.* If God expresses himself in himself, the universe can only be a second degree of expression. Substance already expresses itself in the attributes that constitute *natura naturans,* but attributes in their turn express themselves in modes, which constitute *natura naturata.* Still more reason to ask: Why this second level? Why does God produce a modal universe?

To account for production *a priori,* Spinoza adduces the initial argument that God acts, or produces, as he understands himself (*seipsum intelligit*); understanding himself necessarily, he acts necessarily.[2] His second argument appears sometimes to depend on the first, sometimes to be distinct and complementary. God produces as he exists; necessarily existing, he necessarily produces.[3]

What is the sense of the first argument? What does "understands himself" mean? God does not conceive in his understanding *possibilities,* but understands the necessity of his own nature. Infinite understanding is not the locus of the possible, but the form of the idea that God necessarily has of himself or of his own essence. The *scientia* of God is not a science of the possible, but the knowledge[a] God has of himself and of his own nature. Understanding, then, is to be opposed to conceiving something as possible. Understanding is thus the deduction of properties from what one apprehends as necessary. Thus, from the definition of the circle, we deduce various properties that really follow from this definition. God understands himself; an infinity of properties follow, which fall, necessarily, within the divine understanding. God in understanding his own essence produces an infinity of things, which result from it *as properties result from a definition.* One sees in this argument how modes are assimilated to logically necessary properties that follow from the essence of God as this is understood. When Spinoza congratulates certain Hebrews for having seen that God, God's understanding, and the things he understands, were one and the same thing, he means at once that God's understanding is the *scientia* he has of his own nature, and that this knowledge comprises an infinity of things that necessarily result from this nature.[4]

But why does God understand himself? Sometimes Spinoza presents the proposition as a sort of axiom.[5] The axiom derives from Aristotelian conceptions: God thinks himself, is himself the object of his thought, his knowledge has no other object than himself. Such is the principle opposed to the idea of a divine understanding that thinks "possibles." And many commentators had assembled convincing arguments to show how Aristotle's God, thinking himself, thereby also thinks all the other things that necessarily result from him: the Aristotelian tradition thus tends toward a theism, sometimes even toward a pantheism, which identifies knower, knowledge and known (the Hebrews invoked by Spinoza were Jewish Aristotelians).

Yet Spinoza's theory of the idea of God is too original to be based on a mere axiom or an appeal to some tradition. That God understands himself should follow from the necessity of the divine nature.[6] The notion of expression plays here a decisive role. In his self-expression, God understands himself insofar as he expresses himself. In expressing himself formally in his attributes he understands himself objectively in an idea. God's essence, expressed in the attributes as formal essence, is expressed in ideas as objective essence. Thus Spinoza, from the definition of attribute on, invokes an understanding capable of perceiving. Not that the attribute is "attributed" by understanding: the word "perceiving" sufficiently indicates that understanding grasps nothing that is not in Nature. But as expressing the essence of substance, attributes are necessarily referred to an understanding that understands them objectively, that is, perceives what they express. Thus the idea of God is seen to be grounded in the divine nature itself: because God has as his nature an infinity of attributes, each of which "expresses" an infinite essence, it follows from this expressive nature that God understands himself and, understanding himself, produces all the things that "fall" within an infinite understanding.[7] Expressions are always explications. But the explications of the understanding are only perceptions. It is not understanding that explicates substance, but the explications of substance refer necessarily to an understanding that understands them. God necessarily understands himself, just as he explicates or expresses himself.

Let us consider the second argument: God produces as he exists. Modes are here no longer assimilated to logical properties, but rather to physical affections. The independent development of this line of argument is thus grounded in power: the more power a thing has, the more it can be affected in a great number of ways; but we have proved, either *a posteriori* or *a priori*, that God has an absolutely infinite power of existence. God therefore has the ability to be affected in an infinity of ways, a *potestas* that corresponds to his power or *potentia*. This ability is necessarily exercised, but this cannot be by affections which come from something other than God; thus God necessarily and actively produces an infinity of things which affect him in an infinity of ways.

That God should necessarily produce things tells us also how he produces. Understanding himself as a substance composed of an infinity of attributes, existing as a substance composed of an infinity of attributes, God acts as he understands and as he exists, this then *in* these attributes that express at once his essence and existence. He produces an infinity of things, "in an infinity of modes." That is: The things produced have no existence outside the attributes that contain them. Attributes are univocal conditions of God's existence, and also of his action. Attributes are

univocal or common forms, predicated, in the same form, of creatures and creator, products and producer, formally constituting
the essence of one, formally containing the essence of the others. The principle of necessary production thus reflects a double univocity. A univocity of cause: God is cause of all things *in
the same sense* as he is cause of himself. A univocity of attributes:
God produces through and in the same attributes that constitute
his essence. So Spinoza pursues a constant polemic: he never tires
of showing the absurdity of a God producing things through moral
attributes such as goodness, justice or charity, or indeed through
human attributes such as understanding and will.

   Suppose, by *analogy* with man, that understanding and will
were attributes of God himself.[8] This would not get us very far,
for we would be attributing understanding and will to God only
equivocally: because of the distinction of divine and human
essence, divine and human understanding and will share a "community of name" only, like dog-star and barking dog-animal.
Numerous absurdities follow, according to which God must contain eminently the perfections through which he produces creatures. 1. From the viewpoint of understanding, God will be said
to be "omnipotent" precisely because he is "unable" to create
things with perfections as he understands them, that is, in the
same form as they belong to him. So one purports to demonstrate the omnipotence of God through an impotence.[9] 2. From
the viewpoint of will, it will be said that God might have willed
otherwise, or that things might have been of another nature had
God so willed. God is attributed will, it is made his essence;
but it is supposed at the same time that he might have had a
different will, and so a different essence (unless divine will be
made a pure thing of reason, in which case the contradictions
are only increased); this allows the supposition of two or more
possible gods. So that here variability and plurality are intro-

duced into God, to demonstrate his eminence.[10]

I have simplified Spinoza's criticisms. But I believe that whenever he attacks the image of a God essentially endowed with understanding and will, he is developing the critical implications of his theory of univocity. He wants to show that understanding and will can only be considered attributes of God by analogy. But analogy is unable to conceal the equivocation from which it sets out, or the eminence to which it leads. And the eminence of perfections in God involves, like equivocal attributes, all sorts of contradiction. To God are attributed only those forms that are as perfect in the creatures in which they are implicated, as in God who understands them. God does not produce things because he wills, but because he is. He does not produce because he conceives, conceives things as possible, but because he understands himself, necessarily understands his own nature. In short God acts "by the laws of his nature alone": he could not have produced anything else, or produced things in a different order, except by having a different nature.[11] It may be noted that Spinoza hardly needs, in general, to denounce the incoherence of the idea of creation directly. He has only to ask: How does God produce things, in what conditions? The very conditions of production render it different from a creation, and "creatures" different from creations. As God produces necessarily, and within his own attributes, his productions are necessarily modes of these attributes that constitute his nature.

The logic of expression seems to be one of duplication. Spinoza is too careful a grammarian to allow us to miss the linguistic origins of "expression." Attributes are, as we have seen, names: verbs rather than adjectives. Each attribute is a verb, a primary infinitive proposition, an expression with a distinct sense; but all attributes designate substance as one and the same thing. The traditional distinction between the sense expressed and the object designated (and expressing itself in this sense[b]) thus finds in Spinozism direct application. The distinction necessarily generates a certain movement of expression. For the sense of an initial proposition must in its turn be made the *designatum* of a second, which will itself have a new sense, and so on. Thus the substance they designate is expressed in the attributes, attributes express an essence. Then the attributes are in their turn expressed: they express themselves in modes which designate them, the modes expressing a modification. Modes are truly "participial" propositions which derive from the primary infinitive ones. Thus expression, through its own movement, generates a second level of expression. Expression has within it the sufficient reason of a re-expression. This second level defines production itself: God is said to produce things, as his attributes find expression.[c] So that in the last instance it is always God who, but for the different level of expression, is designated by all things. Attributes designate God, but so also do modes, within the attribute on which they depend. "Some of the Hebrews seem to have seen this, as if through a cloud, when they maintained that God, God's understanding, and the things understood by him are one and the same."[12]

There is an *order* in which God necessarily produces things. This order is that of the expression of attributes. Each attribute is first expressed in its absolute nature: an immediate infinite mode is thus the first expression of an attribute. Then the modified attribute expresses itself, in a mediate infinite mode. Finally the attribute is expressed "in a certain and determinate way," or rather in an infinity of ways which amount to finite existing modes.[13] This last level would remain inexplicable did not infinite modes, within each attribute, contain in them the laws or the principles of the laws according to which corresponding finite modes are themselves determined and ordered.

If there is an order of production, it is the same for all attributes. For God produces things concomitantly in all the attributes that constitute his nature. So that the attributes express themselves in one and the same order, down to the level of finite modes, which must have the same order in different attributes. This identity of order defines a correspondence of modes: to any mode of one attribute there necessarily corresponds a mode of each of the other attributes. This identity of order excludes any relation of real causality. Attributes are mutually irreducible and really distinct; none is cause of another, or of anything whatever in another. Modes therefore involve the concept of their own attribute alone, and not that of any other.[14] The identity of order and the correspondence between modes of different attributes therefore excludes any relation of real causality between these modes, as between their attributes. And on this point there is no serious reason to believe any change occurs in Spinoza's thought: the famous passages of the *Short Treatise* in which Spinoza speaks of an action of one attribute on another, of an effect of one attribute in another, an interaction between modes of different attributes, should not it seems be interpreted in terms of real causality.[15] The context specifies that two attributes (Thought and Extension) act one on another when they are "taken together," or that two modes of different attributes (soul and body) act one on another to the extent that they form "parts of a whole." Nothing in this really goes beyond the assertion of correspondence: if two things are parts of a whole, nothing can change in one without there being some corresponding change in the other, and neither thing can change without the whole itself changing.[16] One may at most see in these passages the stamp of a phase in which Spinoza had not yet sufficiently expressed the difference between his own doctrine and apparently similar doctrines (occasional causality, ideal causality). Spinoza never seems to have admitted the action of a real causality to account for the relation between modes of different attributes.

The principles above lead to a result in which may be recognized Spinoza's first formulation of parallelism: there is an *identity of order* or *correspondence* between modes of different attributes. One may indeed call "parallel" two things or two series of things which bear to each other a constant relation, such that there is nothing in one to which there corresponds nothing in the other, while all real causality between them is excluded. But one should be wary of the word "parallelism," which is not Spinoza's. It seems to be a creation of Leibniz's, who employs it on his own account to designate such a correspondence between autonomous or independent series.[17] So we should not imagine that identity of order is enough to identify Spinoza's system; there is a sense in which it is found in more or less all doctrines that refuse to interpret correspondences in terms of real causality. If the word "parallelism" does adequately characterize Spinoza's philosophy, it does so by itself implying something beside a mere identity of order, something beside a correspondence. And it does so also because Spinoza is not satisfied with this correspondence or this identity as definition of the link that unites modes of different attributes.

Thus Spinoza gives two further formulations that extend the first: *identity of connection or equality of principle, identity of being or ontological unity.* The specifically Spinozist theory is stated thus: "One and the same order, that is, one and the same connection of causes, i.e., that the same things follow one another."[18] One should certainly be in no haste to consider order and connection (*connexio* or *concatenatio*) as strictly synonymous. What is certain is that in the passage just cited, the assertion of an identity of

being amounts to something more than a mere identity of connection; so that it appears likely that connection already involves
something more than order. And indeed, identity of connection
means not only the autonomy of corresponding series, but an
isonomy, that is, an equality of principle between autonomous
or independent series.[d] Consider two corresponding series, but
with unequal principles, that of one being in some way eminent
in relation to that of the other: between a solid and its projection, a line and an asymptote, there is indeed an identity of order
or correspondence, but not, strictly speaking, an "identity of
connection." The points of a curve are not linked together (con-
catenantur) in the same way as those of a straight line.[e] In such
cases one can speak of parallelism only in a very vague sense.
"Parallels," in the strict sense, require an equality of principle
between the two corresponding series of points. When Spinoza
asserts that modes of different attributes have not only the same
order, but also the came connection or concatenation, he means
that the principles on which they depend are themselves equal.
Already in the passages of the *Short Treatise*, if two attributes or
two modes of different attributes are "taken together," this is
because they form equal parts or halves of a whole. Parallelism
is given its strict sense by the equality of attributes, which guarantees that the connection is the same between things whose
order is the same.

Leibniz, then, coins the word "parallelism," but invokes it for
his own purposes in a very general and hardly satisfactory manner:
Leibniz's system does indeed imply a correspondence between
autonomous series, substances and phenomena, solids and projections; but the principles of these series are singularly unequal.
(One may add that Leibniz, when he speaks more exactly, invokes
the image of projection rather than that of parallels.) Spinoza,
on the other hand, does not use the word "parallelism," yet the

word suits his system, as he does suppose the equality of the principles from which independent and corresponding series follow.
Here again one sees well enough the nature of his polemical
intent. By his strict parallelism Spinoza refuses any analogy, any
eminence, any kind of superiority of one series over another, and
any ideal action that presupposes a preeminence: there is no more
any superiority of soul over body, than of the attribute of Thought
over that of Extension. And the third formulation of parallelism,
that which asserts identity of being, goes even further in the same
direction: the modes of different attributes have not only the
same order and the same connection, but the same being; they
are the *same things*, distinguished only by the attribute whose concept they involve. Modes of different attributes are one and the
same modification, differing only in attribute. Through this identity of being or ontological unity, Spinoza refuses the interven-
tion of a transcendent God to make each term in one series agree
with a term in the other, or even to set the series in agreement
through their unequal principles. Spinoza's doctrine is rightly
named "parallelism," but this because it excludes any analogy,
any eminence, any transcendence. Parallelism, strictly speaking,
is to be understood neither from the viewpoint of occasional
causes, nor from the viewpoint of ideal causality, but only from
the viewpoint of an immanent God and immanent causality.

The essence of expression is in play in all this. For the relation of expression goes beyond the relation of causality: it applies
to independent things, and to autonomous series which have, no
less than these, a determinate correspondence, constant and reg-
ular. If Spinoza's philosophy and that of Leibniz have a natural
line of engagement,[f] it is to be found in the idea of expression,
in their respective use of this idea. And we will see that Leibniz's
"expressive" model is always that of asymptote or projection.
The expressive model that emerges in Spinoza's theory is quite

different: a "parallelist" model, it implies the equality of two things that express the same third thing, and the identity of this third thing as expressed in the other two. The idea of expression in Spinoza at once brings together and grounds the three aspects of parallelism.

Parallelism characterizes modes, and modes alone. But it is grounded in substance and the attributes of substance. God produces things in all attributes at once: he produces them in the same order in each, and so there is a correspondence between modes of different attributes. But because attributes are really distinct this correspondence, or identity of order, excludes any causal action of one on another. Because the attributes are all equal, there is an identity of connection between modes differing in attribute. Because attributes constitute one and the same substance, modes that differ in attribute form one and the same modification. One may in a sense see in this the triad of substance "descending" into the attributes and communicating itself to the modes.g Substance expressed itself in attributes, each attribute was an expression, the essence of substance was expressed. Now each attribute expresses itself, the dependent modes are expressions, and a modification is expressed. It will be recalled that the essence they expressed had no existence outside the attributes, but was expressed as the absolute essence of substance, the same for all attributes. The same applies here: a modification has no existence outside the mode that expresses it in each attribute, but it is expressed as a modification of substance, the same for all modes differing in attribute. One and the same modification is thus expressed in the infinity of attributes in "an infinity of modes," which differ only in attribute. Importance must therefore be attached to the terms "mode" and "modification." In principle, a mode is an affection of an attribute, a modification an affection of substance. One is to be understood formally, the other ontologically. Every mode is the form of a modification in an attribute, every modification the being in itself of modes differing in attribute (being in itself is not here opposed to a being for us, but to a formal being). Their correlation may be stated thus: modes differing in attribute express one and the same modification, but this modification has no existence outside the modes expressing it in different attributes. Whence a formulation presented by Spinoza himself as obscure: "God is really the cause of things as they are in themselves (*ut in se sunt*), insofar as he consists of an infinity of attributes.[h] For the present, I cannot explain these matters more clearly."[19] "In itself" obviously does not mean that the things produced by God are substances. The *res in se* is substantial modification; but God does not produce this modification outside the modes that express it in all attributes at once. We see the triad of substance, then, extending to a modal triad (attribute–mode–modification). And this is precisely how Spinoza demonstrates parallelism in the Scholium to II.7: Just as one and the same substance is "comprehended"[i] under different attributes, one and the same thing (modification) is "expressed" in all attributes; as this thing has no existence outside the modes that express it in each attribute, modes differing in attribute have the same order, the same connection, and the same being in themselves.

CHAPTER SEVEN

The Two Powers and the Idea of God

Parallelism, then, seems easy to demonstrate. One need only carry the unity of substance into modification, and the expressive character of attributes into modes, the transposition being grounded in the necessity of production (the second level of expression). But when we consider Part Two, Proposition 7 as a whole, we are disconcerted to find before us a far more complex operation. Thus the text of Enuncia, Proof and Corollary does indeed assert an identity of order, connection and even being, but not between modes expressing the same modification in each attribute. The triple identity is asserted only of ideas, which are modes of Thought, and the thing they represent, which is a mode of some attribute. Such parallelism is *epistemological*: it is established between an idea and its "object" (*res ideata, objectum ideae*). The Scholium, on the other hand, follows the lines indicated above: it deduces an *ontological* parallelism between all modes differing in attribute. But it itself reaches this conclusion only by way of the proof and corollary: it generalizes the case of an idea and its object, extending it to *all* modes differing in attribute.[1]

Several questions arise. In the first place, assuming the two parallelisms go together, why does one have to pass at the outset through an "epistemological" detour? Is it only a detour? What is its sense and importance in the *Ethics* as a whole? Above all, are the two parallelisms reconcilable? The epistemological viewpoint amounts to this: that given a mode in some attribute, there corresponds to it in the attribute of Thought an idea that represents it, and it alone.[2] Far from leading us to the unity of a "modification" expressed by all modes in different attributes, epistemological parallelism directs us rather to the simple unity of an "individual" formed by the mode of a certain attribute and the idea that represents solely this mode.[3] Far from leading us to the unity of all modes differing in their attribute, it directs us to the multiplicity of the ideas corresponding to modes of different attributes. In this sense, "psychophysical" parallelism is a particular case of epistemological parallelism: the soul is the idea of the body, that is to say, the idea of a certain mode of Extension, and of this mode only. The epistemological viewpoint, then, may be stated thus: one and the same individual is expressed by a given mode and by the corresponding idea. But the ontological viewpoint thus: one and the same modification is expressed by all corresponding modes differing in attribute. Of all Spinoza's friends and disciples, it is Tschirnhaus who best emphasizes the difficulty, recognizing that it is at the heart of the system of *expression*.[4] How may the two viewpoints be reconciled? This, most particularly, since epistemology forces us to confer on the attribute of Thought a singular privilege: the attribute must contain as many irreducible ideas as there are modes of different attributes; still more, as many ideas as there are attributes. This privilege seems in flagrant contradiction with all the demands of ontological parallelism.

We must therefore examine the Proof and Corollary of Proposition 7 in detail: "The order and connection of ideas is the same as the order and connection of things." The Proof is simple; it merely invokes the axiom that "The knowledge of an effect depends on, and involves, the knowledge of its cause." Which takes us back, in its turn, to the Aristotelian principle that to know is to know by the cause. In Spinoza's perspective one deduces: (1) To every idea there corresponds some thing (nothing can be known independently of a cause of its being, in essence or in existence); (2) The order of ideas is the same as the order of things (a thing is known only by knowledge of its cause).

But this specifically Spinoza's perspective involves more than just Aristotle's axiom. How otherwise could we understand the fact that Aristotle and many others did not reach a theory of parallelism? Spinoza happily recognizes this: "We have shown that a true idea is simple, or composed of simple ideas; that it shows how and why something is, or has been done; and that its objective effects proceed in the soul according to the formal nature of its object. This is the same as what the ancients said, i.e., that true knowledge proceeds from cause to effect – except that so far as I know they never conceived the soul (as we do here) as acting according to certain laws, like a spiritual automaton."[5] "Spiritual automaton" means first of all that an idea, being a mode of thought, has its (efficient and formal) cause nowhere but in the attribute of Thought. Equally, any object whatever has its efficient and formal cause only in the attribute of which it is a mode, and whose concept it involves. Here then is what sets Spinoza apart from the tradition leading down from Antiquity: all efficient or formal (and *a fortiori* material and final) causality between ideas and things, things and ideas, is excluded. This double exclusion is not referred to an axiom, but is the object of proofs that occupy the beginning of Part Two of the *Ethics*.[6] Spinoza can thus assert the independence of the two series, the series of things and the series of ideas. That to each idea there corresponds some thing is, in this context, an initial element of parallelism.

But only an initial element. For ideas to have the same connection as things, there must also be an idea corresponding to
each thing. We come back to two formulae of the *Short Treatise*:
"No idea can exist unless the thing also exists," but in turn
"There is no thing of which there is not an idea in the thinking
thing."[7] But, to prove that each thing is the object of an idea, we
no longer run up against the difficulties that stopped us in the *a
posteriori* proof. For now we start from an existent God. We know
that this God understands himself: he forms an idea of himself,
he possesses an infinite understanding. But it is enough for this
God to understand himself, to produce things and, producing,
to understand all that he produces.

To the extent that God produces as he understands himself,
all that he produces necessarily "falls" within his infinite understanding. In understanding himself and his own essence, God
also understands all that follows from his essence. So infinite
understanding understands all the attributes of God, as well as
all his affections.[8] Ideas that God forms are ideas of his own
essence, but are also ideas of all that he formally produces in his
attributes. There are thus as many ideas as there are things, each
thing being the object of an idea. One calls a "thing," indeed,
anything that follows formally from the divine substance; things
are explicated through that attribute of which they are a mode.
But as God understands all he produces, to each mode that follows from an attribute there corresponds an idea in God's understanding. Thus ideas themselves flow from the idea of God, *just
as* modes follow or flow from their respective attribute; the idea
of God is thus the cause of all ideas, just as God is himself the
cause of all things.

To every idea there corresponds some thing, and to every thing
an idea. It is just this theme that allows Spinoza to assert an *equal-*

ity of principle: there are in God two equal powers. In Proposition 7, the Corollary is linked to the Proof precisely through the recognition of this equality of powers: "From this it follows that God's power of thinking is equal to his actual power of acting." Thus the argument from powers no longer serves to prove *a posteriori* the existence of God, but plays a decisive role in determining epistemological parallelism. It allows us to go farther still, and to assert an *identity of being* between objects and ideas. This is the point of the Corollary: what follows formally (that is to say, in this or that attribute) from God's infinite nature, is the same as what follows objectively from the idea of God. One and the same thing is formal in the attribute on which it depends within the power of existing and acting, and objective in the idea of God on which it depends within the power of thinking. A mode of an attribute and the idea of that mode are one and the same thing expressed in two ways, under two powers. In the Proof and Corollary taken together we thus find once again the three moments of parallelism: identity of order, identity of connection or equality of principle, and identity of being, but here these apply only to the relations of an idea and its object.

Spinoza's God is a God who both is, and produces, all, like the One and All of the Platonists; but he is also a God who thinks both himself and everything, like Aristotle's Prime Mover. We must on the one hand attribute to God a power of existing and acting identical to his formal essence, or corresponding to his idea. But we must equally, on the other hand, attribute to him a power of thinking identical to his objective essence, or corresponding to his nature. Now this principle of the equality of powers merits close examination, because there is a danger of confusing it with another principle of equality, which concerns the attributes alone. Yet *the distinction of powers and attributes has an essential importance in Spinozism*. God, that is the absolutely infinite, possesses two equal powers: the power of existing and acting, and the power of thinking and knowing. If one may use a Bergsonian formulation, the absolute has two "sides," two halves. If the absolute thus possesses two powers, it does so in and through itself, involving them in its radical unity. Such is not the case with attributes. We know of only two, Extension and Thought, but this because our knowledge is limited, because we are constituted by a mode of Extension and a mode of Thought. The determination of the two powers is on the other hand in no way relative to the limits of our knowledge, any more than it depends on the nature of our constitution. The power of existing we assert of God is an absolutely infinite power: God exists "absolutely," and produces an infinity of things in the "absolute infinity" of his attributes (and so in an infinity of modes).[9] Similarly, the power of thinking is absolutely infinite. Spinoza does not merely say that it is infinitely perfect; God thinks himself absolutely, and thinks an infinity of things in an infinity of modes.[10] Whence the expressions *absoluta cogitatio* to designate the power of thinking, and *intellectus absolute infinitus* to designate infinite understanding; and the thesis according to which an infinity of things in an infinity of modes follows (objectively) from the idea of God.[11] The two powers are thus in no way relative: they are the halves of the absolute, the dimensions of the absolute, the powers of the absolute. Schelling is a Spinozist when he develops a theory of the absolute, representing God by the symbol "A³" which comprises the Real and the Ideal as its powers.[12]

It may be asked: What are the conditions for asserting of God an absolutely infinite power of existing and acting, corresponding to his nature? The conditions are that he should have an infinity of formally distinct attributes which, taken together, constitute this nature itself. We know, it is true, only two attributes. But we also know that the power of existing is not the same as the attribute of Extension: ideas exist no less than bodies, and Thought is no less than Extension a form of existence or "genus." Nor, furthermore, do Thought and Extension taken together suffice to exhaust or fulfill an absolute power of existing. We arrive here at the positive ground of God's infinity of attributes. In an important passage of the *Short Treatise*, Spinoza asserts that "We find in ourselves something which openly indicates to us not only that there are more, but also that there are infinite perfect attributes"; unknown attributes "tell us that they are, though they so far do not tell us what they are."[13] In other words: the very fact of our existence shows us that existence is not exhausted by the attributes we know. As infinite perfection does not bear its reason within itself, God must have an infinity of infinitely perfect attributes, all equal to one another, and each constituting an ultimate or irreducible form of existence. We know that none exhausts the absolute power of existing which belongs to God as sufficient reason.

The absolutely infinite consists, first of all, of an infinity of formally or really distinct attributes. All attributes are equal, none being superior or inferior to any other, and each expressing an infinitely perfect essence. All these formal essences are expressed by the attributes as the absolute essence of substance, are identified, that is, in ontologically single substance. The formal essence is the essence of God as it exists in each attribute. The absolute essence is the same essence, in relation to a substance from which existence necessarily flows, a substance, then, that possesses all attributes. Expression here appears as the relation of form and absolute: each form expresses, explicates or unfolds the absolute, but the absolute contains or "complicates" an infinity of forms. God's absolute essence is the absolutely

119

infinite power of existing and acting; but we only assert this
primary power as identical to the essence of God *conditionally
upon* an infinity of formally or really distinct attributes. The
power of existing and acting is thus absolute formal essence. And
this is how the equality of attributes is to be understood: all
attributes are equal relative to this power of existing and acting
that they condition.[a]

But the absolute has a second power, as it were a second formula or "period" of expression: God understands and expresses
himself objectively. God's absolute essence is formal in the attributes that constitute his nature, and objective in the idea that
necessarily represents this nature. The idea of God thus represents
all formally or really distinct attributes, to the extent that a distinct soul or idea corresponds to each.[14] The same attributes that
are formally distinguished in God are objectively distinguished
in the idea of God. But this idea is nonetheless absolutely unitary,
like the substance constituted by all the attributes.[15] Absolute
objective essence is thus the second power of the absolute itself:
one cannot posit a being as cause of all things, without its objective essence also being the cause of all ideas.[16] God's absolute
essence is objectively the power of thinking and knowing, as it
is formally the power of existing and acting. Another reason to
ask, in this new instance: What are the conditions for attributing
to God this absolutely infinite power of thinking, as identical to
his objective essence?

*It is no more legitimate to confuse the attribute of Thought with
the power of thinking, than to confuse the attribute of Extension with
the power of existing.* And yet there is a passage of Spinoza's that
seems to say the express opposite, identifying the attribute of
Thought with the *absoluta cogitatio.*[17] But Spinoza goes on to specify the sense in which this identification should be understood:
only that the power of thinking has as its sole condition the attri-

bute of Thought. Spinoza does indeed sometimes inquire into the condition of the power of thinking or, which comes to the same thing, into the *possibility* of the idea of God: for God to be able to think an infinity of things in an infinity of ways, for it to be possible for him to form an idea of his essence and of all that follows from it, he must, and need only, have the attribute that is Thought.[18] The attribute of Thought thus suffices to condition a power of thinking equal to the power of existing, which is however conditioned by all attributes (including Thought). One should not rush into attacking Spinoza's inconsistency. For one only finds inconsistency by confusing two very different principles of equality in Spinoza. On the one hand, all attributes are equal; but this should be understood in relation to the power of existing and acting. On the other hand, this power of existing is only one half of the absolute, the other half being a power of thinking equal to it: it is in relation to this second power that the attribute of Thought enjoys certain privileges. By itself it conditions a power equal to that conditioned by all the other attributes. There does not seem to be any contradiction in this, but rather an *ultimate fact*. A fact that in no way concerns our constitution or the limitations of our knowledge. The fact rather of divine constitution or of the unfolding of the absolute. "The fact is" that no attribute suffices to fulfill the power of existing: a thing can exist and act, without being extended or thinking. Nothing, on the other hand, can be known except by thought; the power of thinking and knowing is indeed fulfilled by the attribute of Thought. There would be contradiction had Spinoza first of all posited the equality of all attributes, and then, from the same viewpoint, given to the attribute of Thought powers and functions at variance with such equality. But Spinoza does not proceed in this way: it is the equality of powers that confers special capacities in a domain which is no longer that of the equality of attributes. *The attribute of Thought is to the power of thinking what all attributes (including Thought) are to the power of existing and acting.*

Three consequences follow from the relation (and so, also, from the difference) between the power of thinking and the attribute of Thought. First, the power of thinking is asserted, by nature or participation, of all that is "objective." The objective essence of God is an absolutely infinite power of thinking; and all that flows from that essence participates in this power. *But objective being would amount to nothing did it not itself have a formal being in the attribute of Thought.* Not only the objective essence of what is produced by God, but also the objective essences of attributes, and the objective essence of God himself, are subject to the condition of being "formed" in the attribute of Thought.[19] *Thus the idea of God is but a mode of Thought,* and belongs to *natura naturata.* The modes of the attribute of Thought are not, strictly speaking, the objective essences or objective beings of ideas as such. Modes or products are always ideas taken in their formal being. Thus Spinoza takes great care in giving to the first mode of Thought the name of infinite understanding: for infinite understanding is not the idea of God from some viewpoint or other, but just the formal being of the idea of God.[20] It is true, and one must insist on this point, that objective being would be nothing without this formal being through which it is a mode of the attribute of Thought. Or, if you like, it would be only potential, without this potentiality ever being actualized.

We must still distinguish two viewpoints: *in its necessity* the idea of God is grounded in *natura naturans.* For it belongs necessarily to God, considered in his absolute nature, to understand himself. There attaches to him an absolute power of thinking identical with his objective essence, or corresponding to his idea. The idea of God is thus an objective principle, an absolute principle of all that follows objectively in God. But *in its possibility* the idea of God is grounded only in the *natura naturata* to which it belongs. It can be "formed" only in the attribute of Thought, finds in the attribute of Thought the formal principle on which it depends, precisely because this attribute is the condition of asserting of God the absolutely infinite power of thinking. The distinction between the two viewpoints, that of necessity and that of possibility, seems to me to be of importance in the theory of the idea of God.[21] The nature of God, to which corresponds the power of existing and acting, is grounded in necessity and possibility *at once*: its possibility is established by the formally distinct attributes, and its necessity by these same attributes taken together, ontologically "one." The same does not apply to the idea of God: its objective necessity is established in the nature of God, but its formal possibility in the single attribute of Thought to which, consequently, it belongs as a mode. It will be recalled that divine power is always actual; but the power of thinking corresponding to the idea of God would not, indeed, be actual, did not God produce infinite understanding as the formal being of this idea. Infinite understanding is, in addition, called the Son of God, the Christ.[22] Now in the barely Christian image of Christ as Wisdom, Word or Voice of God, proposed by Spinoza, one may distinguish an aspect in which it agrees objectively with the absolute nature of God, an aspect in which it formally flows from the divine nature regarded under the sole attribute of Thought.[23] So that the question whether Spinoza's God thinks himself in himself is a subtle one, which may only be resolved if we remember that infinite understanding is only a mode.[24] For if God has wisdom or knowledge, it is a knowledge of himself and of his own nature; if he necessarily understands himself, he does so by virtue of his own nature: the power of thinking, and of thinking himself, properly belongs to him, then, absolutely. But this power would remain only potential did not God create in the attribute of Thought the formal being of the idea in which he thinks himself. Thus God's understanding does not belong to his nature, while the power of thinking does belong to that nature. God produces things as he objectively understands himself; but the process of understanding itself necessarily has the form of a product.[25]

Such is the first privilege of the attribute of Thought: it formally contains modes that, taken objectively, represent the attributes themselves. This first privilege is not to be confused with another, which flows from it. A mode that depends on a particular attribute is represented by an idea in the attribute of Thought; but a mode that differs from the first in attribute must be represented by *another idea*. For whatever participates, within this or that attribute, in the power of existing and acting, also participates in the power of thinking, but always in the attribute of Thought. As Schuller says, "the attribute of Thought has a much wider extension than the other attributes."[26] Given a substantial modification, it will be expressed only once in each of the other attributes, but an infinity of times in infinite understanding, and, therefore, in the attribute of Thought.[27] And each idea that expresses it in Thought will represent a mode of one particular attribute, rather than of some other. So that there will be as great a distinction between ideas as between attributes themselves or modes of different attributes: they will have "no connection."[28] There will thus be an objective distinction between ideas, equivalent to the real formal distinction between attributes, or modes differing in attribute. Furthermore, this distinction between ideas will itself be objective and formal, insofar as it is brought into relation with the formal being of the ideas themselves. Thought will thus contain modes which, while belonging to the same attribute, are nevertheless distinguished not modally, but formally or really. This privilege, once again, would remain unintelligible, were it not for the introduction of the special relation between the attribute of Thought and the power of thinking. *Objective formal distinction is the necessary correlate in the idea of God of real formal distinction* as it applies in the nature of God; it designates the act of infinite understanding when it grasps diverse attributes, or corresponding modes of diverse attributes.

In the third place, everything that exists formally has an idea that corresponds to it objectively. But the attribute of Thought is itself a form of existence, and every idea has a formal being in this attribute. Therefore every idea is, in its turn, the object of an idea that represents it; this other idea is the object of a third, and so on *ad infinitum*. In other words: if it be true that every idea that participates in the power of thinking belongs formally to the attribute of Thought, then conversely, every idea that belongs to the attribute of Thought is the object of an idea that participates in the power of thinking. Whence this final apparent privilege of the attribute of Thought, which is the ground of a capacity of ideas to reflect themselves *ad infinitum*. Spinoza sometimes says that the idea of an idea has to the idea the same relation as the idea to its object. This is surprising, insofar as idea and object are the same thing considered under two attributes, while the idea of an idea and the idea itself would then be the same thing under the same attribute.[29] But object and idea are not referred only to two attributes, but referred also to two powers, the power of existing and acting, and the power of thinking and knowing. It is the same with an idea and the idea of that idea: they are certainly referred to the same attribute, but are referred also to two powers, since the attribute of Thought is on the one hand a form of existence, and on the other, the condition of the power of thinking.

Given this situation, one understands how the theory of the idea of an idea develops in two different directions. For an idea and an idea of that idea may be distinguished insofar as we consider the one in its formal being, in relation to the power of existing, and the other in its objective being, in relation to the power of thinking: the *Correction of the Understanding* presents the idea of an idea as another idea, distinct from the first.[30] But every idea is, on the other hand, referred to the power of thinking: even its formal being is only the condition of its participation in that power. From this viewpoint we see the unity of an idea and the idea of that idea, insofar as they are given in God with the same necessity, *by the same power of thinking*.[31] There is consequently only a distinction of reason between the two ideas: the idea of an idea is the form of that idea, referred as such to the power of thinking.

The apparent contradictions of parallelism vanish once two very different arguments are distinguished: that from powers and their equality, and that from attributes and *their* equality. Epistemological parallelism follows from the equality of powers. Ontological parallelism follows from the equality of attributes (in relation to the power of existing). A difficulty does, however, remain. The Scholium to II.7 passes from epistemological to ontological parallelism. The transition is effected simply by generalization: "I understand the same concerning the other attributes." But what account is to be given of this transition? From the fact that an object (in whatever attribute) and its idea (in the attribute of Thought) are one and the same thing (or individual), Spinoza infers that correlative objects in all attributes are one and the

126

same thing (or modification). But it might seem that the argument should lead, not to the unity of a modification, but rather to an infinite and irreducible plurality of "idea–object" pairs.

The difficulty is only resolved by considering the complex status of the idea of God. From the viewpoint of its objective necessity, the idea of God is an absolute principle, with no less unity than absolutely infinite substance. From the viewpoint of its formal possibility, it is only a mode whose principle is to be found in the attribute of Thought. Hence the idea of God is able to communicate something of substantial unity to modes. Indeed, ideas that flow from the idea of God itself – that is to say, modes of thinking that belong to infinite understanding – will have a specifically modal unity. The same modification will thus find expression in an infinity of ways in God's infinite understanding. *Consequently*, the objects represented by these ideas will be objects differing only in attribute: like their ideas, they will express one and the same modification. A mode in some attribute forms, with the idea that represents it, an irreducible "individual"; as does an idea in the attribute of Thought together with the object it represents. But this infinity of individuals correspond to one another, in that they express a single modification. Thus the same modification exists not only in an infinity of modes, but in an infinity of individuals, each of which is constituted by a mode and the idea of that mode.

But why did we have to pass through epistemological parallelism? Why not deduce the unity of substantial modification directly from the unity of substance? Because God produces things in attributes that are formally or really distinct; attributes are indeed expressive, but each finds expression on its own account, as an ultimate and irreducible form. Of course everything leads one to think that production will benefit from a unity deriving from substance itself. For, while each attribute finds expression on its own account, God nonetheless produces in all attributes at once. Everything leads us then to expect that there will be modes in different attributes expressing the same modification. Yet we have no absolute certainty in this matter. One might even conceive as many worlds as there are attributes. Nature would be one in substance, but multiple in its modifications, what is produced in one attribute remaining absolutely different from what is produced in another. It is because of their individual coherence, their specificity, that we are forced to seek a separate ground of the unity of which they are capable. Kant criticized Spinozism for failing to seek a specific principle of the unity of the diverse in modes.[32] (He was thinking of the unity of modes in the same attribute, but the same problem arises with the unity of a modification relative to modes of different attributes.) But the objection seems unfounded. Spinoza was perfectly aware of a particular problem in the unity of modes, and of the need to invoke novel principles to account for the transition from substantial unity to modal unity.

The idea of God provides just such a principle, through its dual aspect. In it one passes from the unity of substance, constituted by all the attributes that express its essence, to the unity of a modification comprehended in infinite understanding, but constituted by the modes that express it in each attribute. To the question: "Why are there not as many worlds as there are attributes of God?" Spinoza simply replies by referring the reader to the Scholium to II.7.[33] And this text embodies, precisely, an argument that turns on infinite understanding (whence the importance of the allusion to "some of the Hebrews"): God's understanding has no less unity than divine substance, and so the things he understands have no less unity than God himself.

CHAPTER EIGHT

Expression and Idea

Spinoza's philosophy is a "Logic." The nature and rules of this Logic constitute his Method. The question whether the Method and Logic of the *Correction of the Understanding* are retained in the *Ethics* in their entirety is an important one, and can only be resolved by examining the *Correction* itself. The treatise consists of two distinct parts. The first concerns the end of Method, or of Philosophy, the final end of thought: it deals primarily with the form of a true idea.[1] The second part is mainly concerned with the means of attaining this end; it deals with the content of a true idea.[2] The first part necessarily anticipates the second, since the end predetermines the means by which one attains it. Each of these points must be analyzed.

The end of Philosophy, or the first part of Method, does not consist in our gaining knowledge of some thing, but in gaining knowledge of our power of understanding. Not of gaining knowledge of Nature, but gaining a conception of, and acquiring, a higher human nature.[3] Which is to say that Method, in its first aspect, is essentially reflexive: it consists solely in the knowledge of pure understanding, of its nature, its laws and its forces.[4] "Method is nothing but a reflexive knowledge, or an idea of an idea."[5] There is in this respect no difference between the *Ethics* and the *Correction of the Understanding*. The object of Method is again the final end of Philosophy. Part Five of the *Ethics* describes this end not as the knowledge of some thing, but as the knowledge of our power of comprehension, of our understanding; from it are deduced the conditions of beatitude,ᵃ which is the full actualization of this power. Whence the title of Part Five: *De Potentia intellectus seu de libertate humana*.

"Because Method is reflexive knowledge itself, this foundation, which must direct our thoughts, can be nothing other than knowledge of what constitutes the *form* of truth."[6] In what does this relation of form and reflection consist? Reflexive consciousness is the idea of an idea. We have seen that the idea of an idea is distinct from that idea itself, insofar as the latter is referred in its formal being to the power of existing, the former in its objective being to the power of thinking. But, from another viewpoint, an idea taken in its formal being already refers to the power of thinking. The formal being of an idea is, indeed, its existence in the attribute of Thought. And this attribute is not only a kind of existence, but also the condition for ascribing to any thing a power of thinking, understanding and knowing. God has within the attribute of Thought an absolutely infinite power of thinking. An idea within the attribute of Thought has a determinate power of knowing or understanding. The power of understanding that belongs to an idea is the power of thinking of God himself insofar as it is "explicated" in this idea. It will thus be seen that the idea of an idea is the idea considered in its form, insofar as it possesses a power of understanding or knowing (as part of the absolute power of thinking). So form and reflection are implicated one in the other.

Thus form is always the form of some idea we actually *have*. And one must add that only truth has a form. Had falsity a form it would be impossible for us to take the false for the true, and so to be mistaken.[7] Form is, then, always the form of some true idea we have. Just to have a true idea is enough for it to be reflected, and to reflect its power of knowing; it is enough to know, to know that one knows.[8] Hence Method presumes that one has some true idea or other. It presupposes an "innate force" of understanding which cannot fail among all its ideas *to have at least one that is true*.[9] It is in no sense the end of Method to furnish us with such an idea, but rather to produce the "reflection" of one we have already, to make us understand our power of knowledge.

But in what does such reflection consist? Form is not in general opposed to content, but formal being to objective or representative being: the idea of an idea is the idea in its form, independently of the object it represents. Thought is indeed, like all attributes, autonomous; so modes of Thought, ideas, are automata. That is to say, they depend in their formal being on the attribute of Thought alone: here they are considered "without relation to the object."[10] So the form of an idea is opposed to its objective or representative content. But it is in no way opposed to some other content that the idea might itself be supposed to possess independently of the object it represents. In fact we should guard against a double mistake concerning both the form and the content of an idea. Suppose we accept the definition of truth as a correspondence of an idea with its object. This certainly tells us nothing of a true idea's form: so how are we to know whether an idea accords with its object? Nor does it tell us anything of a true idea's content; for a true idea, on this definition, will have no more reality or internal perfection than a false one.[11] The conception of truth as correspondence gives us no definition, either formal or material, of truth; it proposes a purely nominal definition, an extrinsic designation. One may perhaps think, then, that "clarity and distinctness" provides a better determination, that is, an internal characterization of truth as it is present *in* an idea. But it does nothing of the sort. Taken in themselves clarity and distinctness do indeed relate an idea's content, but they relate only to its "objective" or "representative" content. They also relate to the form, but only to the form of "psychological consciousness" in the idea. *They thus allow us to recognize a true idea, the very idea presupposed by the Method,* but give us no knowledge of the material content of that idea, nor of its logical form. Moreover, clarity and distinctness cannot take us beyond the duality of form and content. Cartesian clarity is dual, rather than some single thing. Descartes himself asks us to distinguish a material evidence, as it were, the clarity and distinctness of an idea's objective content, and a formal evidence, a clarity attaching to the "ground" of our belief in the idea.[12] This dualism extends into the Cartesian division of understanding and will. In short, Cartesianism fails not only to conceive the true content of ideas as material, and their true form as logical, but fails also to rise to the standpoint of the "spiritual automaton" which implies the identity of these.

Ideas have a logical form that should not be confused with a form of psychological consciousness. They have a material content that should not be confused with their representative content. One has only to discover this true form and true content, to conceive their unity: the soul or understanding as a "spiritual automaton." *Its form, as a form of truth, is one with the content of any true idea*: it is by thinking the content of some true idea which we have that we reflect[b] the idea in its form, and understand our power of thinking. We then see why Method involves a second part, and why the first part necessarily anticipates the second. The first part of Method, its final goal, is concerned with the form of a true idea, the idea of an idea, a reflexive idea. The second is concerned with the content of a true idea, that is, with the adequacy of an idea. This second part is, so to speak, a means subordinate to an end, but also the means on which the realization of that end depends. It inquires: What is an idea's content? That is, what makes an idea adequate?

A true idea is, from the viewpoint of its form, an idea of the idea; from the viewpoint of its matter it is an adequate idea. Just as the idea of an idea is seen to be a *reflexive idea*, an adequate idea is seen to be an *expressive idea*. In Spinoza the term "adequate" never signifies the correspondence of an idea and the object it represents or indicates, but the internal conformity of the idea with something it expresses. What does it express? Let us first consider an idea as the knowledge of some thing. It is only true knowledge to the extent that it bears on the thing's essence: it must "explicate" that essence. But it explicates or explains the essence to the extent that it comprehends[c] the thing through its proximate cause: it must "express" this cause itself, must, that is, "involve" a knowledge of the cause.[13] This conception of knowledge is thoroughly Aristotelian. Spinoza does not merely mean that the effects known depend on causes. He means in Aristotelian manner that knowledge of a thing itself depends on a knowledge of its cause. But this renewal of an Aristotelian principle is inspired by parallelism: that knowledge should thus progress from cause to effect must be understood as the law of an autonomous Thought, the expression of an absolute power on which all ideas depend. It thus amounts to the same as saying that knowledge of an effect, considered objectively, "involves" a knowledge of its cause, or that an idea, considered formally, "expresses" its own cause.[14] *An adequate idea is just an idea that expresses its cause.* Thus Spinoza reminds us that his Method is based on the possibility of linking ideas one to another in a chain, one being the "complete cause" of another.[15] As long as we remain with clear and distinct ideas, we have knowledge of effects only; or to put it differently, we know only properties of things.[16] Only adequate ideas, as expressive, give us knowledge through causes, or through a thing's essence.

One now sees what the second part of Method amounts to. We are still presumed to have a true idea, and to recognize it by its clarity. But, even though the "innate force" of understanding provide us at once with this recognition and this possession, this still leaves us simply in the sphere of chance (*fortuna*). We still have no adequate idea. The whole problem of Method becomes the following: How to extract our true thoughts from the rule of chance? That is: How make a true thought into an adequate idea, linked to other adequate ideas? We set out from a true idea. *And it is best, given our aims, for us to choose a true idea, clear and distinct, which quite obviously depends on our power of thinking, as it has no object in Nature, for example the idea of a sphere (or circle).*[17] We must render this idea adequate, that is, must connect it with its own cause. It is not a matter, as in the Cartesian Method, of knowing a cause from its effect. Rather is it a matter of understanding the knowledge we have of the effect through a knowledge, itself more perfect, of its cause.

It may be objected that we set out in any case from a known effect, that is to say, from an idea that is supposed given.[18] But we do not proceed from properties of the effect to certain properties of the cause, which would be only, as it were, necessary conditions in relation to this effect. Starting from the effect we determine the cause, *even if through a "fiction,"* as the *sufficient reason* of all the properties we conceive the effect to possess.[19] It is in this sense that we know *through* the cause, or that the cause is better known than its effect. Cartesian Method is regressive and analytic. Spinoza's Method is reflexive and synthetic: reflexive because it involves knowledge of an effect through knowledge of its cause; synthetic because it generates all the properties of the effect from the cause known as sufficient reason. We have an adequate idea to the extent that, from a thing, some of whose properties we conceive clearly, we give a *genetic* definition, from which follow all of its known properties (and still others that we do not know). It has often been noted that the only role of mathematics in Spinoza is to provide such a genetic process.[20] The cause as sufficient reason is what, being given, means that all the thing's properties are also given, and, being withdrawn, means that all the properties are withdrawn with it.[21] We define the plane by the movement of a line, the circle by the movement of a line with one endpoint fixed, the sphere by the movement of a semicircle. To the extent that a thing's definition expresses its efficient cause or the genesis of what it defines, the thing's idea itself expresses its own cause, and we have rendered the idea adequate. Thus Spinoza says that the second part of Method is primarily a theory of definition: "The chief point of this second part of the Method is concerned solely with this: knowing the conditions of a good definition...."[22]

Spinoza's Method is thus far already distinct from any analytic procedure, but does at the same time have a certain regressive appearance. Reflection appears similar to analysis in that we first of all "suppose" an idea, in that we start from a supposed knowledge of an effect. We suppose certain properties of the circle to be clearly known; we rise to the sufficient reason from which all the properties flow. But in determining the reason of the circle as the movement of a line about one of its endpoints, we have not yet reached a thought formed through itself or "absolutely." For such a movement is not contained in the concept of the line, and is itself *fictitious*, calling for a cause that determines it. Whence, if the second part of Method amounts primarily to a theory of definition, it is not to be reduced to such a theory. A final problem presents itself: *How exorcize the supposition with which one began?* How thereby extricate oneself from a fictitious sequence? How construct the real itself, rather than remaining on the level of mathematical entities or things of reason? We reach the positing of a principle on the basis of a hypothesis; *but the principle must be of such a nature as to free itself entirely from the hypothesis,* to ground itself, and ground the movement by which we reach it; it must *as soon as possible* render obsolete the pre-supposition from which we started in order to discover it. Spinoza's Method, in its opposition to Descartes, poses a problem closely analogous to Fichte's, reacting against Kant.[23]

Spinoza recognizes that he cannot immediately set out "the truths of Nature" in their due order.[24] That is to say, he cannot immediately set out the succession of ideas as they would have to succeed one another, for the Real to be reproduced by the power of Thought alone. One should not see in this any inadequacy of Method, but rather a requirement of Spinoza's Method, its way of taking its time. For Spinoza does also recognize that he can *very quickly* reach the absolute principle from which all ideas flow in due order: the Method will only be perfect when we possess the idea of the perfect Being; "So in the beginning we must take the greatest care that we arrive at knowledge of such a Being *as quickly as possible*." We must "begin *as soon as possible* from the first elements, i.e., from the source and origin of Nature"; "As for order, to unite and order all our perceptions, it is required that we ask *as soon as possible, and as reason demands,* whether there is a certain Being, and at the same time, what sort of being it is, which is the cause of all things, so that its objective essence may also be the cause of all our ideas."[25] Some commentators change the form of these passages; and they are also sometimes explained as belonging to an imperfect phase of Spinoza's thought. This is not the case: that one cannot begin from the idea of God, that one cannot from the outset install oneself in God, is a constant of Spinozism. There are real differences between the *Ethics* and the *Correction of the Understanding*, but they do not concern this point (but only the means used to reach the idea of God as quickly as possible).

What is the theory in the *Correction of the Understanding*? If we consider an infinite regress, that is an infinite sequence of things that do not exist by their own nature, or whose ideas are not formed through themselves, we recognize that the concept of such a regression is in no way absurd. Yet at the same time – and this is the real sense of the classic proof *a posteriori* – it would be absurd not to recognize the following: that things that do not exist by their own nature are determined in their existence (and in the production of their effects) by something that itself does exist necessarily and does produce its effects through itself. It is always God who determines any cause to produce its effect; so God is never, properly speaking, a "distant" or "remote" cause.[26] Thus we do not start from the idea of God, but we reach it very quickly, at the beginning of the regression; for without it we would not even understand the possibility of a series, its efficiency and actuality. *Whence it little matters that we proceed through a fiction.* The introduction of a fiction may indeed help us to reach the idea of God as quickly as possible without falling into the traps of infinite regression. In conceiving the sphere, for example, we form an idea to which no object in Nature corresponds. We explain it by the movement of a semicircle: the cause is certainly fictitious, since nothing in Nature is produced in such a way; it is nonetheless a "true perception," but this to the extent that it is conjoined with the idea of God as the principle which ideally determines the semicircle to motion, that is, which determines that cause to produce the idea of the sphere.

Everything changes, however, once we arrive, by this means,

at the idea of God. For we form this idea through itself and absolutely. "If there is a God, or something omniscient, he can feign nothing at all."[27] Starting from the idea of God we deduce all other ideas, one from another, in "due order." Not only is this order now one of progressive synthesis, but, taken in this order, ideas can no longer amount to things of reason, and all fiction is excluded. They are necessarily ideas of "real or true things," ideas to which there corresponds some thing in Nature.[28] The production of ideas, starting from the idea of God, is of itself a reproduction of all the things in Nature; the sequence of ideas has no need to copy the sequence of things, insofar as ideas are themselves produced on their own account, from the idea of God.[29]

Ideas do indeed "represent" some thing, but they represent a thing precisely because they "express" their own cause, and express the idea of God as determining that cause. All ideas, says Spinoza, express or involve God's essence, and are thereby ideas of real or true things.[30] We are no longer caught in a regressive process that connects a true idea to its cause, if only fictitiously, in order to rise as quickly as possible to the idea of God: that process could only legitimately determine the content of true ideas. We are now following a progressive procedure, from which all fiction is excluded, and going from one real being to another, deducing ideas one from another, starting from the idea of God: ideas are then linked according to their own content; but their content is also determined by this sequence; *we grasp the identity of form and content*, we are sure that the sequence of ideas reproduces reality as such. We will later see just how the deduction works in detail. It is enough for the moment to consider how the idea of God, as an absolute principle, frees itself from the hypothesis from which we began in order to rise to it, and grounds a sequence of adequate ideas that is identical to the construction of reality. The second part of the Method provides not merely a theory of genetic definition, but closes in a theory of productive deduction.

Spinoza's Method comprises, then, three general heads, each strictly implicated in the others. The first part is concerned with the end of thinking, which consists not so much in knowing some thing, as knowing our power of knowing. Thought is from this viewpoint considered in terms of its form: the form of a true idea is an idea of the idea or a reflexive idea. The formal definition of truth is that a true idea is the idea *insofar as it is explained by our power of knowing*. Method, in this first aspect, is itself reflexive.

The second part of Method is concerned with the means of realizing this end: some true idea or other is supposed given, but we must make of it an adequate idea. Adequation constitutes the matter of truth. The definition of an adequate idea (the material definition of truth) is: an idea *insofar as it expresses its own cause, and insofar as it expresses God's essence as determining that cause*. An adequate idea is thus an expressive idea. In this second aspect, Method is genetic: the cause of an idea is determined as the sufficient reason of all the properties of a thing. This part of Method leads us to the highest thought, that is, leads us as quickly as possible to the idea of God.

The second part concludes with a third and last head, concerning the unity of form and content, end and means. One finds in Spinoza as in Aristotle that formal and material definitions, considered in general, fragment the real unity of a complete definition. Between an idea and an idea of the idea there is only a distinction of reason: in reality reflexive and expressive ideas are one and the same thing.

How should we understand this last unity? An idea never has as its cause an object it represents; rather does it represent an object because it expresses *its own* cause. An idea has, then, a content, expressive and not representative, that is to be referred solely to the power of thinking. But the power of thinking is what constitutes the form of an idea as such. The concrete unity of the two appears when all ideas are deduced one from another, materially from the idea of God, formally according to the power of thinking alone. From this viewpoint the Method is deductive: form, as logical form, and content, as expressive content, are conjoined in the sequence of ideas. One should note the extent to which Spinoza insists on this unity of that sequence. At the very point where he says that Method does not set out to give us knowledge of some thing, but to give us knowledge of our power of knowing, he adds that we do not know the latter except through knowing as many things, linked one to another, as possible.[31] Conversely, when he shows that our ideas are causes one of another, he deduces from this that all have as cause our power of knowing or thinking.[32] It is above all the term "spiritual automaton" that testifies to this unity. The soul is a kind of spiritual automaton, which is to say: In thinking we obey only the laws of thought, laws that determine both the form and the content of true ideas, and that make us produce ideas in sequence according to their own causes and through our own power, so that in knowing our power of understanding we know through their causes all the things that fall within this power.[33]

In what sense is the idea of God "true"? One cannot say that it expresses its own cause: formed absolutely, that is, without the help of other ideas, it *expresses infinity*. So it is in relation to the idea of God that Spinoza announces: "The form of the true thought must be placed in the same thought itself without relation to other things."[34] It may, however, seem odd that Spinoza

140

does not restrict the application of such a principle to the idea of God, but extends it to all thoughts. To the extent that he adds: "We must not say that this difference [of true and false] arises from the fact that the true thought is knowing things through their first causes. In this, indeed, it differs greatly from the false." I believe this difficult passage should be thus understood: Spinoza recognizes that true knowledge is obtained through the cause, but considers that here again we have only a material definition of truth. An adequate idea is an idea that expresses its cause; but we still do not know what constitutes the form of truth, what provides a formal definition of truth itself. Here as elsewhere, we should not altogether identify *what expresses itself* and *what is expressed*: what is expressed is the cause, but what expresses itself is once again our power of knowing or understanding, the power of our understanding. Hence Spinoza says "What constitutes the form of the true thought must be sought in the same thought itself, and must be deduced from the nature of the understanding."[35] Hence also he goes on to say that the third kind of knowledge has as its formal cause nothing but the soul or understanding itself.[36] It is the same with the idea of God: what is expressed is infinity, but what expresses itself is the absolute power of thinking. So it was necessary to integrate the viewpoint of form with that of matter, in order to finally conceive the concrete unity of the two as it appears in the succession of ideas. In this way only can we arrive at a complete definition of truth, and understand the phenomenon of expression in ideas as a whole. Not only the idea of God, but all ideas, are formally explained through the power of thinking. An idea's content is reflected in its form, just as what is expressed relates or is attributed to what expresses itself. All ideas follow at once materially from the idea of God, and formally from the power of thinking: their succession translates the unity of their two derivations.

141

We have a power of knowing, understanding or thinking only to the extent that we participate in the absolute power of thinking. Which implies both that our soul is a mode of the attribute of Thought, and is a part of infinite understanding. The two points involve, and give a new form to, a classic problem: What is the nature of our idea of God? According to Descartes, for example, we do not "comprehend" God, but we nonetheless have a clear and distinct idea of him; for we "understand" what is meant by infinity, if only negatively, and "conceive" an infinite thing in a positive manner, albeit only partially. So our knowledge of God is limited in only two ways: through our not knowing God in his entirety, and through the fact that we do not know how what we do know of him finds its place in his eminent unity.[37] There is definitely no question of saying that Spinoza does away with all limitation. But, even though he sometimes expresses himself in a manner close to that of Descartes, he interprets the limits of our knowledge in an entirely novel context.

The Cartesian conception presents, on the one hand, that mixture of negation and affirmation which one always finds in methods of analogy (one recalls Descartes's explicit declarations against univocity). In Spinoza, on the other hand, the radical critique of eminence, the positing of the univocity of attributes, have as their immediate consequence that our idea of God is not only clear and distinct, but also adequate. For the things we know of God belong to God in the same form as that in which we know them, that is, in a form common to God who possesses them, and to creatures who imply and know them. It nevertheless remains the case, in Spinoza as in Descartes, that we know only a part of God: we know only two of these forms, only two attributes, since our body implies no attribute other than Extension and our ideas none other than Thought. "Therefore this idea of the body involves the knowledge of God insofar only as he is considered under the attribute of Extension.... Therefore the idea of this idea involves the knowledge of God, insofar as he is considered under the attribute of Thought, and not insofar as he is considered under any other."[38] In Spinoza, furthermore, the very idea of parts of God is better grounded than in Descartes, divine unity being perfectly consistent with a real distinction between attributes.

Yet even on this second point the difference between Descartes and Spinoza remains fundamental. For, even before knowing a part of God, our soul is itself "a part of God's infinite understanding": for we have a power of understanding or knowing only to the extent that we participate in the absolute power of knowing corresponding to the idea of God. Consequently *it is enough for there to be something common to the whole and the part for this something to give us an idea of God that is not only clear and distinct, but adequate.*[39] This idea we are given is not an idea of God in his entirety. It is nevertheless adequate, because it is in the part as it is in the whole. So it is no surprise that Spinoza sometimes says that God's existence is not known to us through itself: he means that such knowledge is necessarily afforded to us through "common notions," without which it would not even be clear and distinct, but thanks to which it is adequate.[40] When Spinoza recalls, on the other hand, that God makes himself known immediately, that he is known through himself and not through something else, he means that the knowledge of God has need neither of signs nor of processes of analogy: this knowledge is adequate because God possesses all the things that we know to belong to him, and possesses them in the same form in which we know them.[41] What is the relation between these common notions that give us knowledge of God and these forms, themselves common or univocal, under which we know God? Such an analysis must be postponed until a later point, since it goes beyond the problem of adequation.

143

CHAPTER NINE

Inadequacy

What follows from Spinoza's theory of truth? We must first of all look for its converse[a] in his conception of inadequate idea. *An inadequate idea is an inexpressive idea.* But how is it possible for us to have indequate ideas? Their possibility only appears once we determine the conditions of our having ideas in general.

Our soul is itself an idea. It is in this respect an affection[b] or modification of God within the attribute of Thought, just as our body is an affection or modification of God within the attribute of Extension. The idea constituting our soul or mind is present in God. He possesses it, but possesses it only through being affected by another idea, which is its cause. He has it only by "conjointly" having another idea, an idea, that is, of something else. "The cause of one singular idea is another idea, or God, insofar as he is considered to be affected by another idea; and of this also he is the cause, insofar as he is affected by another, and so on, *ad infinitum.*"[1] Not only does God possess all ideas, as many of them as there are things; but all these ideas, as they are in God, express their own cause, and express God's essence as determining that cause. "All ideas are in God; and, insofar as they are related to God, are true, and adequate."[2] We can, furthermore, already begin to sense that, as for this idea which constitutes our soul, *we do not possess it.* Or we do not at least possess it immediately; for it is in God only insofar as he also possesses an idea of something else.

All modes participate in the power of God: just as our body participates in the power of existing, our soul participates in the power of thinking. All modes are also parts, a part of the power of God, a part of Nature. So they necessarily come under the influence of other parts. Other ideas necessarily act on our soul, just as other bodies act on our body. We have here "affections" of a second sort, relating no longer to the body itself, but to what happens in the body; no longer to the soul (the idea of the body), but to what happens in the soul (an idea of what happens in the body).[3] This is the sense in which *we have* ideas; for although the ideas of this sort of affection are in God, they are there only insofar as he explicates himself through our soul alone, independently of the other ideas he has; they are thus in us.[4] If we have a knowledge of external bodies, of our own body, of our soul itself, it is solely through these ideas of affections. They alone are given us: we perceive external bodies only insofar as they affect us, we perceive our own body only insofar as it is affected, we perceive our soul through the idea of an idea of an affection.[5] What we call an "object" is only the effect an object has on our body; what we call "me" is only the idea we have of our own body and our soul insofar as they suffer an effect. The given here appears as the most intimate and vital as well as the most confused relation between our knowledge of bodies, our knowledge of our own body and our knowledge of ourself.

Let us consider the ideas we have corresponding to the effect of an object on our body. On the one hand, they depend on our power of knowing, that is, on our soul or mind, as their formal cause. But we have no idea of our body, or of our soul, independently of the effects they suffer. We are thus incapable of under-

standing ourselves as the formal cause of our ideas and they appear
to be altogether the result of chance.[6] On the other hand, they
have as material causes ideas of external things. But we do not
have these ideas of external things either; they are in God, but
not insofar as he constitutes our soul or mind. We do not therefore possess our ideas in conditions such that they can express
their own (material) cause. Our ideas of affections do of course
"involve" their own cause, that is, the objective essence of the
external body; but they do not "express" or "explain" it. They
similarly involve our power of thinking, but are not explained
by it, and are referred to chance. *So the word "involve" is here no
longer a correlate of "explain" or "express,"* but is opposed to these,
designating the mixture of external body and our own body in
affections of which we have ideas. Spinoza's usual formulation of
this is: our ideas of affections *indicate* a state of our body, but do
not *explain* the nature or essence of the external body.[7] This is
to say, the ideas we have are signs, indicative images impressed
in us, rather than expressive ideas formed by us: perception or
imagination, rather than comprehension.

An image is, in the strictest sense, an imprint, a trace or physical impression, an affection of the body itself, the effect of some
body on the soft and fluid parts of our own body; in the figurative
sense, an image is the idea of an affection which makes an object
known to us only by its effect. But such knowledge is not knowledge at all, it is at best recognition. And from this there follow
the characteristics of indication in general: the primary "thing
indicated" is never our essence, but always a momentary state of
our changing constitution; the secondary (or indirect) thing indicated is never the nature or essence of some external thing, but
is rather an appearance that only allows us to recognize a thing
by its effect, to rightly or wrongly assert its mere presence.[8] The
fruits of chance and of encounters, serving for recognition, purely

indicative, the ideas we have are inexpressive, that is to say, inadequate. An inadequate idea is neither an absolute privation or an absolute ignorance: it involves a lack of knowledge.[9]

Our knowledge is doubly lacking: we lack knowledge both of ourselves, and of the object that produces in us an affection of which we have an idea. An inadequate idea is thus an idea that involves, both formally and materially, the privation of knowledge of its own cause. So it remains inexpressive: "truncated," like a conclusion without premises.[10] What is here fundamental is that Spinoza shows *how* a conclusion may thus be detached from its two premises. We find ourselves naturally in a situation in which the ideas we have are necessarily inadequate, because they cannot express their cause nor be explained by our power of knowing. On all points, the knowledge of external bodies, the knowledge of our soul or mind, the knowledge of our duration, and that of things, we have only inadequate ideas.[11] "When we look at the sun, we imagine it as about two hundred feet away from us, an error that does not consist simply in this imagining, but in the fact that while we imagine it in this way, we are ignorant of its true distance and of *the cause of this imagining.*"[12] An image is thus an idea in us that cannot express its own cause, that is, the idea from which it derives, which is not available to us: its material cause. But nor does an image express its formal cause, nor can it be explained by our power of knowing. Thus Spinoza says that an image, or idea of an affection, is like a conclusion without premises: there are indeed two premises, material and formal, and the image involves our lack of knowledge of these.

Our problem is now transformed. The question is no longer "Why do we have inadequate ideas?" but rather "How do we come to form adequate ideas?" In Spinoza it is the same with truth as with freedom: they are not given to us in principle, but appear as the result of a long activity through which we produce adequate ideas, liberated from the sequence of external necessity.[13] Spinoza's inspiration is in this respect profoundly empiricist. One is always struck by the diverse inspirations of empiricists and rationalists. One group is surprised by what fails to surprise the others. If we listen to the rationalists, truth and freedom are, above all, rights; they wonder how we can lose these rights, fall into error or lose our liberty. Thus rationalism finds in the Adamic tradition, which sets up as its principle the image of a free and rational Adam, a theme that suits its preoccupations particularly well. From an empiricist viewpoint everything is inverted: what is surprising is that men sometimes manage to understand truth, sometimes manage to understand one another, sometimes manage to free themselves from what fetters them. One may recognize Spinoza's empiricist inspiration simply by the vigor with which he opposes the Adamic tradition, his conception of freedom and truth as final products revealed only at the end. One of the paradoxes in Spinoza — and this is not the sole instance in which we will see it at work — is to have rediscovered the concrete force of empiricism in applying it in support of a new rationalism, one of the most rigorous versions ever conceived. Spinoza asks: How do we come to form and produce adequate ideas, when we necessarily have so many inadequate ones which divert our power and cut us off from what we might achieve?

We must distinguish two aspects of inadequate ideas: they "involve privation" of the knowledge of their cause, but are at the same time effects that in some way "involve" that cause. Under the first aspect an inadequate idea is false; but under the second it contains *something positive*, and so something true.[14] We imagine, for example, that the sun is two hundred feet away. This idea of an affection is incapable of expressing its own cause: it does not explain the nature or essence of the sun. It does nevertheless involve this essence "insofar as the body is affected by it." It is all very well to know the true distance of the sun, but it will still continue to affect us in such a way that we see it two hundred feet away: as Spinoza says, the mistake may be eliminated, but not our imagination. There is thus something positive in an inadequate idea, a sort of indication that we can grasp clearly. This is, in fact, how we are able to have some idea of its cause: having clearly grasped the conditions in which we see the sun, we can clearly infer that it is an object far enough away to appear small, rather than a small object seen at close range.[15] If one does not bear this positive character in mind, several of Spinoza's theses become incomprehensible: in the first place, the thesis that one can naturally have a true idea, as required by the Method before it sets to work. But more importantly, since falsity has no form, one could not otherwise understand how an inadequate idea could itself give rise to the idea of an idea, could have, that is to say, a form that must be referred to our power of thinking.[16] The faculty of imagination is defined by the conditions in which we naturally have ideas, inadequate ideas; it is nonetheless in one of its aspects a *virtue*; it involves our power of thinking even though it is not explained by it; an image involves its own cause, even though it does not express it.[17]

It is not of course enough simply to grasp what is positive in an idea of an affection in order to have an adequate idea. But this is the first step. For from this positivity we can form the idea of *what is common* to the affecting and affected bodies, to the external body and our own. And we will see that this "common notion" is itself necessarily adequate: it belongs to the idea of our body as to that of the external body; it is then in us as it is in God; it expresses God and is explained by our power of thinking. But from this common notion there follows in turn an idea of the affection that is itself adequate: the common notion is necessarily the cause of an adequate idea of the affection that is distinct only in "its reason" from that idea of the affection from which we began. This complex mechanism does not, then, amount to the elimination of our inadequate ideas, but to using what is positive in them to form the largest possible number of adequate ideas, and ensuring that what inadequate ideas remain are restricted to the smallest part of our selves. In short, we must ourselves accede to conditions in which we can produce adequate ideas.

I do not yet wish to analyze this mechanism by which we may reach adequate ideas. Our question was simply: What is an adequate idea? And its converse: What is an inadequate idea? An adequate idea is an idea that expresses its own cause and is explained by our own power. An inadequate idea is inexpressive and unexplained: an impression that has not yet become an expression, an indication that has not yet become an explanation. This brings out the intention that underlies the whole of Spinoza's doctrine of truth: *to substitute a conception of adequacy for the Cartesian conception of clarity and distinctness.* Spinoza's terminology in this relation does, it is true, vary: sometimes he uses the word "adequate" to mark the insufficiency of clarity and distinctness, thus emphasizing the need to advance beyond the Cartesian criteria; sometimes he himself uses the words "clear and distinct," but applying them only to ideas that follow from an idea that is itself adequate; he sometimes uses them, finally, to designate such an adequate idea, but in that case has even more reason to give them an implicit meaning altogether different from Descartes's.[18]

Spinoza's doctrine of truth is never, in any case, detached from a polemic, whether direct or indirect, directed against the

Cartesian theory. Considered in themselves clarity and distinctness allow us at the most to recognize some true idea that we have, recognize, that is, what is positive in an idea that is still inadequate. But forming an adequate idea takes us beyond clarity and distinctness. A clear and distinct idea does not in itself constitute real knowledge, any more than it contains its own ground within itself: the sufficient reason of clarity and distinctness is to be found only in adequacy, and a clear and distinct idea constitutes real knowledge only to the extent that it follows from an idea that is itself adequate.

We have here, once again, a point of agreement between Spinoza and Leibniz, which helps to define the Anticartesian reaction. Leibniz's remark that *knowledge is a species of expression* could have come from Spinoza.[19] Of course they do not conceive of the nature of adequacy in the same way, because they neither understand nor use the concept of expression in the same way. But under three essential heads they show a real if unintentional agreement. First of all Descartes, in his conception of the clear and distinct, restricted himself to the representative content of ideas; he did not rise to the conception of an infinitely deeper expressive content. He didn't conceive adequacy as the necessary and sufficient reason of clarity and distinctness: didn't conceive expression, that is to say, as the basis of representation. Second, Descartes got no farther than the form of psychological consciousness in ideas; he didn't get as far as the logical form through which an idea is explained, by which ideas are linked one to another. And finally he had no conception of the unity of form and content, that is, of the "spiritual automaton" which reproduces reality in producing ideas in their due order. Descartes taught us that truth was present in ideas. But what use to us is such knowledge, if we don't know what is present in true ideas? A clear and distinct idea is still inexpressive, and remains unexplained. Good enough for recognition, but unable to provide a real principle of knowledge.

We have seen what are the three principal points established by Spinoza's theory of ideas: the representative content is but an appearance, determined by a deeper expressive content; the form of psychological consciousness is superficial in relation to true logical form; the spiritual automaton, manifested in the concatenation of ideas, is the unity of logical form and expressive content. Now, these three points are also Leibniz's principal theses. Whence his liking for Spinoza's term "spiritual automaton." He himself understands it in the sense of the autonomy of individual thinking substances. But even for Spinoza the automatism of a mode of Thought does not exclude a sort of autonomy in its power of understanding (indeed the power of understanding is a part of the absolute power of thinking, insofar as the latter is explicated through the former). All the differences between Leibniz and Spinoza take away nothing from their agreement on these fundamental principles which, above all else, constitute the Anticartesian revolution.

Leibniz's criticism of Descartes is well known: clarity and distinctness on their own allow us to *recognize* an object, but give us no true knowledge of the object; they fall short of its essence, bearing only on external appearances or extrinsic characteristics through which we can only "conjecture" that essence; they fall short of a cause that shows us why the thing is necessarily what it is.[20] Spinoza's criticism, while less familiar, nonetheless proceeds along the same lines, denouncing above all the insufficiency of the Cartesian idea: clarity and distinctness by themselves give us only an indeterminate knowledge; they fall short of a thing's essence, bearing only on *propria*; they fall short of a cause from which all the thing's properties would together follow, leading us only to recognize an object, the presence of an object, from the effect it has on us; a clear and distinct idea does not express its own cause, gives us no knowledge of that cause "except what we consider in the effect."[21] In all this, Spinoza and Leibniz are fighting a common cause, a continuation of what had set them against the Cartesian ontological proof, the search for a sufficient reason singularly lacking throughout Cartesianism. Each of them, proceeding differently, discovers *the expressive content of ideas, and their explicative form.*

CHAPTER TEN

Spinoza Against Descartes

Cartesianism relies on a certain sufficiency of clear and distinct ideas. Such sufficiency is the ground of Descartes's Method, but is on the other hand itself demonstrated by applying that Method itself. Descartes asserts his preference for *analysis*. In an important passage he says that analytic method has the merit of showing us "how effects depend on causes."[1] The claim might appear paradoxical, lending to analysis what belongs to synthesis, did one not examine its precise significance. We have, according to Descartes, a clear and distinct knowledge of an effect *before* having a clear and distinct knowledge of its cause. I know for example that I exist as a thinking being before knowing the cause of my existence. Of course, a clear and distinct knowledge of an effect presupposes a certain knowledge of its cause, but only a confused one. "If I say $4 + 3 = 7$, this is a necessary conception, because we cannot distinctly conceive the number 7 without including in it 3 and 4 *confusa quadam ratione*."[2] A clear and distinct knowledge of an effect presupposes, then, a confused knowledge of its cause, and never depends on a more perfect knowledge of the cause. Rather does a clear and distinct knowledge of a cause depend on the clear and distinct knowledge of its effect. This is the basis of the *Meditations* – of their order, in particular, and of their analytic Method in general: a method of inference or implication.

So if this Method shows us how effects depend on causes, it does so as follows: from a clear knowledge of an effect, we render clear the knowledge of the cause it confusedly implied, and thence show that the effect would not be what we know it to be, did it not have such a cause on which it necessarily depends.[3] In Descartes, then, two themes are fundamentally linked: the theoretical sufficiency of clear and distinct ideas, and the practical possibility of passing from a clear and distinct knowledge of an effect to a clear and distinct knowledge of its cause.

That an effect depends on its cause is not in question. The question relates to the best way of showing this. Spinoza says: It is possible to start from a clear knowledge of an effect; but from it we will arrive only at a clear knowledge of its cause, we will know nothing of the cause beyond what we consider in its effect, and will never obtain an adequate knowledge. The *Correction of the Understanding* contains a fundamental criticism of the Cartesian Method, of the process of inference or implication it uses, and of the alleged sufficiency of the clarity and distinctness to which it appeals. Clear ideas give us nothing apart from some knowledge of a thing's properties, and lead us to nothing apart from a negative knowledge of its cause. "There is the perception that we have when the essence of a thing is inferred from another thing, but not adequately"; "We understand nothing about the cause except what we consider in the effect. This is sufficiently evident from the fact that then the cause is explained only in very general terms: *Therefore there is something, Therefore there is some power*, etc. Or also from the fact that the terms express the cause negatively: *Therefore it is not this, or that*, etc."; "We infer one thing from another in this way: after we clearly perceive that we feel such a body, and no other, then, I say, we infer clearly that the soul is united to the body, which union is the cause of such a sensation; but we cannot understand absolutely from this what that sensation and union are"; "Although such a conclusion is certain, it is still not sufficiently safe."[4] There is not one line among these that is not directed against Descartes and his Method. Spinoza does not believe in the sufficiency of clarity and distinctness, because he doesn't believe there is any satisfactory way of proceeding from the knowledge of an effect to a knowledge of its cause.

Clear and distinct ideas are not enough, one must advance to adequate ideas. That is: it is not enough to show how effects depend on causes, one must show how true knowledge of an effect itself depends on knowing its cause. This is the definition of the *synthetic* Method. On all these points Spinoza stands as an Aristotelian against Descartes: "This is the same as what the ancients said, i.e., that true knowledge proceeds from cause to effect."[5] Aristotle showed how scientific knowledge was to be had through causes. He didn't just say that knowledge must discover causes, reach the cause on which a known effect depends; he said that an effect is not known, except to the extent that its cause is already, and better, known. A cause is not only prior to its effect because it is its cause, but prior also from the viewpoint of knowledge, needing to be better known than the effect.[6] Spinoza takes up this thesis: "For really, knowledge of the effect is nothing but acquiring a more perfect knowledge of its cause."[7] Not "more perfect" than that which we had at first, but more perfect than that which we have of the effect itself, and prior to that which we have of the effect. Knowledge of an effect may be said to be clear and distinct, but knowledge of its cause is more perfect, that is, adequate; and clarity and distinctness are only well grounded insofar as they follow from adequacy as such.

To know by causes is the only way to know essence. The cause is, so to speak, the middle term on which the connection of subject and attribute is grounded, the principle or reason from which follow all properties belonging to a thing. Thus the search for a cause coincides, as in Aristotle, with the search for a definition. Whence the importance of the scientific syllogism whose premises give us the formal cause or definition of a phenomenon, and whose conclusion gives us its material cause or definition. A total definition is one that combines form and matter in a unitary statement, in such a way that the object's unity is no longer fragmented, but rather affirmed in an intuitive concept. On all these points Spinoza seems to remain an Aristotelian: he emphasizes the importance of the theory of definition, he presents the search for definitions and the search for causes as identical, and he asserts the concrete unity of a total definition comprehending both the formal and material causes of a true idea.

Descartes was not unaware of the claims of the Aristotelian kind of synthetic method: the proof it embodies, he says, is often "of effects from their causes."[8] Descartes means that while the synthetic method always claims to gain knowledge through causes, it doesn't always succeed. His basic objection is the following: How can the cause itself be understood? We can understand *through* causes in Geometry, but only because its matter is clear and conforms to our senses. Descartes admits this (whence his use of the word "often").[9] So does Aristotle: point, line, even unit, are principles or "subject-genera," indivisibles accessible through intuition; their existence is known and their meaning understood.[10] But what happens in other cases, for example in Metaphysics, when we have to deal with real beings? How is a cause, principle or middle term to be found? Aristotle himself seems to refer us to an inductive process, hardly distinguishable from abstraction, and beginning with a confused perception of the effect. In this sense it is the effect that is best known, best known

to us as against "best known absolutely." When Aristotle sets out
the way to advance to a middle term or causal definition, he begins from a confused whole and abstracts from it a "proportionate"
universal. So that the formal cause is always a specific abstract
characteristic, which has its origin in confused sensory material.
In this light, the unity of formal and material causes remains for
Aristotle a pure ideal, as does unity of an intuitive concept.

Descartes's position may then be put thus: the synthetic
method has an exaggerated ambition, and gives us no means of
knowing real causes. It actually begins from a confused knowledge of an effect, and advances to abstractions which are wrongly
presented to us as causes, and so, despite its pretensions, merely
examines causes through their effects.[11] The analytic method, on
the other hand, has a more modest intent. But, as it begins by
eliciting a clear and distinct perception of the effect, it provides
us with a means of inferring from that perception a true knowledge of the cause; it is thus able to show how the effects themselves depend on their causes. The synthetic method is therefore
only legitimate on the condition of not being left to function
alone, but coming after the analytic method, and based on a
prior knowledge of real causes. The synthetic method on its own
gives us no knowledge, it is not a method of discovery; its utility lies in the exposition of knowledge, the exposition of what
has already been "discovered."[a]

It may be noted that Descartes never considers setting the two
methods apart by relating synthesis to the order of being, and
analysis to the order of knowing. Nor does Spinoza. It would then
be unsatisfactory, and misleading, to oppose Descartes to Spinoza
by saying that the former follows the order of knowledge and the
latter the order of being. It does of course follow from the definition of the synthetic method that its order coincides with that
of being. But this consideration is of little importance. The prob-

lem is simply to know whether the synthetic method is capable, from the outset and by itself, of giving us knowledge of the principles it presupposes. Can it *make known* to us what is? The problem then is simply: What is the true method from the viewpoint of knowledge?[12] Here Spinoza's Anticartesianism is fully manifest: according to him, the synthetic method is the only real method of discovery, the only effective method in the order of knowing.[13] But such a position is only tenable if Spinoza thinks he has the means, not only to refute Descartes's objections, but also to overcome the difficulties of Aristotelianism. And indeed, when he presents what he calls the third "mode of perception" in the *Correction of the Understanding*, he brings together in this *imperfect* mode or genus two very disparate procedures, each equally condemned as insufficient.[14] The first consists in inferring a cause from a clearly perceived effect: one recognizes Descartes's analytic method and its process of implication. But the second consists in "inferring something from some universal, which some property always accompanies": one recognizes Aristotle's synthetic method and its deductive process starting from a middle term conceived as a specific characteristic. If Spinoza can, not without a certain irony, thus bring together Descartes and Aristotle, *it is because it comes to the same thing, more or less, to abstract a universal from a confused knowledge of an effect, and to infer a cause from a clear knowledge of its effect.* Neither of these procedures leads to adequacy. Descartes's analytic method is insufficient, but Aristotle had no more satisfactory a conception of the synthetic method.

What was lacking in the Ancients, says Spinoza, was the conception of the soul as a sort of spiritual automaton, that is, of thought as determined by its own laws.[15] It is parallelism, then, that provides for Spinoza the means of overcoming the difficulties of Aristotelianism. The formal cause of an idea is never an abstract universal. Universals, whether genera or species, do indeed involve a power of imagination, but this power is reduced as we come to understand more and more things. The formal cause of a true idea is our power of understanding; and the more things we understand, the less we form these fictions of genera and species.[16] If Aristotle identifies formal cause with specific universal, it is because he remains at the *lowest level* of the power of thinking, without discovering the laws that permit thought to go from one real being to another "without passing through abstract things." On the other hand, the material cause of an idea is not a confused sensory perception: the idea of a particular thing always has its cause in another idea of a particular thing, which is determined to produce it.

With the Aristotelian model before him, Descartes could not grasp the possibilities of the synthetic method. In one of its aspects, it is true, that method gives us no knowledge of things; but it would be wrong to conclude that its only role was expository. In its primary aspect, the synthetic method is reflexive, that is, gives us knowledge of our power of knowing. It is true, also, that the synthetic method *invents or feigns* a cause on the basis of an effect; but far from seeing a contradiction here, we should recognize a minimal regression which allows us, *as quickly as possible*, to reach the idea of God as the source of all other ideas. In this second aspect the method is constructive or genetic. That is, the ideas that follow from the idea of God are ideas of real beings: their production is at the same time the deduction of reality; the form and matter of truth become identified in the concatenation of ideas. The method is, in this third aspect, deductive. Reflection, genesis and deduction, these three moments together constitute the synthetic method. It is on these that Spinoza counts, both to advance beyond Cartesianism and to make good the inadequacies of Aristotelianism.

Let us now turn to the theory of Being: we see Spinoza's opposition to Descartes shifting, but remaining no less radical. It would indeed be surprising if analytic and synthetic methods implied the same conception of being. Spinoza's ontology is dominated by the notions of a *cause of itself*, *in itself* and *through itself*. These terms are to be found in Descartes himself; but the difficulties he encountered in their use should teach us something about the incompatibilities of Cartesianism and Spinozism.

Caterus and Arnauld had already objected against Descartes that he used "through itself" negatively, to denote only the absence of a cause.[17] Even were we to admit with Arnauld that, if God is assigned no cause, this is because of the full positivity of his essence and is not related to the imperfection of our understanding, we still cannot conclude that he has being through himself "positively as through a cause," that he is (that is to say) cause of himself. Descartes does, it is true, consider this polemic to be largely a matter of words. He asks only that one accord him the full positivity of God's essence: this conceded, one recognizes that this essence plays a role *analogous* to that of a cause. There is a positive reason for God not to have a cause, a formal cause, then, for his not having an efficient cause. Descartes explains his thesis in the following terms: God is his own cause, but this *in another sense* than that in which an efficient cause is the cause of its effect; he is cause of himself in the sense that his essence is a formal cause; and his essence is said to be a formal cause, not directly but by analogy, insofar as it plays in relation to his existence a role analogous to that of an efficient cause in relation to its effect.[18]

This theory rests on three closely linked notions: *equivocation* (God is cause of himself, but in another sense than that in which he is the efficient cause of the things he creates; so that being is not affirmed in the same sense of everything that is, divine and created substance, substances and modes, and so on); *eminence* (God thus contains all reality, but eminently, in a form other than that of the things he creates); and *analogy* (God as cause of himself is not, then, grasped as he is in himself, but by analogy: it is by analogy with an efficient cause that God may be said to be cause of himself, or to be "through himself" as through a cause). These theses are not so much explicitly formulated by Descartes as received and accepted as a Scholastic and Thomist legacy. But, although they are never discussed, they nonetheless have an essential importance, are everywhere present in Descartes, and indispensable to his theories of Being, of God and of creatures. The full sense of his Metaphysics is not to be found in them, but without them a lot of its sense would be lost. Whence the readiness of Cartesians to present a theory of analogy: rather than thereby attempting to reconcile their master's work with Thomism, they are developing an essential component of Cartesianism which had remained implicit in Descartes himself.

One can always imagine fanciful links between Descartes and Spinoza. One may claim, for example, to find monistic and even pantheistic tendencies in the Cartesian definition of substance ("what requires only itself to exist"). This is to neglect the implicit role of analogy in Descartes's philosophy, which is enough to warn against any such temptation: as in Saint Thomas, the act of existing is in the case of created substances something analogous to what it is in the divine substance.[19] And it does indeed seem that the analytic method ends naturally in an analogical conception of being; its procedure itself leads spontaneously to the positing of being as analogical. It is hardly surprising then that Cartesianism, in its own way, comes upon a difficulty already present in the most orthodox Thomism: despite its ambitions, analogy never manages to free itself from the equivocation from which it starts, or from the eminence to which it leads.

163

According to Spinoza, God is cause of himself in no other sense than that in which he is cause of all things. *Rather is he cause of all things in the same sense as cause of himself.*[20] Descartes says either too much, or too little: too much for Arnauld, but too little for Spinoza. For one cannot employ "through itself" positively, while using "cause of itself" by simple analogy. Descartes recognizes that if God's essence is cause of his existence, it is so in the sense of a formal rather than an efficient cause. The formal cause is indeed immanent essence, coexisting with its effect, and inseparable from it. But we still then need some positive reason why God's existence has no efficient cause and is identical with his essence. Descartes finds this reason in a mere property: God's immensity, superabundance or infinity. But such a property cannot play the part of a rule of proportionality in an analogical judgment. Because the property designates nothing in God's nature, Descartes is stuck at an indirect determination of self-causality: this is asserted in a sense other than efficient causality, but is also asserted by analogy with it. What then is missing in Descartes, is a reason through which self-causality can be arrived at in itself, and directly grounded in the concept or nature of God. This reason is what Spinoza discovers in distinguishing the divine nature from *propria*, absolute from infinite. The attributes are the immanent formal elements that constitute God's absolute nature. And these attributes, in constituting God's essence also constitute his existence; in expressing his essence they also express the existence that necessarily flows from it; his existence is therefore the same as his essence.[21] The attributes thus constitute the formal reason that makes substance in itself a cause of itself, directly, and not by analogy.

The cause of itself is approached first of all in itself; this is the condition for "in itself" and "through itself" to take on a perfectly positive sense. Self-causality is, as a consequence, no longer

asserted *in another sense* than efficient causality; rather is efficient causality asserted in the same sense as self-causality. Thus
God produces as he exists: on the one hand, he produces necessarily; on the other, he necessarily produces within the same
attributes that constitute his essence. Here we come again upon
the two aspects of Spinozist univocity, univocity of cause and
univocity of attributes. There has been a suggestion from the
outset of this analysis that Spinozism cannot be considered apart
from the contest it carries on against negative theology, and
against any method proceeding through equivocation, eminence
and analogy. Spinoza condemns not only the introduction of
negativity into being, but all false conceptions of affirmation in
which negativity still remains as well. It is these survivals that
Spinoza finds and contests in Descartes and the Cartesians. Herein
lies the sense of Spinoza's concept of immanence; it expresses
the double univocity of cause and attribute, that is, the unity of
efficient and formal cause, and the identity of an attribute as
constituting the essence of substance, and as implied by the
essences of creatures.

It should not be thought that in thus reducing creatures to
modifications or modes Spinoza takes away from them all their
own essence or power. The univocity of cause does not mean *that
self-causality and efficient causality have one and the same sense, but
that both are asserted in the same sense of a cause.* The univocity of
attributes does not mean that substance and modes have the same
being or the same perfection: substance is in itself, and modifications are in substance as in something else. What is in another
thing and what is in itself are not asserted in the same sense, but
being is formally asserted in the same sense of what is in itself
and what is in something else: the same attributes, taken in the
same sense, constitute the essence of one and are implied by
the essence of the other. Further still, this common being is not

in Spinoza, as in Duns Scotus, a neutralized being, indifferent between finite and infinite, between *in-se* and *in-alio*. Rather is it the qualified Being of substance, in which substance remains in itself, but modes also remain as in something else. Immanence is thus the new figure that the theory of univocity takes on in Spinoza. The synthetic method naturally leads to the positing of this common being or immanent cause.

In Descartes's philosophy certain axioms constantly reappear. Principal among these is that nothing has no properties. It follows from this, from the viewpoint of quantity, that every property is the property of some being: everything is thus a being or a property, a substance or a mode. Also, from the viewpoint of quality, every reality is a perfection. From the viewpoint of causality there must be as much reality in a cause as in its effect; otherwise something would be produced from nothing. And finally, from the viewpoint of modality, there can strictly speaking be no accidents, accidents being properties that do not necessarily imply the being to which they attach. It belongs to Spinoza to have given a new interpretation to all these axioms in accord with his theory of immanence and the requirements of the synthetic method. And it seems to Spinoza that Descartes had not grasped the full sense and consequences of the proposition that nothing has no properties. On the one hand, any plurality of substances becomes impossible: there are neither unequal limited substances nor equal unlimited substances, for "they would have to have something they had from nothing."[22] It is not enough, on the other hand, just to say that every reality is a perfection. One must also recognize that everything in the nature of a thing is reality, that is, perfection; "To say that the nature of the thing required this [limitation], and therefore it could not be otherwise, is to say nothing. For the nature of the thing cannot require anything unless it exists."[23] One should not imagine

166

that a substance might undergo some limitation of its nature as a result of its own possibility.

There is no more any contingency of modes in relation to substance than a possibility of substance dependent on its attribute. It is not enough to show, with Descartes, that accidents are not real. In Descartes the modes of a substance remain accidental, because they require an external causality to somehow "put" them in that substance itself. In fact, the opposition of mode and accident already shows that necessity is the sole affection of being, its sole modality: God is cause of all things in the same sense as cause of himself; thus everything is necessary, from its essence or from its cause. It is of course true that a cause is more perfect than its effect, substance more perfect than modes; but, although it has more reality, a cause never contains the reality of its effect in any other form or any other way than that on which the effect itself depends. In Descartes one passes from the superiority of the cause to the superiority of certain forms of being over others, and so to the equivocation or analogy of reality (since God contains reality in a form superior to that involved in creatures). It is this transition that grounds the concept of eminence; but it is radically illegitimate. Against Descartes, Spinoza posits the equality of all forms of being, and the univocity of reality which follows from this equality. The philosophy of immanence appears from all viewpoints as the theory of unitary Being, equal Being, common and univocal Being. It seeks the conditions of a genuine affirmation, condemning all approaches that take away from Being its full positivity, that is, its formal community.[b]

CHAPTER ELEVEN

Immanence and the Historical

Components of Expression

Two questions now arise. What are the logical links between immanence and expression? And how was the idea of expressive immanence historically formed within specific philosophical traditions? (Such traditions may well be complex, themselves combining very diverse influences.)

Everything may, it seems, be traced back to the Platonic problem of participation. Plato proposed various hypothetical schemes of participation: to participate was to be a part; or to imitate; or even to receive something from a demon.... Participation was understood, according to these schemes, either materially, or imitatively, or demonically. But the difficulties in each case seem to have the same root: the principle of participation was always sought by Plato on the side of what participates. It usually appears as an accident supervening on what is participated from outside, as a violence suffered by what is participated. If participation consists in being a part, it is difficult to see how what is participated suffers no division or separation. If to participate is to imitate, there must be some external artist who takes the Idea as his model. And it is difficult to see, indeed, what role an intermediary, whether artist or demon, might in general have, other than that of forcing the sensible to reproduce the intelligible, while also forcing the Idea to allow itself to be participated by something foreign to its nature. Even when Plato considers the participation of Ideas in one another, the corresponding power is taken as a power of participating, rather than of being participated.

The primary Postplatonic task was to invert the problem. A principle that would make participation possible was sought, but one that would make it possible from the side of the participated itself. Neoplatonists no longer start from the characteristics of what participates (as multiple, sensible and so on), asking by what violence participation becomes possible. They try rather to discover the internal principle and movement that grounds participation in the participated as such, from the side of the participated as such. Plotinus reproaches Plato for having seen participation from its lesser side.[1,a] The participated does not in fact enter into what participates in it. What is participated remains in itself; it is participated insofar as it produces, and produces insofar as it gives, but has no need to leave itself to give or produce. Plotinus formulates the program of starting at the highest point, subordinating imitation to a genesis or production, and substituting the idea of a *gift* for that of a violence. What is participated is not divided, is not imitated from outside, or constrained by intermediaries which would do violence to its nature. Participation is neither material, nor imitative, nor demonic: it is emanative. Emanation is at once cause and gift: causality by donation, but by productive donation. True activity comes from what is participated; what participates is only an effect, receiving what it is given by its cause. An emanative cause is a donative Cause, a donative Good, a donative Virtue.

When we seek the internal principle of participation *on the side* of what is participated, we necessarily find it "above" or "beyond" participation. There is no question of the principle that makes participation possible itself being participated or participable. Everything emanates from this principle, it gives forth everything. But it is not itself participated, for participation occurs only through what it gives, and in what it gives. This was the basis of Proclus's elaboration of his profound theory of the Imparticipable; participation only occurs through a principle that is itself imparticipable, but that gives participation in things. And Plotinus had already shown that the One is necessarily above its gifts, that it gives what does not belong to it, or is not what it gives.[2] Emanation has in general a triadic form: giver, given and recipient. To participate is always to participate through what is given. So we must recognize not only the genesis of what participates, but also that of what is participated itself, which accounts for the fact of its being participated. A double genesis, of the given and what receives it: the effect that receives determines its own existence when it fully possesses what is given to it; but it does not fully possess it except by turning toward the giver. The giver is above its gifts as it is above its products, participable through what it gives, but imparticipable in itself or as itself, thereby grounding participation.

We are now already able to determine the characteristics by which emanative and immanent cause have something in common logically, as well as fundamental differences. Their common characteristic is that neither leaves itself: they produce *while remaining in themselves.*[3] When defining immanent causality, Spinoza insists on this definition, which to some extent assimilates immanence to emanation.[4] But their difference relates to the way the two causes produce things. *While an emanative cause remains in itself, the effect it produces is not in it, and does not remain in it.* Plotinus says of the One as first principle or cause of causes:

"It is because *there is nothing in it* that all things come from it."[5] In reminding us that an effect is inseparable from its cause, he is thinking of a continuity of flow or radiation, and not of the actual inherence of any content. The emanative cause produces through what it gives, but is beyond what it gives: so that an effect comes out of its cause, exists only in so coming out, and is only determined in its existence through turning back toward the cause from which it has come. Whence the determination of the effect's existence is inseparable from a conversion[b] in which the cause appears as the Good within a perspective of transcendent finality. A cause is immanent, on the other hand, when its effect is "immanate" in the cause, rather than emanating from it. What defines an immanent cause is that its effect is in it – in it, of course, as in something else, but still being and remaining in it. The effect remains in its cause no less than the cause remains in itself. From this viewpoint the distinction of essence between cause and effect can in no way be understood as a degradation. From the viewpoint of immanence the distinction of essence does not exclude, but rather implies, an equality of being: it is the same being that remains in itself in the cause, and in which the effect remains as in another thing.

Plotinus also says that the One has "nothing in common" with the things that come from it.[6] For an emanative cause is superior not only to its effect, but superior also to what it gives the effect. But why exactly is the first cause the One? Giving being to all that is, it is necessarily beyond being or substance. So emanation, in its pure form, always involves a system of the One-above-being; the first hypothesis of the *Parmenides*[c] dominates all Neoplatonism.[7] Nor is emanation any more separable from a negative theology, or a method of analogy that respects the eminence of principle or cause. Proclus shows that, in the case of the One itself, negation generates affirmations applicable to what the One gives and what proceeds from it. Furthermore, at each stage of emanation, one must recognize the presence of an imparticipable from which things proceed and to which they revert. Emanation thus serves as the principle of a universe rendered hierarchical; the difference of beings is in general conceived as a hierarchical difference; each term is as it were the image of the superior term that precedes it, and is defined by the degree of distance that separates it from the first cause or first principle.

Between emanative and immanent cause there thus appears a second distinction. Immanence for its part implies a pure ontology, a theory of Being in which Unity is only a property of substance and of what is. What is more, pure immanence requires as a principle the equality of being, or the positing of equal Being: not only is being equal in itself, but it is seen to be equally present in all beings. And the Cause appears as everywhere equally close: there is no remote causation. Beings are not defined by their rank in a hierarchy, are not more or less remote from the One, but each depends directly on God, participating in the equality of being, receiving immediately all that it is by its essence fitted to receive, irrespective of any proximity or remoteness. Furthermore, pure immanence requires a Being that is univocal and constitutes a Nature, and that consists of positive forms, common to producer and product, to cause and effect. We know that immanence does not do away with the distinction of essences; but there must be common forms that constitute the essence of substance as cause, while they contain the essences of modes as effects. Thus the superiority of causes subsists within the viewpoint of immanence, but now involves no eminence, involves, that is, no positing of any principle beyond the forms that are themselves present in the effect. Immanence is opposed to any eminence of the cause, any negative theology, any method of analogy, any hierarchical conception of the world. With immanence all is affirmation. The Cause is superior to its effect, but not superior to what it gives to the effect. Or rather, it "gives" nothing to the effect. Participation must be thought of in a completely positive way, not on the basis of an eminent gift, but on the basis of a formal community that allows the distinction of essences to subsist.

If there is such a great difference between emanation and immanence, how can they be historically assimilated, if only in a partial manner? This happens because in Neoplatonism itself, under Stoic influences, a truly immanent cause does in fact come to be combined with emanative causality.[8] At the level of the One, the metaphors of sphere and radiation already offer an important corrective to the theory of a strict hierarchy. But it is above all the first emanation that presents us with an idea of immanent causality. From the One emanate Intelligence and Being; and not only is there a mutual immanence of Being and Intelligence, but Intelligence contains all intelligences and all intelligibles, just as Being contains all beings and all genera of being. "Full of the beings which it has generated, Intelligence[d] as it were swallows them up again, by keeping them in itself."[9] Of course from Intelligence, in its turn, there emanates a new hypostasis. But Intelligence does not constitute such an emanative cause except to the extent that it has reached its own limit of perfection; and this it reaches only as an immanent cause. Being and Intelligence are still the One, but a One that is and that knows, the One of the second hypothesis in the *Parmenides*, a One in which the Multiple is present, and which is itself present in the Multiple. Plotinus shows that Being is identical to number in the state of unity, that beings are identical to number in the state of development (that is to number as "explicated"[10]). There is already in Plotinus an equality of Being correlative with the supereminence of the One.[11] Damascius develops the description of this aspect of Being – in which the Multiple is collected, concentrated, *comprised* in the One, but in which the One also *explicates* itself in the Many – to great lengths.

Such is the origin of a pair of notions that take on greater and greater importance in the philosophies of the Middle Ages and Renaissance: *complicare* and *explicare*.[12] All things are present to God, who complicates them. God is present to all things, which explicate and implicate him. A co-presence of two correlative movements comes to be substituted for a series of successive subordinate emanations. For things remain in God while explicating and implicating him, no less than God remains in himself, in complicating them. The presence of things to God constitutes an inherence, just as the presence of God to things constitutes an implication. An equality of being is substituted for a hierarchy of hypostases; for things are present to the same Being, which is itself present in things. Immanence corresponds to the unity of complication and explication, of inherence and implication. Things remain inherent in God who complicates them, and God remains implicated in things which explicate him. It is a complicative God who is explicated through all things: "God is the universal complication, in the sense that everything is in him; and the universal explication, in the sense that he is in everything."[13] Participation no longer has its principle in an emanation whose source lies in a more or less distant One, but rather in the immediate and adequate expression of an absolute Being that comprises in it all beings, and is explicated in the essence of each. Expression comprehends all these aspects: complication, explication, inherence, implication. And these aspects of expression are also the categories of immanence. Immanence is revealed as expressive, and expression as immanent, in a system of logical relations within which the two notions are correlative.

From this viewpoint the idea of expression accounts for the real activity of the participated, and for the possibility of participation. It is in the idea of expression that the new principle of immanence asserts itself. Expression appears as the unity of the multiple, as the complication of the multiple, and as the explication of the One. God expresses *himself* in the world; the world is the expression, the explication, of a God-Being or a One who is. The world is carried into God in such a way that it loses its limits or finitude, and participates directly in divine infinity. The metaphor of a circle whose center is everywhere and circumference nowhere applies to the world itself. The relation of expression does not ground between God and world an identity of essence, but an equality of being. For it is the same Being that is present in the God who complicates all things according to his own essence, and in the things that explicate him according to their own essence or mode. So that God must be defined as identical to Nature *complicative*, and Nature as identical to God *explicative*. But this equality or identity in distinction constitutes two moments within expression as a whole: God expresses himself in his Word, his Word expresses the divine essence; but the Word in its turn expresses itself in the Universe, the Universe expressing all things in the way belonging to each essentially. The Word is the expression of God, the language of his expression; the Universe is the expression of this expression, the face of expression, its physiognomy. (This classic theme of a double expression is to be found in Eckhardt: God expresses himself in the Word, which is a silent inward speech; and the Word expresses itself in the world, which is externalized speech and face.[14])

I have tried to show how an expressive immanence of Being was grafted onto the emanative transcendence of the One. Yet in Ploti-

nus and his successors this immanent causality remains subordinate
to emanative cause. Being or Intelligence do indeed "explicate
themselves," but self-explication is only found in what is already
multiple, and not in the first principle. "Intelligence explicated[h]
itself because it wanted to possess everything – how much better
it would have been for it not to want this, for it thereby became
the second principle."[15] Immanent Being, immanent Thought,
cannot constitute an absolute, but presuppose as first principle an
emanative cause and transcendent end from which all flows, and
to which all reverts. This first principle, the One above Being,
does of course contain all things virtually: *it is explicated* but does
not *explicate itself*, in contrast to Intelligence and to Being.[16] It is
not affected by what expresses it. So that for the limiting development of Neoplatonism we have to wait until the Middle Ages,
Renaissance and Reformation, when we see immanent causality
taking on ever greater importance, Being in competition with the
One, expression in competition with, and sometimes tending to
supplant, emanation. It has often been asked what makes the
philosophy of the Renaissance "modern"; I fully agree with Alexandre Koyré's thesis, that the specific category of expression
characterizes the mode of thinking of such philosophy.

One must however recognize that this expressionist tendency
was never fully worked through. It was encouraged by Christianity, by its theory of the Word, and above all by the ontological
requirement that the first principle be a Being. But Christianity
also repressed it, through the still more powerful requirement
that the transcendence of the divine being be maintained. Thus
one sees philosophers constantly threatened by the accusation of
immanentism and pantheism, and constantly taking care to avoid,
above all else, such an accusation. Already in Erigena one has to
admire the philosophically subtle contrivances by which the
claims of an expressive immanence, an emanative transcendence

and an exemplary creation *ex nihilo*, are all reconciled. The transcendence of a creator God is in fact saved through an analogical conception of Being, or at least through an eminent conception of God which sets limits to the implications of an equality of being. The principle of equality of being is itself interpreted analogically; transcendence is preserved by drawing on all the resources of symbolism. The inexpressible is, then, maintained at the heart of expression itself. Not that one goes back to Plotinus, to the positing of an ineffable One above Being. For it is the same God, the same infinite being, who asserts and expresses himself in the world as immanent cause, and who remains inexpressible and transcendent as the object of a negative theology that denies of him all that is affirmed of his immanence. Thus, even in these conditions, immanence appears as a theoretical limit, corrected through the perspectives of emanation and creation. The reason for this is simple: expressive immanence cannot be sustained unless it is accompanied by a thoroughgoing conception of univocity, a thoroughgoing affirmation of univocal Being.

Expressive immanence is grafted onto the theme of emanation, which in part encourages it, and in part represses it. And it interacts no less, under similar conditions, with the theme of creation. Creation, in one of its aspects, seems to relate to the same concern as Emanation: it is here a question, once again, of finding a principle of participation on the side of the participated itself. Ideas are placed in God: rather than being referred to some lower power that might take them as models, or force them to descend into the sensible order, they themselves have an exemplary character. While representing God's infinite being, they also represent all that God wishes, and is able, to do. Ideas in God *are exemplary likenesses*; things created *ex nihilo* are *imitative likenesses*. Participation is an imitation, but the principle of imitation is to be found on the side of the model or what is imitated: Ideas are not distinguished in relation to God, but in relation to the things whose possible participation in God himself they ground. (Malebranche defines Ideas in God as principles of expression, representing God as participable or imitable.)

This was the line taken by Saint Augustine. And here again, the concept of expression comes forward to determine the status of both exemplary and imitative likeness. It is Bonaventure who, following Augustine, attaches the greatest importance to this double determination: the two likenesses together constitute the concrete whole of "expressive" likeness. God expresses himself in his Word or in an exemplary Idea; but the exemplary Idea expresses the multiplicity of creatable and created things. This is the paradox of expression as such: intrinsic and eternal, it is one in relation to what expresses itself, and multiple in relation to what is expressed.[17] Expression is like a radiation that leads us from God, who expresses himself, to the things expressed. As itself expressive (rather than expressed), it extends equally to all things without limitation, like the divine essence itself. We here again find an idea of equality, which enables Bonaventure to deny any hierarchy among Ideas as they are in God. Indeed the theory of expressive likeness implies a certain immanence. Ideas are in God, therefore things are in God through their exemplary likenesses. But must not the things themselves be in God, as imitations? Is there not a certain inherence of a copy in its model?[18] One can escape such a conclusion only by maintaining a strictly analogical conception of being (Bonaventure himself constantly opposes expressive likeness and univocal likeness or likeness of univocity).

Most of the authors cited thus far belong to two traditions at once: those of emanation and imitation, emanative cause and exemplary cause, Pseudo-Dionysius and Augustine. But these two lines meet in the concept of expression. This may already be seen in Erigena, who forges a philosophy of expression that is sometimes "similitudinous" (turning on likeness) and sometimes "emanative." *Emanation leads us to expression as explication. Creation leads us to expression as likeness.* And expression does in fact have this dual aspect: on the one hand it is a mirror, a model, a resemblance; on the other a seed, a tree, a branch. But these metaphors come in the end to nothing. The idea of expression is repressed as soon as it surfaces. For the themes of creation or emanation cannot do without a minimal transcendence, which bars "expressionism" from proceeding all the way to the immanence it implies. Immanence is the very vertigo of philosophy, and is inseparable from the concept of expression (from the double immanence of expression in what expresses itself, and of what is expressed in its expression).

The significance of Spinozism seems to me this: it asserts immanence as a principle and frees expression from any subordination to emanative or exemplary causality. *Expression itself no longer emanates, no longer resembles anything.* And such a result can be obtained only within a perspective of univocity. God is cause of all things in the same sense that he is cause of himself; he produces as he formally exists, or as he objectively understands himself. He thus produces things in the very forms that constitute his own essence. But the same attributes that formally constitute God's essence contain all the formal essences of modes, and the idea of God's essence comprehends all objective essences, or all ideas. Things in general are modes of divine being, that is, they implicate the same attributes that constitute the nature of this being. Thus all likeness is univocal, defined by the presence in both cause and effect of a common property. The things that are produced are not imitations any more than their ideas are models. There is nothing exemplary even in the idea of God, since this is itself, in its formal being, also produced. Nor conversely do ideas imitate things. In their formal being they follow from the attribute of thought; and if they are representative, they are so only to the extent that they participate in an absolute power of thinking which is in itself equal to the absolute power of producing or acting. Thus all imitative or exemplary likeness is excluded from the relation of expression. God expresses himself in the forms that constitute his essence, as in the idea that reflects it. Expression characterizes both being and knowing. But only univocal being, only univocal consciousness, are expressive. Substance and modes, cause and effects, only have being and are only known through common forms that actually constitute the essence of the one, and actually contain the essence of the others.

Spinoza therefore sets apart two domains which were always confused in earlier traditions: that of expression and of the expressive knowledge which is alone adequate; and that of signs, and of knowledge by signs, through apophasis or analogy. Spinoza distinguishes different sorts of signs: indicative signs, which lead us to infer something from the state of our body; imperative signs, which lead us to grasp laws as moral laws; and revelatory signs, which themselves lead us to obey them and which at the very most disclose to us certain "*propria*" of God. But whatever its sort, knowledge through signs is never expressive, and remains of the first kind. Indication is not an expression, but a confused state of involvement in which an idea remains powerless to explain itself or to express its own cause. An imperative sign is not an expression, but a confused impression which leads us to believe that the true expressions of God, the laws of nature, are so many commandments. Revelation is not an expression, but a cultivation of the inexpressible, a confused and relative knowledge through which we lend God determinations analogous to our own

(Understanding, Will), only to rescue God's superiority through his eminence in all genera (the supereminent One, etc.). Through univocity, Spinoza gives the idea of expression a positive content, opposing it to the three sorts of sign. The opposition of expressions and signs is one of the fundamental principles of Spinozism.

Expression had also to be freed from all trace of emanation. Neoplatonism drew part of its force from the thesis that production is not carried out by composition (addition of species to genus, reception of a form in matter), but by distinction and differentiation. But Neoplatonism was constrained by various requirements: distinction had to be produced from the Indistinct or the absolutely One, and yet to be actual; it had to be actual, and yet not numerical. Such requirements explain Neoplatonist efforts to define the status of indistinct distinctions, undivided divisions, unplurifiable pluralities. Spinoza, on the other hand, finds another solution in his theory of distinctions. In conjunction with univocity, the idea of a formal distinction, that is to say, a real distinction that is not and cannot be numerical, allows him immediately to reconcile the ontological unity of substance with the qualitative plurality of its attributes. Far from emanating from an eminent Unity, the really distinct attributes constitute the essence of absolutely single substance. Substance is not like a One from which there proceeds a paradoxical distinction; attributes are not emanations. The unity of substance and the distinction of attributes are correlates that together constitute expression. The distinction of attributes is nothing but the qualitative composition of an ontologically single substance; substance is distinguished into an infinity of attributes, which are as it were its actual forms or component qualities. Before all production there is thus a distinction, but this distinction is also the composition of substance itself.

The production of modes does, it is true, take place through

differentiation. But differentiation is in this case purely quantitative. If real distinction is never numerical, numerical distinction is, conversely, essentially modal. Number is of course more
suitably applied to things of reason than to modes themselves.
Yet it remains that modal distinction is quantitative, even if number does not well explain the nature of such quantity. This is
well seen in Spinoza's conception of participation.[19] Theories of
emanation and creation agreed in refusing any material sense to
participation. In Spinoza, on the other hand, the principle of participation itself requires us to interpret it as a material and quantitative participation. To participate is to have a part in, to be a
part of, something. Attributes are so to speak dynamic qualities to
which corresponds the absolute power of God. A mode is, in its
essence, always a certain degree, a certain quantity, of a quality.
Precisely thereby is it, within the attribute containing it, a part
so to speak of God's power. Being common forms, attributes are
the conditions of substance having an omnipotence identical with
its essence, and also of modes possessing a part of this power identical with their essence. God's power expresses or explicates itself
modally, but only in and through such quantitative differentiation. Man thus loses in Spinozism all the privileges owed to a
quality supposed proper to him, which belonged to him only
from the viewpoint of imitative participation. Modes are distinguished quantitatively: each mode expresses or explicates God's
essence, insofar as that essence explicates itself through the
mode's essence, that is, divides itself according to the quantity
corresponding to that mode.[20]

Modes of the same attribute are not distinguished by their
rank, by their nearness to, or distance from God. They are quantitatively distinguished by the quantity or capacity of their respective essences which always participate directly in divine
substance. A certain hierarchy does of course appear to persist

in Spinoza between infinite immediate mode, infinite mediate mode, and finite modes. But Spinoza constantly reminds us that *God is never, strictly speaking, a remote cause.*[21] God, considered under some attribute, is the proximate cause of the corresponding infinite immediate mode. As for the infinite mode Spinoza calls mediate, it derives from the already modified attribute; *but the first modification is not interposed as an intermediate cause within a system of emanations*, it appears as the modality in which God himself produces in himself the second modification. If we consider the essences of finite modes, we see that they do not form a hierarchical system in which the less powerful depend on the more powerful, but an actually infinite collection, a system of mutual implications, in which each essence conforms with all of the others, and in which all essences are involved in the production of each. Thus God directly produces each essence together with all the others. That is, existing modes themselves have God as their direct cause. An existing finite mode must of course be referred to something else besides an attribute; its cause lies in another existing mode, whose own cause lies in another, and so on *ad infinitum*. But God is the power that, in each case, determines a cause to have such an effect. We never enter into infinite regress; we have only to consider a mode together with its cause in order to arrive directly at God as the principle that determines that cause to have such an effect. Thus God is never a remote cause, even of existing modes. Whence Spinoza's famous phrase "insofar as...." Things are always produced directly by God, but in various modalities: insofar as he is infinite, insofar as he is modified by a modification that is itself infinite, insofar as he is affected by a particular modification. A hierarchy of modalities of God himself is substituted for a hierarchy of emanations; but in each modality God expresses himself immediately, produces his effects directly. Every effect is thus in God, and remains in God; and God, furthermore, is himself present in each of his effects.

Substance first of all expresses itself in itself. This first expression is formal or qualitative. Substance expresses itself in formally distinct, qualitatively distinct, really distinct attributes; each attribute expresses the essence of substance. Here again we find the double movement of complication and explication: substance "complicates" its attributes, each attribute explicates the essence of substance, and substance explicates itself through all its attributes. This first expression, prior to any production, is as it were the constitution of substance itself. A principle of equality here finds its first application: not only is substance equal to all its attributes, but each attribute is equal to the others, none is superior or inferior. *Substance expresses itself to itself.* It expresses itself in the idea of God, which comprises all attributes. In expressing or explicating himself, God understands himself. This second expression is objective. It involves a new application of the principle of equality: the power of thinking, corresponding to the idea of God, is equal to the power of existing, which corresponds to the attributes. The idea of God (the Son or Word) has a complex status: objectively equal to substance, it is in its formal being only a product. It thus leads us to a third expression: *Substance re-expresses itself, attributes in their turn express themselves in modes.* This expression is the production of the modes themselves: God produces as he understands; he cannot understand himself without producing an infinity of things, and without also understanding all that he produces. God produces things within the same attributes that constitute his essence, and thinks all he produces within the same idea that comprises[k] his essence. All modes are thus expressive, as are the ideas corresponding to those modes. Attributes "complicate" the essences of modes, and explicate themselves through them, just as the Idea of God comprises all ideas and explicates itself through them. This third expression is quantitative. And, like quantity itself, it has two forms: intensive in the essences of modes, and extensive when the modes pass into existence. The principle of equality here finds its final application: not in an equality of modes to substance itself, but in a superiority of substance which involves no eminence. Modes are expressive precisely insofar as they imply the same qualitative forms that constitute the essence of substance.

PART THREE

The Theory of Finite Modes

CHAPTER TWELVE

Modal Essence:

The Passage from Infinite

to Finite

One finds in Spinoza the classic identification of attribute and quality. Attributes are eternal and infinite qualities: as such they are indivisible. Extension is indivisible *qua* substantial quality or attribute. Each attribute is indivisible *qua* quality. But each attribute–quality has an infinite quantity that is for its part divisible in certain conditions. This infinite quantity of an attribute constitutes a matter, but a purely modal matter. An attribute is thus divided modally, and not really. It has modally distinct parts: modal, rather than real or substantial parts. This applies to Extension as to the other attributes: "Is there no part in Extension prior to all its modes? None, I reply."[1]

But it appears from the *Ethics* that the word "part" must be understood in two ways. Sometimes it is a question of parts of a power, that is, of intrinsic or intensive parts, true degrees, degrees of power or intensity. Modal essences are thus defined as degrees of power (Spinoza here joins a long Scholastic tradition, according to which *modus intrinsecus = gradus = intensio*[2]). But it is also, at times, a question of extrinsic or extensive parts, external to one another, and acting on one another from outside. Thus the simplest bodies are the ultimate extensive modal divisions of Extension. (It should not be thought that Extensivity belongs only to Extension: the modes of Extension are defined essentially by degrees of power, and an attribute such as Thought itself has extensive modal parts, ideas that correspond to the simplest bodies.[3,a])

It is as though to each attribute there belonged two quantities, each in itself infinite, but each in its own way divisible in certain conditions: an intensive quantity, which divides into intensive parts, or degrees, and an extensive quantity, which divides into extensive parts. It is hardly surprising, then, that beside the qualitative infinity of attributes, which relates to substance, Spinoza alludes to two strictly modal quantitative infinities. In a letter to Meyer he writes "Certain things [are infinite] in virtue of the cause on which they depend, yet when they are considered abstractly they can be divided into parts and viewed as finite; *certain others*, lastly, are said to be infinite or, if you prefer, indefinite, because they cannot be equated with any number, yet they can be conceived as greater or less."[4,b] But we then face many problems: In what do these two infinities consist? How, and in what conditions, do they allow of division into parts? How are they related, and what are the relations of their respective parts?

What is it that Spinoza calls a modal essence, a particular or singular essence? His position may be stated thus: A mode's essence is not a logical possibility, nor a mathematical structure, nor a metaphysical entity, but a physical reality, a *res physica*. Spinoza means that the essence, *qua* essence, has an existence. *A modal essence has an existence distinct from that of the corresponding mode.* A mode's essence exists, is real and actual, even if the mode whose essence it is does not actually exist. Whence Spinoza's conception of a nonexistent mode: this is not something possible, but an object whose idea is necessarily comprised in the idea of God, just as its essence is necessarily contained in an attribute.[5] The idea of nonexistent modes is thus the necessary objective correlate of modal essence. Every essence is the essence of something; the essence of a mode is the essence of something which must be conceived in infinite understanding. One cannot say of the essence itself that it is only possible, nor can one say that a nonexistent mode tends, by virtue of its essence, toward existence. On these two points Spinoza and Leibniz are radically opposed: in Leibniz an essence or individual notion is a logical possibility, inseparable from a certain metaphysical reality, that is, from a "claim to existence," a tendency to exist.[6] In Spinoza this is not the case: an essence is not a possibility, but possesses a real existence that belongs to it itself; a nonexistent mode lacks nothing and claims nothing, but is conceived in God's understanding as the correlate of its real essence. Neither a metaphysical reality nor a logical possibility, *the essence of a mode is a pure physical reality*.

Modal essences therefore, no less than existing modes, have efficient causes. "God is the efficient cause, not only of the existence of things, but also of their essence."[7] When Spinoza shows that a mode's essence does not involve existence, he of course primarily means that its essence is not the cause of a mode's existence. But he also means that the mode's essence is not the cause of its own existence.[8,c]

Not that there is any real distinction between an essence and *its own* existence; the distinction of essence and existence is sufficiently grounded once it is agreed that an essence has a cause that is itself distinct. From this it does indeed follow that the essence exists necessarily, but this by virtue of its cause (and not through itself). One may recognize here the principle of a famous thesis of Duns Scotus's (and of Avicenna before him): existence necessarily accompanies essence, but this by virtue of the latter's cause; it is not thereby included or involved in essence, but added to it. It is not added to it as a really distinct actuality, but only as a sort of ultimate determination resulting from the essence's cause.[9] In short, essence always has the existence due to it by virtue of its cause. Thus in Spinoza, the following two propositions go together: *Essences have an existence or physical reality*; *God is the efficient cause of essences*. An essence's existence is the same as its being-caused. So that one should not confuse Spinoza's theory with an apparently analogous Cartesian theory: when Descartes says that God produces even essences, he means that God is not subject to any law, that he creates everything, even possibility. Spinoza, on the other hand, means that essences are not possibles, but that they have a fully actual existence that belongs to them by virtue of their cause. Essences of modes can only be assimilated to possibles to the extent that we consider them abstractly, that is, divorce them from the cause that makes them real or existing things.

If all essences *agree*, this is just because they are not causes one of another, but all have God as their cause. When we consider them concretely, referring them all to the cause on which they depend, we posit them all together, coexisting and agreeing.[10] All essences agree in the existence or reality resulting from their cause. One essence can only be separated from the others abstractly, by considering it independently of the principle of production which comprehends all. Thus essences form a total system, an actually infinite whole. One may say of this whole, as in the letter to Meyer, that it is infinite through its cause. We must then ask: How are the essences of modes distinct, if they are inseparable one from another? How are they singular, when they form an infinite whole? Which amounts to asking: In what does the physical reality of essences as such consist? This problem concerning at once individuality and reality poses, as is well known, many difficulties for Spinozism.

Spinoza does not appear to have had any clear solution at the outset, nor even a clear statement of the problem. Two famous passages of the *Short Treatise* argue that, as long as the corresponding modes do not themselves exist, their essences are not distinct from the attribute containing them, and are furthermore not distinct one from another – that they do not, then, have in themselves any principle of individuality.[11] Individuation takes place only through a mode's existence, not through its essence. (And yet the *Short Treatise* already requires the hypothesis of modal essences that are in themselves singular, and makes full use of this hypothesis.)

But these two passages of the *Short Treatise* should perhaps be taken as ambiguous, rather than as thoroughly excluding any singularity and distinction of essences as such. For the first passage seems to say that as long as a mode doesn't exist, its essence exists solely as contained *in* its attribute; but the idea of the essence cannot itself contain a distinction that is not in Nature; thus it cannot represent a nonexistent mode as if it were distinct *from* its attribute and from other modes. And the second passage, that as long as a mode doesn't exist, the idea of its essence cannot involve any distinct existence; as long as the whole wall is white, one cannot apprehend anything distinct from it or distinct in it. (This thesis is not even abandoned in the *Ethics*: as long as a mode doesn't exist, its essence is contained in its attribute, its idea comprised in the idea of God; this idea cannot then involve a distinct existence, nor can it be distinguished from other ideas.[12])

"Being distinct from" is bluntly opposed in all this to "being contained in." As contained only in their attribute, modal essences are not distinct from it. *Distinction, then, is taken in the sense of extrinsic distinction.* The argument is as follows. Modal essences are contained in their attribute; as long as a mode does not exist, no extrinsic distinction between its essence and the attribute, or between its essence and other essences, is possible. Thus no idea can represent or apprehend modal essences as extrinsic parts of the attribute, or as parts external one to another. This position may seem odd, because it supposes that, conversely, extrinsic distinction is not incompatible with existing modes, and is even, indeed, required by them. We will postpone the analysis of this point and simply note here that an existing mode has duration, and that while it endures it is no longer simply contained in its attribute, just as its idea is no longer simply comprised in the idea of God.[13] It is through duration (and also, in the case of modes of Extension, through figure and place) that existing modes have their strictly extrinsic individuation.

As long as the wall is white, no shape is distinguished from or in it. That is: in such a state the quality is not affected by anything extrinsically distinct from it. But there remains the question of knowing whether there is another type of modal distinction, presenting an intrinsic principle of individuation. Furthermore, one might well consider that individuation through the existence of a mode is insufficient. We cannot distinguish existing things except insofar as we suppose their essences distinct; similarly, any extrinsic distinction seems to presuppose a prior intrinsic one. So a modal essence should be singular in itself, even if the corresponding mode does not exist. But how? Let us return to Scotus: whiteness, he says, has various intensities; these are not added to whiteness as one thing to another thing, like a shape added to the wall on which it is drawn; its degrees of intensity are intrinsic determinations, intrinsic modes, of a whiteness that remains univocally the same under whichever modality it is considered.[14]

This seems also to be the case for Spinoza: modal essences are intrinsic modes or intensive quantities. An attribute remains as a quality univocally what it is, containing all the degrees that affect it without modifying its formal reason. Modal essences are thus distinguished from their attribute as intensities of its quality, and from one another as different degrees of intensity. One may be permitted to think that, while he does not explicitly develop such a theory, Spinoza is looking toward the idea of a distinction or singularity belonging to modal essences as such. The difference of being (of modal essences) is at once intrinsic and purely quantitative; for the quantity here in question is an intensive one. Only a quantitative distinction of beings is consistent with the qualitative identity of the absolute. And this quantitative distinction is no mere appearance, but an internal difference, a difference of intensity. So that each finite being must be said to *express the absolute*, according to the intensive quantity that constitutes its essence, according, that is, to the degree of its power.[15] Individuation is, in Spinoza, neither qualitative nor extrinsic, but quantitative and intrinsic, intensive. There is indeed, in this sense, a distinction of modal essences, both from the attribute that contains them, and one from another. Modal essences are not distinct in any extrinsic way, being contained in their attribute, but they have nonetheless a type of distinction or singularity proper to them, within the attribute that contains them.

Intensive quantity is infinite, and the system of essences an actually infinite series. We are here dealing with infinity "through a cause." This is the sense in which an attribute contains, that is, complicates, the essences of all its modes; it contains them as the infinite series of degrees corresponding to its intensive quantity. Now it is easy to see that this infinity is in a sense indivisible: one cannot divide it into extensive or extrinsic parts, except through abstraction. (But by abstraction we separate essences from their cause and from the attribute that contains them, considering them as simple logical possibilities, and taking from them all physical reality.) Modal essences are thus in fact inseparable, and are characterized by their total agreement. But they are nevertheless singular and particular, and distinguished from one another intrinsically. In their concrete system, all essences are involved in the production of each: this applies not merely to the lowest degree of essence, but to the highest also, since the series is actually infinite. Yet in this concrete system each essence is produced as an irreducible degree, necessarily apprehended as a singular unity. Such is the system of "complication" of essences.

Modal essences are, then, parts of an infinite series. But this in the very special sense of intensive or intrinsic parts. One should not give Spinoza's particular essences a Leibnizian interpretation. Particular essences are not microcosms. They are not all contained in each, but all are comprised in the production of each. A modal essence is a *pars intensiva*, and not a *pars totalis*.[16] As such, it has an expressive power, but such expressive power must be understood in a way very different from the way it is understood by Leibniz. For the status of modal essences relates to a strictly Spinozist problem, concerning absolutely infinite substance. This is the problem of passing from infinite to finite. Substance is, so to speak, the absolute ontological identity of all qualities, absolutely infinite power, the power of existing in all forms, and of thinking all forms. Attributes are infinite forms or qualities, and as such indivisible. So the finite is neither substantial nor qualitative. But nor is it mere appearance: it is modal, that is, quantitative. Each substantial quality has intensive modal quantity, itself infinite, which actually divides into an infinity of intrinsic modes. These intrinsic modes, contained together as a whole in an attribute, are the intensive parts of the attribute itself. And they are thereby parts of God's power, within the attribute that contains them. It is in this sense, as we have already seen, that modes of a divine attribute necessarily participate in God's power: their essence is itself part of God's power, is an intensive part, or a degree of that power. Here again the reduction of creatures to the status of modes appears as the condition of their essence being a power, that is, of being an irreducible part of God's power. Thus modes are in their essence expressive: they express God's essence, each according to the degree of power that constitutes its essence. The individuation of the finite does not proceed in Spinoza from genus to species or individual, from general to particular; it proceeds from an infinite quality to a corresponding quantity, which divides into irreducible intrinsic or intensive parts.

CHAPTER THIRTEEN

Modal Existence

We know that the existence of a modal essence is not the same as the existence of the corresponding mode. A modal essence can exist without the mode itself existing: its essence is not the cause of a mode's existence. A mode's existence thus has as it cause another mode, itself existing.[1] But this infinite regression in no way tells us in what that existence consists. If, however, it be true that an existing mode "needs" a great number of other existing modes, this already suggests that it is itself composed of a great number of parts, parts that come to it from elsewhere, that begin to belong to it as soon as it comes to exist by virtue of an external cause, that are renewed in the play of causes while the mode exists, and that cease to belong to it when it passes away.[2] So we can now say in what a mode's existence consists: *to exist is to actually possess a very great number [plurimae] of parts*. These component parts are external to the mode's essence, and external one to another: they are extensive parts.

I do not think that there are, for Spinoza, any existing modes that are not actually composed of a very great number of extensive parts. There are no existing bodies, within Extension,[a] that are not composed of a very great number of simple bodies. And the soul, insofar as it is the idea of an existing body, is itself composed of a great number of ideas which correspond to the body's component parts, and which are extrinsically distinct from one another.[3] The faculties, furthermore, which the soul possesses insofar as it is the idea of an existing body, are genuine extensive parts, which cease to belong to the soul once the body itself ceases to exist.[4] Here then, it seems, are the primary elements of Spinoza's scheme: a mode's essence is a determinate degree of intensity, an irreducible degree of power; a mode exists, if it actually possesses a very great number of extensive parts corresponding to its essence or degree of power.

What does Spinoza mean by "a very great number"? The letter to Meyer provides a valuable clue: there are magnitudes that are called infinite or, better, indefinite, because "the parts cannot be determined or expressed by any number"; "they cannot be equated with any number, but exceed every number that can be given."[5] Here we recognize the second infinity, modal and quantitative, of the letter to Meyer: a strictly extensive infinity. Spinoza gives a geometrical example: the sum of the unequal distances between two nonconcentric circles[b] exceeds any number that may be given. This infinite quantity has three distinctive characteristics, although these are it is true negative, rather than positive. It is not, in the first place, constant or equal to itself: it can be conceived as both greater and less (Spinoza explains in another passage: "In the whole space between two circles having different centers we conceive twice as many parts as in half that space, and yet the number of the parts, of the half as well as of the whole, exceeds any assignable number"[6]). Extensive infinity is thus an infinity necessarily conceived as greater or less. But in the second place, it is not strictly speaking "unlimited": for it relates to something limited. There is a maximum and a minimum distance between two nonconcentric circles, and these distances attach to a perfectly limited and determinate space. In the third place, finally, this quantity is not infinite through the multitude of its parts, for "if the infinity were inferred from the multitude of parts, we should not be able to conceive a greater multitude of parts, but their multitude ought to be greater than any given one." It is not from the number of its parts that the quantity is infinite, but rather because it is infinite that it divides into a multitude of parts exceeding any number.

One may note that number never adequately expresses the nature of modes. It may be useful to identify modal quantity and number; indeed one must do so, if it is to be opposed to substance and substantial qualities. I did so when presenting modal distinction as a numerical distinction. But number is, in fact, only a way of imagining quantity, or an abstract way of thinking of modes. Modes, insofar as they flow from substance and its attributes, are something more than phantoms of imagination, something more than things of reason. Their being is quantitative, rather than numerical, strictly speaking. If one considers the primary modal infinity, intensive infinity, it is not divisible into extrinsic parts. The intensive parts it intrinsically includes, modal essences, are not separable one from another. Number separates them from one another, and from the principle of their production, and thereby grasps them abstractly. If one considers the second infinity, extensive infinity, it is of course divisible into the extrinsic parts that compose existing things. But these extrinsic parts always come in infinite collections; their sum always exceeds any given number. When we explain them by number, we lose our hold on the real being of existing modes, and grasp only fictions.[7]

Thus the letter to Meyer presents, among other things, the special case of an extensive modal infinity, variable and divisible. This exposition is important in itself; Leibniz congratulated Spinoza on having gone further on this point than many mathe-

maticians.[8] But from the viewpoint of Spinozism itself, the question is: What is the bearing of this theory of the second modal
infinity on the system as a whole? The answer seems to be that
extensive infinity relates to modal existence. Indeed, when
Spinoza asserts in the *Ethics* that composite modes have a *very
great number* of parts, he understands by "very great number" an
unassignable number, that is, a plurality exceeding any number.
The essence of such a mode is itself a degree of power; but whatever degree of power constitutes its essence, the mode cannot
exist unless it actually has an infinity of parts. If one considers a
mode whose degree of power is double that of the previous one,
its existence is composed of an infinity of parts, which is itself
the double of the previous infinity. There is in the limit an infinity of infinite wholes, a whole of all the wholes, the whole, so
to speak, of existing things both contemporaneous and successive. In short, the characteristics assigned by Spinoza to the second modal infinity, in his letter to Meyer, find an application only
in the theory of existing modes developed in the *Ethics* – and
there find general application. Existing modes have an infinity
(a very great number) of parts; their essences or degrees of power
always correspond to a limit (a maximum or minimum); all
existing modes taken together, not only contemporaneous but
also successive ones, constitute the greatest infinity, itself divisible into infinities greater or less than one another.[9]

We have yet to discover whence come these extensive parts, and
in what they consist. They are not atoms: for not only do atoms
imply a void, but an infinity of atoms could not correspond to
something limited. Nor are they the virtual components of divisibility to infinity: these could not form greater or lesser infinities. To go from the hypothesis of infinite divisibility to that of

atoms is to run "from Charybdis to Scylla."[10] The ultimate extensive parts are in fact the actual infinitely small parts of an infinity that is itself actual. Positing an actual infinity in Nature is no less important for Spinoza than for Leibniz: there is no contradiction between the idea of absolutely simple ultimate parts and the principle of infinite division, as long as this division is *actually infinite*.[11] We must then consider that an attribute has not only an infinite intensive quantity, but an infinite extensive quantity also. It is the extensive quantity that is actually divided into an infinity of extensive parts. These are extrinsic parts, acting one on another from outside, and externally distinguished. *As a whole, and in all their relations, they form an infinitely changeable universe, corresponding to God's omnipotence. But in this or that determinate relation they form greater or lesser infinite wholes, corresponding to this or that degree of power, in other words, to this or that modal essence.* They always come in infinities: an infinity of parts, however small, always corresponds to a degree of power; and the whole universe corresponds to the Power that comprises all these degrees.

This is how we should understand Spinoza's analysis of the modes of Extension. The attribute of Extension has an extensive modal quantity that actually divides into an infinity of simple bodies. These simple bodies are extrinsic parts which are only distinguished from one another, and which are only related to one another, through movement and rest. Movement and rest are precisely the form of extrinsic distinction and external relation between simple bodies. Simple bodies are determined from outside to movement or rest *ad infinitum*, and are distinguished by the movement and rest to which they are determined. They are always grouped in infinite wholes, *each whole being defined by a certain relation*[c] *of movement and rest.* It is through this relation that an infinite whole corresponds to a certain modal essence (that is, to a certain degree of power), and thus constitutes the very existence of that mode of Extension.[d] If one considers all these infinite wholes in all their relations as a whole, one has "the sum of all the variations of matter in movement," or "the face of the whole universe" under the attribute of Extension. This face or sum corresponds to God's omnipotence insofar as the latter comprises all the degrees of power or all the modal essences in this same attribute of Extension.[12]

This scheme enables us to clear up certain contradictions which some have thought to find in Spinoza's physics, or to find rather in his *Ethics*, inconsistencies between its physics of bodies and its theory of essences. Thus Rivaud noted that a simple body is always, and only, determined to movement and to rest from outside; whence its state must be referred to an infinite collection of simple bodies. But how, then, reconcile this status of simple bodies with that of essences? "A particular body, or a simple body at least, has then no eternal essence. Its reality seems to be subsumed into that of an infinite system of causes"; "We sought a particular essence, and we find only an infinite chain of causes none of whose terms appears to have any essential reality of its own"; "This consequence, which appears to be forced on us by the passages just cited, seems to contradict the most clearly ascertained principles of Spinoza's system. What is to become of the eternity of essences, unreservedly asserted on so many occasions? How can a body, however small, however transitory its being, exist without a nature of its own, a nature without which it can neither arrest nor transmit any movement it receives? What has no essence at all cannot exist, and every essence is, by definition, immutable. A soap bubble that exists at some given moment, must necessarily have an eternal essence, without which it could not be."[13]

Yet there is no need to seek an essence for each extensive part. An essence is a degree of intensity. But extensive parts and degrees of intensity (or intensive parts) in no way correspond term for term. To every degree of intensity, however small, there correspond an infinity of extensive parts that have, and must have, between them purely extrinsic relations. Extensive parts come in greater or lesser infinities, but always come in an infinity; there is no question of each having an essence, because even to a minimal essence there correspond an infinity of parts. The soap bubble does indeed have an essence, but each part of the infinite collection that in some relation composes it, does not. In other words, in Spinoza, *there is no existing mode that is not actually infinitely composite*, whatever be its essence or degree of power. Spinoza says that composite modes have a "very great number" of parts; but what he says of composite modes must be understood of all existing modes, for there are no incomposite existing modes, all existence is by definition composite. Should one then say that simple extensive parts exist? Should one say that in Extension there exist simple bodies? If by this one means existence singly, or as a number together, the absurdity is obvious. Strictly speaking, simple parts have neither an essence nor an existence of their own. They have no internal essence or nature; they are extrinsically distinguished one from another, extrinsically related to one another. They have no existence of their own, but existence is composed of them: to exist is to actually have an infinity of extensive parts. In greater or lesser infinities they compose, in different relations, the existence of modes whose essences are of greater or lesser degree. Not only Spinoza's physics, but Spinozism as a whole, becomes unintelligible if one doesn't distinguish what belongs to essences, what belongs to existences, and the correspondence between them, which is in no way term for term.

We now have the elements of an answer to the question of how an infinity of extensive parts can compose the existence of a mode. Thus a mode exists, for example, in Extension when an infinity of simple bodies, corresponding to its essence, actually belong to it. But how can they correspond to its essence, or belong to it? Spinoza's answer remains identical from the *Short Treatise* on: they do so *in a certain relation of movement and rest.* A given mode "comes to exist," comes into existence, when an infinity of extensive parts enter into *a given* relation: it continues to exist as long as this relation holds. Extensive parts are thus grouped together in various collections on various levels of relation, corresponding to different degrees of power. Extensive parts form a greater or lesser infinite whole, insofar as they enter into this or that relation; in any given relation they correspond to some modal essence and compose the existence of the corresponding mode itself; in some other relation they form part of another whole, correspond to another modal essence, and compose the existence of another mode. Such is the doctrine of the *Short Treatise* concerning the coming into existence of modes.[14] The *Ethics* puts it still more clearly: little does it matter if the component parts of an existing mode are each moment renewed; the whole remains the same insofar as it is defined by a relation through which any of its parts belong to that particular modal essence. An existing mode is thus subject to considerable and continual alteration: but it little matters, either, that the division between its parts of movement and rest, or of speed and slowness of movement, should alter. A given mode will continue to exist as long as the same relation subsists in the infinite whole of its parts.[15]

It must then be recognized that a modal essence (a degree of power) expresses itself eternally in a certain relation, with its various different levels. But the mode does not come into existence until an infinity of extensive parts are actually determined to enter into this relation. These parts may be determined to enter into another relation; they are then integrated into another infinite whole, greater or lesser, corresponding to another modal essence, and composing the existence of another mode. Spinoza's theory of existence involves, then, three components: *a singular essence*, which is a degree of power or intensity; *a particular existence*, always composed of an infinity of extensive parts; and *an individual form* that is the characteristic or expressive relation which corresponds eternally to the mode's essence, but through which also an infinity of parts are temporarily related to that essence. In an existing mode, the essence is a degree of power; this degree expresses itself in a relation; and the relation subsumes an infinity of parts. Whence Spinoza's formulation according to which the parts, being under the domination of one and the same nature, are "forced, as this nature demands, to adapt themselves to one another."[16]

A modal essence expresses itself eternally in a relation, but we should not confuse the essence and the relation in which it expresses itself. A modal essence is not the cause of the existence of the mode itself: the proposition takes up, in Spinoza's terms, the old principle that a finite being's existence does not follow from its essence. But what is the new sense of this principle as seen from Spinoza's viewpoint? It means that for all that a modal essence expresses itself in a characteristic relation, it is not the essence that determines an infinity of extensive parts to enter into that relation. (A mere nature does not establish its dominance by itself, or itself force the parts to adapt themselves to one another so as to conform with the relation in which it expresses itself.) For extensive parts determine one another from outside and *ad infinitum*; they have none but an extrinsic determination. A mode comes into existence, not by virtue of its essence, but by virtue of purely mechanical laws which determine an infinity of some extensive parts or other to enter into a precise given relation, in which its essence expresses itself. A mode ceases to exist as soon as its parts are determined to enter into another relation, corresponding to another essence. Modes come into existence, and cease to exist, by virtue of laws external to their essences.

What are these mechanical laws? In the case of Extension they amount ultimately to the laws of communication of movement. If we consider the infinity of simple bodies, we see that they are always grouped in constantly changing infinite wholes. But the whole of all these wholes remains fixed, this fixity being defined by the total quantity of movement, that is, by the total proportion of movement and rest, which contains an infinity of particular relations. Simple bodies are never separable from some one or other of these relations, through which they belong to some whole. But the total proportion always remains fixed, while these relations are made and unmade according to the laws of composition and decomposition.

Take two composite bodies, each possessing, in a certain relation, an infinity of simple bodies or parts. When they meet it may happen that the two relations can be directly combined. Then the parts of one adapt to the parts of the other in a third relation composed of the two previous ones. Here we have the formation of a body more composite still than the two from which we began. In a famous passage, Spinoza shows how chyle and lymph combine their respective relations to form, as a third relation, the blood.[17] And, in more or less complex conditions, this process is that of all generation or formation, that is, of all coming into existence. Parts come together in different relations; each relation already corresponds to a modal essence; two relations combine in such a way that the parts that meet enter into a third relation, corresponding to a further modal essence. The corresponding mode thereby comes into existence. But it may happen that the two relations cannot be directly combined. The bodies that meet are either mutually indifferent, or one, through its relation, decomposes the relation in the other, and so destroys the other body. This is the case with a toxin or poison, which destroys a man by decomposing his blood. And this is the case with nutrition, but in a converse sense: a man forces the parts of the body by which he nourishes himself to enter into a new relation that conforms with his own, but which involves the destruction of the relation in which that body existed previously.

Thus there are laws of composition and decomposition of relations which determine both the coming into existence of modes, and the end of their existence. These eternal laws in no way affect the eternal truth of each relation: each relation has an eternal truth, insofar as an essence expresses itself in it. But the laws of composition and decomposition determine the conditions in which a relation is actualized – that is, actually subsumes extensive parts – or, on the other hand, ceases to be actualized. Whence we must, above all, avoid confusing essences and relations, or a law of production of essences and a law of composition of relations. It is not the essence that determines the actualization of the relation in which it expresses itself. Relations are composed and decomposed according to their own laws. The order of essences is characterized by a total conformity. Such is not the case with the order of relations. All relations are of course combined *ad infinitum*, but not in just any way. Some given relation does not combine with just any other given relation. The laws of composition that apply to characteristic relations, and that regulate the coming into existence of modes, pose many problems. Such laws are not contained in the modal essences themselves. Was Spinoza thinking of these laws when he wrote, as early as the *Correction of the Understanding*, of laws inscribed in attributes and infinite modes "as in their true codes"?[18] (The

complexity of this passage prevents me from adducing it here.)
And then, do we know these laws, and if so, how? Spinoza does
seem to admit that we have to pass through an empirical study
of bodies in order to know their relations, and how they are
combined.[19] Whatever be the answers to these questions, it is
enough provisionally to note the irreducibility of the order of
relations to the order of essences themselves.

A mode's existence does not, then, follow from its essence. When
a mode comes into existence, it is determined to do so by a
mechanical law that composes the relation in which it expresses
itself, which constrains, that is to say, an infinity of extensive parts
to enter into that relation. Coming into existence should never
be understood in Spinoza as a transition from possible to real:
an existing mode is no more the realization of a possible, than a
modal essence is such a "possible." Essences necessarily exist, by
virtue of their cause; the modes whose essences they are necessarily come into existence by virtue of causes that determine parts
to enter into the relations corresponding to those essences.
Necessity everywhere appears as the only modality of being, but
this necessity has two components. We have seen that the distinction between an essence and its own existence should not be
interpreted as a real distinction, nor should that of an essence
and the existence of the mode itself. An existing mode is just its
own essence itself insofar as the essence actually possesses an
infinity of extensive parts. Just as the essence exists by virtue of
its cause, so the mode itself exists by virtue of the cause that
determines its parts to belong to it. But the two forms of causality we are thus led to consider force us to define two types of
modal position,[e] and two types of modal distinction.

Modal essences were characterized above as intensive realities. They were distinguished from their attribute and from one another only through a very special type of distinction, an intrinsic one. They existed only as contained in their attribute, and their ideas existed only as comprised in the idea of God. All such essences were "complicated" in their attribute; this was the form in which they existed and expressed the essence of God, each according to its degree of power. But when modes come into existence, they acquire extensive parts. They acquire a size and duration: each mode endures as long as its parts remain in the relation that characterizes it. We must therefore recognize that existing modes are *extrinsically* distinct from their attribute, and *extrinsically* distinct from one another. The *Metaphysical Thoughts* defined "the being of existence" as "the essence itself of things outside God," as opposed to "the being of essence" that designated things as they are "comprehended in the attributes of God."[20] This definition corresponds perhaps more closely than one might imagine to the thought of Spinoza himself. In this respect it presents several important characteristics.

It reminds us first of all that the distinction between essence and existence is never a real distinction. The being of essence (the existence of essence) is its position in an attribute of God. The being of existence (the existence of a thing itself) is also a positing of essence, but an extrinsic position, *outside* the attribute. And I do not believe that this thesis is abandoned in the *Ethics*. The existence of a particular thing is the thing itself, no longer as simply contained in its attribute, no longer as simply comprehended in God, but as having duration, as having a relation with a certain extrinsically distinct time and place.[21] It might be objected that such a conception is radically opposed to immanence. For, from the viewpoint of immanence, modes do not cease to belong to substance, to be contained in it, when they come into existence. But the point is so obvious that it should not detain us long.

Spinoza doesn't say that existing modes are no longer contained in substance, but rather that they are "are no longer only" contained in substance or attribute.[22] The difficulty is easily resolved *if we consider that extrinsic distinction remains always and only a modal distinction.* Modes do not cease to be modes once they are posited outside their attribute,[f] for this extrinsic position is purely modal rather than substantial. If a passing comparison with Kant be permissible, it will be recalled that Kant explains that, although space is the form of exteriority, this form is no less internal to me than the form of interiority: it presents objects as external to us and to one another, and this without any illusion, but itself is completely internal to us.[23] Similarly Spinoza, in an altogether different context, talking of an altogether different matter, says that extensive quantity belongs to an attribute no less than intensive quantity, but that it is a strictly modal form of exteriority. It presents existing modes as external to the attribute, and as external one to another. It is nonetheless contained, along with all existing modes, in the attribute it modifies. The idea of an extrinsic modal distinction is in no way inconsistent with the principle of immanence.

What then does such an extrinsic modal distinction amount to? When modes are posited extrinsically they cease to exist in the *complicated* form that they have while their essences are contained solely in their attribute. Their new existence is an *explication*: they explicate the attribute, each "in a certain and determinate way." That is: each existing mode explicates the attribute in the relation that characterizes it, in a way extrinsically distinct from other ways in other relations. An existing mode is thus no less expressive than its essence, but is so in another manner. An attribute no longer expresses itself only in the modal essences that it complicates or contains according to their degrees of power; it also expresses itself in existing modes that explicate it in a certain and determinate manner, that is, according to the relations corresponding to their essences. Modal expression as a whole is constituted by this double movement of complication and explication.[24]

CHAPTER FOURTEEN

What Can a Body Do?

The expressive triad corresponding to finite modes comprises an essence as a degree of power; a characteristic relation in which it expresses itself; and the extensive parts subsumed in this relation, which compose the mode's existence. But we find in the *Ethics* a strict system of equivalences that leads us to a second modal triad: the essence as a degree of power; a certain capacity to be affected in which it expresses itself; and the affections that, each moment, exercise that capacity.

What are these equivalences? An existing mode actually possesses a very great number of parts. But the nature of extensive parts is such that they "affect one another" *ad infinitum*. From this one may infer that an existing mode is affected in a very great number of ways. Spinoza proceeds from the parts to their affections, and from these affections to the affections of the existing mode as a whole.[1] Extensive parts do not belong to a given mode except in a certain relation. And a mode is said to have affections by virtue of a certain capacity of being affected. A horse, a fish, a man, or even two men compared one with the other, do not have the same capacity to be affected: they are not affected by the same things, or not affected by the same things in the same way.[2] A mode ceases to exist when it can no longer maintain

217

between its parts the relation that characterizes it; and it ceases to exist when "it is rendered completely incapable of being affected in many ways."[3] In short, relations are inseparable from the capacity to be affected. So that Spinoza can consider two fundamental questions as equivalent: *What is the structure* (fabrica) *of a body?* And: *What can a body do?* A body's structure is the composition of its relation. What a body can do corresponds to the nature and limits of its capacity to be affected.[4]

This second triad characterizing finite modes well shows how modes express substance, participate in it, and even, in their own way, reproduce it. God was defined by the identity of his essence and an absolutely infinite power (*potentia*); as such he had a *potestas*, that is, a capacity to be affected in an infinity of ways; and this capacity was eternally and necessarily exercised, God being cause of all things in the same sense as cause of himself. An existing mode has, for its part, an essence that is identical to a degree of power; as such it has an ability to be affected, a capacity to be affected in a very great number of ways. While the mode exists this capacity is exercised in varying ways, but is always necessarily exercised under the action of external modes.

What, from these various viewpoints, is the difference between an existing mode and divine substance? One must not, in the first place, confuse an "infinity of ways" with a "very great number of ways." A very great number is indeed an infinity, but one of a special kind: a greater or lesser infinity that relates to something limited. God is, on the other hand, affected in an infinity of ways, and this is infinity through a cause, since God is the cause of all his affections. This is a strictly unlimited infinity, which comprises all modal essences and all existing modes.

A second difference is that God is the cause of all his affections, and so cannot suffer them. It would be wrong indeed to confuse affection and suffering or passion.[b] An affection is not a

WHAT CAN A BODY DO?

passion, except when it cannot be explained by the nature of the affected body: it then of course involves the body, but is explained by the influence of other bodies. Affections that can be completely explained by the nature of the affected body are active affections, and themselves actions.[5] Let us apply the principle of this distinction to God: there are no causes external to God; God is necessarily the cause of all his affections, and so all these affections can be explained by his nature, and are actions.[6] Such is not the case with existing modes. These do not exist by virtue of their own nature; their existence is composed of extensive parts that are determined and affected from outside, *ad infinitum*. Every existing mode is thus inevitably affected by modes external to it, and undergoes changes that are not explained by its own nature alone. Its affections are at the outset, and tend to remain, passions.[7] Spinoza remarks that childhood is an abject state, but one common to all of us, in which we depend "very heavily on external causes."[8] The great question that presents itself in relation to existing finite modes is thus: Can they attain to active affections, and if so, how? This is the "ethical" question, properly so called. But, even supposing that a mode manages to produce active affections, while it exists it cannot eliminate all its passions, but can at best bring it about that its passions occupy only a small part of itself.[9]

A final difference concerns the very content of the word "affection," according to whether it be applied to God or to modes. For God's affections are those modes themselves, modal essences or existing modes. Their ideas express the essence of God as their cause. But the affections of modes are as it were a second degree of affection, affections of affections: for example, a passive affection that we experience is just the effect of some body on our own. The idea of such an affection does not express its cause, that is to say, the nature or essence of the external body:

rather does it indicate the present constitution of our own body, and so the way in which our capacity to be affected is being at that moment exercised. An affection of our body is only a corporeal image, and the idea of the affection as it is in our mind an inadequate idea, an imagining. And we have yet another sort of affection. From a given idea of an affection there necessarily flow "affects" or feelings (*affectus*).[10,c] Such feelings are themselves affections, or rather a new kind of idea of an affection. One should resist attributing to Spinoza intellectualist positions he never held. An idea we have indicates the present state of our body's constitution; while our body exists, it endures, and is defined by duration; its present state is thus inseparable from a previous state with which it is linked in a continuous duration. Thus *to every idea that indicates an actual state of our body, there is necessarily linked another sort of idea that involves the relation of this state to the earlier state.* Spinoza explains that this should not be thought of as an abstract intellectual operation by which the mind compares two states.[11] Our feelings are in themselves ideas which involve the concrete relation of present and past in a continuous duration: they involve the changes of an existing mode that endures.

A mode thus has affections of two sorts: states of a body or ideas that indicate these states, and changes in the body or ideas indicating these changes. The second kind are linked to the first, and change with them: one senses how, beginning with an initial affection, our feelings become linked with our ideas in such a way that our whole capacity to be affected is exercised at each moment. But all this turns, ultimately, on a certain characteristic of modes, and of man in particular: the first ideas he has are passive affections, inadequate ideas or imaginings; the affects or feelings that flow from them are thus passions, feelings that are themselves passive. One cannot see how a finite mode, especially at the beginning of its existence, could have any but inadequate ideas; and one cannot, consequently, see how it could experience any but passive feelings. The link is well marked by Spinoza: an inadequate idea is an idea of which we are not the cause (it is not formally explained by our power of understanding); this inadequate idea is itself the (material and efficient) cause of a feeling; we cannot then be the adequate cause of this feeling; but a feeling of which we are not the adequate cause is necessarily a passion. [12] Our capacity to be affected is thus exercised, from the beginning of our existence, by inadequate ideas and passive feelings.

An equally profound link may be found between ideas that are adequate, and active feelings. An idea we have that is adequate may be formally defined as an idea of which we are the cause; were it then the material and efficient cause of a feeling we would be the adequate cause of that feeling itself; but a feeling of which we are the adequate cause is an action. Thus Spinoza can say that "Insofar as our mind has adequate ideas, it necessarily does certain things, and insofar as it has inadequate ideas, it necessarily undergoes other things"; "The actions of the mind arise from adequate ideas alone; the passions depend on inadequate ideas alone." [13] Hence the properly ethical question is linked to the methodological question of how we can become active. How can we come to produce adequate ideas?

One already senses the fundamental importance of that area of the *Ethics* that concerns existential changes of finite modes, or expressive changes. These changes are of several kinds, and must be understood on various levels. Consider a mode with a given essence and a given capacity to be affected. Its passive affections (inadequate ideas and passive feelings) are constantly changing. However, insofar as its capacity to be affected is exercised by passive affections, this capacity itself appears as a *force or power of suffering*. The capacity of being affected is called a power of suffering insofar as it is actually exercised by passive affections. The body's power of suffering has as its equivalent in the mind the power of imagining and of experiencing passive feelings.

Let us now assume that the mode, as it endures, comes to exercise (at least partially) its capacity of being affected by active affections. In this aspect the capacity appears as a *force or power of acting*. The power of understanding or knowing is the power of acting proper to the soul. But *the capacity to be affected remains constant, whatever the relative proportion of active and passive affections*. And so we arrive at the following conjecture: that the proportion of active and passive feelings is open to variation, within a fixed capacity of being affected. If we manage to produce active affections, our passive affections will be correspondingly reduced. And as far as we still have passive affections, our power of action will be correspondingly "inhibited." In short, for a given essence, for a given capacity to be affected, the power of suffering and that of acting should be open to variation in inverse proportion one to the other. Both together, in their varying proportions, constitute the capacity to be affected.[14]

We must next introduce another level of possible variation. For the capacity to be affected does not remain fixed at all times and from all viewpoints. Spinoza suggests, in fact, that the relation that characterizes an existing mode as a whole is endowed with a kind of elasticity. What is more, its composition, as also its decomposition, passes through so many stages that one may almost say that a mode changes its body or relation in leaving behind childhood, or on entering old age. Growth, aging, illness: we can hardly recognize the same individual. And is it really indeed the same individual? Such changes, whether imperceptible or abrupt, in the relation that characterizes a body, may also be seen in its capacity of being affected, as though the capacity and the relation enjoy a margin, a limit, within which they take form and are deformed.[15] Here we see the full significance of the passages of the letter to Meyer that allude to the existence of a maximum and a minimum.

Thus far we have proceeded as though the power of suffering and the power of acting formed two distinct principles, their exercise being inversely proportional within a given capacity to be affected. This is indeed the case, but only in relation to the fundamental limits of that capacity. It is the case so long as we consider affections abstractly, without concretely considering the essence of the affected mode. Why? We find ourselves here at the threshold of a problem explored by Leibniz as well as Spinoza. It was not by chance that Leibniz, on first reading the *Ethics*, spoke with admiration of Spinoza's theory of the affections, his conception of action and passion. And one should see here a coincidence between the developments of their respective philosophies, rather than an influence of Spinoza on Leibniz.[16] Such coincidence is in fact more remarkable than any influence. On one level, Leibniz sets out the following thesis: a body's force, which is called "derivative," is double: a force of acting and a force of suffering, active force and passive force; the active force remains "dead," or becomes "alive," according to what obstacles or inducements, registered by the passive force, it encounters. But on a deeper level Leibniz asks: should passive force be conceived as distinct from active force? Is its principle autonomous, does it have any positivity, is it in any way assertive? The reply is that only active force is strictly real, positive and affirmative. Passive force asserts nothing, expresses nothing but the imperfection of the finite. It is as though active force had taken up all that is real, positive or perfect in finitude itself. Passive force has no autonomy, but is the mere limitation of active force. There would be no such force without the active force that it limits. It amounts to the inherent limitation of active force; and ultimately to the limitation of an even deeper force, that is, of an *essence* that asserts and expresses itself solely in active force as such.[17]

Spinoza also sets out an initial thesis: the power of suffering and the power of acting are two powers which vary correlatively, while the capacity of being affected remains fixed; the power of acting is dead or alive (Spinoza says: inhibited or helped) according to the obstacles or opportunities that it finds on the side of passive affections. But this thesis, if physically true, is not metaphysically true. Already in Spinoza, at a deeper level, the power of suffering expresses nothing positive. In every passive affection there is something imaginary which inhibits it from being real. We are passive and impassioned only by virtue of our imperfection, in our imperfection itself. "For it is certain that the agent acts through what he has, and that the patient[d] suffers through what he does not have"; "Suffering,[d] when the agent and the patient are different, is a palpable imperfection."[18] We suffer external things, distinct from ourselves; we thus ourselves have a distinct force of passion and action. But our force of suffering is simply the imperfection, the finitude, the limitation of our force of acting itself. Our force of suffering *asserts* nothing, because it *expresses* nothing at all: it "involves" only our impotence, that is to say, the limitation of our power of action. Our power of suffering is in fact our impotence, our servitude, that is to say, *the lowest degree of our power of acting*: whence the title of Part Four of the *Ethics*, "On Human Servitude." The power of imagination is indeed a power or virtue, says Spinoza, but would be all the more so, did it depend on our nature, that is, were it active, rather than amounting only to the finitude or imperfection of our power of action, or, in short, our impotence.[19]

We still do not know how we may come to produce active affections; and so we do not know our power of action. And yet we may already say that the power of action is the only real, positive and affirmative form of our capacity to be affected. As long as our capacity to be affected is exercised by passive affections, it is reduced to a minimum, and exhibits only our finitude or limitation. It is as though a disjunction had appeared in the finite mode's existence: the negative falling on the side of passive affections, and the active affections expressing all that is positive in finite modes. Active affections are indeed the only ones that really and positively exercise our capacity to be affected. The power of action is, on its own, the same as the capacity to be affected as a whole; the power of action by itself expresses essence, and active affections, by themselves, assert essence. In existing modes, essence is the same as power of action, and the power of action the same as the capacity to be affected.

One finds in Spinoza a reconciliation of two fundamental principles. In the physical view a capacity to be affected remains fixed for a given essence, whether it be exercised by active affections or passive ones; a mode is thus always as perfect as it can be. But in the ethical view the power of being affected is fixed only within general limits. While exercised by passive affections, it is reduced to a minimum; we then remain imperfect and impotent, cut off, in a way, from our essence or our degree of power, cut off from what we can do. It is indeed true that an existing mode is always as perfect as it can be: but this only relative to the affections actually belonging to its essence. It is indeed true that the passive affections we experience exercise our capacity to be affected; but this, having reduced it to a minimum, having cut us off from what we can do (our power of action). The expressive changes of finite modes consist, then, not only in mechanical changes in the affections it experiences, but also in dynamic changes in the capacity to be affected, and in "metaphysical" changes of their essence itself: while a mode exists, its very essence is open to variation, according to the affections that belong to it at a given moment.[20]

Whence the importance of the ethical question. _We do not even know of what a body is capable_, says Spinoza.[21] That is: _We do not even know of what affections we are capable, nor the extent of our power_. How could we know this in advance? From the beginning of our existence we are necessarily exercised by passive affections. Finite modes are born in conditions such that they are cut off in advance from their essence or their degree of power, cut off from that of which they are capable, from their power of action. We can know by reasoning that the power of action is the sole expression of our essence, the sole affirmation of our power of being affected. But this knowledge remains abstract. We do not know what this power is, nor how we may acquire or discover it. And we will certainly never know this, if we do not concretely try to become active. The _Ethics_ closes with the following reminder: most men only feel they exist when they are suffering something. They can bear existence only as suffering things; "as soon as [the ignorant man] ceases to be acted on, he ceases to be."[22]

Leibniz made a habit of characterizing Spinoza's system by the impotence in which its creatures found themselves: the theory of modes was only a means of taking from creatures all their activity, dynamism, individuality, all their authentic reality. Modes were only phantasms, phantoms, fantastic projections of a single Substance. And Leibniz uses this characterization, presented as a criterion, to interpret other philosophies, denouncing in them either the first signs of an incipient Spinozism, or the consequences of a hidden one: thus Descartes is the father of Spinozism, through his belief in inert passive Extension; the Occasionalists are involuntary Spinozists to the extent that they withdraw from things any action and any principle of action. His criticism of a generalized Spinozism is skillful; but one cannot be sure that Leibniz himself subscribed to it (for how then could he have so admired Spinoza's theory of action and passion in modes?).

What is clear, at any rate, is that everything in Spinoza's work contradicts such an interpretation. Spinoza constantly reminds us that one cannot, without misrepresenting them, confuse modes with things of reason or "aids to imagination." When speaking of modifications, he seeks specifically modal principles, whether arguing from the unity of substance to the ontological unity of modes differing in attribute, or arguing from the unity of substance to the systematic unity of the modes contained in one and the same attribute. And above all, the very idea of the mode is in no sense a way of taking from creatures any power of their own: rather is it, according to Spinoza, the only way of showing how things "participate" in God's power, that is, how they are parts of divine power, but singular parts, intensive quantities or irreducible degrees. As Spinoza says, man's power is a "part" of the power or essence of God, but this only insofar as God's essence *explicates itself* through the essence of man.[23]

Leibniz and Spinoza do in fact have a common project. Their philosophies constitute two aspects of a new "naturalism." This naturalism provides the true thrust of the Anticartesian reaction. In a fine passage, Ferdinand Alquié has shown how Descartes dominated the first half of the seventeenth century by succeeding in the venture of a mathematical mechanical science, whose first effect was to devaluate Nature by taking away from it any virtuality or potentiality, any immanent power, any inherent being. Cartesian metaphysics completes the venture, because it seeks Being outside Nature, in a subject which thinks it and a God who creates it.[24] With the Anticartesian reaction, on the other hand,

227

it is a matter of re-establishing the claims of a Nature endowed with forces or power. But a matter, also, of retaining the chief discovery of Cartesian mechanism: every power is actual, in act; the powers of Nature are no longer virtualities referred to occult entities, to souls or minds through which they are realized. Leibniz formulates the program perfectly: to counter Descartes by restoring to Nature the force of action and passion, but this without falling back into a pagan vision of the world, an idolatry of Nature.[25] Spinoza's program is very similar (with this difference, that he does not rely on Christianity to save us from idolatry). Spinoza and Leibniz take issue with Boyle as the representative of self-satisfied mechanism. Did Boyle wish only to teach us that everything happens in bodies through shape and movement, that would be a meager lesson, being well known since Descartes.[26] Which, for a given body, are these shapes, which these movements? Why *such* a shape, *such* a movement? One thus sees that mechanism does not exclude the idea of a nature or essence of each body, but rather requires it, as the sufficient reason for a given shape or a given movement, or a given proportion of movement and rest. The Anticartesian reaction is, throughout, a search for sufficient reasons: a sufficient reason for infinite perfection, a sufficient reason for clarity and distinctness, and a sufficient reason, indeed, for mechanism itself.

The new program is realized by Leibniz on three different levels. On the first everything happens in bodies mechanically, through shape and movement. But these bodies are "aggregates," actually and infinitely composite, governed by laws. And movement has no distinctive mark in a body at a given moment: nor are its patterns discernable at particular moments. The movements themselves presuppose forces of passion and action, without which bodies would be no more distinguished than would patterns of movement. Or, if you will, the mechanical laws themselves presuppose an inner nature in the bodies they govern. For these laws could not be "executed," did they confer on bodies a mere extrinsic determination, and were they imposed on them independently of what they are: thus the working of a law cannot be understood simply in terms of God's will, as the Occasionalists believed, but must also be understood *in terms of the body itself.* Hence derivative forces must be attributed to the aggregates as such: "the internal nature of things is no different from the force of acting and suffering."[27] But nor does the derivative force, in its turn, contain its own reason: it is only momentary, although it links that moment to earlier and later ones. It must be referred to a law governing the series of moments, which is a sort of primitive force or individual *essence.* These essences, simple and active, are the source of the derivative forces attributed to bodies. Indeed they amount to a genuine metaphysics of Nature, which does not merely enter into physics, but corresponds to such physics itself.

Spinoza's realization of the naturalist program is closely analogous. Mechanism governs infinitely composite existing bodies. But this mechanism must in the first place be referred to a dynamic theory of the capacity to be affected (the power of acting and suffering); and in the last instance to the theory of the particular essences that express themselves in the variations of this power of action and passion. In Spinoza as in Leibniz three levels may be distinguished: mechanism, force and essence. So the real opposition between the two philosophies should not be sought in Leibniz's very general criticism that Spinozism takes from creatures all power and all activity. Leibniz, while linking them to this pretext, himself reveals the true reasons for his opposition. And these are in fact practical reasons, relating to the problem of evil, to providence and to religion, relating to the practical conception of the role of philosophy as a whole.

These divergences certainly do, however, have a speculative form. I believe what is essential, in this respect, concerns the role of *conatus* in Spinoza and in Leibniz. According to Leibniz, *conatus* has two senses: physically it designates a body's tendency toward movement; metaphysically, the tendency of an essence toward existence. Spinoza could not share such a view. Modal essences are not "possibles"; they lack nothing, are all that they are, even if the corresponding modes do not exist. They thus involve no tendency to come into existence. A *conatus* is indeed a mode's essence (or degree of power) *once the mode has begun to exist.* A mode comes to exist when its extensive parts are extrinsically determined to enter into the relation that characterizes the mode: then, and only then, is its essence itself determined as a *conatus.* Thus *conatus* is not in Spinoza the effort to persevere in existence, once existence is granted. It designates existential function of essence, that is, the affirmation of essence in a mode's existence. Nor then, when we consider an existing body, can its *conatus* be a tendency toward movement. Simple bodies are determined to movement from outside; they could not be so determined were they not also capable of being determined to rest. One constantly finds in Spinoza the ancient thesis according to which movement would be nothing, were rest not something as well.[28] A simple body's *conatus* can only be the effort to preserve the state to which it has been determined; and a composite body's *conatus* only the effort to preserve the relation of movement and rest that defines it, that is, to maintain constantly renewed parts in the relation that defines its existence.

The dynamic characteristics of *conatus* are linked with its mechanical ones. A composite body's *conatus* is also the effort to maintain the body's ability to be affected in a great number of ways.[29] But, since passive affections exercise in their own way our capacity of being affected, we make an effort to persevere in exist-

230

ence, not only insofar as we may be supposed to have adequate ideas and active feelings, but also insofar as we have inadequate ideas and experience passions.[30] An existing mode's *conatus* is thus inseparable from the affections experienced by the mode each moment. From this two consequences follow.

Any affection whatever is said to determine our *conatus* or essence. *Conatus*, as determined by an affection or feeling we actually experience, is called "desire"; as such it is necessarily accompanied by consciousness.[31] To the linkage of feelings with ideas, we must add the further linkage of desires with feelings. As long as our capacity to be affected remains exercised by passive affections, our *conatus* is determined by passions, or, as Spinoza puts it, our desires themselves "are born" from passions. But, even in this case, our power of action comes into play. For we must distinguish what determines us, and that to which we are determined. A given passive affection determines us to do this or that, to think of this or that, and thereby to make an effort to preserve our relation or maintain our power. Sometimes we make an effort to ward off an affection we do not like, sometimes to hold on to an affection we like, and this always with a desire that is all the greater, the greater the affection itself.[32] But "that to which" we are thus determined is explained by our nature or essence, and must be referred to our power of action.[33] Passive affections do, it is true, testify to our impotence, and cut us off from that of which we are capable; but it is also true that they *involve* some degree, however low, of our power of action. If we are to some extent cut off from that of which we are capable, this is because our power of action is immobilized, fixated, determined to engage itself in a passive affection. Our *conatus* is thus always identical with our power of acting itself. The variations of *conatus* as it is determined by this or that affection are the dynamic variations of our power of action.[34]

231

What is the real difference between Leibniz and Spinoza, from which all the practical oppositions follow? In Spinoza no less than in Leibniz the idea of an expressive Nature forms the basis of a new naturalism. In Spinoza no less than in Leibniz, expression in Nature means that mechanism is superseded in two ways. Mechanism calls, on the one hand, for a dynamism of the capacity to be affected, defined by the variations of a power of action and passion; and, on the other, for the positing of singular essences defined as degrees of power. But the two philosophies do not at all proceed in the same way. If Leibniz recognizes in things an inherent force of their own, he does so by making individual essences into so many substances. In Spinoza, on the other hand, this is done by defining particular essences as modal, and more generally, by making things themselves modes of a single substance. But the distinction is far from clear. For in Leibniz mechanism is in fact referred to something deeper through the requirements of a finality that remains partly transcendent. If essences are determined as substances, if they are inseparable from the tendency to come into existence, that is because they are caught in an order of finality as the context in which they are chosen by God, or even just subject to such choice. And the finality that thus presides over the constitution of the world is found again in its details: derivative forces reflect an analogous harmony, in virtue of which this world is the best, even down to its parts themselves. And not only are there principles of finality that govern substances and derivative forces, but there is also an ultimate agreement between mechanism itself and finality. Hence expressive Nature is in Leibniz a Nature whose different levels are hierarchically related, harmonized and, above all, "symbolize one another." Expression is never divorced in Leibniz from a symbolization whose principle is always finality or ultimate agreement.

In Spinoza mechanism is referred to something deeper, but this through the requirements of an absolutely immanent pure causality. Causality alone leads us to consider existence, and causality is itself enough to resolve the question. From the viewpoint of immanent causality, modes are but appearances devoid of force and essence. Spinoza relies on such causality, properly understood, to endow things with a force or power of their own, belonging to them precisely as modes. As opposed to that of Leibniz, Spinoza's dynamism and "essentialism" deliberately excludes all finality. Spinoza's theory of *conatus* has no other function than to present dynamism for what it is by stripping it of any finalist significance. If Nature is expressive, it is not so in the sense that its different levels symbolize one another; sign, symbol and harmony are excluded from the true powers of Nature. *The complete modal triad may be presented thus*: a modal essence expresses itself in a characteristic relation; this relation expresses a capacity to be affected; this capacity is exercised by changing affections, just as the relation is effected by parts which are renewed. Between these different levels of expression, one finds no ultimate correspondence, no moral harmony. One finds only the necessary concatenation of the various effects of an immanent cause. So there is in Spinoza no metaphysics of essences, no dynamic of forces, no mechanics of phenomena. Everything in Nature is "physical": a physics of intensive quantity corresponding to modal essences; a physics of extensive quantity, that is, a mechanism through which modes themselves come into existence; a physics of force, that is, a dynamism through which essence asserts itself in existence, espousing the variations of the power of action. Attributes explicate themselves in existing modes; modal essences, themselves contained in the attributes, are explicated in relations or powers; these relations are effected by their parts, and these powers by the

233

affections that explicate them in their turn. Expression in Nature is never a final symbolization,[e] but always, and everywhere, a causal *explication*.

CHAPTER FIFTEEN

The Three Orders and

the Problem of Evil

An attribute expresses itself in three ways: in its absolute nature (its immediate infinite mode), as modified (its infinite mediate mode) and in a certain and determinate way (a finite existing mode).[1] Spinoza himself presents us with two infinite modes of Extension: movement and rest, and the face of the whole universe.[2] What does he mean by this?

We know that relations of movement and rest must themselves be considered in two ways: both as eternally expressing the essences of modes, and as temporarily subsuming extensive parts. From the first viewpoint movement and rest, in comprising all relations, also contain all essences as they are in their attribute. Thus Spinoza asserts in the *Short Treatise* that movement and rest comprise the essences even of things that do not exist.[3] More plainly still, he argues that movement affects Extension before the latter has any extrinsic modal parts. In order to allow that there should indeed be movement in the "altogether infinite," it is enough to recall that there is never any movement on its own, but only ever movement and rest together.[4] This recollection is Platonic: the Neoplatonists often insisted on a simultaneous presence of movement and rest, without which movement would itself be unthinkable in the whole.

From the second viewpoint, the various relations of movement and rest group together changing infinite collections of
extensive parts. They thus determine the conditions for modes to
come into existence. Each relation that is actualized constitutes
the form of an existing individual. But there is no relation that
does not itself combine with some other to form, in a third relation, a further individual at a higher level. And this *ad infinitum*,
so that the universe as a whole is a single existing individual,
defined by the total proportion of movement and rest, comprising all relations combined *ad infinitum*, the collection of all
collections under all relations. This individual is, by its form, the
"*facies totius universi*, which, although it varies in infinite ways,[a]
yet remains always the same."[5]

All relations combine *ad infinitum* to form this *facies*. But they
combine according to their own laws, laws comprised in the infinite mediate mode. Which is to say that the relations do not just
combine in any way at all; any given relation cannot be combined
with just any other. Thus we saw how laws of composition were
also laws of decomposition; and when Spinoza says that the *facies*
remains the same while changing in infinite ways, he is alluding
not only to the composition of relations, but also to their destruction and decomposition. These decompositions do not however
(any more than compositions) affect the eternal truth of the relations involved. A relation is composed when it begins to subsume
its parts; it decomposes when it ceases to be realized in them.[6]
Decomposition, destruction amount then only to this: when two
relations do not directly combine, the parts subsumed in one
determine the parts of the other to enter (according to some law)
into some new relation that can be combined with the first.[b]
Thus we see that everything in the order of relations is, in a

way, just composition. Everything in Nature is just composition. When poison decomposes the blood, it does so simply according to a law that determines the parts of the blood to enter into a new relation that can be combined with that of the poison. Decomposition is only the other side of composition. But the question of why there should be this other side remains. Why do the laws of composition also amount to laws of destruction? The answer must be that existing bodies do not encounter one another *in the order* in which their relations combine. There is a combination of relations in any encounter,[c] but the relations that combine are not necessarily those of the bodies that meet. Relations combine *according to laws*; but existing bodies, being themselves composed of extensive parts, meet *bit by bit*. So parts of one of the bodies may be determined to take on a new relation imposed by some law while losing that relation through which they belonged to the body.

If we consider the order of relations in itself, we see it purely as an order of composition. If it determines destruction as well, it does so because bodies meet in an order that is not that of their relations. Whence the complexity of Spinoza's notion of the "Order of Nature." We must in any existing mode distinguish three things: its essence as a degree of power; the relation in which it expresses itself; and the extensive parts subsumed in this relation. To each of these orders there corresponds an order of nature.

There is in the first place an order of essences, determined by degrees of power. This order is one of total conformity: each essence agrees with all others, all being comprised in the production of each. They are eternal, and none could perish without all the others perishing also. The order of relations, as an order of composition according to laws, is very different. It determines the eternal conditions for modes to come into existence, and to continue to exist while the composition of their relation is maintained. All relations are combined *ad infinitum*, but a given relation cannot be combined with just any other. We must, in the third place, consider the order of encounters. This is an order of local and temporary partial agreement and disagreement. Existing bodies meet in their extensive parts, bit by bit. Two bodies that meet may have relations that combine directly according to a law (may, that is, agree); but it may be the case, if two relations cannot combine, that one of the bodies is so determined as to destroy the other's relation (the bodies then disagree). This order of encounters thus effectively determines the moment when a mode comes into existence (when the conditions set by the relevant law are fulfilled), the duration of its existence, and the moment of its death or destruction. Spinoza defines it as at once "the Common Order of Nature," as the order of "extrinsic determinations" and "chance encounters," and as the order of passions.[7]

It is indeed a common order, since all modes are subject to it. It is the order of passions and extrinsic determinations, since it determines the affections we experience each moment, which are produced by the external bodies we encounter. And Spinoza can call it "fortuitous" (*fortuitus occursus*) without thereby introducing the least contingency. For the order of encounters is itself perfectly determinate: its necessity is that of extensive parts and their external determination *ad infinitum*. But it is fortuitous in relation to the order of relations; the laws of composition no more themselves determine which bodies meet, and how, than essences determine the laws by which their relations are combined. The existence of this third order poses all sorts of problems in Spinoza. For, taken as a whole, it coincides with the order of relations. If one considers the infinite sum of encounters over the infinite duration of the universe, each involves a composition of relations, and all relations are combined, together with all encounters. But the two orders in no way coincide in their detail: if we consider a body with a definite given relation, it must necessarily encounter bodies whose relation cannot combine with its own, and will always eventually meet one whose relation destroys its own. Thus there is no death that is not *brutal, violent and fortuitous*; but this precisely because each is altogether *necessary* within the order of encounters.

Two sorts of "encounters" must be distinguished. The first sort occurs when I meet a body whose relation combines with my own. (This itself may happen in various ways: sometimes the body encountered has a relation that naturally combines with one of my component relations, and may thus contribute to the maintenance of my overall relation; sometimes the relations of two bodies may agree so well that they form a third relation within which the two bodies are preserved and prosper.) Whatever the case, a body whose relation is preserved along with my own is said to "agree with my nature," to be "good," that is, "useful," to me.[8] It produces in me an affection that is itself good, which itself agrees with my nature. The affection is passive because it is explained by the external body, and the idea of the affection is a passion, a passive feeling. But it is a feeling of joy, since it is produced by the idea of an object that is good for me, or agrees with my nature.[9] But when Spinoza sets out to define this joyful passion "formally," he does so by saying that it increases or aids our power of action, is our power of acting itself as increased or aided by an external cause.[10] (And we know what is good only insofar as we perceive something to affect us with joy.[11])

What does Spinoza mean by this? He has certainly not forgotten that our passions, of whatever kind, are always the mark

239

of our impotence: they are explained not by our own essence or power, but by the power of some external thing; they thus involve some impotence on our part.[12] All passion cuts us off from our power of action; as long as our capacity to be affected is exercised by passions, we are cut off from that of which we are capable. Thus Spinoza says that joyful passions are passions only insofar as "a man's power of acting is not increased to the point where he conceives himself and his actions adequately."[13] That is to say, our power of action is not yet increased to the point that we are active. We are still impotent, still cut off from our power of action.

But our impotence is only the limitation of our essence and power of action itself. In involving our impotence, our passive feelings involve some degree, however low, of our power of action. Indeed any feeling at all determines our essence or *conatus*. It thus determines us to desire, *that is, to imagine, and to do, something that flows from our nature.* When the feeling affecting us itself agrees with our nature, our power of action is then necessarily increased or aided. For the joy is *added* to the desire that follows from it, so that the external thing's power encourages and increases our own.[14] *Conatus*, being our effort to persevere in existence, is always a quest for what is useful or good for us; it always involves some degree of our power of action, with which indeed it may be identified: this power is thus increased when our *conatus* is determined by an affection that is good or useful to us. We do not cease to be passive, to be cut off from our power of action, but we tend to become less cut off, we come nearer to this power. Our passive joy is and must remain a passion: it is not "explained" by our power of action, but it "involves" a higher degree of this power.

Insofar as the feeling of joy increases our power of action, it determines us to desire, imagine, do, all we can in order to preserve this joy itself and the object that procures it for us.[15] Love is in this manner linked with joy, and other passions with love, so that our capacity to be affected is completely exercised. Thus, if we consider such a succession of joyful affections, following one from another, beginning with an initial feeling of joy, we see that our capacity to be affected is exercised in such a way that our power of action continually increases.[16] But it never increases enough for us to come into its real possession, for us to become active, to become the adequate cause of the affections that exercise our capacity to be affected.

Let us now pass on to the second kind of encounter. I meet a body whose relation cannot be combined with my own. The body does not agree with my nature, is contrary to it, bad or harmful. It produces in me a passive affection which is itself bad or contrary to my nature.[17] The idea of such an affection is a feeling of sadness, a sad passion corresponding to a reduction of my power of action. And we know what is bad only insofar as we perceive something to affect us with sadness. It might, however, be objected that various cases should be distinguished. Everything in such an encounter seems to depend on the respective essences or powers of the bodies that meet one another. If my body has essentially a greater degree of power, it will destroy the other, decompose its relation. And the reverse will be the case if it has a lesser degree of power. The two cases do not seem to correspond to a single pattern.

But this objection is in fact abstract, for we cannot when considering existence take any account of degrees of power considered absolutely. If we consider essences or degrees of power in themselves, we know that none can destroy any other, that all agree. When, on the other hand, we consider conflicts and incompatibilities between existing modes, we have to bring in all sorts of concrete factors, which prevent us from saying that the mode with stronger essence or degree of power will definitely triumph. Indeed, existing bodies that meet one another are not only defined by their overall relations: meeting in their various parts, bit by bit, it is necessarily some of their partial or component relations that meet first. A body less strong than my own may be stronger than one of my components, and may thereby be enough to destroy me, should the component in question be a vital one.

Thus Spinoza reminds us that the contest between modes, *according* to their degree of power, is not to be understood as relating to these degrees of power themselves: there is no contest between essences as such.[18] But conversely, when Spinoza shows that there are always bodies more powerful than my own in existence which can destroy me, one need not necessarily think that such bodies have an essence whose degree of power is greater than my own, or a greater perfection. A body can be destroyed by another of less perfect essence if the conditions of their encounter (that is, the partial relation within which it takes place) favor such destruction. In order to know in advance the result of a contest, one would have to know under which relation the two bodies were to meet, under which relation the two incompatible relations were to confront one another. One would need an infinite knowledge of Nature, which we do not have. At any rate, a feeling of sadness, if only a partial one, always comes into any encounter I have with a body that does not agree with my nature, this from the fact that the body always injures me in one of my partial relations. This feeling of sadness is, furthermore, our only way of knowing that the other body does not agree with our nature.[19] Whether or not we will triumph changes nothing, for we do not know this in advance. We triumph if we manage to ward off this feeling of sadness, to destroy, then, the body that so affects us. We are defeated if sadness takes us over more and

more, in all our component relations, this marking the destruction of our overall relation.

But how, beginning with the first feeling of sadness, is our
capacity to be affected exercised? Sadness, no less than joy, determines our *conatus* or essence. That is, out of sadness is born a
desire, which is hate. This desire is linked with other desires,
other passions: antipathy, derision, contempt, envy, anger and so
on. But here again, as determining our essence or *conatus*, sadness involves something of our power of action. As determined
by sadness, *conatus* is still the quest for what is useful or good
for us: we endeavor to triumph, that is, to act so as to make the
parts of the body that affects us with sadness take on a new relation that may be reconciled with our own. We are thus determined to do everything to ward off sadness and destroy the object
that is its cause.[20] And yet our power of action is said in this case
to be "diminished." For the feeling of sadness is not added to the
desire that follows from it: rather is the desire inhibited by this
feeling, so that the external thing's power *is subtracted* from our
own.[21] Thus affections rooted in sadness are linked one to another
in exercising our capacity to be affected, and this in such a way
that our power of action is further and further diminished, tending toward its lowest degree.

We have proceeded thus far as though two chains[d] of affections, joyful and sad, corresponded to the two sorts of encounter, good and bad. But this is still an abstract view. If one takes
account of the concrete factors of existence, one sees a constant
interplay between the two chains: extrinsic relations[e] are so
arranged that an object can always be a cause of sadness or joy
accidentally.[22] We may both love and hate the same object, not
only by virtue of these relations, but also by virtue of the complexity of the relations of which we are ourselves intrinsically
composed.[23] A joyful chain may always, furthermore, be inter-

rupted by destruction, or even simply by the sadness of the loved object itself. A sad chain, conversely, may be interrupted by the sadness or destruction of the thing hated: "He who imagines that what he hates is destroyed will rejoice," "He who imagines what he hates to be affected with sadness will rejoice."[24] We are always determined to seek the destruction of an object that makes us sad; but to destroy it is to give the parts of the object a new relation that agrees with our own; we then experience a joy which increases our power of action. And with the two sequences thus in constant interaction, our power of action never ceases to vary.

We must also take account of other concrete factors. For the first sort of encounter, good encounters with bodies whose relation combines directly with our own, remains altogether hypothetical. The question is, once we exist *is there any chance of us naturally having good encounters, and experiencing the joyful affections that follow from them?* The chances are in fact slight enough. In speaking of existence, we must not consider essences or degrees of power absolutely; nor must we consider abstractly the relations in which these express themselves. For an existing mode always exists as already affected by objects in partial and particular relations; it exists as determined to this or that. There has always been some accommodation of partial relations between it and external things, such that the mode's characteristic relation can barely be grasped, or is singularly deformed. Thus man should in principle agree perfectly with man. But in reality men agree very little in their natures, one with another; this because they are determined to such a degree by their passions, by objects which affect them in various ways, that they do not naturally meet in relations that can in principle be combined.[25] "Because they are subject to feelings which far surpass human power or virtue, they are often drawn in different directions and are contrary to one another."[26] Indeed a man may be drawn so far as to be in

some sense contrary to himself: his partial relations may be subject to such accommodations, be so far transformed under the
action of imperceptible external causes, that he "takes on another
nature, contrary to the former," another nature that determines
him to suppress the first.[27]

There is, then, very little chance of our naturally having good
encounters. We seem to be determined to much contest, much
hatred, and to the experience of only partial or indirect joys
which do not sufficiently disrupt the chain of our sorrows and
hatreds. Partial joys are "titillations"[f] which only increase our
power of action at one point by reducing it everywhere else.[28]
Indirect joys are those we experience in seeing a hated object
sad or destroyed; but such joys remain imprisoned in sadness.
Hate is in fact a sadness, itself involving the sadness from which
it derives; the joys of hatred mask this sadness and inhibit it, but
can never eliminate it.[29] We now seem farther than ever from
coming into possession of our power of action: our capacity to
be affected is exercised not only by passive affections, but, above
all, by sad passions, involving an ever lower degree of the power
of action. This is hardly surprising, as Nature is not constructed
for our convenience, but in a "common order" to which man,
as a part of Nature, is subject.

We have however made some progress, albeit abstract. We
started from a primary Spinozist principle, the opposition of
passions and actions, of passive affections and active affections.
This principle itself presented two aspects. In the first it was a
matter, almost, of real opposition: active and passive affections,
and so the power of action and the power of suffering, varied
inversely within a fixed capacity of being affected. But on a
deeper level the real opposition was simply a negation: passive
affections reflected only the limitations of our essence, involved
our impotence, did not relate to the mind except insofar as it

itself involved a negation. In this aspect only active affections could effectively or positively exercise our capacity to be affected; the power of action was thus identical to this capacity itself: as for passive affections, they cut us off from that of which we were capable.

Passive affections were opposed to active ones because they were not explained by our power of action. Yet, involving the limitations of our essence, they in some sense involved the lowest degree of that power. They are in their own way our power of action, but this in a state of involvement, unexpressed, unexplained. In their own way they exercise our capacity to be affected, but do so by reducing it to a minimum: the more passive we are, the less we are capable of being affected in a great number of ways. If passive affections cut us off from that of which we are capable, *this is because our power of action is reduced to attaching itself to their traces*, either in the attempt to preserve them if they are joyful, or to ward them off if they are sad. As involving a reduced power of action, they sometimes increase it, sometimes reduce it. The increase may proceed indefinitely, but we will never come into full possessiong of our power of action until we have active affections. But the opposition of actions and passions should not conceal the other opposition that constitutes the second principle of Spinozism: that of joyful passive affections and sad passive affections. One increases our power, the other diminishes it. We come closer to our power of action insofar as we are affected by joy. The ethical question falls then, in Spinoza, into two parts: *How can we come to produce active affections?* But first of all: *How can we come to experience a maximum of joyful passions?* ✗ 𝄢 2 7 3

What is evil? There are no evils save the reduction of our power of action and the decomposition of a relation. And the reduction of our power of action is only an evil because it threatens and diminishes the relation that is our composition. So we are left with the following definition of evil: it is the destruction, the decomposition, of the relation that characterizes a mode. Hence evil can only be spoken of from the particular viewpoint of an existing mode: there is no Good or Evil in Nature in general, *but there is goodness and badness*, useful and harmful, for each existing mode. Evil is what is bad from the viewpoint of this or that mode. Being ourselves men, we judge evil from our viewpoint; and Spinoza often reminds us that he is speaking of good and bad only in relation to human ends. We hardly think, for example, of speaking of an evil when we destroy the relation in which some animal exists in order to nourish ourselves. But we do speak of "evil" in two cases: when our body is destroyed, our relation decomposed, under the action of some other thing; or when we ourselves destroy a being like ourselves, that is, a being whose resemblance to us is enough to make us think it agreed with us in principle, and that its relation was in principle compatible with our own.[30]

Evil being thus defined from our viewpoint, we see that the same applies from all other points of view: *evil is always a bad encounter*, evil is always the decomposition of a relation. The typical case of such decomposition is the action of a poison on our body. The evil suffered by a man is always, according to Spinoza, *of the same kind as indigestion, intoxication or poisoning.* And evil done to a man by some thing, or by another man, always operates like a poison, like a toxic or indigestible matter. Spinoza insists on this, in interpreting the celebrated case of Adam's eating of the forbidden fruit. We should not think, says Spinoza, that God forbade Adam anything. He simply revealed to him that such a fruit was capable of destroying his body and decomposing his relation: "just as he reveals also to us through our natural understanding[h] that poison is deadly to us."[31] Spinoza's theory of evil would have remained obscure had not one of his correspondents, Blyenbergh, led him to clarify his position. Not that Blyenbergh himself avoids misunderstandings – misunderstandings that so try Spinoza's patience that he eventually gives up the attempt to dispel them. But on one essential point Blyenbergh well understands Spinoza's thought: "You avoid the things I call vice...as we avoid eating food that our nature finds disgusting."[32] *Evil as a bad encounter, evil as poisoning*, constitutes the basis of Spinoza's theory.

So if it be asked what evil amounts to in the order of relations, one has to reply that evil is nothing. For there is nothing, in the order of relations, but composition. It cannot be said that the combining of some relations or others is an evil: any combination of relations is good from the viewpoint of the relations combined, that is, simply from the positive viewpoint. When a poison decomposes my body, it is because a natural law determines the parts of my body in contact with the poison to take on a new relation which combines with that of the toxic body. Nothing in this is evil from Nature's viewpoint. To the extent that the poison is determined by a law to have an effect, that effect is not an evil, since it consists of a relation which itself combines with that of the poison. Similarly, when I destroy a body, even one similar to my own, this is because *in the relation and in the circumstances in which I encounter it*, it doesn't agree with my nature: so I am determined to do everything in my power to impose on the parts of that body a new relation in which they will agree with me. Thus the wicked man, like the virtuous one, seeks what is useful or good to him (if there is some difference between them it does not lie here). Whence Blyenbergh's first misunderstanding consists in believing that, according to Spinoza, the wicked man is determined to do evil. We are, it is true, always determined;

our *conatus* is itself determined by the affections we experience. But we are never determined to do evil; we are determined to seek what is good for us in our encounters, in the circumstances in which those encounters take place. To the extent that we are determined to produce an effect, the effect is necessarily combined with its cause, and contains nothing that could be called "evil."[33] In short, evil is nothing because it expresses no composition of relations, no law of composition. In any encounter, whether I destroy or be destroyed, there takes place a combining of relations that is, as such, good. Thus if one considers the order of encounters as a whole, one may say it coincides with the order of relations as a whole. And one may say that evil is nothing in the order of relations themselves.

If we then ask what evil amounts to in the order of essences, here again it is nothing. Consider our death or destruction: our relation is decomposed, ceases, that is, to subsume its extensive parts. But these extensive parts are in no way constituents of our essence; our essence itself, having its full reality in itself, has never presented the least tendency to come into existence. Once we exist, of course, our essence is a *conatus*, an attempt to persevere in existence. But this *conatus* is only the state such an essence *is determined* to take on in existence, insofar as the essence determines neither existence itself, nor the duration of existence. And so, being the attempt to persevere in existence indefinitely, the *conatus* involves no definite period: the essence is not more or less perfect accordingly as the mode succeeds in persevering for a longer or shorter period in existence.[34] Lacking nothing while the mode does not yet exist, the essence is deprived of nothing when it ceases to exist.

Consider, on the other hand, the evil we do when we destroy another body similar to our own. Take the action of beating (that is, lifting the arm, clenching the fist and moving the arm up and down): one can see that it expresses something of an essence insofar as the human body can do it while maintaining its characteristic relation. In this sense the action "is a virtue, which is conceived from the structure of the human body."[35] Then, if the action is aggressive, threatening or destroying the relation that defines another body, that is indeed the mark of an encounter between two bodies whose relations are incompatible in this respect, but expresses no essence. One says that my intention itself was wicked. But *the wickedness of the intention lies solely in the fact that I join the image of such an action to the image of a body whose relation is destroyed by such an action.*[36] There is "evil" only to the extent that the action has as its object something or someone whose relation does not combine with that on which the action depends. This case is once again analogous to that of a poison.

The difference between two famous matricides, Nero killing Agrippina, and Orestes killing Clytemnestra, may serve to enlighten us. Orestes is *not* considered guilty because Clytemnestra, having begun by killing Agamemnon, put herself in a relation that could no longer be combined with that of Orestes. Nero *is* considered guilty because he had to be wicked to view Agrippina in a relation absolutely incompatible with his own, and to link the image of Agrippina to the image of an action that would destroy her. But nothing in all this expresses an essence.[37] All that we see is the encounter of two bodies in incompatible relations, the connection of the image of an act with the image of a body whose relation is incompatible with that of the act. The same act could be a virtue, had it for its object something whose relation combined with its own (thus there are greetings that look like beatings). Whence Blyenbergh's second misunderstanding: he thinks that according to Spinoza an evil becomes a good, a crime a virtue, to the extent that it expresses an essence, be it even Nero's. And Spinoza only partly disabuses him. This not just because he is impatient with Blyenbergh's blundering, even insolent, demands, but above all because an "amoralist" thesis such as Spinoza's can make itself understood only by means of a certain amount of provocation.[38] In fact a crime expresses nothing of essence, expresses no essence, not even Nero's.

Evil thus appears only in the third order of Nature, that of encounters. It corresponds only to the fact that the relations combined when two bodies meet are not always those of the bodies themselves. We have seen, moreover, that evil amounts to nothing in the order of encounters taken as a whole. Again, it is nothing in the limiting case in which a relation is decomposed, since such destruction affects neither the reality of the essence in itself, nor the eternal truth of the relation. There remains, then, but one case in which evil seems to amount to something. While it exists, and according to the encounters it experiences, a given existing mode goes through changes corresponding to variations in its power of action; but, when its power of action diminishes, the existing mode *passes from greater to lesser perfection*.[39] Does not evil reside in this "passage to a lesser perfection"? As Blyenbergh says, there must be some evil when one is deprived of a better condition.[40] Spinoza's famous reply is that there is no privation in the passage to a lesser perfection: privation is only a negation. Evil is nothing even in this last order. A man becomes blind; a man previously inspired by a desire for good is overcome by a sensual appetite. We have no reason to say that he is deprived of a better state, since that state no more belongs to his nature at the moment in question than to those of a stone or the devil.[41]

This reply clearly presents certain problems. Blyenbergh fiercely criticizes Spinoza for having confused two very different sorts of comparison: comparisons between things that do not share the same nature, and comparisons between different states of one and the same thing. It does not, true enough, belong to a stone's nature to see, but sight does belong to man's nature. Thus his main objection is that Spinoza attributes to a thing's essence an instantaneous character foreign to it; "on your view nothing else pertains to an essence than what it has *at that moment* when it is perceived."[42] If this be the case then any transition forward or backward in time becomes unintelligible.

Blyenbergh argues as though Spinoza had said that a being is always as perfect as it can be, *given the essence it has at any given moment*. Here, then, is his third misunderstanding. For Spinoza says something completely different: A being is always as perfect as it can be, *given the affections that, at any particular moment, belong to its essence*. Blyenbergh is clearly confusing "belonging to its essence" and "constituting its essence." At each moment the affections I am experiencing belong to my essence, in that they exercise my capacity of being affected. While a mode exists its essence is as perfect as it can be, given the affections that, at any particular moment, are exercising its capacity to be affected. If some given affections are exercising my capacity at some particular moment, then it cannot at the same time be exercised by any other affections: there is an incompatibility, exclusion, negation, but no privation. Let us return to the example of the blind man. Either one imagines a blind man who still has luminous sensations, but is blind in the sense that he can no longer act according to these sensations, and what luminous sensations remain to him are altogether passive. In such a case only the relative proportion of active and passive affections will have changed, his capacity to be affected remaining constant. Or one imagines a blind man who has lost all luminous affections. In that case his capacity to be affected has indeed been reduced. But the same conclusion follows: any existing mode is as perfect as it can be, given the affections that exercise its capacity to be affected and cause it to vary within the limits compatible with existence. In short, there is in Spinoza no contradiction between the "necessitarian" view according to which the capacity to be affected is at each moment necessarily exercised, and the "ethical" view according to which it is exercised at each moment in such a way that the power of action increases or diminishes, our capacity itself varying with it. As Spinoza says, there is nowhere any privation, but there are nonetheless passages between greater and lesser perfections.[43]

Evil is not anything in any sense. To be is *to express oneself, to express something else or to be expressed*. Evil is nothing, being in no way expressive. Above all, it expresses nothing. It expresses no law of composition, no composition of relations; it expresses no essence; it expresses no privation of some better state of existence. To evaluate the originality of this position, one must oppose it to other ways of *denying* evil. One may call "rationalist moralism" (optimism) a tradition that has its sources in Plato, and its fullest development in the philosophy of Leibniz; Evil is nothing because only Being is, or rather because Being, superior to existence, determines all that is. The Good, or the Better, *make things be*. Spinoza's position has nothing to do with this tradition: it amounts to rationalist "amoralism." For according to Spinoza, Good has no more sense than Evil: in Nature there is neither Good nor Evil. Spinoza constantly reminds us of this: "If men were born free, they would form no concept of good and evil so long as they remained free."[44] The question of Spinoza's atheism is singularly lacking in interest insofar as it depends on arbitrary definitions of theism and atheism. The question can only be posed in relation to what most people call "God" from a religious viewpoint: a God, that is to say, inseparable from a *ratio boni*, proceeding by the moral law, acting as a judge.[45] Spinoza is clearly an atheist in this sense: the moral pseudo-law is simply the measure of our misunderstanding of natural laws; the idea of rewards and punishments reflects only our ignorance of the true relation between an act and its consequences; Good and Evil are inadequate ideas, and we form conceptions of them only to the extent that our ideas are inadequate.[46]

But because there is no Good or Evil, this does not mean that all distinctions vanish. There is no Good or Evil in Nature, but there are good and bad things for each existing mode. The moral opposition of Good and Evil disappears, but this disappearance does not make all things, or all beings, equal. As Nietzsche puts it, " '*Beyond Good and Evil*'... at least this does *not* mean 'Beyond Good and Bad.'"[47] There are increases in our power of action, reductions in our power of action. The distinction between good things and bad provides the basis for a real ethical difference, which we must substitute for a false moral opposition.

CHAPTER SIXTEEN

The Ethical Vision of the World

When Spinoza says that we do not even know what a body can do, this is practically a war cry. He adds that we speak of consciousness, mind, soul, of the power of the soul over the body; we chatter away about these things, but do not even know what bodies can do.[1] Moral chattering replaces true philosophy.

This declaration is important in several respects. As long as we speak of a power of the soul over the body we are not really thinking of a capacity or power. What we really mean is that the soul, from its own eminent nature and special finality, has higher "duties": it must command the body's obedience, according to the laws to which it is itself subject. As for the body's power, this is either a power of execution, or the power to lead the soul astray, and entice it from its duties. In all this we are thinking morally. The moral view of the world appears in a principle that dominates most theories of the union of soul and body: when one of these acts, the other suffers. This is, in particular, the principle of real action in Descartes: the body suffers when the soul acts, and the soul in its turn suffers when the body acts.[2] And, while denying real action, Descartes's successors do not relinquish the idea behind this principle: preestablished harmony, for example, preserves an "ideal action" between soul and body, according to which one always suffers when the other acts.[3] From such viewpoints we have no means of *comparing* the powers of soul and body; and having no way of comparing them we are quite unable to *assess* either of them.[4]

If parallelism is a novel doctrine, this is not because it denies a real action of soul on body. It is because it overturns the moral principle by which the actions of one are the passions of the other. "The order of actions and passions of our body is, by nature, at one with the order of actions and passions of the mind."[5] What is a passion in the mind is *also* a passion in the body, what is an action in the mind is *also* an action in the body. Parallelism thus excludes any eminence of the soul, any spiritual and moral finality, any transcendence of a God who might base one series on the other. And parallelism is in this respect practically opposed not only to the doctrine of real action, but to the theories of preestablished harmony and occasionalism also. We ask "Of what is a body capable? Of what affections, passive as well as active? How far does its power extend?" Thereby, and thereby only, can we know of what a soul is in itself capable, what is its power. Thereby we find a means of "comparing" the power of the soul with that of the body, and so find a means of assessing the power of the soul considered in itself.

To reach an *assessment* of the power of the soul in itself, one must pass through a *comparison* of powers: "To determine what is the difference between the human mind and the others, and how it surpasses them, it is necessary for us, as we have said, to know the nature of its object, i.e., of the human body.... I say in general, that in proportion as a body is more capable than others of doing many things at once, or being acted on in many ways at once, so its mind is more capable than others of perceiving many things at once. And in proportion as the actions of a body depend more on itself alone, and as other bodies concur with it less in acting, so its mind is more capable of understanding distinctly."[6] In order to really think in terms of power, one must consider the matter in relation to the body, one must in the first place free the body from that relation of inverse proportionality which makes all comparison of powers impossible, and thereby also makes impossible any assessment of the power of the soul considered in itself. The question, "What can a body do?" must be taken as a model. *The model implies no devaluation of Thought relative to Extension, but merely a devaluation of consciousness relative to thought.* One recalls Plato saying that materialists, if at all intelligent, should speak of power rather than of bodies. But it is true, conversely, that intelligent dynamists must first speak of bodies, in order to "think" power. The theory of power according to which actions and passions of the body accompany actions and passions of the soul amounts to an ethical vision of the world. The substitution of ethics for morality is a consequence of parallelism, and shows its true significance.

The question of what a body can do makes sense taken alone, since it implies a new conception of the embodied individual, of species, and of genera. As we will see, its biological significance should not be neglected. But *taken as a model*, its primary significance is juridical and ethical. All a body can do (its power) is also its "natural right." If we manage to pose the problem of rights at the level of bodies, we thereby transform the whole philosophy of rights in relation to souls themselves. Everyone seeks, soul and body, what is useful or good for them. If someone happens to encounter a body that can combine with his own in a favorable relation, he tries to unite with it. When someone encounters a body whose relation is incompatible with his own, a body that affects him with sadness, he does all in his power to ward off the sadness or destroy the body, that is, to impose on the parts of that body some new relation that accords with his own nature. Thus affections at each moment determine *conatus*, but *conatus* is at each moment a seeking of what is useful in terms of the affections that determine it. *Whence a body always goes as far as it can, in passion as in action*; and what it can do is its right. The theory of natural rights implies a double identification of power with its exercise, and of such an exercise of power with a right. "The rights of an individual extend to the utmost limits of his power as it has been conditioned."[7] This is the very meaning of the word *law*: the law of nature is never a rule of duty, but the norm of a power, the unity of right, power and its exercise.[8] There is in this respect no difference between wise man and fool, reasonable and demented men, strong man and weak. They do of course differ in the kind of affections that determine their effort to persevere in existence. But each tries equally to preserve himself, and has as much right as he has power, given the affections that actually exercise his capacity to be affected. The fool is himself a part of Nature, and in no way disturbs its order.[9]

This conception of natural right is inherited directly from Hobbes. (The question of the fundamental differences between Spinoza and Hobbes arises on another level.) What Spinoza owes to Hobbes is a conception of natural right thoroughly opposed to the classic theory of natural law.[a] If we take as our guide Cicero, who combines within him Platonic, Aristotelian and Stoic traditions, we see that the natural law of Antiquity presents various characteristics: 1. It defines a being's nature by its perfection, within an order of ends (thus man is "naturally" reasonable and sociable). 2. It follows that the state of nature is not, for man, a state preceding society, even in principle, but rather a life in conformity with nature in a "good" civil society. 3. What is then primary and unconditional in such a state are "duties"; for natural powers are only potential, and always require an act of reason to determine and realize them in relation to ends they are to serve. 4. This itself grounds the authority of the wise man; for the wise man is the best judge of the order of ends, of duties that follow from it, and of the offices and actions that it falls to each to exercise and carry out. One can foresee the use Christianity would make of this conception of natural law: law would become inseparable from natural theology and even Revelation.[10]

It belongs to Hobbes to have brought forward four basic theses to set against those just cited. These novel theses transform the philosophical problem of right precisely by taking the body as their mechanical and dynamical model. Spinoza adopts these theses, integrating them within his own system where they are seen in a new light. 1. The law of nature is no longer referred to a final perfection but to an initial desire, to the strongest "appetite"; detached from the order of ends, it is deduced from appetite as its efficient cause. 2. Reason, from this viewpoint, enjoys no privilege: the fool tries no less than a reasonable being to persevere in his being; and desires or actions born of reason exemplify this effort no more than do the desires or passions of the fool. What is more, *nobody is born reasonable.* Reason may perhaps apply and preserve the law of nature, but is in no sense its principle or motive force. Similarly, *nobody is born a citizen.*[11] The civil state may preserve the law of nature, but the state of nature is in itself presocial, precivil. Further still, *nobody is born religious*: "The state of nature is, both in nature and in time, prior to religion. No one knows by nature that he owes any obedience to God...."[12] 3. What then is primary and unconditional is power or right. "Duties," of whatever sort, are always secondary relative to the affirmation of our power, to the exercise of our power, the preservation of our right. And power is no longer referred to an act that determines and realizes it in relation to an order of ends.

My power is itself actual, because the affections that I experience each moment, whatever these may be, have full right to determine and exercise it. 4. It follows that nobody has the authority to decide my rights. Everyone in the state of nature, whether wise man or fool, judges what is good or bad, and what is necessary to his preservation. Whence natural right is not opposed "to strifes, hatred, anger, treachery, or, in general, anything that appetite suggests."[13] And if it comes about that we are led to renounce our natural right, this will not happen through the recognition of the wise man's authority, but through our own consent to this renunciation, from fear of a greater evil or hope of a greater good. The principle of consent (pact or contract) becomes the principle of political philosophy, and replaces the rule of authority.

Thus defined, the state of nature itself shows us what makes it intolerable. The state of nature is not viable, as long as the natural right corresponding to it remains theoretical and abstract.[14] In the state of nature I live at the mercy of encounters. It is true enough that my power is determined by the affections that each moment exercise my capacity to be affected, true enough that I always have all the perfection of which I am capable, given those affections. But in the state of nature my capacity to be affected is exercised in such conditions that not only do I experience passive affections which cut me off from my power of action; these passive affections are, moreover, predominantly sad, and continually reduce this power itself. There is no chance of my encountering bodies that combine directly with my own. It would be all very well to prevail in various encounters with bodies opposed to me; but such triumphs, such joys of hate, would not eliminate the sadness involved in hatred; and, above all, I could never be sure winning the next encounter, and would thus be affected by a perpetual fear.

There could be only one way of making the state of nature

viable: by striving to *organize its encounters*. Whatever body I meet, I seek what is useful. But there is a great difference between seeking what is useful through chance (that is, striving to destroy bodies incompatible with our own) and seeking to organize what is useful (striving to encounter bodies agreeing in nature with us, in relations in which they agree). Only the second type of effort defines *proper or true utility*. [15] This endeavor does of course have its limits: we will still be determined to destroy certain bodies, if only in order to subsist; we cannot avoid all bad encounters, we cannot avoid death. But we can strive to unite with what agrees with our nature, to combine our relation with those that are compatible with it, to associate our acts and thoughts with the images of things that agree with us. From such an effort we have a right, by definition, to expect a maximum of joyful affections. Our capacity to be affected will be exercised in such conditions that our power of action will increase. And if it be asked what is most useful to us, this will be seen to be man. For man in principle agrees in nature with man; man is absolutely or truly useful to man. Everyone, then, in seeking what is truly useful to him, also seeks what is useful to man. The effort to organize encounters is thus first of all the effort to form an association of men in relations that can be combined. [16]

There is in Nature neither Good nor Evil, there is no moral opposition, but there is an ethical difference. This ethical difference appears in various equivalent forms: that between the reasonable man and the foolish, the wise and the ignorant, free man and slave, strong and weak. [17] And wisdom or reason have in fact no other content but strength, freedom. This ethical difference does not relate to *conatus*, since fools and the weak, no less than reasonable men and the strong, strive to persevere in their being. *It relates to the kind of affections that determine our* conatus. The free, strong and reasonable man is in principle fully defined by

261

his possession of a power of action and the presence in him of adequate ideas and active affections; the slave and the weak man, on the other hand, have only those passions that derive from their inadequate ideas, and cut them off from their power of action.

But ethical difference is first expressed on a simpler, preparatory or preliminary level. Before coming into full possession of his power, *the strong free man* may be recognized by his joyful passions, by affections that increase his power of action; *the slave or weak man* may be recognized by his sad passions, by affections based on sadness which diminish his power of action. We must, it seems, distinguish two stages of reason or freedom: increasing our power of action by striving to experience a maximum of joyful passive affections; and thence passing on to a final stage in which our power of action has so increased that it becomes capable of producing affections that are themselves active. The link between the two stages remains, to be sure, mysterious. But the existence of the first stage is not, at least, in doubt. A man who is to become reasonable, strong and free, begins by doing all in his power to experience joyful passions. He then strives to extricate himself from chance encounters and the concatenation of sad passions, to organize good encounters, combine his relation with relations that combine directly with it, unite with what agrees in nature with him, and form a reasonable association between men; all this in such a way as to be affected with joy. The description of the reasonable and free man in Part Four of the *Ethics* identifies the striving of reason with this art of organizing encounters, or forming a *totality* of compatible relations.[18]

Reason, strength and freedom are in Spinoza inseparable from a development, a formative process, a culture.[c] Nobody is born free, nobody is born reasonable.[19] And nobody can undergo for us the slow learning of what agrees with our nature, the slow effort of discovering our joys. Childhood, says Spinoza, is a state of impotence and slavery, a state of foolishness in which we depend in the highest degree on external causes, and in which we necessarily have more of sadness than of joy; we are never more cut off from our power of action. The first man, Adam, corresponds to the childhood of humanity. This is why Spinoza so forcefully opposes the Christian, and then rationalist, traditions which present Adam to us as reasonable, free and perfect before his fall. Rather should we imagine Adam as a child: sad, weak, enslaved, ignorant, left to chance encounters. "It must be admitted that it was not in the first man's power to make a right use of reason, but that, like us, he was subject to passions."[20] That is to say: *It is not sin that explains weakness, but our initial weakness that explains the myth of sin.* Spinoza presents three theses concerning Adam, which together form a systematic whole: 1. God forbade Adam nothing, but simply revealed to him that the fruit was a poison that would destroy his body if it came into contact with it. 2. As his understanding was weak like a child's, Adam perceived this revelation as a prohibition; he disobeyed like a child, not understanding the natural necessity of the relation between action and consequence, believing the laws of Nature to be moral laws which it is possible to violate. 3. How can we imagine Adam free and reasonable, when the first man must necessarily be affected by passive feelings, not having had time to undergo the long formative process presupposed by reason no less than by freedom?[21]

The state of reason, in its initial aspect, already has a complex relation to the state of nature. On the one hand the state of nature is not subject to the laws of reason: reason relates to the proper and true utility of man, and tends solely to his preservation; Nature on the other hand has no regard for the preservation of man and comprises an infinity of other laws concerning the universe as a whole, of which man is but a small part. But the state of reason is not, on the other hand, of another order than the state of nature itself. Reason, even in its "commandments," demands nothing contrary to Nature: it demands only that everyone should love themselves, seek what is useful to themselves, and strive to preserve their being by increasing their power of action.[22] There is thus no artificiality or conventionality in reason's endeavor. Reason proceeds not by artifice, but by a natural combination of relations; it does not so much bring in calculation, as a kind of direct recognition of man by man.[23] The question of knowing whether creatures supposed reasonable, or in the process of becoming so, need to mutually commit themselves through a sort of contract, is a highly complex one; but even if there is a contract on this level, it implies no conventional renunciation of natural rights, no artificial limitation. The state of reason is one with the formation of a higher kind of body and a higher kind of soul, enjoying natural rights corresponding to their power: indeed, should two individuals completely combine their relations, they would naturally form an individual twice as great, having twice as great a natural right.[24] The state of reason in no way either does away with or limits natural rights, but raises them to a power without which such rights would remain unreal and abstract.

What then does the difference between the state of reason and the state of nature come down to? In the order of nature each body meets others, but its relation cannot necessarily combine with those of the bodies it encounters. The correspondence of encounters and relations occurs only at the level of Nature as a whole; it occurs between whole and whole in the infinite mediate mode. When however we rise higher in the order of essences, we witness an effort which prefigures that of Nature as a whole. The highest essences already strive in their existence to make *their own* encounters correspond to relations that are compati-

ble with *theirs*. This endeavor, which cannot wholly succeed, constitutes the striving of reason. A reasonable being may in this
sense be said, in its way, to reproduce and express the effort of
Nature as a whole.

How can men come to meet one another in relations that are
compatible, and so form a reasonable association? If man agrees
with man, this is so only insofar as he is supposed *already* reasonable.[25] As long as they live by chance encounters, as long as
they are affected by chance passions, men are led in various directions and so have no chance of meeting in relations that agree:
they are opposed one to another.[26] We can, it is true, avoid this
conflict to the extent that we bring into play a very slow learning process, a very slow empirical education. But we then fall
immediately into another difficulty. In the first place, the bur-
den of present encounters is always there to threaten the annihi-
lation of reason's effort. Moreover, this effort will at best succeed
at the close of life; "nevertheless they are in the meanwhile bound
to live."[27] Thus reason would amount to nothing and would never
come into its own power, did it not find help in a power of
another kind, which joins with it, and which prepares and accompanies its development. This other kind of power is that of the
State or City.[d]

The City is, in fact, in no way a reasonable association. It
differs from such an association in three ways. 1. The motive
force of its formation is not an affection of reason, that is to say
an affection produced in us by another man in a relation that is
perfectly compatible with our own. The motive is anxiety or fear
of the state of nature, hope of a greater good.[28] 2. The whole
that is reason's ideal is constituted by relations that directly and
naturally combine, by powers or rights that are naturally addi-

265

tive. This is not the case in the City: men being unreasonable, each must "renounce" his natural rights. Such renunciation alone makes possible the formation of a whole that itself takes on the sum of these rights. This is the civil "pact" or "contract."[29] The sovereign City then has power enough to institute indirect conventional relations through which citizens *are forced* to agree and be compatible. 3. Reason is the principle of an ethical distinction between "those who live under its guidance" and those who remain guided by feeling, those who free themselves and those who remain slaves. But the civil state distinguishes only the just and the unjust, accordingly as they obey or do not obey its laws. Having renounced their right to judge what is good and bad, citizens rely on a State that rewards and punishes. Sin and obedience, justice and injustice are strictly social categories; moral opposition finds in society both its principle and its domain.[30]

And yet there is a great similarity between the City and Reason's ideal. In Spinoza as in Hobbes the sovereign is defined by his natural right, equal to his power, equal, that is, to all the rights relinquished by the contracting parties. But such a sovereign is not, as in Hobbes, a third party who gains by the contract made by individuals. The sovereign is the whole; the contract is made between individuals who transfer their rights to the whole they form by contracting. Thus Spinoza describes the City as a collective person, with common body and soul, "a multitude which is guided, as it were, by one mind."[31] That the process of its formation is very different from that of reason, that it is prerational, does not prevent the City from imitating and preparing the way for reason. Indeed there is not, nor can there be, any irrational totality contrary to reason. The sovereign has of course the right to demand all it wishes, everything within its power; it is the sole judge of the laws it institutes and can neither do wrong nor disobey. But precisely because it is a whole, it can preserve itself as such only insofar as "it tends toward the end that sound reason teaches all men to pursue": the whole cannot preserve itself unless it tends toward something that has at least the appearance of reason.[32] The contract by which individuals alienate their rights has no motivation but interest (the fear of a greater evil, the hope of a greater good); if the citizens begin to fear the City above all else, they find themselves once more in a state of nature, while the City loses its power, a prey to the factions it has stirred up. The City's own nature thus determines it to aim as far as possible for reason's ideal, to strive to make the sum of its laws conform to reason. And the City will agree all the more with reason, the less sad passions (sadness or even hope) it produces in its citizens, relying rather on joyful affections.[33]

We must in all this understand a "good" City. For it is with cities as with individuals: many causes, sometimes imperceptible, intervene to pervert nature and precipitate ruin. But, from the viewpoint of the good City, two further considerations may be added to those above. In the first place, what does it mean for a citizen to "renounce his natural rights"? Not, obviously, to renounce persevering in being. But rather to renounce being determined by *any personal affections whatever*. Abandoning his right to personally judge what is good and what bad, the citizen thereby commits himself to *common collective affections*. But given these affections he continues personally to persevere in his being, and to do all in his power to preserve his existence and look after his interests.[34] Spinoza is thus able to say that each, as a member of the City, renounces his natural rights, and yet entirely preserves these natural rights in the civil state.[35] In the second place, *affections of reason* are not subject to the City's rule: the power of knowing, thinking and expressing one's thought remains an inalienable natural right, which the City cannot compromise with-

267

out reintroducing between itself and its subjects relations of simple violence.[36]

The "good" City both takes the place of reason for those who have none, and prepares, prefigures and in its way imitates the work of reason. It is the City that makes possible the development of reason itself. One should not take as signs of excessive optimism Spinoza's two propositions that, everything considered and despite everything, the City is the best environment in which man can become reasonable, and that it is also the best environment in which a reasonable man can live.[37]

In an ethical vision of the world it is always a matter of capacity and power, and never of anything else. Law is identical to right. True natural laws are norms of power rather than rules of duty. Thus the moral law that purports to prohibit and command, involves a kind of mystification: the less we understand the laws of nature, that is, the norms of life, the more we interpret them as orders and prohibitions – to the point that the philosopher must hesitate before using the word "law," so much does it retain a moral aftertaste: it would be better to speak of "eternal truths." Moral laws or duties are in truth purely civil, social. Society alone orders and prohibits, threatens and gives us to hope, rewards and punishes. Reason does of course on its own account involve a *pietas* and a *religio*; and there are of course precepts, rules or "commands" of reason. But the list of such commands is enough to show that they are not duties but norms of life, relating to the soul's "strength" and its power of action.[38] It can of course also happen that such norms coincide with the laws of ordinary morality; but such coincidences are on the one hand not particularly numerous; and on the other, when reason enjoins or denounces something analogous to what morality orders or prohibits, it is always for reasons very different from those of morality.[39] The *Ethics* judges feelings, conduct and intentions by relating them, not to transcendent values, but to modes of existence they presuppose or imply: there are things one cannot do or even say, believe, feel, think, unless one is weak, enslaved, impotent; and other things one cannot do, feel and so on, unless one is free or strong. *A method of explanation by immanent modes of existence* thus replaces the recourse to transcendent values. The question is in each case: Does, say, this feeling, increase our power of action or not? Does it help us come into full possession of that power?

To do all we can is our ethical task properly so called. It is here that the *Ethics* takes the body as model; for every body extends its power as far as it can. In a sense every being, each moment, does all it can. "What it can do" is its capacity to be affected, which is necessarily and constantly exercised by the thing's relations with other beings. But in another sense, our capacity to be affected may be exercised in such a way that we are cut off from our power of action, and such that this incessantly diminishes. In this second sense it can happen that we live cut off from "what we can do." This indeed is the fate of most men, most of the time. *The weak man, the slave, is not someone of lesser strength in absolute terms.* The weak man is he who, whatever his strength, remains cut off from his power of action, kept in slavery or impotence. To do all we can amounts to two things: How exercise our capacity to be affected in such a way that our power of action increases? And how increase this power to the point where, finally, we produce active affections? There are weak men and strong, slaves and free men. There is no Good and Evil in Nature, there is no moral opposition, but there is an ethical difference. The difference lies in the immanent existing modes involved in what we feel, do and think.

This ethical conception has a fundamental critical aspect.

Spinoza belongs to a great tradition: the practical task of philosophy consists in denouncing all myths, all mystifications, all "superstitions," whatever their origin. I believe that this tradition always involves a naturalist philosophy. *Superstition* is everything that keeps us cut off from our power of action and continually diminishes it. The source of superstition is thus the concatenation of sad passions, fear, the hope linked to fear, the anxiety that delivers us over to phantoms.[40] Spinoza knows, like Lucretius, that there are no joyful myths or superstitions. Like Lucretius he sets the image of a positive Nature against the uncertainty of gods: *what is opposed to Nature is not Culture, nor the state of reason, nor even the civil state, but only the superstition that threatens all human endeavor.* And like Lucretius again, Spinoza assigns to philosophy the task of denouncing all that is sad, all that lives on sadness, all those who depend on sadness as the basis of their power. "In despotic statecraft, the supreme and essential mystery is to hoodwink the subjects, and to mask the fear, which keeps them down, with the specious garb of religion, so that they may fight as bravely for slavery as for safety...."[41] The devaluation of sad passions, and the denunciation of those who cultivate and depend on them, form the practical object of philosophy. Few themes of the *Ethics* reappear more constantly than this one: that all that is sad is bad and enslaves us; all that involves sadness expresses tyranny.

"No deity, nor anyone else, unless he be envious, takes pleasure in my lack of power and my misfortune; nor does he ascribe to virtue our tears, sighs, fear, and other things of that kind, which are signs of a weak mind. On the contrary, the greater the joy with which we are affected, the greater the perfection to which we pass, i.e., the more we must participate in the divine nature." "He who rightly knows that all things follow from the necessity of the divine nature, and happen according to the eternal laws and rules of Nature, will surely find nothing worthy of hate, mockery or disdain, nor anyone whom he will pity. Instead he will strive, as far as human virtue allows, to act well, as they say, and rejoice." "The superstitious know how to reproach people for their vices better than they know how to teach them virtues, and they strive, not to guide men by reason, but to restrain them by fear, so that they flee the evil rather than love virtues. Such people aim only to make others as wretched as they themselves are, so it is no wonder that they are generally burdensome and hateful to men." "One who has been badly received by a lover thinks of nothing but the inconstancy and deceptiveness of women, and their other, often sung vices. All of these he immediately forgets as soon as his lover receives him again. One therefore, who is anxious to moderate his feelings and appetites from the love of freedom alone will strive, as far as he can, to come to know the virtues and their causes, and to fill his mind with the gladness which arises from the true knowledge of them, but not at all to consider men's vices, or to disparage men, or to enjoy a false appearance of freedom." "A free man thinks of nothing less than of death, and his wisdom is a meditation on life, not on death."[42]

One may see Spinoza, through the scholia of Part Four of the *Ethics*, forming a truly ethical conception of man, founded on joy and joyful passions. This he opposes to a superstitious or satirical conception, founded on sad passions alone: "instead of an *Ethics*, they have generally written a satire."[43] At a deeper level Spinoza denounces oppressive powers, which can rule only through inspiring in man the sad passions from which they profit ("those who know only how to break men's minds...")[44]. Some sad passions are of course socially useful: among them fear, hope, humility, even remorse. But this only insofar as we do not live by the guidance of reason.[45] It remains the case that every passion is in itself bad insofar as it involves sadness: even *hope*, even confidence.[46] A City is so much the better the more it relies on joyful affections; the love of freedom should outweigh hope, fear and confidence.[47] Reason's only commandment, the sole requirement of *pietas* and *religio*, is to link a maximum of passive joys with a maximum of active ones. For joy is the only passive affection that increases our power of action, and of all affections joy alone can be active. The slave may be recognized by his sad passions, and the free man by his joys, passive and active. The sense of joy is revealed as the truly ethical sense; it is to the practical sphere what affirmation itself is to the speculative. Spinoza's naturalism is defined by speculative affirmation in his theory of substance, and by practical joy in his conception of modes. A philosophy of pure affirmation, the *Ethics* is also a philosophy of the joy corresponding to such affirmation.

CHAPTER SEVENTEEN

Common Notions

Spinoza's philosophy does not fix itself in God, or find its natural starting point in God. The conditions in which we have ideas seem to condemn us to having only inadequate ones, and the conditions in which we are affected seem to condemn us to experience only passive affections. The affections that naturally exercise our capacity to be affected are passions that reduce it to a minimum, and cut us off from our essence or our power of action.

Yet there appears in this pessimistic assessment of existence a first glimmer of hope: the radical distinction of action and passion should not lead us to overlook a prior distinction between two kinds of passions. Any passion does of course keep us cut off from our power of action, but this to a greater or lesser extent. As long as we are affected by passions we have not come into full possession of our power of action. But joyful passions lead us closer to this power, that is, increase or help it; sad passions distance us from it, that is, diminish or hinder it. The primary question of the *Ethics* is thus: What must we do in order to be affected by a maximum of joyful passions? Nature does not favor us in this respect. But we should rely on the efforts of reason, the very slow empirical effort which finds in the City the conditions that make it possible: reason in the first principle of its development, or in its initial aspect, is the effort to organize encounters in such a way that we are affected by a maximum of joyful passions. For joyful passions increase our power of action; reason is the power of understanding, the power of action belonging to the soul; so joyful passions agree with reason, and lead us to understand, or determine us to become reasonable.[1]

But it is not enough for our power of action to increase. It might increase indefinitely, joyful passions might follow indefinitely from joyful passions, without us coming into full possession of our power of action. A sum of passions does not make an action. It is not enough, then, just to accumulate joyful passions; we must find the means, through such accumulation, to win the power of action and so at last experience active affections of which we are the cause. The second principal question of the *Ethics* is thus: What must we do to produce in ourselves active affections?

1. Active affections, when they occur, are necessarily joyful: there is no active sadness, since all sadness is the diminution of our power of action; only joy can be active.[2] So if our power of action increases to the point that we come into its full possession, our subsequent affections will necessarily be active joys.[3] 2. Active joy is "another" feeling than passive joy.[4] And yet Spinoza suggests that the distinction between the two is one of reason only.[5] The two feelings differ only in their causes; passive joy is produced by an object that agrees with us, and whose power increases our power of action, but of which we do not yet have an adequate idea. Active joy we produce by ourselves, it flows from our power of action itself, follows from an adequate idea in us. 3. To the extent that passive joys increase our power of action, they *agree with* reason. But since reason is the soul's power of action, those joys that are active are *born* of reason. When Spinoza suggests that what agrees with reason may also be born

of it, he means that from every passive joy there may arise an active joy distinguished from it only by its cause.[6]

Consider two bodies that agree entirely, two bodies, that is to say, all of whose relations can be combined: they are like parts of a whole, the whole exercising a *general function* in relation to these parts, and the parts having a *common property* as belonging to the whole. Thus two bodies that agree entirely have an identical structure. Because all their relations may be combined, they have an analogy, similarity or community of composition. Now consider bodies agreeing less and less, or bodies opposed to one another: their constitutive relations can no longer be directly combined, but present such differences that any resemblance between the bodies appears to be excluded. There is still however a similarity or community of composition, but this *from a more and more general viewpoint* which, in the limit, brings Nature as a whole into play. One must in fact take account of the "whole" formed by the two bodies, not with one another directly, but together with all the intermediary terms that allow us to pass from one to the other. As all relations are combined in Nature as a whole, Nature presents a similarity of composition that may be seen in all bodies from the most general viewpoint. One may pass from one body to another, however different, simply by changing the relation between its ultimate parts. For it is only relations that change in the universe as a whole, whose parts remain the same.

We thus arrive at what Spinoza calls a "common notion." A common notion is always an idea of a similarity of composition in existing modes. But there different kinds of such notions. Spinoza says that common notions may be more or less useful, more or less easily formed and also more or less universal — that is, they are organized in terms of the greater or lesser generality of their viewpoints.[7] One may in fact distinguish two main varieties of common notion. The less universal (but also the most useful) are those representing a similarity of composition between bodies that directly agree, and this from their own viewpoint. One common notion, for example, represents "what is common to a human body and to *certain* external bodies."[8] Through such notions we understand agreements between modes: they go beyond an external perception of agreements observed by chance, to find in a similarity of composition the necessary internal reason for an agreement of bodies.

At the other extreme the most universal common notions also represent a similarity or community of composition, but now between bodies that agree from a very general viewpoint, and not from *their own* viewpoint. They thus represent "what is common to all things," for example extension, or movement and rest — that is, the universal similarity of relations as combined *ad infinitum* from the viewpoint of Nature as a whole.[9] These notions also have their use, for they allow us to understand disagreements themselves, giving us a necessary internal reason for them. In fact, they allow us to determine the viewpoint beyond which a very general agreement between two bodies ends; they show us how and why opposition appears when we adopt a "less universal" viewpoint on these same two bodies. We are able, by making an experiment in thought, to vary a relation up to the point where the corresponding body takes on a nature in some sense "contrary" to its own; we can thereby understand the nature of disagreements between bodies with these or those relations. Thus, when assigning a role to all common notions taken as a whole, Spinoza says they internally determine the mind to understand the agreements of things, as well as their differences and oppositions.[10]

Spinoza carefully distinguishes common notions, on the one hand, and transcendental terms (being, thing, something) or universal notions (genera and species, man, horse, dog) on the other.[11] And yet common notions are themselves universal, "more or less" universal according to their degree of generality; one must then suppose that Spinoza is not attacking what is universal, but only a certain conception of abstract universality. Similarly, Spinoza is not criticizing the notions of genus and species in general; he himself speaks of horse and dog as natural types, of man himself as a normative type or model.[12] Here again, we must suppose that he is attacking only a certain abstract determination of genera and species. An abstract idea has, indeed, two aspects that reflect its inadequacy. In the first place it retains only gross sensible differences between things: we choose a sensible characteristic that is easily imagined; we distinguish objects possessing it from those that do not; we identify all those possessing it; as for minor differences, we pass over these, precisely because objects become confused once their number exceeds the capacity of our imagination. Second, a sensible differential characteristic is extremely variable: it is accidental, depending on the way objects affect each of us in chance encounters. "Those who have often regarded men's stature with wonder will understand by the word *man* an animal of erect stature. But those who have been accustomed to consider some other characteristic will form another general image of men – for example, that man is an animal capable of laughter, or a featherless biped, or a rational animal."[13] And the kind of characteristic selected changes not only from individual to individual, but also among the different objects affecting the same individual: certain objects are defined by their sensible form, others by their use or function, their manner of being and so on. On all counts, abstract ideas are thoroughly inadequate: they are images that are not explained by

277

our power of thinking, but that involve, rather, our impotence; images that do not express the nature of things, but indicate, rather, the variability of our human constitution.

In all this Spinoza is clearly attacking, not just the procedures of common sense, but the Aristotelian tradition also. The attempt to define genera and species through differences first appears in Aristotelian biology; and those sensible differences vary considerably in nature when different animals are in question. Against this tradition Spinoza proposes a grand principle: to consider structures, rather than sensible forms or functions.[14] But what is the meaning of "structure"? It is a system of relations between the parts of a body (these parts not being organs, but the anatomical components of those organs). By inquiring how these relations vary from one body to another, we have a way of directly determining the resemblances between two bodies, however disparate they may be. The form and function of an organ in a given animal depend solely on the relations between its organic parts, that is, between fixed anatomical components. In the limit Nature as a whole is a single Animal in which only the relations between the parts vary. For the examination of sensible differences is substituted an examination of intelligible similarities, which allow us to understand resemblances and differences between bodies "from the inside." Spinoza's common notions are biological, rather than physical or mathematical, ideas. They really do play the part of Ideas in a philosophy of Nature from which all finality has been excluded. (Spinoza's comments on this aspect of common notions are, indeed, rare. But then his comments on all aspects of common notions are rare, and we will see why. His suggestions nevertheless suffice to make him a forerunner of Geoffroy Saint-Hilaire, in the development of the great principle of compositional unity.[15])

Common notions are *general* rather than *abstract* ideas. And as such they are necessarily "adequate." Take the case of the less universal notions: what is common to my body and to certain external bodies is "equally" in each of these bodies; the idea is thus present in God, not only insofar as he has an idea of those external bodies, but also insofar as he simply has the idea of my body; thus I myself have the idea of something common to various bodies, and have it as it is in God.[16] As for the more universal notions: what is common to all things is "equally" in the part and in the whole, the idea is thus present in God, and so on.[17] These proofs underlie the two aspects in which common notions in general are necessarily adequate; in other words, *common notions are ideas that are formally explained by our power of thinking and that, materially, express the idea of God as their efficient cause.* They are explained by our power of thinking because, being in us as they are in God, they fall within our own power as they fall within the absolute power of God. They express the idea of God as their cause because, since God possesses them as we possess them, they necessarily "involve" God's essence. Indeed when Spinoza says that all ideas of particular things necessarily involve the eternal infinite essence of God, he means particular things as they are in God, and so ideas of things as possessed by God.[18] Among the ideas we *have*, the only ones capable of expressing God's essence, or of involving knowledge of this essence, are thus ideas that are in us as they are in God: in short, common notions.[19]

Several important consequences follow from this: 1. We were asking how we might attain adequate ideas. Everything about existence condemned us to having only inadequate ideas: we had ideas neither of ourselves, nor of external bodies, but only ideas of affections, indicating the effect of some external body on us. But precisely from such an effect, we can form the idea of what is common to some external body and our own. Given the conditions of our existence this is for us the only possible way of reaching an adequate idea. *The first adequate idea we have* is a common notion, the idea of "something common." 2. This idea is explained by our power of understanding or thinking. But the power of understanding is the soul's power of action. We are therefore active insofar as we form common notions. The forming of a common notion marks the point at which we enter into *full possession* of our power of action. It thereby constitutes the second stage of reason. Reason in its initial development is the effort to organize encounters on the basis of perceived agreements and disagreements. The very activity of reason is the effort to conceive common notions, and so to intellectually understand agreements and disagreements themselves. When we form a common notion our soul is said "to use reason": we come into the possession of our power of action or of understanding, we become reasonable beings. 3. A common notion is our first adequate idea. But whatever it be, it leads us directly to another adequate idea. An adequate idea is expressive, and what it expresses is the essence of God. Any common notion gives us direct knowledge of God's eternal infinite essence. Any adequate, that is to say, expressive idea, gives us knowledge of what it expresses, that is, adequate knowledge of God's essence itself.

There is, though, a danger of common notions appearing to intervene miraculously, unless we explain how we come to form them. *How do they come to break the concatenation of inadequate ideas to which we had seemed condemned?* "Common" does not of course mean merely something common to two or more bodies, but something common also to minds capable of forming an idea of it. Spinoza first of all reminds us that common notions can be more common or less common in different minds.[20] And even if they be identified with innate ideas, innateness in no way does away with the effort of forming them, a *causa fiendi* we need in order to rediscover what is already given only in principle. That common notions are in us as they are in God means only that, if we form them, we *have* them as God *has* them. But how, indeed, do we form them, in what favorable circumstances? How do we arrive at our power of action?

As long as we retain a speculative viewpoint, the problem remains insoluble. There seems to be a danger of two mistaken interpretations of the theory of common notions: overlooking their biological sense in favor of their mathematical one, and, above all, overlooking their practical sense in favor of their speculative content. The latter mistake may be explained by the way Spinoza himself introduces his system of common notions. For Part Two of the *Ethics* does indeed consider such notions from a purely speculative viewpoint, and therefore presents them in logical order, proceeding from the most universal to the least universal.[21] But there Spinoza is only showing that *if* we form common notions, they are necessarily adequate ideas. The cause and order of their formation is still unknown to us, as is their practical nature and function, which is merely suggested in Part Two.[22] It is true that all bodies have something in common, be it only extension, and movement and rest. Bodies that do not agree and are opposed to one another have nevertheless something in common, namely a very general similarity of composition which brings into play Nature as a whole under the attribute of Extension.[23] This indeed is why the presentation of common notions in logical order begins with the most universal: begins, then, with bodies very disparate one from another, and very opposed one to another. But if it be true that two opposed bodies have something in common, one can never, on the other hand, be opposed to the other or bad for the other through what it has in common with it: "No thing can be evil through what it has in common with our nature; but insofar as it is evil for us, it is contrary to us."[24] When we experience a bad affection, a sad passive affection produced in us by a body that disagrees with us, *nothing induces us to form the idea* of what is common to that body and our own. The opposite is the case when we experience a joyful affection: a thing being good to the extent that it agrees with our nature, the joyful affection itself induces us to form the corresponding common notion. The first common notions we form are thus the least universal, those, that is, that apply to our body and to another that agrees directly with our own and affects it with joy. If we consider the order in which common notions are formed, we must begin from the least universal; for the most universal, applying to bodies opposed to our own, have no *inductive principle* in the affections we experience.

In what sense are we here taking "induce"? What is in question is a kind of *occasional cause*.[a] Adequate ideas are formally explained by our power of understanding or action. But everything that is explained by our power of action depends only on our essence, and is thus "innate." But innateness had already, in Descartes, involved a kind of occasionalism. What is innate is active; but it can only become actual if it finds a favorable occasion among affections that come from outside us, among passive affections. Spinoza's scheme seems then to be as follows:

When we encounter a body that agrees with our own, when we experience a joyful passive affection, we are induced to form the idea of what is common to that body and our own. Thus Spinoza is led, in Part Five of the *Ethics*, to recognize the special part played by joyful passions in the formation of common notions: "*So long as we are not torn by feelings contrary to our nature* [feelings of sadness, provoked by contrary objects that do not agree with us], the power of the mind by which it strives to understand things is not hindered. So long, then, the mind has the power of forming clear and distinct ideas."[25] It is enough, in fact, for the hindrance to be lifted for the power of action to become actual, and for us to come into possession of what is innate in us. One can see why it was not enough just to accumulate joyful passions, in order to become active. The passion of love is linked to the passion of joy, and other feelings and desires are linked to love. All increase our power of action, but never to the point that we become active. These feelings must first become "secure"; we must first of all avoid sad passions which diminish our power of action; this is reason's initial endeavor. But we must then break out of the mere concatenation of passions, even joyful ones. For these still do not give us possession of our power of action; we have no adequate idea of objects that agree in nature with us; joyful passions are themselves born of inadequate ideas, which only indicate a body's effect on us. We must then, *by the aid of joyful passions*, form the idea of what is common to some external body and our own. For this idea alone, this common notion, is adequate. This is the second stage of reason; then, and then only, do we understand and act, and we are reasonable: this not through the accumulation of joyful passions as passions, but by a genuine "leap," which puts us in possession of an adequate idea, by the aid of such accumulation.

Why do we become active when we form a common notion or have an adequate idea? An adequate idea is explained by our power of understanding, and so by our power of action. It puts us in possession of this power, but how does it do this? We should remember that inadequate ideas also involve a concatenation of ideas that follow from them. A mind that forms an adequate *idea* is the adequate *cause* of the ideas that follow from it: this is the sense in which it is active.[26] What, then, are the ideas that follow from the common notion which we form by the aid of joyful passions? Joyful passions are ideas of the affections produced

by a body that agrees with our own; our mind by itself forms
the idea of what is common to that body and our own; *from this
flows an idea of the affection, a feeling, which is no longer passive,
but active.* Such a feeling is no longer a passion, because it follows from an adequate idea in us; it is itself an adequate idea.
It is distinct from the passive feeling from which we began, but
distinct only in its cause: its cause is no longer an inadequate
idea of an object that agrees with us, but the necessarily adequate idea of what is common to that object and ourselves. Thus
Spinoza can say: "A feeling which is a passion ceases to be a
passion as soon as we form a clear and distinct [adequate] idea
of it."[27] For we form a clear and distinct idea of it insofar as we
attach it to the common notion as to its cause; it is then active,
and dependent on our power of action. Spinoza does not mean
that all passion disappears: what disappears is not the passive
joy itself, but all the passions, all the desires linked to it and
connected with the idea of the external thing (the passion of
love, and so on).[28]

Any feeling determines our *conatus* to do something on the
basis of an idea of an object; *conatus*, thus determined, is called
a desire. But as long as we are determined by a feeling of passive
joy, our ideas are still irrational, since they are born of inadequate
ideas. But as well as passive joy we now have an active joy distinct only in its cause; from this active joy are born desires that
belong to reason, since they proceed from an adequate idea.[29]
"All the appetites, or desires, are passions only insofar as they arise
from inadequate ideas, and are counted as virtues when they are
aroused or generated by adequate ideas. For all the desires by
which we are determined to do something can arise as much from
adequate ideas as from inadequate ones."[30] Desires of reason thus
replace irrational desires, or rather, a rational concatenation of
desires is substituted for an irrational one: "We have the power

of ordering and connecting the affections of the body according to the order of the understanding."[31]

This whole process as described by Spinoza falls into four phases: (1) passive joy, which increases our power of action, and from which flow desires and passions based on a still inadequate idea; (2) the formation, by the aid of these joyful passions, of a common notion (an adequate idea); (3) active joy, which follows from this common notion and is explained by our power of action; (4) this active joy is added to the passive joy, but *replaces* the passions of desire born of the latter by desires belonging to reason, which are genuine actions. Spinoza's project is thus realized not by suppressing all passion, but by the aid of joyful passions restricting passions to the smallest part of ourselves, so that our capacity to be affected is exercised by a maximum of active affections.[32]

Spinoza shows at the opening of Part Five of the *Ethics* that a feeling ceases to be a passion once we form a clear and distinct (adequate) idea of it; and that we form a clear and distinct idea of it as soon as we attach it to a common notion as to its cause. Spinoza doesn't however apply this principle only to the feeling of joy, but asserts its applicability to *any* feeling: "There is no affection of the body of which we cannot form a clear and distinct concept."[33] The proof of this proposition is very concise: "Those things that are common to all can only be conceived adequately, and so...." Let us consider, then, the case of sadness. Spinoza obviously does not mean that sadness, being an inevitable passion, is itself common to all men or to all beings. He does not forget that a common notion is always the idea of something positive: nothing is common through mere impotence or through imperfection.[34] Spinoza means that, even in the case of a body that does not agree with our own, and affects us with sadness, we can form an idea of what is common to that body and our

285

own; the common notion will simply be very universal, implying a much more general viewpoint than that of the two bodies
confronting each other. It has nonetheless a practical function:
it makes us understand why these two bodies in particular do not
agree from their *own* viewpoint. "We see that sadness over some
good which has perished is lessened as soon as the man who has
lost it realizes that this good could not, in any way, have been
kept."[35] (The man in fact understands that his own body and the
external one could not have combined their relations in a dura-
ble way except in different circumstances: had there been intermediary terms, bringing into play the whole of Nature, from
whose viewpoint such a combination would have been possible.)
But when a very universal common notion makes us understand
a disagreement, a feeling of active joy again flows from this: *an
active joy always follows from what we understand.* "Insofar as we
understand the causes of sadness, it ceases to be a passion."[36] It
thus appears that, even if we begin from a sad passion, the basic
pattern of the earlier scheme is retained: sadness; forming a common notion; active joy flowing from it.

In Part Two of the *Ethics* Spinoza considers the speculative
content of common notions: he supposes them given or poten-
tially given; it is thus natural for him to proceed in a logical order
from the most universal to the least universal. At the opening of
Part Five he analyzes the practical function of common notions,
supposed given: that function consists in such notions being the
causes of adequate ideas of affections, that is, of active joys. The
principle applies to the most universal common notions as to the
least universal, and one can thus consider all common notions
taken together, in the unity of their practical function.

All is changed, though, when Spinoza asks later in Part Five
how we come to form common notions, we who seem condemned to inadequate ideas and passions. We then see that our

initial notions are necessarily the least universal ones. They are those that apply to my body and another body that agrees (or some other bodies that agree) with it; *these alone have a chance of being formed from the passive joys I experience*. The most universal, on the other hand, apply to all bodies, and so to very different bodies that are opposed to one another. But the sadness or opposition produced in us by a body that does not agree with our own never provides *the occasion to form* a common notion. So the process of forming common notions runs thus: We at first seek to experience a maximum of joyful passions (reason's initial endeavor). So we seek to avoid sad passions, to escape their concatenation and to avert bad encounters. We then, subsequently, use joyful passions to form corresponding common notions, whence flow active joys (the second effort of reason). These common notions are among the least universal, since they apply only to my body and to bodies that agree with it. But they strengthen our ability to avoid bad encounters; and above all they put us in possession of our power of action and understanding. *Thus, third,* we become capable of forming more universal common notions that apply in all cases, even to bodies opposed to us; we become capable of understanding even our sadness, and of drawing from such understanding an active joy. We can cope with bad encounters which we cannot avoid, and reduce the sadness that necessarily remains with us. But it must not be forgotten that, despite their general identity of practical function (that of producing active joys), common notions are all the more useful, all the more effective, for being less universal, proceeding from joyful passions.[37]

All common notions have the same speculative content: they involve a certain generality without abstraction. They all have the same practical function: as necessarily adequate ideas they are such that active joy necessarily flows from them. But they in no way share the same speculative and practical roles, when one considers the conditions in which they are formed. The first common notions we form are the least universal, since the principle of their induction lies in our joyful passions. We come into our power of action on the level of the "least universal": we accumulate passive joys, finding in them an opportunity to form common notions, from which flow active joys. The increase of our power of action thus presents us with the opportunity of coming into that power, or of becoming truly active. Having come into our true activity in some cases, we become capable of forming common notions even in less favorable cases. There is a whole learning process involved in common notions, in our *becoming active*: we should not overlook the importance in Spinozism of this formative process; we have to start from the least universal common notions, from the first we have a chance to form.

CHAPTER EIGHTEEN

Toward the Third Kind of Knowledge

The different kinds of knowledge are also different ways of living, different modes of existing. The first kind (imagination) is constituted by all inadequate ideas and passive affections in their concatenation.[1] This initial knowledge corresponds first of all to the *state of nature*: I perceive objects through chance encounters, and by the effect they have on me. Such an effect is but a "sign," a varying "indication." Such knowledge is had through *vague experience*,[a] and "vague" relates, etymologically, to the random character of encounters.[2] Here we know only Nature's "common order," know only the effects of encounters between parts according to purely extrinsic determinations.

But the *civil state* also belongs to the first kind of knowledge. Already in the state of nature, imagination forms universal abstract ideas, which retain this or that sensible characteristic of an object. The characteristic is designated by a name, which serves as a sign either for objects resembling the first, or for objects habitually linked with it.[3] But along with language and the civil state a second sort of sign develops, which is imperative rather than indicative. Signs appear to tell us what we *must* do to obtain a given result, achieve a given end: this is knowledge by *hearsay*. Thus, in Spinoza's famous example, a sign represents the operation we "must" perform on three numbers in order to find a fourth. Whether a law of nature or a technical rule, any law inevitably appears to us in a moral form just insofar as we have only an inadequate knowledge of it; a law seems to us a moral one, or of a moral type, whenever we make its effect depend on an imperative sign (rather than on the constitutive relations of things).

It is signs that give the first kind of knowledge its unity. They characterize a state of thought that is still inadequate, involved, unexplained. One must include even the *religious state* within this first kind of knowledge and existence, the state, that is, of man in relation to a God who gives him a revelation. This state differs from the state of nature no less than does the civil state itself: "No one knows by nature that he owes any obedience to God, nor can he attain thereto by any exercise of his reason, but solely by revelation confirmed by signs."[4] This religious state belongs nonetheless to the first kind of knowledge, precisely because it is part of our inadequate knowledge, because it is based on signs and manifests itself in the form of laws which demand and order things. Revelation is itself explained by the inadequate character of our knowledge, and bears only on certain of God's *propria*. The signs of Revelation constitute a third sort of sign and characterize the religion of the prophets, religion of the first kind or of imagination.

The second kind of knowledge corresponds in the *Ethics* to the state of reason: a knowledge of common notions and through common notions. This is where the real break between different kinds of knowledge appears in the *Ethics*: "Knowledge of the second and third kinds, and not of the first kind, teaches us to distinguish the true from the false."[5] We enter, with common notions, into the domain of *expression*: these notions are our first adequate ideas, they draw us out of the world of inadequate signs. And because any common notion leads us to the idea of the God whose essence it expresses, the second kind of knowledge also involves a second kind of religion: no longer a religion of imagination, but one of understanding. The expression of Nature replaces signs, love replaces obedience; this is no longer the religion of the prophets but, on its various levels, the religion of Solomon, the religion of the Apostles, and the true religion of Christ founded on common notions.[6]

But what exactly do we know of these notions? Common notions do not of course constitute the essence of any particular thing. And yet one cannot define simply them by their generality. *The notions apply to particular existing modes, and have no sense independently of such application.* Representing (from more or less general viewpoints) the similarity of composition of existing modes, they are for us the only means of reaching an adequate knowledge of the characteristic relations of bodies, of the combination of these relations and of the laws of composition. Once again, this is well seen in the case of numbers: in the second kind of knowledge we do not apply rules known by hearsay, as one would obey a moral law; by understanding the rule of proportionality through a common notion, we grasp the way that the constitutive relations of three given numbers are combined. Thus common notions give us knowledge of the positive order of Nature as an order of constitutive or characteristic relations by which bodies agree with, and are opposed to, one another. Laws of Nature no longer appear as commands and prohibitions, but for what they are: eternal truths, norms of composition, rules for the realization of powers. This order of Nature expresses God as its source; and the more we know things according to this order, the more our ideas themselves express God's essence. All our knowledge expresses God, when it is governed by common notions.

Common notions are one of the fundamental discoveries of the *Ethics*. We must here attach great importance to the chronology. Ferdinand Alquié has recently insisted that the introduction in the *Ethics* of common notions marks a decisive point in the development of Spinozism.[7] Indeed, nothing is made of them either in the *Short Treatise* or in the *Correction of the Understanding*. Things are already known in the *Short Treatise* to have characteristic relations, but the discovery of these is entrusted to "reasoning," and there is no mention of common notions.[8] In addition, what there corresponds to the second kind of knowledge (the second "mode of consciousness") does not constitute an adequate knowledge, but only a right belief. And the third "mode of perception," which in the *Correction of the Understanding* corresponds to the second kind of knowledge, still amounts only to a clear knowledge, rather than an adequate one: and it is not in the least defined by common notions but by a Cartesian type of inference and an Aristotelian type of deduction.[9]

However, one does find in the *Correction of the Understanding*, in *an altogether different context*, a foreshadowing of, and approximation to, what will later become common notions. Thus a famous passage speaks of "fixed and eternal things" which, from being omnipresent, are for us "like universals, or genera of the definitions of singular, changeable things": one recognizes in these the most universal notions, extension, movement, rest, which are common to all things. And when the remainder of the passage argues for still other "aids" necessary for the understanding of singular changing things, one thinks of the role of less universal common notions.[10] If the passage raises many difficulties, this is because it is written from the viewpoint of the highest mode of perception or kind of knowledge, relating to essences themselves: laws are inscribed in fixed and eternal things, says

Spinoza, as in their true codes; but these laws seem to be the laws of production of essences as well as the laws of composition of relations. [11]

How can we explain Spinoza's conflation here of such different sorts of law? I would suggest that he only had an intimation of common notions as he progressed in the composition of the *Correction of the Understanding*. But he had by then already and otherwise defined the third mode of perception (corresponding to what would become the second kind of knowledge). So constant and eternal things, playing the part of universals, found a place only on the level of the highest kind or mode of perception: and they were thus also taken as the principles of our knowledge of essences. Another role would have been possible, but Spinoza would then have had to go back and recast his description of modes of perception in terms of his new idea. This would partly explain why Spinoza gave up the idea of completing the *Correction of the Understanding* precisely at the point where he came to the exposition of what he himself calls common properties. The hypothesis would also allow us to date Spinoza's full development of the theory of common notions between the abandoning of the *Correction of the Understanding* and the composition of the *Ethics*. This full possession would then have induced a desire to modify the *Treatise*, reformulating the theory of the second kind or third mode of perception, by giving an autonomous and distinct development of common notions; thus Spinoza, in the *Ethics*, speaks of a treatise in which he proposes to develop these points. [12]

When Spinoza discovers that common notions are our first adequate ideas, a gap opens between the first and second kinds of knowledge. The existence of such a gap should not however lead us to overlook a whole system of correspondences between the two kinds, without which the forming of an adequate idea

293

or a common notion would remain incomprehensible. We have seen in the first place that the civil state was a substitute for reason, prepared the way for reason, and imitated it. This would be impossible did not moral laws and imperative signs, despite the contradictions they involve, coincide in a way with the true positive order of Nature. So it was indeed the laws of Nature that the prophets grasped and transmitted, even though they inadequately understood them. Similarly, a society's primary endeavor is to choose signs and institute laws that correspond as a whole, as far as possible, to the order of Nature, and, above all, to man's survival in that order. The variability of signs becomes in this respect an advantage, and opens up to us possibilities that do not belong to understanding on its own account, but rather to imagination. [13] What is more, reason would never come to form common notions, that is, come into its power of action, did it not try to find itself in that first effort that consists in selecting joyful passions. Before becoming active we must select and link together passions that increase our power of action. But such passions are related to images of objects that agree in nature with us; these images themselves are, once more, inadequate ideas, mere indications which give us knowledge of objects through the effect they have on us. Reason would not then "find" itself, were its first effort not traced out in the frame of the first kind of knowledge, using all the resources of imagination.

If we consider their origin, common notions find in imagination the very conditions of their formation. Considered, moreover, in their practical function, they apply only to things that can be imagined. Thus they may themselves, in some respects, be likened to images. [14] *The application of common notions implies, in general, a strange harmony between reason and imagination, between the laws of reason and those of imagination.* Spinoza analyzes various cases. He had shown in Parts Three and Four of the

294

Ethics under which particular laws of imagination a passion becomes more or less intense, more or less strong. Thus our feeling toward something we simply imagine is stronger than the feeling we experience when we believe the thing to be necessary or
necessitated. [15] But the fundamental law of reason amounts precisely to considering things as necessary: common notions allow
us to understand the necessity of the agreements and disagreements between bodies. Reason thus profits from one of the fea-
tures of imagination: the more we understand things as necessary,
the less we feel the strength or intensity of passions rooted in
imagination.[16] Imagination is subject to a law according to which
it always initially asserts the presence of its object, is then affected
by causes that exclude such a presence, and enters into a kind
of "vacillation," thinking of its object only as possible, or even
contingent. The process of imagining an object thus contains
within it the principle of its own dissipation over time. But reason's law is to form common notions, that is, ideas of properties
"which we always regard as present." [17] Reason here satisfies the
demands of imagination better than can imagination itself. Imagination, carried along by its fate, which is to be affected by varying causes, doesn't manage to maintain the presence of its object.
Reason doesn't only diminish the relative strength of passions:
"taking time into account" the active feelings born of reason
or of common notions are in themselves stronger than any of
the passive feelings born of imagination.[18] By imagination's law,
a feeling is so much the stronger, the more causes act together
to provoke it. [19] But a common notion, by its law, applies or
relates to several things, or images of things easily associated
with them: it is therefore frequent and lively.[20] It thus diminishes the intensity of feelings of imagination, since it determines
the mind to consider several objects. And these objects associated with the notion are like so many causes favorable to the

feeling of reason which flows from the notion.[21]

Necessity, presence and frequency are the three characteristics of common notions. And these characteristics ensure that the notions in a certain way impose themselves on the imagination, either reducing the intensity of passive feelings, or guaranteeing the liveliness of active ones. Common notions use the laws of imagination to free us from imagination itself. Their necessity, presence and frequency allow them to intervene in the movement of imagination, and divert its course to their own ends. It is not too much to speak here of a *general harmony* of imagination and reason.

The greater part of the Ethics – *more precisely, down to V.21 – is written from the viewpoint of the second kind of knowledge.* For it is only through common notions that we come to have adequate ideas and an adequate knowledge of God himself. This does not amount to a condition of any knowledge, but to a condition of our knowledge, insofar as we are finite existing modes composed of a soul and a body. We who have at first only inadequate ideas and passive affections, can come into our power of understanding and action only by forming common notions. All our knowledge comes to us through such notions. Whence Spinoza can say that not even God's existence is known through itself, but "must necessarily be inferred from notions so firmly and incontrovertibly true, that no power can be postulated or conceived sufficient to impugn them."[22] The same admission is to be found in the *Ethics*: Part One gives us knowledge of God, and of all things as they depend on God; but this knowledge is itself of the second kind.[23]

All bodies agree in certain things, such as extension, movement and rest. The ideas of extension, movement and rest are for us very universal common notions, since they apply to all existing bodies. We may then ask whether the idea of God should itself be considered as a common notion, as the most universal of all? Many passages appear to suggest this.[24] But it is not however the case: our idea of God is closely related to common notions, but is not itself one of them. The idea of God is in a sense opposed to common notions in that they always apply to things that can be imagined, while God cannot be imagined.[25] Spinoza says only that common notions lead us to the idea of God, that they necessarily "give" us knowledge of God, and that without them we would not have such knowledge.[26] For, a common notion is an adequate idea; an adequate idea is an idea that is expressive; and what it expresses is God's very essence. The relation of the idea of God to common notions is thus one of expression. Common notions express God as the source of all the constitutive relations of things. As it relates to these notions that express it, the idea of God is the basis of religion of the second kind. For active feelings, active joys, flow from common notions; and they do so "accompanied by the idea of God." The love of God is just such joy so accompanied.[27] Reason's highest endeavor, insofar as it conceives common notions, is thus to know God and to love him.[28] (But this God connected with common notions does not have to respond to our love; he is an impassive God, who gives us nothing in return. For, however active, joys flowing from common notions are inseparable from those passive joys resulting from imagination which initially increased our power of action, and served us as the occasional causes of our action. And God is himself free of passions: he feels no passive joy, nor any active joy of the type that presupposes a passive joy.[29])

One recalls the methodological principle of the *Correction of the Understanding*, that we cannot start from the idea of God, but must reach it as quickly as possible. And the "quickest possible" way was there presented thus: we had to begin from what was positive in some idea we had; we strove to make that idea adequate; it was adequate when referred to its cause, when it expressed its cause; but in expressing its cause it also expressed the idea of God as determining that cause to produce such an effect. We were thus in danger of entering an infinite regression from cause to cause: God was expressed at each level as what determined that level of causality.

I believe it is wrong to contrast the *Ethics* and the *Correction of the Understanding* on this point. *The* Ethics *begins with God as absolutely infinite substance no more than does the* Correction. The *Ethics* does not begin from God as something unconditioned; we have seen the role of its opening propositions in this respect. The project of the *Ethics* is the same as that of the *Correction of the Understanding*: to rise as quickly as possible to the idea of God, without falling into an infinite regression, without making God himself into a remote cause. So if the *Ethics* is to be contrasted with the *Correction of the Understanding*, this should not be in terms of any change of method, or still less any change of principles, but only insofar as the *Ethics* has found less artificial and more concrete means. These means (up to V.21) are common notions. We no longer start from what is positive in some idea or other, in order to try and form an adequate idea: such a procedure is very unsure and remains indeterminate. We start from what is positive in a joyful passion; this determines us to form a common notion, as our first adequate idea. We then form more and more general common notions, which together constitute the system of reason; but each common notion, on its own level, expresses God and leads us to knowledge of God. Every common notion expresses God as the source of the relations combined together in the bodies to which the notion applies. It should not be said that the most universal notions better express God than less universal ones. And, above all, one should not suggest that the idea of God is itself a common notion, the most universal of all: but each notion leads us to it, each expresses it, the least universal along with the most universal. In the system of expression God is never a remote cause.

The idea of God thus plays in the *Ethics* a pivotal role. Everything turns about it, everything changes along with it. Spinoza announces that "besides" the second kind of knowledge, there is a third.[30] He furthermore presents the second kind as the driving force of the third: the second kind determines us to enter into the third, to "form" the third.[31] But how does the second kind so determine us? *Only the idea of God can explain the transition*, which appears in the *Ethics* at V.20–21. 1. Every common notion leads us to the idea of God. As related to the common notions which express it, the idea of God itself belongs to the second kind of knowledge. It represents, in this respect, an impassive God; but the idea accompanies all the joys that flow from our power of understanding (insofar as this power proceeds through common notions). The idea of God is thus the limiting point of the second kind of knowledge. 2. But although it necessarily relates to common notions, the idea of God is not itself a common notion. So it propels us into a new element. We can come to the idea of God only through the second kind of knowledge; but in arriving at the idea we are determined to leave behind the second kind of knowledge, and enter into a new state. In the second kind of knowledge, the idea of God serves as a basis of the third; and by "basis" must be understood the true driving force, the *causa fiendi*.[32] This idea of God will itself then change in content, taking on another content in the third kind of knowledge to which it determines us.

Two of the characteristics of a common notion are to apply to several existing modes, and to give us knowledge of the relations through which existing modes agree or are opposed. In the limiting case, it is understandable how the idea of an attribute initially appears to be a common notion: the idea of extension is a very universal notion in that it applies to all existing bodies; and the idea of the infinite modes of Extension makes known to us the agreement of all bodies from the viewpoint of Nature as a whole. But the idea of God, which is joined to, or "accompanies" all common notions, leads us to a reappraisal of attributes and modes. Here again, the *Ethics* follows the *Correction of the Understanding*: the idea of God affects our entry into the domain of "real beings" and their connection. An attribute is no longer understood merely as a *common property* of all the *existing modes* corresponding to it, but as what constitutes the *singular essence* of divine substance, and as what contains all the *particular essences* of its modes. The third kind of knowledge is defined as proceeding "from an adequate idea of the formal essence of certain attributes of God to the adequate knowledge of the essence of things."[33] Attributes are still common forms; what has changed is the sense of the word "common." Common no longer means more general, that is, applicable to several existing modes, or to all existing modes of a certain kind. Common means univocal: attributes are univocal, or common to God whose singular essence they constitute, and to the modes whose particular essences they contain. In short, a fundamental difference appears between the second and third kinds of knowledge: ideas of the second kind are defined by their general function; they apply to existing modes and give us knowledge of the composition of the relations that characterize those modes. Ideas of the third kind are defined by their singular nature; they represent God's essence and give us knowledge of particular essences as these are contained in God himself.[34]

We are ourselves existing modes. Our knowledge is subject to the condition that we must pass through common notions to reach ideas of the third kind. Far from being able to deduce the relation that characterizes a mode from its essence, we must first know the relation, if we are to come to know the essence. We must similarly conceive Extension as a common notion before understanding it as constituting God's essence. The second kind of knowledge is for us the efficient cause of the third kind; and in the second kind it is the idea of God that allows us to pass from second to third kind. We begin by forming common notions that express God's essence; only then can we understand God as expressing himself in essences. This condition of our knowledge is not a condition of all knowledge: the true Christ does not proceed through common notions. He adapts or conforms what he teaches us to common notions, but his own knowledge is directly of the third kind; God's existence is thus known to him through itself, as are all essences, and the order of essences.[35] Thus Spinoza says that, unlike Christ, we do not know God's existence through itself.[36] In the natural situation of our existence we are filled with inadequate ideas and passive affections; we will never reach any adequate idea or active joy, if we do not first form common notions. Yet it should not be concluded that God is known to us only *indirectly*. Common notions have nothing to do with signs; they simply constitute the conditions in which we ourselves attain to the third kind of knowledge. Thus the proofs of God's existence are not indirect proofs: in them the idea of God is still grasped in its relation to common notions, but it determines us, precisely, to "form" the third kind of knowledge, to enter into a direct vision.

CHAPTER NINETEEN

Beatitude

The first kind of knowledge has as its object only encounters between parts of bodies, seen in terms of their extrinsic determinations. The second kind rises to the composition of characteristic relations. But the third kind alone relates to eternal essences: the knowledge of God's essence, of particular essences as they are in God, and as conceived by God. (We thus rediscover in the three kinds of knowledge the three aspects of the order of nature: the order of passions, that of the composition of relations and that of essences themselves). Now essences have various characteristics. They are in the first place particular essences, and so irreducible one to another: each is a real being, a *res physica*, a degree of power or intensity. Thus Spinoza can oppose the third kind of knowledge to the second, by saying that the second shows us in general terms that everything that exists depends on God, but the third alone allows us to understand the dependence of some given essence in particular.[1] On the other hand, however, each essence agrees with all others. For all essences are involved in the production of each. This is not a case of more or less general relative agreement between existing modes, but of an agreement that is at once singular and absolute, of each essence with all others.[2] So the mind cannot know an essence, that is, know a

303

thing *sub specie aeternitatis*, without being determined to know still more things, and to desire more and more such knowledge.[3] Essences are, lastly, expressive: not only does each essence express all the others in the principle of its production, but it expresses God as this principle itself, containing all essences, and the principle on which each particular essence depends. Each essence is a part of God's power, and is thus conceived through God's essence itself, insofar as God's essence is explicated through *that* essence.[4]

The highest knowledge thus has three elements. An adequate idea, first, of ourselves and of our own essence (an idea expressing the essence of our body *sub specie aeternitatis*): everyone forms an idea of their own essence, and it is of such an idea that Spinoza is thinking when he says that the third kind of knowledge shows us how some essence *in particular* depends on God.[5] An adequate idea, second, of the greatest number of possible things, this again in their essence or *sub specie aeternitatis*. And an adequate idea, third, of God, as containing all essences, and comprising all in the production of each (and so in the production of our own essence in particular).

Myself, things and God are the three ideas of the third kind. From them flow joys, a desire and a love. Joys of the third kind are active joys: for they are explained by our own essence and are always "accompanied" by an adequate idea of this essence. Everything we understand within the third kind of knowledge, including the essences of other things and that of God, we understand on the basis of conceiving our own essence (that of our body) *sub specie aeternitatis*.[6] The third kind of knowledge thus has no other *formal cause* than our power of action and of understanding, the power of thinking, that is, of God himself, insofar as he is explicated through our own essence.[7] In the third kind of knowledge all ideas have as their formal cause our power of understanding. All the affections that follow from these ideas are thus of the nature of active affections, active joys.[8] I must conceive God's essence as affecting mine, and essences as affecting one another; but an essence has no affections that are not formally explained by the essence itself, that are not, then, accompanied by the idea of oneself as formal cause or by the consideration of one's power of action.

From the joy that flows from an adequate idea of ourselves is born a *desire*, a desire to know ever more things in their essence or *sub specie aeternitatis*. And there is born, above all, a *love*. For in the third kind of knowledge the idea of God is, in its turn, the material cause of all ideas. All essences express God as that through which they are conceived: the idea of my own essence represents my power of action, but my power of action is just the power of God himself insofar as it is explicated through my essence. There is thus no joy of the third kind which is not accompanied by the idea of God as its material cause: "From the third kind of knowledge there necessarily arises an intellectual Love of God. For from this kind of knowledge there arises joy, accompanied by the idea of God as cause."[9]

But how are active joys of the third kind to be distinguished from those of the second kind? Joys of the second kind are already active, since they are explained by some adequate idea that we have. They are, then, explained by our power of understanding or action. They imply our full possession of this power. But although this power seems incapable of any increase, it still lacks a certain quality, a particular qualitative difference characterized by the degree of power or intensity of our own essence itself. Indeed, so long as we remain with the second kind of knowledge, our adequate ideas still do not include one of ourselves, our essence, the essence of our body. This limitation is seen to be important once one recalls the starting point of the problem of knowledge: we do not immediately have an adequate idea of ourselves or our body, because this idea is only in God insofar as he is affected by ideas of other bodies; we do not therefore know our own body except through necessarily inadequate ideas of affections, and we do not know ourselves except through ideas of these ideas; as for ideas of external bodies, as for the idea of our own body or our own mind, we do not *have* these, in the immediate conditions of our existence. Now, the second kind of knowledge does indeed give us adequate ideas; but these are only ideas of properties common to our body and external bodies. They are adequate because they are in a part as they are in the whole, and because they are in us, in our mind, as they are in the ideas of other things. But they in no way amount to an adequate idea of *ourselves*, nor to an adequate idea of some *other thing*.[10] They are explained by our essence but do not themselves constitute an idea of this essence. With the third kind of knowledge, on the other hand, we come to form adequate ideas of ourselves and of other things as they are in God, and as conceived by God. The active joys that flow from ideas of the third kind are thus of a different nature from those that flow from ideas of the second kind. And, more generally, Spinoza is now able to distinguish two forms of the mind's activity, two modes in which we are active and feel ourselves to be active, two expressions of our power of understanding: "It is of the nature of reason to conceive things *sub specie aeternitatis* [second kind of knowledge], and it also pertains to the nature of the mind to conceive the body's essence *sub specie aeternitatis* [third kind], and beyond *these two*, nothing else pertains to the mind's essence."[11]

All affections, whether passive or active, are affections of an essence to the extent that they exercise the capacity to be affected in which the essence expresses itself. But passive affec-

tions, whether of sadness or joy, are *adventitious*, being produced
from outside; active affections, active joys, are *innate* because they
are explained by our essence or our power of understanding.[12]
And yet it is as though what is innate had two different dimensions, which account for the difficulties we experience in coming upon it or finding it. In the first place, common notions are
themselves innate, as are the active joys that flow from them. But
this does not stop them having to be formed, and formed either
more or less easily, and so being more or less common to different minds. The apparent contradiction disappears, if we consider
that we are born cut off from our power of action or understanding: we must, in our existence, come into what belongs to our
essence. We cannot, in particular, form common notions, even
the most general of these, unless we find a starting point in joyful passions which initially increase our power of action. Thus
the active joys that flow from common notions find as it were
their occasional causes in passive affections of joy: in principle
innate, they nonetheless depend on adventitious affections as
their occasional causes. But God himself immediately possesses
an infinite power of action incapable of any increase. God therefore no more experiences any passion, not even a joyful one, than
he has inadequate ideas. But the question also arises of knowing
whether common notions, and the active joys that flow from
them, are in God. Being adequate ideas, common notions are
indeed in God, but this only insofar as he has other ideas that
necessarily contain them (these other ideas are for us those of
the third kind).[13] So neither God, nor Christ who is the expression of his thought, think *through* common notions. Common
notions cannot, then, serve in God as the principles of joys corresponding to those we experience in the second kind of knowledge:
God is free of passive joys, and he doesn't even experience those
active joys of the second kind that presuppose an increase in the

power of action as their occasional cause. Thus *according to the ideas of the second kind we have of them*, God experiences no feelings of joy.[14]

Ideas of the third kind are not only explained by our essence, they consist of the idea of this essence itself, and of its relations (its relation to the idea of God, its relations with the ideas of other things, *sub specie aeternitatis*). From the idea of our essence as formal cause, and the idea of God as material cause, we can conceive all ideas as they are in God. In the third kind of knowledge we form ideas and active feelings that are in us as they are immediately and eternally in God. We think as God thinks, we experience the very feelings of God. We form the idea of ourselves as it is in God, and form at least in part the idea of God as it is in God himself: ideas of the third kind thus constitute a deeper dimension of what is innate, and joys of the third kind are the only true affections of an essence in itself. We do of course appear to *reach* the third kind of knowledge.[15] But what here serve us as occasional causes are common notions themselves, and so something adequate and active. The "transition" is only an appearance; in reality we are simply finding ourselves as we are immediately and eternally in God. "The mind has had eternally the same perfections which, in our fiction, now come to it."[16] Those joys that follow from ideas of the third kind are therefore the only ones that deserve the name of *beatitude*: they are no longer joys that increase our power of action, nor even joys that still presuppose such an increase, but joys that derive absolutely from our essence, as it is in God, and as conceived by God.[17]

We must further ask: What is the difference between the idea of God of the second kind, and that of the third kind? The idea of God belongs to the second kind of knowledge only through its relation to the common notions that express it. And the conditions of our knowledge are such that we "reach" the idea of

God through common notions. But the idea of God is not itself one of these notions. It is this idea, then, that leads us out of the second kind of knowledge and reveals to us a new content of knowledge: no longer common properties, but God's essence, my essence and all the other essences that depend on God. Now, insofar as the idea of God relates to common notions, it represents a sovereign being who experiences no love and no joy. But in determining us to the third kind of knowledge, it itself receives new qualifications corresponding to this kind of knowledge. The active joys we experience in the third kind of knowledge are the joys experienced by God himself, because the ideas from which they flow are in us as they are eternally and immediately in God. No contradiction should be seen, then, between the two kinds of love whose descriptions succeed one another in Part Five of the *Ethics*: the love of a God who cannot love us, as he experiences no joy, and the love of a God who is himself joyful, who loves himself and loves us with the same love by which we love him. It is enough, as the context suggests, to relate the initial passages to the second kind of knowledge, and the others to the third kind.[18]

Proceeding as they do from the idea of ourselves as it is in God, our active joys are part of God's joys. Our joy is the joy of God himself insofar as he is explicated through our essence. And the love of the third kind which we feel for God is "a part of the infinite love by which God loves himself." The love we feel for God is the love God feels for himself insofar as he is explicated through our own essence, and so the love he feels for our essence itself.[19] *Beatitude* designates the possession not only of an active joy as it is in God, but of an active love as it is in God also.[20] The word "part" must in all this always be understood in an explicative or expressive manner: a part is not a component, but an expression and explication. Our essence is a part of God, and the idea of our essence a part of the idea of God, only to the extent that God's essence explicates itself through ours. And it is in the third kind of knowledge that the system of expression takes on its final form. This final form of expression is the identity of speculative and practical affirmation, the identity of Being and Joy, of Substance and Joy, of God and Joy. Joy manifests the unfolding of substance itself, its explication in modes and the consciousness of this explication. The idea of God is no longer simply expressed by common notions in general, but is what expresses and explicates itself in all essences according to their own principle of production. It expresses itself in each essence in particular, but each essence comprises all other essences in the law of its production. The joy we feel is the joy God himself feels insofar as he has an idea of our essence; the joy God feels is that which we ourselves feel insofar as we have ideas as they are in God.

Once we come to exist in duration, and so "during" our existence itself, we can come into the third kind of knowledge. But we can only succeed in doing so according to a strict order, which corresponds to the optimal exercise of our capacity to be affected: 1. We begin with inadequate ideas which come to us, and passive affections which flow from them, some increasing our power of action, others diminishing it; 2. We then form common notions as a result of an effort of selection among these passive affections themselves; active joys of the second kind follow from common notions, and an active love follows from the idea of God as it relates to common notions; 3. We then form adequate ideas of the third kind, and the active joys and active love that follow from these ideas (beatitude). But it is a vain hope, while we exist in duration, to have only active joys of the third kind, or just active affections in general. We will always have passions, and sadness together with our passive joys. Our knowledge will always pass through common notions. All that we can strive toward is to have proportionately more joyful passions than sad ones, more active joys of the second kind than passions, and the greatest possible number of joys of the third kind. It is all a question of the relative proportions of the different kinds of feeling that exercise our capacity to be affected: a matter of making inadequate ideas and passions take up only *the smallest part of ourselves.*[21]

Duration relates to the existence of modes. It will be recalled that a mode's existence is constituted by extensive parts which are determined, in a certain relation, to belong to the mode's essence. Thus duration is measured by time: a body exists as long as it possesses extensive parts in the relation that characterizes it. As soon as encounters arrange these parts differently, the body itself ceases to exist, its parts forming other bodies with different relations. It is therefore obvious that we cannot eliminate all passion during our existence: for our extensive parts are determined and affected from outside *ad infinitum.* To the parts of the body there correspond *faculties* of the soul, faculties of experiencing passive affections. Thus imagination corresponds to the actual imprint of some body in our own, and memory to the succession of imprints in time. Memory and imagination are true parts of the soul. The soul has extensive parts which belong to it only to the extent that it is the idea of a body that is itself composed of extensive parts.[22] The soul "endures" to the extent that it expresses the actual existence of a body that endures. And the soul's faculties themselves involve a power, a power of suffering, a power of imagining things according to the affections they produce in our body, and so a power of conceiving things in duration, and in relation to time.[23]

Extensive parts belong to an essence within a certain relation and during a certain time; but they do not constitute that essence.

The essence itself has an altogether different nature. In itself the essence is a degree of power or intensity, an intensive part. Nothing seems to me more mistaken than a mathematical interpretation of particular essences in Spinoza. An essence does, it is true, express itself in a relation, but it is not the same as that relation. A particular essence is a physical reality; thus affections are affections of an essence and the essence itself the essence of a body. The physical reality is an intensive reality, an intensive existence. One sees from this that essence does not endure. Duration is predicated in relation to extensive parts, and is measured by the time during which these parts belong to the essence. But the essence has in itself an eternal reality or existence; it has no duration, nor any time to mark the end of such duration (no essence can destroy any other). Spinoza actually says that essence is *conceived* "by a certain eternal necessity."[24] But this formulation does not, in its turn, permit of any intellectualist or idealist interpretation. Spinoza simply means that a particular essence is not of itself eternal. Divine substance alone is eternal by virtue of itself; an essence is only eternal by virtue of a cause (God), from which its existence or reality as an essence derives. It is thus necessarily conceived through that cause; and is thus necessarily conceived with the eternal necessity deriving from that cause. It should come as no surprise that Spinoza consequently speaks of "the idea which expresses the essence of this or that human body *sub specie aeternitatis.*" He doesn't mean that the body's essence exists only as an idea. The mistake in the idealist interpretation is to turn against parallelism an argument that is an integral part of it, or to understand as a proof of ideality a purely causal argument. If an idea in God expresses the essence of this or that body, it is because God is the cause of essences; it follows that an essence is necessarily conceived through this cause.[25]

A body exists and endures as long as it actually possesses

extensive parts. But it has an essence that is, so to speak, an eternal intensive part (a degree of power). The soul itself has extensive parts, insofar as it expresses the existence of a body in duration. But it also has an eternal intensive part, which is, so to speak, the idea of the body's essence. The idea that expresses the body's essence constitutes the soul's intensive part or essence, and is necessarily eternal. The soul has in this respect a faculty, that is a power, explained by its own essence: an active power of understanding, of understanding things through the third kind of knowledge *sub specie aeternitatis*. Insofar as it expresses the body's actual existence in duration, the soul has the power to conceive other bodies in duration; insofar as it expresses the body's essence, it has the power to conceive other bodies *sub specie aeternitatis*.[26]

Spinozism thus asserts a difference of nature between duration and eternity. If Spinoza avoids using the concept of *immortality* in the *Ethics*, this is because it seems to him to involve the most tiresome confusions. Three arguments may be found, variously employed, in a tradition of immortality which runs from Plato to Descartes. Theories of immortality rest, in the first place, on a certain postulated simplicity of the soul: the body alone is conceived as divisible; the soul is immortal because it is indivisible, its faculties not being its parts. The immortality of this absolutely simple soul is, in the second place, conceived in duration: the soul already existed before the body began to exist, and endures when the body ceases to exist. Thus theories of immortality often involve the assumption of a purely intellectual memory, by which the soul separated from the body can be conscious of its own duration. Finally, immortality thus defined cannot be the object of a direct experience while the body endures. In what form does the soul survive the body, what are the modalities of survival, what are the faculties of the soul once it is disembodied? Only a *revelation* can tell us in our present state.

These three principles find in Spinoza an avowed opponent. Theories of immortality always involve a confusion of duration with eternity. The postulate of the soul's simplicity, in the first place, itself always involves a confused idea of the union of soul and body. Comparing soul and body, one opposes the simplicity of the soul taken as a whole to the divisibility of the body, also taken as a whole. It is seen that the body has extensive parts while it exists, but it is not seen that the soul also has such parts insofar as it is the idea of an existing body. One sees (more or less clearly) that the soul has an absolutely simple and eternal intensive part which constitutes its essence, but one doesn't see that this also expresses the body's essence, which is no less simple and eternal. "Immortality" invites us, in the second place, to think in terms of succession, and renders us incapable of conceiving the soul as a composite of coexisting things. We do not see that while the body exists, duration and eternity themselves "coexist" in the soul as two elements different in nature. The soul endures insofar as there belong to it extensive parts that do not constitute its essence. The soul is eternal insofar as there belongs to it an intensive part that defines its essence. We should not imagine that the soul endures beyond the body: it endures while the body itself endures, and it is eternal insofar as it expresses the body's essence. While the soul is the idea of an existing body, there coexist in it extensive parts that belong to it in duration, and an intensive part that constitutes it in eternity. Finally, we have no need of any revelation in order to know in what modes the soul survives, and how. The soul eternally remains what it already is in its essence during the body's existence: an intensive part, a degree of power or power of understanding, an idea that expresses the body's essence *sub specie aeternitatis*. Thus the soul's eternity can indeed be the object of a direct experience. To feel and experience that we are eternal, it is enough to enter into the third kind of knowledge, that is, to form the idea of ourselves as it is in God. This idea is just the idea that expresses the body's essence; to the extent that we form it, to the extent that we have it, we *experience* that we are eternal. [27]

What happens when we die? Death is a subtraction, a cutting-back. We lose all the extensive parts that belonged to us in a certain relation; our soul loses all the faculties it possessed insofar as it expressed the existence of a body itself endowed with extensive parts. [28] But for all that these parts and faculties belonged to our essence they *constituted* nothing of it: our essence considered simply as such loses none of its perfection when we lose the elements of extension of which our existence was composed. The part of us that remains, however great (that is, whatever its degree of power or intensive quantity), is in any case more perfect than all the extensive parts which perish, and conserves all its perfection when those extensive parts disappear. [29] When, furthermore, our body has ceased to exist, when our soul has lost all those parts that related to the body's existence, we are no longer in a state in which we can experience passive affections. [30] Our essence is no longer kept in a state of involvement, we can no longer be cut off from our power: all that remains, indeed, is our power of understanding or action. [31] The ideas we have are necessarily adequate ideas of the third kind, as they are in God. Our essence adequately expresses God's essence, and the affections of our essence adequately express our essence. *We become completely expressive*, nothing remains that is "involved" or merely "indicated." While we existed we could have only a certain number of active affections of the third kind, themselves related to active affections of the second kind, which were in turn related to passive affections. We could hope for only partial beatitude. But death seems to put us in a situation where we can only be affected by affections of the third kind, which are themselves explained by our essence.

This point does, it is true, still raise many problems. 1. In what sense are we, after death, still affected? Our soul has lost everything that belonged to it as the idea of an existing body. But there does remain the idea of our existing body's essence. There does remain the idea of our body's essence as it is in God. We ourselves have the idea of this idea as it is in God. Our soul is thus affected by the idea of itself, by the idea of God, and by the idea of other things *sub specie aeternitatis*. As all essences agree with each essence, as they all have as their cause the God who comprises all in the production of each, affections that flow from ideas of the third kind are necessarily active and intensive affections, which are explained by the essence of whoever experiences them, while they at the same time express God's essence. 2. But if we are still affected after death, does this not mean that our capacity to be affected, and our characteristic relation themselves subsist along with our essence? Our relation can indeed be destroyed or decomposed, but this only in the sense that it no longer subsumes extensive parts. The extensive parts that belonged to us are determined to enter into other relations incompatible with our own. But the relation that characterizes us does nonetheless have an eternal truth insofar as our essence expresses itself in it. It is the eternal truth of the relation which remains along with our essence. (And so common notions are still included in the ideas of essences.) Our capacity to be affected may similarly be said to be destroyed, but this in the sense that it can no longer be exercised by passive affections.[32] It has nonetheless an eternal power, which is the same as our power of action or understanding. And it is the capacity to be affected in its eternal power which remains along with our essence.

But how can we conceive that we in any case enjoy after death

active affections of the third kind, as though necessarily rediscovering what was eternally innate in us? Leibniz presents several criticisms of Spinoza's conception of eternity: he complains
of its geometric character, with the ideas of essences as analogues
of mathematical forms or shapes; he complains that it conceives
of eternity as without memory or imagination, the eternity, at
best, of a circle or a triangle. But a third criticism seems more
important, posing as it does what is in the end the real problem
with Spinozism: if Spinoza were right, there would be no point
in perfecting oneself in order to leave behind one a still more
perfect eternal essence (as though that essence or Platonic idea
"were not already in Nature, whether I try to resemble it or not,
and as though it would be any use to me after death, if I were no
longer anything, to have resembled such an idea"[33]). The question is, effectively: What is the use of existing if we in any case
rejoin our essence after death, in such conditions that we experience intensively all the active affections corresponding to it?
In losing existence we lose nothing: we lose only our extensive
parts. But what is the use of our efforts while in existence if our
essence is in any case just what it is, a degree of power unaffected
by the extensive parts that were only temporarily and externally
related to it?

In fact our capacity to be affected will not, according to
Spinoza, be exercised (after death) by active affections of the
third kind, if we did not succeed during existence itself in experiencing a maximum proportion of active affections of the second kind and (already) of the third. Spinoza can thus consider
that he entirely preserves the positive content of the notion of
salvation. Existence itself is still conceived as a kind of test. Not,
it is true, a moral one, but a physical or chemical test, like that
whereby workmen check the quality of some material, of a metal
or of a vase.

317

While in existence we are composed of an eternal intensive part, constituting our essence, and extensive parts which belong to us in time within a certain relation. What matters is the relative importance of these two kinds of components. Suppose that we succeed, while still in existence, in experiencing active affections: our extensive parts are themselves affected by affections that are explained by our essence alone; the passions that remain are proportionately less than these active affections. That is: our capacity to be affected is exercised by a proportionately greater number of active affections than passive ones. Now active affections are explained by our essence; passive affections are explained by the infinite play of extrinsic determinations of our extensive parts. One may conclude that, of the two elements that make us up, the intensive part of ourselves has taken on a much greater relative importance than the extensive parts. When in the end we die, what perishes is "of no moment in relation to what remains."[34] The more we know things by the second and third kinds of knowledge, the greater, relatively, is the eternal part of ourselves.[35] It goes without saying that this eternal part, taken in itself independently of the extensive parts that are added to it to make up our existence, is an absolute. But suppose that during our existence we remain exercised and determined by passive affections. Of the two elements that make us up, the extensive parts will have relatively more importance than the eternal intensive part. And we will lose all the more in dying; whence he only who has something to fear from it fears death, he who loses relatively more by dying.[36] Our essence remains no less the absolute it is in itself; the idea of our essence remains no less what it is absolutely in God. But the capacity to be affected which eternally corresponds to it remains empty: having lost our extensive parts we have lost all the affections explained by them. But we have no other affections. When we die our essence remains, but as something abstract; our essence remains unaffected.

The reverse is the case if we have made our intensive part the most important element of ourselves. In dying we lose little: we lose our remaining passions, since these were explained by our extensive parts; to some extent we also lose common notions and active affections of the second kind, for these have no independent role except as they relate to existence; and lastly, active affections of the third kind can no longer impose themselves on our extensive parts, since these no longer belong to us. But our capacity to be affected remains with us eternally, accompanying our essence and the idea of our essence; so this capacity is necessarily and absolutely exercised by affections of the third kind. During our existence we have made our intensive part relatively the most important portion of ourselves; after our death the active affections explained by this part exercise our capacity to be affected absolutely; what remains of ourselves is absolutely realized. Our essence as it is in God, and the idea of our essence as conceived by God, are completely affected.

There are no such things as the moral sanctions of a divine Judge, no punishments or rewards, but only the natural consequences of our existence. During our existence our capacity to be affected is, it is true, always and necessarily exercised: but this either by passive affections or active ones. But if our capacity is completely exercised while we exist by passive affections, then it will remain empty, and our essence will remain abstract, once we have ceased to exist. It will be absolutely realized by affections of the third kind if we have exercised it with a maximum proportion of active affections. Whence the importance of this "test" that is existence: while existing we must select joyful passions, for they alone introduce us to common notions and to the active joys that flow from them; and we must make use of common notions as the principle that introduces us while still existing to ideas and joys of the third kind. Then, after death, our essence will have all the affections of which it is capable; and these will all be of the third kind. Such is the difficult path of salvation. Most men remain, most of the time, fixated by sad passions which cut them off from their essence and reduce it to the state of an abstraction. The path of salvation is the path of expression itself: to become expressive – that is, to become active; to express God's essence, to be oneself an idea through which the essence of God explicates itself, to have affections that are explained by our own essence and express God's essence.

The Theory of Expression in

Leibniz and Spinoza:

Expressionism in Philosophy

A philosophy's power is measured by the concepts it creates, or whose meaning it alters, concepts that impose a new set of divisions on things and actions. It sometimes happens that those concepts are called forth at a certain time, charged with a collective meaning corresponding to the requirements of a given period, and discovered, created or recreated by several authors at once. Such is the case with Spinoza, Leibniz and the concept of expression. This concept takes on the force of an Anticartesian reaction led by these two authors, from their two very different viewpoints. It implies a rediscovery of Nature and her power and a recreating of logic and ontology: a new "materialism" and a new "formalism." The concept of expression applies to Being determined as God, insofar as God expresses himself in the world. It applies to ideas determined as true, insofar as true ideas express God and the world. It applies, finally, to individuals determined as singular essences, insofar as singular essences express themselves in ideas. So that the three fundamental determinations, *being, knowing* and *acting* or *producing*, are measured and systematized by this concept. Being, knowing and acting are the three forms of expression. This is the age of "sufficient reason": and the three branches of sufficient reason, the *ratio essendi, ratio*

321

cognoscendi and *ratio fiendi* or *agendi*, find in expression their common root.

The concept of expression rediscovered by Spinoza and Leibniz is not, however, a new one: it already had behind it a long philosophical history. But a rather hidden, and a rather forbidden[a] history. I have tried, indeed, to show how the theme of expression crept into the two great theological traditions of emanation and creation. It did not impinge on these traditions as a third concept competing with the two others from outside, but rather appeared at a particular moment in their development, bearing in it the constant threat of diverting or taking over the traditions for its own ends. It is in short a specifically philosophical concept of immanence, which insinuates itself among the transcendent concepts of emanative or creationist theology. It brings with it a specifically philosophical "danger": pantheism or immanence – the immanence of its expression in what expresses itself, and of what is expressed in its expression. It claims to penetrate into the deepest things, the "arcana," to use a word of which Leibniz was fond. It at once gives back to Nature its own specific depth[b] and renders man capable of penetrating into this depth. It makes man commensurate with God,[c] and puts him in possession of a new logic: makes him a spiritual automaton equal to a combinatorial world. Born of the traditions of emanation and creation it makes of these two enemies, questioning the transcendence of a One above Being along with the transcendence of a Being above his Creation. Every concept has in it a virtual apparatus of metaphor. The metaphorical apparatus of expression comprises mirror and seed.[1] Expression as *ratio essendi* is reflected in the mirror as *ratio cognoscendi* and reproduced in the seed as *ratio fiendi*. But the mirror then seems to absorb both the being reflected in it, and the being that sees this image. The seed, or branch, seems to absorb both the tree from which it comes, and the tree that comes from it. And what is this strange existence that is "held" in the mirror, and that is implied, involved,[d] in the seed – what is it that is *expressed*, that entity which one can barely say exists? We saw that the concept of expression had, so to speak, two sources: one of them ontological, relating to *the expression of God*, and born within the traditions of emanation and creation, but bringing these profoundly into question; the other logical, relating to *what is expressed by propositions*, born within Aristotelian logic, but questioning and shaking it. Both meet in the problem of divine Names, of the Logos or Word.

If in the seventeenth century Leibniz and Spinoza, one starting from a Christian tradition and the other from a Jewish one, both came upon the concept of expression and set it in a new light, they obviously did so within the context of their own time, and in terms of the problems posed by their respective systems. Let me first try to bring out what is common to the two systems, and the reasons for their reintroduction of the concept of expression.

What, in concrete terms, they criticize in Descartes is his having constructed too "fast," too "easy" a philosophy. Descartes proceeds so quickly in all areas that he misses sufficient reasons, essences or true natures: he everywhere stops at what is relative. *This, first of all, with God*: Descartes's ontological proof is based on infinite perfection and rushes to its conclusion; but infinite perfection is a *proprium*, altogether insufficient to show what God's nature is, and how that nature is possible. His *a posteriori* proofs are, similarly, based on considering the actual quantities of reality in things, and do not rise as far as any dynamic principle on which these might depend. *Then with ideas*: Descartes discovers criteria of clarity and distinctness; but "clear-and-distinct" is once more a *proprium*, an extrinsic determination of ideas which tells us nothing of the nature and possibility of the thing of which we have an idea, or of thought as such. Descartes stops

323

at the representative content of ideas, and at the form of the psychological consciousness that thinks them: he thus misses the true immanent content of ideas, along with their true logical form, and the unity of the two in the spiritual automaton. He tells us that truth is present in clear and distinct ideas; but what is present in a true idea? The extent to which this second critical current merges with the first is easily seen: for if one stops at clarity and distinctness one can only measure ideas against one another, and compare them with things, by considering their quantities of reality. Having only an extrinsic characterization of ideas, one gets no further than extrinsic characteristics within Being. Moreover distinctness, taken as a norm of ideas, prejudges the status of distinctions between the things represented by ideas: it is on the basis of his criterion of clarity and distinctness that Descartes, from the whole store of Scholastic distinctions, keeps only real distinction, which is according to him necessarily numerical, distinctions of reason, according to him necessarily abstract, and modal distinction, according to him necessarily accidental. *Finally, with individuals and their actions*: Descartes understands human individuals as real composites of soul and body, that is of two heterogeneous terms, supposed really to act on one another. Is it not then inevitable that so many things should according to Descartes be "incomprehensible"? Not just this composite itself, but the workings of causality within it, as well as infinity, and freedom? One and the same move reduces Being to the platitude of infinite perfection, things to the platitude of quantities of reality, ideas to the platitude of real causality – and rediscovers all the depth of the world, but this, then, in an incomprehensible form.

Now whatever the differences between Leibniz and Spinoza, and their different interpretations of expression in particular, the fact is that they both use this concept to advance, on all the lev-

els just noted, beyond what they consider the inadequacy or facility of Cartesianism, and to restore the demand for a sufficient
reason operating absolutely. Not that they retreat from Descartes.
There are for them Cartesian discoveries that are beyond question: starting, precisely, with the properties of infinite perfection,
of a thing's quantity of reality, of clarity and distinctness, of mechanism and so on. Spinoza and Leibniz are Postcartesians in the
same sense that Fichte, Schelling and Hegel are Postkantians. It
is a question for them of reaching the foundation from which
flow all the properties just enumerated, of rediscovering an
absolute that measures up to Cartesian "relativism." How do they
go about this, and why is the concept of expression the best
suited to their task?

Infinite perfection as a *proprium* must be left behind for absolute infinity as a nature. And the first ten propositions of the
Ethics show that God necessarily exists, but does so because
absolute infinity is possible or noncontradictory: thus Spinoza
proceeds by showing that, among all the nominal definitions at
the beginning of the *Ethics*, the sixth definition is real. But this
reality is constituted by the coexistence of all the infinite forms
that introduce distinction into the absolute without introducing
number. These constitutive forms of God's nature, a nature of
which infinite perfection is only a property, are the expression
of the absolute. God is represented as infinitely perfect, but he
is constituted by these deeper forms; he *expresses himself* in these
forms, these attributes. The way Leibniz proceeds is formally similar: the same leaving behind of infinity for the absolute. Not, of
course, that Leibniz's absolute Being is the same as Spinoza's. But
once again it is a matter of demonstrating the reality of a definition, and reaching a divine nature that goes beyond any property.
Here again this nature is constituted by simple distinct forms in
which God expresses himself, and which express themselves in

325

infinite positive qualities.[2] Similarly, in Spinoza as in Leibniz, it is as we have seen the discovery of intensive quantities or quantities of power, as deeper than quantities of reality, that transforms *a posteriori* procedures, by introducing into them expressivity.

Let us pass to the second point, concerning knowledge and ideas. What is common to Leibniz and Spinoza is the criticism of Cartesian clarity-and-distinctness, as applying to recognition and to nominal distinctions, rather than to true knowledge through real definitions. Real knowledge is discovered to be a *kind* of expression: which is to say both that the representative content of ideas is left behind for an immanent one, which is truly expressive, and that the form of psychological consciousness is left behind for an "explicative" logical formalism. And the spiritual automaton presents the unity[e] of this new form and new content. We are ourselves ideas, by virtue of our expressive capacity: "We can therefore define our essence or idea as that which includes everything which we express. And since it expresses our union with God himself, it has no limits and nothing is beyond it."[3]

As for the third point, we must rethink the individual defined as a composite of soul and body. For though the supposition of a real causality may be the simplest way of understanding the phenomena associated with such a composite, its actions and passions, it is not for all that the most convincing or intelligible way. It overlooks the rich and deep world of *noncausal correspondences*. It is possible, moreover, that real causality is established and reigns only in certain regions of this world of noncausal correspondences, and actually presupposes it. Real causality might be merely a particular case of some more general principle. One feels that soul and body have at once a sort of identity that removes the need for any real causality between them, and a heterogeneity, a heteronomy, that renders it impossible. The identity or quasi-identity is an "invariance," and the heteronomy is that between two varying series, one of which is corporeal, the other spiritual. Now real causality enters into each of these series on their own account; but the relation between the two series, and their relation to what is invariant between them, depends on noncausal correspondence. If we then ask what concept can account for such a correspondence, that of expression appears to do so. For while the concept of expression adequately applies to real causality, in the sense that an effect expresses it cause, and knowledge of the effect expresses a knowledge of its cause, the concept nonetheless goes farther than causality, since it brings a correspondence and a resonance into series that are altogether foreign to one another. So that real causality is a species of expression, but merely a species subsumed under a more fundamental genus. This genus directly explains the possibility of distinct and heterogeneous series (expressions) expressing the same invariant (what is expressed), by establishing in each of the varying series the same concatenation of causes and effects. Expression takes its place at the heart of the individual, in his soul and in his body, his passions and his actions, his causes and his effects. And Leibniz by *monad*, no less than Spinoza by *mode*, understands nothing other than an individual as an expressive center.

If the concept of expression does indeed have this triple importance, from the viewpoints of universal Being, of specific knowledge and of individual action, the importance of what Leibniz and Spinoza have in common cannot be exaggerated. This even though they part company over the use and interpretation of the concept on each point. And differences of content are already prefigured by differences of form and emphasis. I have noted that no explicit definition or demonstration of expression is to be found in Spinoza (even though such a definition and such a demonstration are implicit throughout his work). In Leibniz, on the other hand, one finds passages that deal explicitly with what is

comprised in the category of expression, and how far it extends.g
But it is Leibniz, strangely enough, who gives the category such
an extension that it comes to cover everything, including the
world of signs, of similarities, of symbols and harmonies[4] – while
Spinoza greatly refines its sense, and strictly opposes expressions
to signs or analogies.

One of Leibniz's clearest texts in this regard is "Quid sit
idea."[5] Having defined expression as a correspondence of *habitus*
between two things, Leibniz distinguishes two main types of natural expression: those that imply a certain similarity (for example, a drawing), and those that involve a certain law or causality
(for example, a projection). But it seems that in each case one
of the terms in the relation of expression is always superior to
the other: either because it enjoys the identity reproduced by the
second, or because it involves the law that the other develops.
And it in each case "concentrates" in its unity what the other
"disperses in multiplicity." Expression, according to Leibniz,
grounds just such a relation of One and Many in every domain:
what expresses itself is "endowed with true unity" in relation to
its expressions; or, which comes to the same thing, expression is
a unity in relation to the multiplicity and divisibility of what is
expressed.[6] But a certain area of confusion or obscurity is thus
introduced into expression: the superior term, through its unity,
expresses *more distinctly* what the other in its multiplicity expresses *less distinctly*. This indeed is how a division is made into
causes and effects, actions and passions: when a floating body is
said to be the cause of "an infinite number of movements by the
parts of the water," rather than the reverse, this is because the
body has a unity that allows a more distinct explanation of what
is happening.[7] Moreover, since the second term is expressed in
the first, the latter as it were carves its own distinct expression
out of a dim area which surrounds it on all sides and in which it

is plunged: thus each monad traces its distinct partial expression against the background of a confused total expression; it confusedly expresses the whole world, but clearly expresses only a part of it, set apart or determined by the relation, itself expressive, which it bears to its body. The world expressed by each monad is a continuum in which there are singularities, and it is around these singularities that monads take form as expressive centers. The same applies to ideas: "Our soul reflects only upon more extraordinary phenomena which are distinguished from the others, it does not have a distinct thought about any when it is thinking equally about all."[8] Thus our thought does not reach what is absolutely adequate, the absolutely simple forms that are in God, but stops at relatively simple forms and terms (simple, that is, relative to the multiplicity they involve). And the same is even true of God, "of God's different viewpoints" in the areas of his understanding that relate to possible creations: the different creatable worlds form the dim background against which God creates the best, by creating monads or expressions which best[h] express him. Even in God, or in certain areas of his understanding at least, Unity comes with a "zero" that makes creation possible. We must then take account of two basic factors in Leibniz's conception of expression: *Analogy*, which primarily expresses different types of unity relative to the multiplicities they involve, and *Harmony*, which primarily expresses the way a multiplicity corresponds in every case to an underlying unity.[9]

This all forms a "symbolic" philosophy of expression, in which expression is inseparable from signs of its transformations, and from the obscure areas in which it is plunged. What is distinct and what confused vary in each expression (mutual expression means, in particular, that what one monad expresses confusedly, another expresses distinctly). *Such a symbolic philosophy is necessarily a philosophy of equivocal expressions.* And rather than opposing

Leibniz to Spinoza by citing the Leibnizian themes of possibility and finality, it seems to me essential to bring out this concrete point concerning the way Leibniz understands and operates with the phenomenon of expression, for all the other themes and concepts flow from it. Leibniz, in order at once to save the richness of the concept of expression and avert the pantheist "danger" attaching to it, seems to have found a new formulation according to which creation and emanation are two real species of expression, or correspond to two dimensions of expression: *creation* to the originary constitution of analogous expressive unities ("combinations of unity with zero"), and *emanation* to the derivative series that evolve the multiplicities expressed in each type of unity (involutions and evolutions, then, "transproductions" and "metaschematisms").[10]

Spinoza, though, gives expression an altogether different dynamic interpretation. For what is essential for Spinoza is to separate the domain of signs, which are always equivocal, from that of expressions, where univocity must be an absolute rule. Thus we have seen how the three types of signs (the indicative signs of natural perception, the imperative signs of the moral law and of religious revelation) were decisively rejected as inadequate; and with them went all the language of analogy – that which gave God an understanding and will, along with that which gave things an end. At the same time we become capable of forming and grasping an absolutely adequate idea, since its conditions are set by the strict reign of univocity: an adequate idea is an expressive idea, that is to say, a distinct idea that has freed itself from the obscure and confused background from which in Leibniz it was inseparable. (I tried to show in concrete terms how the selection was effected by Spinoza, through the process of forming common notions, in which ideas cease to be signs, becoming univocal expressions.) Whatever the terms involved in the relation of expression, one can never say that one expresses distinctly what another expresses confusedly. This is not, above all, the way to make the division into active and passive, action and passion, cause and effect; for, contrary to the traditional principle, actions go with actions, passions with passions. If Leibniz's preestablished harmony and Spinoza's parallelism both break with the assumption of a real causality between soul and body, the fundamental difference between them still lies here: the division into actions and passions remains in Leibniz what it was according to the traditional assumption (the body suffering when the soul acts, and vice versa) – while Spinoza in practice overturns all this division, asserting a parity between the soul's passions and the body's, and between the body's actions and the soul's. For the relation of expression holds in Spinoza only between equal terms. Herein lies the true sense of his parallelism: no series is ever eminent. The cause does of course, within its series, remain more perfect than its effect, and the knowledge of the cause, within its series, more perfect than that of the effect; but far from perfection implying an "analogy" or "symbolization" in which the more perfect term would exist *on* another qualitative level than the less perfect, it implies only an immanent quantitative process in which the less perfect exists *in* the more perfect, that is, *in* and *under* the same univocal form that constitutes the essence of the more perfect term. (This is also, as we have seen, the sense in which Leibniz's theory of qualitative individuation should be opposed to Spinoza's theory of quantitative individuation, without our concluding, of course, that a mode has any less autonomy than a monad.)

In Spinoza as in Leibniz the relation of expression applies, essentially, to Unity and Multiplicity. But one would look in vain through the *Ethics* for some sign of the Multiple, as imperfect, implying any confusion relative to the distinctness of the One that

331

expresses itself in it. A greater or lesser perfection never implies, for Spinoza, a change of form. Thus the multiplicity of attributes is strictly equivalent[i] to the unity of substance: by such strict equivalence we must understand that the attributes are *formally* what substance is *ontologically*. This equivalence does not entail the forms of attributes introducing any numerical distinction of substances; rather is their own formal distinction equivalent to all of the ontological difference between them and the single substance. And if we consider the multitude of modes in each attribute, those modes involve the attribute, but this without the attribute taking on any other form than that in which it constitutes the essence of substance: the modes involve and express the attribute *in the very form* in which it involves and expresses the divine essence. Thus Spinozism brings with it a remarkable theory of distinctions which, even when it borrows Cartesian terminology, speaks a quite different language: so real distinction is in effect nonnumerical formal distinction (as in the attributes); modal distinction is in effect an intensive or extensive numerical distinction (as in the modes); the distinction of reason is an objective formal one (as in ideas). Leibniz in his own theory multiplies the types of distinction, but this in order to secure all the resources of symbolization, harmony and analogy. Spinoza's language, on the other hand, is always that of univocity: first of all, the *univocity of attributes* (in that attributes are, in the same form, both what constitute the essence of substance, and what contain modes and their essences); second, *univocity of causation* (in that God is cause of all things in the same sense that he is cause of himself); then *univocity of ideas* (in that common notions are the same in a part as in the whole). Univocity of being, univocity of production, univocity of knowing; common form, common cause, common notion — these are the three figures of the Univocal that combine absolutely in an idea of the third kind.

Far from expression being, in Spinoza, consistent with creation and emanation, it rather excludes these, relegates them to the order of inadequate signs or equivocal language. Spinoza accepts the truly philosophical "danger" of immanence and pantheism implicit in the notion of expression. Indeed he throws in his lot with that danger. In Spinoza *the whole theory of expression supports univocity*; and its whole import is to free univocal Being from a state of indifference or neutrality, to make it the object of a pure affirmation, which is actually realized in an expressive pantheism or immanence. Here, I feel, lies the real opposition between Spinoza and Leibniz: *the theory of univocal expressions in the one should be opposed to the theory of equivocal expressions in the other.* All the other oppositions (necessity and finality, necessary and possible) flow from it, and are abstract in relation to it. For philosophical differences do indeed have their concrete origins, in specific ways of *evaluating* some phenomenon: in this case, that of expression.

But whatever the importance of this opposition, we must return to what is common to Leibniz and Spinoza, to that use of the notion of expression which presents the whole force of their Anticartesian reaction. This notion of expression is essentially triadic: we must distinguish what expresses itself, the expression itself and what is expressed. The paradox is that "what is expressed" *has no existence* outside its expression, yet bears no resemblance to it, but relates *essentially* to what expresses itself as distinct from the expression itself. Expression thus bears within it a double movement: one either takes what is expressed as involved, implicit, wound up, in its expression, and so retains only the couple "expresser–expression"; or one unfolds, explicates, unwindsʲ expression so as to restore what is expressed (leaving the couple "expresser–expressed"). Thus there is in Leibniz, first of all, a divine expression: God expresses himself in absolute

333

forms or absolutely simple notions, as in some divine Alphabet; such forms express unlimited qualities related to God as constituting his essence. God then re-expresses himself on the level of possible creation: here he expresses himself in individual or relatively simple notions, monads, corresponding to each of his "viewpoints." These expressions in their turn express the whole world, that is, the totality of the chosen world, which is related to God as the manifestation of his "glory" or his will. One sees, in Leibniz, that the world has no existence outside the monads that express it, while yet God brings the world, rather than the monads, into existence.[11] These two principles are in no way contradictory, but reflect the double movement by which the world as expressed is implicit in the monads that express it, and by which, conversely, monads in their evolution reconstitute their continuous background together with the singularities about which they are themselves constituted. Subject to all the reservations already noted, the same account may be applied to Spinoza. Within the triad of substance God expresses himself in his attributes, the attributes expressing the unlimited qualities that constitute his essence. In the modal triad God re-expresses himself, or the attributes in their turn express themselves: they express themselves in modes, modes expressing modifications as modifications of substance, constituting the same world through every attribute. This constant triadic character means that the concept of expression cannot be referred either to causality within Being, or to representation in ideas, but goes beyond both, which are seen to be particular cases of expression. For with the dyad of cause and effect, or that of idea and object, there is always associated a third term that transposes one dyad into the other. An effect does of course express its cause; but at a deeper level causes and effects form a series that must itself express something, and something identical (or similar) to what another parallel series

334

expresses. Real causality is thus located in expressive series between which there are noncausal correspondences. Similarly, an idea represents an object, and in a way expresses it; but at a deeper level idea and object express something that is at once common to them, and yet belongs to each: a power, or the absolute in two of its powers,[k] those of thinking or knowing, and being or acting. Representation is thus located in a certain extrinsic relation of idea and object, where each enjoys an expressivity over and above representation. In short, what is expressed everywhere intervenes as a third term that transforms dualities. Beyond real causality, beyond ideal representation, what is expressed is discovered as a third term that makes distinctions infinitely more real and identity infinitely better thought. What is expressed is sense[l]: deeper than the relation of causality, deeper than the relation of representation. The body has a mechanism in reality, there is an automatism of thought in the order of ideality; but we learn that the corporeal mechanism and the spiritual automaton are most *expressive* when they find their "sense" and their "correspondence" in the necessary reason that was everywhere lacking in Cartesianism.

It is hard, in the end, to say which is more important: the differences between Leibniz and Spinoza in their evaluation of expression; or their common reliance on this concept in founding a Postcartesian philosophy.

A Formal Study of the Plan of the *Ethics*, and of the Role of Scholia in its Realization: The Two *Ethics*

Theme	Consequence	Corresponding Expressive Concept
Part One		Speculative Affirmation
1–8 There are not several substances with the same attribute, and numerical distinction is not real.	These eight propositions are not hypothetical but categorical; it is thus false that the *Ethics* 'begins' with the idea of God.	The first triad of substance: attribute, essence, substance.
9–14 Real distinction is not numerical, there is only one substance, with all attributes.	Only here do we reach the idea of God as absolutely infinite substance; and Definition 6 is shown to be real.	The second triad of substance: perfect, infinite, absolute.

337

15–36	Power or production: the processes of production and the nature of their products (modes).	Immanence means both univocity of attributes and univocity of cause (God is cause of all things in the same sense that he is cause of himself).	The third triad of substance: essence as power, that of which it is the essence, and the capacity to be affected (by modes).
	PART TWO		Ideas as expressive.
1–7	The epistemological parallelism of idea and object, and the ontological parallelism of soul and body.	From substance to modes, the transfer of expressivity: the role of the idea of God in this transfer.	The modal triad: attribute, mode, modification.
8–13	The conditions of ideas: ideas God has on the basis of his nature, and those we have on the basis of our nature and our body.	Aspects of God in relation to ideas: God insofar as he is infinite, insofar as he is affected by many ideas, and insofar only as he has a given idea.	Adequacy and inadequacy.
Exposition of Physics	The model of the body.	Extensive parts, relations of movement and rest, composition and decomposition of such relations.	First individual modal triad: essence, characteristic relation, extensive parts.

14–36	The conditions in which we have ideas mean that they are necessarily inadequate: idea of oneself, idea of one's body, ideas of other bodies.	Inadequate ideas are "indicative" and 'involved," as opposed to adequate ideas, which are expressive and explicative: chance, encounters and the first kind of knowledge.	The inexpressive character of inadequate ideas.
37–49	How are adequate ideas possible? What is common to all, or to several, bodies.	Common notions, as opposed to abstract ideas. How common notions lead to the idea of God: the second kind of knowledge, and reason.	The expressive character of adequate ideas, from the point of view of their form, and from that of their matter.

PART THREE		Practical joy.
1–10	What follows from ideas: affections or feelings. *Conatus* as determined by such affections.	The distinction of two sorts of affections, active and passive; actions follow from adequate ideas and passions from inadequate ones.	Second individual modal triad: essence, capacity to be affected, the affections that exercise this capacity.
11–57	The distinction between two sorts of affections, active	The two lines of joy and of sadness: their developments,	Augmenting and diminishing the power to act.

46–73	Good and bad according to this criterion of reason.	Continuation of the critique of sadness.	Free man and slave, strong man and weak, reasonable man and madman.

PART FIVE

Practical joy and speculative affirmation.

1–13	How we can actually come to form adequate ideas (common notions). How joyful passive affections lead us to them. How we thereby diminish sadness, and form an adequate idea of all passive affections.	We thus arrive at the second kind of knowledge, thanks to certain opportunities afforded by the first kind.	Reason's second aspect: forming common notions, and the active affections of joy that follow. Becoming active.
14–20	The idea of God, at the limit of the second kind of knowledge.	From common notions to the idea of God.	The impassive God as understood through the second kind of knowledge.
21–42	This idea of God in its turn leads us out of the second kind of knowledge, and into the third kind: the reciprocating God of the third	There are as many parts of the soul as there are types of affection: not only passive affections of sadness and joy, but also active joyful	The *Ethics* has proceeded thus far through common notions, and common notions only. But it now changes, and speaks from

341

| kind of knowledge, adequate ideas of oneself, of one's body, and of other bodies. | affections of the second kind, and even active joyful affections of the third kind. Whence it is inferred what is mortal and what eternal in the soul: the side that dies and the side that remains, extensive parts and intensive essence. | the point of view of the third kind of knowledge. The unity, in this third kind of knowledge, of practical joy and speculative affirmation: becoming expressive, beatitude, reciprocity, univocity. |

An extensive study should be undertaken of the *Ethics'* formal procedures and of the role of each component (Definition, Axiom, Postulate, and so on). I wish here only to consider the special and complex function of scholia.

The first major scholium in the *Ethics* is the second to I.8. It sets out to give *another* proof of Proposition 5, which states that there cannot be several substances of the same attribute. As we saw in Chapter One above, it runs as follows: (1) Numerical distinction implies an external cause; (2) But it is impossible for a substance to have an external cause, because any substance is in itself and conceived through itself; (3) There cannot therefore be two or more numerically distinct substances within the same attribute.

The Proof in Proposition 5 itself had proceeded differently and more concisely: two substances with the same attribute must be distinguished by their modes, which is absurd. But Proposition 6, following Proposition 5, had shown that external causality cannot *therefore* apply to substance. And Proposition 7, that a substance is *therefore* cause of itself. And Proposition 8 concluded that a substance is *therefore* necessarily infinite.

Thus the group formed by Propositions 5–8, and the Scholium to Proposition 8, proceed then in inverse manner. The sequence of propositions starts from the nature of substance in order to infer its infinity, that is, the impossibility of applying to it numerical distinctions. The Scholium starts from the nature of numerical distinction, and infers the impossibility of applying it to substance.

Now one might think that the scholium, in order to prove that substance cannot admit any external causality, might do well to invoke Propositions 6 and 7. But this is in fact impossible. For 6 and 7 presuppose 5, and the scholium would not then be another proof. Yet it does invoke Proposition 7, and this at some length. But it does so in an altogether novel way: it sees in it a purely axiomatic content, completely detaching it from its demonstrative context. "If men would attend to the nature of substance, they would have no doubt at all of the truth of Proposition 7. Indeed, this proposition would be an axiom for everyone, and would be numbered among the common notions..." The Scholium can therefore provide a proof quite independent of that given in the group formed by Propositions 5–8.

We may identify three characteristics in such a scholium: 1. It sets out a second proof, which is *positive* and *intrinsic* in relation to an initial proof which proceeded negatively, extrinsically. (Thus Proposition 5 simply invoked the anteriority of substance in order to infer the impossibility of assimilating modal distinction to substantial distinction. And the Scholium to 8 infers the impossibility of assimilating numerical to substantial distinction, but does so from intrinsic and positive characteristics of number and substance.) 2. The Scholium is *ostensive* since it is independent of earlier proofs and is to be substituted for them, retaining only certain propositions in an axiomatic guise, detached from their demonstrative sequence. (A scholium does of course sometimes invoke proofs, but not from among the group that it serves to "double"[a]). 3. Whence comes, then, the evidential character which allows us to treat the propositions that are taken up anew, independently of their initial context and their proofs, as axioms? The new character comes from *polemical* arguments in which Spinoza attacks, often violently, those whose minds are too confused to understand, or who, even, have some interest in maintaining confusion. (Already in Proposition 8 he fiercely scolds those who cannot understand Proposition 7 in itself, and who are prepared to believe that trees talk, and that men are born from stones).

In short, scholia are positive, ostensive and aggressive. Given their independence relative to the propositions they double, one might say that the *Ethics* was written twice, in two different tones, on two levels, at the same time. For in their own discontinuous way the scholia jump one to another, echo one another, reappear in the preface to some Part of the *Ethics*, or in the conclusion to another, forming a broken line which runs right through the work at a certain depth, but which rises to the surface only at particular points (of fracture). The Scholium to I.8, for example, forms such a line together with those to I.15, I.17, I.33, II.3 and II.10: these deal with the different kinds of disfigurement to which God is subjected by man. Similarly, the Scholium to II.13, which sets up the model of the body, jumps to that at III.2, and ends up in the Preface to Part Five. A broken line of scholia, similarly, forms a kind of hymn to joy, constantly interrupted, in which those who live on sadness, those whose interest lies in our sadness, and those who need human sadness to secure their power are violently denounced: IV.45s2, IV.50s, IV.63s and V.10s. Similarly, again, the couple free man–slave of IV.66s reappears in the couple strong man–weak of IV.73s, then in that of wise man–fool with which the *Ethics* closes at V.42s. And V.4s and V.20s, finally, form a royal road which leads us into the third kind of knowledge.

The main "turning points" of the *Ethics* are bound, therefore, to appear in its scholia. For the continuity of propositions and proofs can derive its prominent points, its various impulses, its changes of direction, only from the emergence of something that expresses itself in the scholia – scholia as stratum, as current – and that generates those fractures where it emerges. Examples of such turning points are found at II.13s (introducing the model of the body), III.57s (the model of active joys), IV.18s (the model of reason) and V.20s,36s (the third kind of knowledge).

There are thus as it were two *Ethics* existing side by side, one constituted by the continuous line or tide of propositions, proofs and corollaries, and the other, discontinuous, constituted by the broken line or volcanic chain of the scholia. The first, in its implacable rigor, amounts to a sort of terrorism of the head, progressing from one proposition to the next without worrying about their practical consequences, elaborating its *rules* without worrying about individual *cases*. The other assembles the indignation and the joys of the heart, presenting practical joy, setting out the practical struggle against sadness, expressing itself at each point by saying "such is the case." The *Ethics* is in this sense a double book. There may be some interest in reading the second *Ethics* underneath the first, by jumping from one scholium to another.

Let us return to the three characteristics of scholia: they are positive, ostensive and aggressive. These characteristics obviously overlap within a given scholium, but we may consider them separately.

That a scholium proceeds positively may, as we saw, mean that it relies on intrinsic characteristics, while the corresponding proof rests on merely extrinsic properties. A particularly clear example appears at III.7, concerning the "soul's vacillation": this is defined in the Proof of the Proposition by the play of external causes that provoke it, but in the Scholium by the diversity of the internal relations of which we are composed. It may also mean that a scholium proceeds *a priori*, while the proof is *a posteriori*: thus at II.1 the Proof is based on modes, but the Scholium rests on the possibility of directly thinking a quality as infinite. Similarly, at I.11 the scholium presents an *a priori* argument based "on the same principle" as the *a posteriori* method of the Proof. Or again, take the Scholium on parallelism, which is so important, at II.7: while the Proof proceeds from effect to cause to infer that the order of knowledge is the same as that of things, while Proof and Corollary together rise from this identity of order in modes to an equality of powers in God, the Scholium, conversely, begins from the ontological unity of substance and infers the equality of powers and the identity of order. (There is as we saw a dislocation between these two ways of proceeding, which is only resolved by Spinoza's ostensive invocation of the idea of God in the Scholium: this brings us, already, to the second characteristic of scholia.)

But, to conclude the consideration of the first characteristic, it must be added that the positivity of scholia also appears in a particularly complex manner: the scholium may proceed within the order of real definitions, while proposition and proof develop the consequences of nominal definitions: thus Propositions 9 and 10 of Part One establish the purely logical possibility of one and the same being having an infinity of attributes, each of which is conceived through itself, but they invoke only Definitions 3 and 4, which are nominal definitions of substance and attribute. The Scholium, on the other hand, invokes Definition 6 which is, as we saw, the only real definition among all those that open Part One. Furthermore, since a real definition is one that one should be able to *prove* real, one that grounds the "real" possibility of its object (transcendental as opposed to merely logical possibility), the Scholium to Proposition 10 does actually take on this task, and proves that Definition 6 is indeed real: the distinction between attributes cannot, from its positive characteristics, be numerical. And here again, an ostensive use is made of Proposition 9, abstracted from its context.

The positive character of scholia thus has three aspects, intrinsic, *a priori* or real. Let us consider their second characteristic, that of being ostensive. It also has various aspects, the principal one having already been noted. This principal, axiomatic, aspect consists in a scholium's invoking of an earlier proposition in abstraction from the continuous chain of propositions and proofs, to give it a new, directly polemical force: this is seen in the Scholia to I.8 (using Proposition 7), to I.10 (using Proposition 9), to II.3 (invoking the idea of God), and to II.7 (invoking the Hebrews).... The second aspect does, it is true, seem to go less far, for scholia sometimes present only an example of the corresponding proposition: consider II.8 (the example of lines within a circle), IV.40 (the odd example of the action of striking), IV.63 (the example of the healthy man and the sick).... But most of Spinoza's examples seem to go beyond mere examples in two different ways, taking on two higher and more fundamental functions, paradigmatic and casuistic. Thus at II.13s, then at III.2s the *model* of the body is set out: not so the body can serve as a model for thought, disrupting the parallelism or relative autonomy of Thought and Extension; but it is introduced as an example that takes on a paradigmatic function, showing "in parallel" how much there is in Thought itself that is beyond consciousness. The same applies to the model of human nature which is first introduced at IV.18s, and developed at V.10s and V.20s. And applies, lastly, to the model of the third kind of knowledge, introduced at II.40s and in the last lines of II.40s, and fully formulated at V.36s.

The casuistic function of the pseudoexample appears, on the other hand, in all the scholia that present, in relation to the preceding proof, the form of "this is just the case...." Here again we have no mere example, but rather a strict assigning of the conditions in which the object of the corresponding proof is actually realized: the scholium determines a case that falls under the rule contained in the corresponding proof not as one case among others, but as the case that fulfills the rule and meets all its conditions. The conditions are sometimes restrictive, and a scholium, far removed from the corresponding proposition, may remind us that the proposition and its proof must be understood in a restricted sense (II.45s, IV.33s, etc.). But there is on a deeper level something in this aspect of scholia that coincides with their positive way of proceeding, since, for mistakes and passions at least, it is impossible to obtain a real definition independently of the conditions in which the object previously indicated in proposition and proof can actually exist, impossible also to bring out what is positive in a mistake or passion if these conditions are not determined in the scholium. Scholia of this type proceed, then, in the form of a "fiat": this is how the thing comes about.... Thus the Scholium to II.35 explains how error, defined in the Proposition as a privation, actually comes about, and thereby already has a certain positivity in the conditions in which it does come about. And thus II.44, having enunciated and proved that it is only imagination that considers things to be contingent, the scholium in its turn sets out to demonstrate "the conditions in which this comes about" (*qua ratione fiat*). This manner of proceeding is generalized in Part Three: while propositions and proofs trace in their continuous progress the movement in which

348

affections are linked to and derived from one another, the scholia introduce halts, like photographs suddenly taken, freezing the progress in temporary immobility, in a snapshot showing that such a familiar affection or faculty does actually correspond, in such conditions, to what the proposition was discussing. This had already been done in Part Two, with memory (II.18s), and with common notions (II.40s1). But in Part Three there is a proliferation of scholia embodying formulations like "Thus we know how it can happen...," "We see that it may happen...," "This happens because...." At the same time, affections and faculties find their names: not just the Memory and Common Notions of Part Two, but the names of all the affections that are to be collected together in the closing definitions, in a sort of echo of all the scholia: Joy, Sadness, Love, Hate and so on. As though the movement of propositions, proofs and corollaries were continually driving forward the tide of affections, which only, however, formed its waves and crests in the scholia. As though propositions, proofs and corollaries spoke the most elevated language, impersonal and little caring to identify that of which it was speaking, since what it was saying was in any case grounded in a higher truth – while the scholia baptized, gave names, identified, pointed out and denounced, echoing in the depths what the "other" language set forth and moved forward.

The second, ostensive, character of scholia thus has, in its turn, three principal aspects, axiomatic, paradigmatic and casuistic. And these constantly bring into play the last characteristic of scholia, which is to be polemical or aggressive. This final characteristic itself has various aspects: sometimes it is a matter of analyzing the *speculative confusion* or intellectual stupidity of those who disfigure God, taking him as a "king," giving him understanding and will, ends and projects, shapes and functions, and so on (scholia, above all, in Part One). Sometimes it is a matter of determining the conditions in which *sensory error*, and the passions flowing from it, come about (this above all in the scholia of Parts Two and Three). Sometimes it is a matter of denouncing *practical evil*, that is, sad passions, their contagiousness, the interests of those who profit by them – such denunciation taking place above all in Part Four, but this in relation to the more general project of the *Ethics* as recalled in the prefaces and conclusions to various Parts. The polemic thus has within it three aspects, speculative, sensory and practical. It is hardly surprising that all these aspects, and all the characteristics to which they attach, confirm and overlap one another. The major scholia bring them all together. A scholium always has a positive intention, but can only fulfill it by the aid of an ostensive procedure, and this can itself only be founded on a polemical base. The ostensive procedure in its turn divides into the polemical argument which gives it its full force, and the positive principle it serves. It may be asked how the positive movement of scholia can be reconciled with polemical, critical and negative argument. The answer is that the great force of Spinoza's polemical power evolves in silence, far from all discussion, and in order to serve a higher affirmation and a higher "ostensivity." Negation serves only, according to Spinoza, to deny what is negative, to deny what denies and obscures. Polemic, negation, denunciation are there only to deny what denies, misleads, hides – what profits from error, lives on sadness, thinks in negative terms. Thus the most polemical of the scholia bring together, in their particular style and tone, the two supreme registers[b] of speculative affirmation (of substance) and practical joy (in modes): a double language, inviting a double reading of the *Ethics*. What is most important in the greatest scholia is their polemic, but its power is all the more developed for being in the service of speculative affirmation and practical joy, and for bringing them together in univocity.

350

Notes

A Note on References

The titles of Spinoza's writings are cited in abbreviated form as follows:

E   *Ethics*

TP   *Theologico-Political Treatise*

CU   *Treatise on the Correction of the Understanding*

ST   *Short Treatise on God, Man, and His Well-Being*

P   *Political Treatise*

D   *Principles of Descartes' Philosophy*

M   *Metaphysical Thoughts*

In general, passages are located in terms of section and subsection as defined by Spinoza or his original editors, but for citations from TP and the Letters, the place in the Van Vloten and Land edition is also given, and reference to the Letters follows the enumeration given in that edition. Where these divisions apply, "e," "p," "c," "s," refer to a proposition's Enunciation, Proof, Corollary and Scholium respectively, while entire Propositions are referred to simply by Part and number; "n" stands for Note. Thus "E IV.4,5e,c2p,s; IV Preface nn2,3" would refer the reader to the whole of the fourth Proposition of Part IV of the *Ethics*, and to the Enunciation, Proof of the second Corollary, and Scholium at IV.5, together with the second and third Notes to the Preface of Part V. All other divisions are cited in unabbreviated form.

English versions are based on existing translations (TP, P: Elwes; Letters not in Curley I: Wolf; all other works: Curley) with occasional revision where this is required by Deleuze's argument and does not conflict with the Latin or Dutch original. The page or pages where a quoted passage appears in these English versions is given within square brackets at the close of the passage. Where italics occur, these have always been introduced by Deleuze.

The standard edition of Descartes's works is also cited in abbreviated form:

AT *Oeuvres de Descartes*, ed. C. Adam and P. Tannery, 11 vols. (Paris, 1897-1909).

English versions have been made by the present translator from the seventeenth-century French versions used by Deleuze, which present considerable textual variation from the Latin originals on which the available English translations are based.

The following works also are cited in abbreviated form:

PS *Die Philosophischen Schriften von G. W. Leibniz*, ed C. I. Gerhardt, 7 vols. (Berlin, 1875-90).

Loemker Leibniz, *Philosophical Papers and Letters*, ed. and tr. Leroy S. Loemker, 2nd ed. (Dordrecht, 1969).

INTRODUCTION: THE ROLE AND IMPORTANCE OF EXPRESSION

1. The formulations given in the *Ethics* are: (1) *aeternam et infinitatem certam essentiam exprimit* (I.10s); (2) *divinae substantiae essentiam exprimit* (I.19p), *realitatem sive esse substantiae exprimit* (I.10s); (3) *existentiam exprimunt* (I.10c). The three sorts of formulation are brought together at I.10s, where one finds very subtle distinctions and transitions between the various terms.

2. E I.19, 20p.

3. E I.36p [439] (and 25c: *Modi quibus Dei attributa certo et determinato modo exprimuntur*).

4. E I.16p.

5. E II.1p [448].

6. TP iv (II.136 [59]).

7. CU 108 (*infinitatem exprimunt*).

8. E V.29e,p.

9. Cf. ST II.xx.4 (*uytgedrukt*); I. Dialogue II.12 (*vertoonen*); I.vii.10 (*vertoond*).

10. CU 76.

11. E I.8s2: *Verum uniuscuiusque rei definitionem nihil involvere neque exprimere praeter definitae naturam*; CU 95: *Definitio, ut dicatur perfecta, debebit intimam essentiam rei explicare.*

12. E I.19p,20p.

13. E II.45,46p.

14. Chapter Nine.

15. Cf. Alexandre Koyré, *La Philosophie de Jacob Boehme* (Paris, 1929) and, more particularly, *Mystiques, spirituels, alchimistes du XVIᵉ Siècle Allemand* (Paris, 1947).

16. Cf. Foucher de Careil, *Leibniz, Descartes et Spinoza* (1862). Among more recent writers, E. Lasbax is representative of those who have pushed furthest the identification of Spinozist expression with Neoplatonic emanation: *La Hiérarchie dans l'univers chez Spinoza* (Paris, 1919).

17. Erdmann, following Hegel, sees the attributes as forms either of understanding or sensibility (*Versuch einer wissenschaftlichen Darstellung der neueren Philosophie*, Berlin, 1836; *A History of Philosophy*, tr. W. S. Hough, London, 1890).

18. Fritz Kaufmann, "Spinoza's System as a Theory of Expression," *Philosophy and Phenomenological Research*, (September, 1940).

19. André Darbon, *Etudes spinozistes* (Paris, 1946) pp. 117–18.

20. Letters 2,4 (to Oldenburg), ST I.ii.1.

21. Letters 82 (from Tschirnhaus), 83 (to Tschirnhaus).

22. CU 72, 95.

23. CU 72: "To form the concept of a sphere, I feign a cause at will, say that a semicircle is rotated around its centre, and that the sphere is, as it were, produced by this rotation. This idea, of course, is true, and even though we may know that no sphere in Nature was ever produced in this way, neverthe-

less, this perception is true, and a very easy way of forming the concept of a sphere. Now it must be noted that this perception affirms that the semicircle is rotated, which affirmation would be false if it were not joined to the concept of a sphere..." [32].

24. E V.23s; TP xiii: "If any tell us it is not necessary to understand the divine attributes, but that we must believe them simply without proof, he is plainly trifling. For what is invisible and can only be perceived by the mind, can be seen with no other eyes than proofs. Whoever, then, has no proof, can see absolutely nothing of these things" (II.240 [178]).

CHAPTER ONE: NUMERICAL AND REAL DISTINCTION

1. Cf. Merleau-Ponty in *Les Philosophes célèbres* (Paris, 1956), p. 136.

2. E I.5.

3. This is how Spinoza presents the Cartesian position (M II.V): "We need to recall what Descartes has taught (*Principles* I.48,49), viz. that there is nothing in nature but substances and their modes. From this a threefold distinction of things is deduced (I.60–62), viz. *real*, *modal*, and *of reason*" [323].

4. Descartes, *Principles* I.53.

5. *Principles* I.60–62.

6. Cf. Suarez, *Metaphysicarum disputationum* d.VIII. The only distinctions recognized by Suarez were real, modal and of reason – he criticized Duns Scotus's formal distinction in terms very similar to those employed by Descartes.

7. Descartes, *Principles* I.56.

8. *Principles* I.63–64.

9. On these paragraphs, 63 and 64, see the discussion between F. Alquié and M. Gueroult in the proceedings of the Royaumont colloquium: *Descartes* (Paris, 1967), pp. 32–56.

10. Descartes, *Replies to the Fourth Objections*, AT IX.175.

11. This tripartite formulation is given in Letter 2 (to Oldenburg, III.5 [166]).

12. Letter 81 (to Tschirnhaus), III.241; cf. also Letter 12 (to Meyer), III.41: number does not adequately express the nature of modes as an infinity, that is,

as they depend on substance.

13. E I.15s [422].

14. ST I.ii.19-22.

15. E I.5-7,8e.

16. E I.8s2 [416: with "nature" for "attribute"].b

17. E I.10s [416].

18. Cf. P. Lachièze-Rey's interpretation in *Les Origines cartésiennes du Dieu de Spinoza*[2] (Paris, 1934), p. 151: "Nor does such a use of the distinction in any way imply its admissibility, according to Spinoza. It remains solely a means of demonstration, given a hypothesized plurality of substances, intended to nullify any possible consequences of such hypothetical plurality."

19. Letter 9 (to De Vries, III.32). In the *Ethics* the first argument appears almost verbatim at I.9, the second, less directly, at I.11s.

20. Cf. Letter 64 (to Schuller, III.206).

21. E I.10s: "But if someone now asks by what sign we shall be able to distinguish the diversity of substances, let him read the following propositions, which show that in Nature there exists only one substance, and that it is absolutely infinite. So that sign would be sought in vain."

22. ST I.vii.9-10.

23. Cf. Régis, *Refutation de l'opinion de Spinoza touchant l'existence et la nature de Dieu* (Paris, 1704).

24. M II.v [323, 325].

CHAPTER TWO: ATTRIBUTE AS EXPRESSION

1. Letter 2 (to Oldenburg, III.5): *quod concipitur per se et in se*. Thus Delbos's assertion that in this letter an attribute is defined as a substance seems unfounded (cf. "La Doctrine spinoziste des attributs de Dieu," *L'Année Philosophique*, 1912).

2. Cf. 1. ST Appendix I.4c2; 2. ST I.ii.17n5 [i.e., 17nf. according to Curley [70], who reproduces as "note d" a remark disregarded by Van Vloten and Land and by Gebhardt, as being an early interpolation — TR] and First Dialogue, 9; 3. ST I.ii *passim* and 17n5.

3. ST I.ii.17 [70].

4. Letter 10 (to De Vries, III.34 [196]).

5. ST I.ii.17n5 [70].

6. Letter 9 (to De Vries, III.33 [195-96]).

7. E II.1-2: Spinoza demonstrates that Thought and Extension are attributes. The *a posteriori* method appears in the Proof itself, the *a priori* one in the Scholium.

8. For the criticism of equivocation, see E I.17c2: If will and understanding were attributed essentially to God, this would be equivocally, and so purely verbally, more or less as the word "dog" indicates a heavenly constellation. For the criticism of eminence, see Letter 56 (to Boxel, III.190): If a triangle could speak, it would say that God was eminently triangular – here Spinoza is replying to Boxel's contention that only eminence and analogy can save us from anthropomorphism.

9. II.10cs: The inadequate definition of essence (as that without which a thing can neither be nor be conceived) is to be found in Suarez: cf. Gilson, *Index scholastico-cartésien*, pp. 105-6.

10. Letter 6 (to Oldenburg, III.25).

11. Cf. 1. E I.3e; 2. E I.17s. A difference of viewpoint has sometimes been adduced to reconcile these two passages (the viewpoints of immanent and transitive causality, etc.): cf. Lachièze-Rey, *Les Origines cartésiennes*, pp. 156-59n.

12. Letter 4 (to Oldenburg, III.11): "As for your contention that God has nothing formally in common with created things, etc., I have maintained the complete opposite of this in my definition" (the definition, that is, of God as a substance consisting of an infinity of *attributes*). Letter 64 (to Schuller, III.206): "Can a thing be produced by another whose essence and existence are different? For things which are so different from one another *appear* to have nothing in common. *But* since all individual things, except those which are produced by things like themselves, differ from their causes in essence as well as in existence, I see here no reason for doubt." (Spinoza then refers to the definition of "mode," E I.25c.)

13. ST I.vii.6 (cf. also I.i.9n4; iii.1n1).

14. ST I.vii.1n1 [88].

15. ST I.vii.6 [89].

16. Cf. ST I.iii–vi.

17. ST I.vii.

18. TP xiii (III.241 [179]).

19. TP ii (II.115): Adam, for example, knew that God was cause of all things, but not that he was omniscient and omnipresent.

CHAPTER THREE: ATTRIBUTES AND DIVINE NAMES

1. On all of these points, see Maurice de Gandillac's introduction to the *Oeuvres complètes du Pseudo-Denys* (Paris, 1943); and *La Philosophie de Nicolas de Cues* (Paris, 1941). In the latter work De Gandillac well shows how negative theology on the one hand, and analogy on the other, each combines affirmation and negation, but this in converse ways: "In a converse manner to Dionysius, who reduced affirmations themselves to disguised negations, Saint Thomas... principally uses apophasis to rise from this or that prior negation to some positive attribute. From the impossibility of divine movement, he draws for example a proof of divine Eternity; from the exclusion of matter he forms a decisive argument in favor of the coincidence in God of essence and existence" (p. 272).

2. TP vii (II.185): "The path which [this method] teaches us, as the true one, has never been tended or trodden by men, and has thus, by the lapse of time, become very difficult, and indeed almost impassable" [113–14]. And viii (II.191): "I fear that I am attempting my task too late..." [120].

3. TP ii (II.113): "Everyone has been extremely hasty in affirming that the prophets knew everything within the scope of human intellect; and, although certain passages of Scripture plainly affirm that the prophets were in certain respects ignorant, such persons would rather say that they do not understand the passages than admit that there was anything which the prophets did not know; or else they try to wrest the Scriptural words away from their evident meaning" [33].

4. Cf. TP xiv: the list of "dogmas of faith." It will be noted that, even from the viewpoint of "*propria*," revelation remains limited. Everything turns about

justice and charity. Infinity, in particular, does not seem to be revealed in Scripture; cf. ii, where Spinoza sets out what was unknown to Adam, to Abraham and to Moses.

5. On the two senses of the "Word of God," see TP xii. The *Short Treatise* had already opposed immediate communication and revelation through signs: II.xxiv.9-11.

6. TP i (II.95).

7. TP iv (II.139); Letter 19 (to Blyenbergh, III.65).

8. Cf. TP ii–iii.

9. TP xiii (II.239-40).

10. TP iv (II.144 [67]).

11. E I, Definition 6, Explanation: "If something is only infinite in its own kind, we can deny infinite attributes of it."

12. Letter 4 (to Oldenburg, III.10 [171]).

13. ST II.xix.5.

14. See the repeated formulations in the *Short Treatise* (especially I.i), according to which attributes are affirmed, and affirmed of a Nature which is itself positive; and see CU 96: "Every definition must be affirmative" [40].

15. See L. Robinson's remarks on this point, and the texts of Cartesians cited by him: *Kommentar zu Spinozas Ethik* (Leipzig, 1928).

16. ST I.ii.5n [67]. On the imperfection of Extension according to Descartes, see, for example, *Principles* I.23.

17. Letter 9 (to De Vries, III.33 [195-96]).

18. The distinction in the logic of propositions between "what is expressed" (the sense) and "what is designated" (*designatum, denominatum*) is by no means recent, although it reappears in many modern philosophers. Its origin is to be found in Stoic logic, which distinguishes the *expressible* and the *object*. Ockham, in his turn, distinguishes the thing as such (*extra animam*) and the thing as *expressed* in the proposition (*declaratio, explicatio* and *significatio* are synonymous with *expressio*). Some of Ockham's followers take the distinction even further, and rediscover Stoic paradoxes, making the "expressed" into a nonexistent entity, irreducible either to the thing or the proposition: see H. Elie,

358

Le Complexe signifiable (Paris, 1936). These paradoxes of expression play a major role in modern logic (Meinong, Frege, Husserl), but their source is ancient.

19. Duns Scotus, *Opus Oxoniense* (Vivès edition): for the critique of eminence and analogy, I.iii.1–3; on the univocity of being, I.viii.3. It has often been noted that univocal being allows the distinction of its "modes" to subsist: when it is considered in its individuating modalities (infinite and finite), rather than in its nature as Being, it ceases to be univocal. Cf. E. Gilson, *Jean Duns Scot* (Paris, 1952), pp. 89, 629.

20. *Opus Oxoniense* I.viii.4 (a2n13).

21. *Ibid.* I.ii.4, viii.4 (cf. Gilson, Ch. 3).

22. De Gandillac, "Duns Scot et la Via Antiqua," in *Le Mouvement doctrinal du IXe au XIVe siècle* (Paris, 1951), p. 339.

23. *Opus Oxoniense* I.ii.4 (a5n43): formal distinction is *minima in suo ordine, id est inter omnes quae praecedunt intellectionem.*

24. *Ibid.* II.iii.1: the distinct form has a real being, *ista unitas est realis, non autem singularis vel numeralis.*

25. Gilson, *Jean Duns Scot*, p. 251.

26. Suarez, *Metaphysicarum disputationum* d.VII.

27. Caterus had in the *First Objections* to the *Meditations* invoked formal distinction in relation to soul and body. Descartes replies: "As for the formal distinction which this very learned theologian says he takes from Scotus, I reply, in brief, that it is no different from the modal, and only covers incomplete beings..." (AT IX.94–95).

28. There is really no need to inquire whether Spinoza had read Duns Scotus. It is hardly likely that he had. But we do know, even from the inventory of what remained of his library, his taste for metaphysical and logical treatises of the *quaestiones disputatae* variety. Those treatises always included expositions of Scotist univocity and formal distinction. Such expositions belong to the commonplaces of sixteenth- and seventeenth-century logic and ontology; see for example Heerebord's *Collegium logicum* (1649). From the work of Gebhardt and Revah we also know of the probable influence on Spinoza of Juan of Prado, and Juan of Prado definitely knew Duns Scotus; see I. Revah, *Spinoza et le Dr. Juan*

de Prado (Paris and The Hague, 1959), p. 45.

One might add that the problems of a negative or positive theology, of analogy or univocity of being, and of the corresponding status of distinctions, are in no way confined to Christian thought. One finds them just as alive in the Jewish thought of the Middle Ages. Some commentators have underlined the influence of Chasdaï Crescas on Spinoza's theory of extension. More generally, though, Crescas seems to have elaborated a positive theology involving the equivalent of a formal distinction between the attributes of God; see G. Vajda, *Introduction à la pensée juive du Moyen Age* (Paris, 1947), p. 174.

29. *Opus Oxoniense* I.iii.2 (a4n6): *Et ita neuter ex se, sed in utroque illorum includitur; ergo univocus.*

CHAPTER FOUR: THE ABSOLUTE

1. ST I.ii.2-5, nn2,3; E I.8p.

2. ST Appendix II.11 [155].

3. ST I.ii.6 [67]. That there should be no "two equal substances" does not contradict the equality of attributes: the two principles imply one another.

4. Descartes, *Third Meditation*, AT IX.38, 40.

5. *Replies to the First Objections*, AT IX.91.

6. The earliest of Leibniz's texts that relate to this matter date from 1672 (*Leibnitiana*, ed. Jagodinsky [Kazan, U.S.S.R., 1913-15], p. 112). See also the note of 1676 "Quod ens perfectissimum existit" (Loemker 14.I), PS VII.261.

7. *Replies to the Second Objections*: "Or you feign some other possibility, on the side of the object itself, which, if it does not correspond to the former, can never be known by human understanding..." (AT IX.118).

8. Such appears to be the position of the authors of the second set of objections (cf. AT IX.101).

9. *Replies to the Second Objections* (AT IX.112).

10. *Ibid.* (AT IX.108). This is one of the fundamental principles of Thomism: *De Deo et creaturis nil univoce praedicatur.*

11. *Third Meditation* (AT IX.36).

12. Cf. Leibniz, Letter to Princess Elizabeth (1678) and "Meditations on

Knowledge, Truth and Ideas" (1684; Loemker 33).

13. On the nominal character of a definition of God by infinite perfection, see Letter 60 (to Tschirnhaus, III.200).

14. E I.11pp1,2.

15. E I.10s: "It is far from absurd to attribute many attributes to one substance..." [416].

16. ST I.i.1.

17. ST I.i.2. (On the ambiguity of the formulation, and its translation, see Appuhn's note in the Garnier version, p. 506 [his suggestions are in turn taken up by Curley – TR]).

18. ST I.i.1n2 [61–62].

19. E I.20p,c.

20. Cf. G. Friedmann, *Leibniz et Spinoza* (Paris, 1946), pp. 66–70.

21. Leibniz, "Ad Ethicam..." (Loemker 20), PS I.139–52.

22. Cf. "Quod ens..."; Letter to Princess Elizabeth, "Meditations on Knowledge, Truth and Ideas."

23. Cf. Leibniz, "Elementa calculi" (Loemker 26.I), "Plan de la science générale," "Introductio ad encyclopaedium arcanum," in *Opuscules et fragments inédits*, ed. Couturat (Paris, 1903).

24. E I.10s [416].

25. Letters 2, 4 (to Oldenburg, III.5,10–11), 35, 36 (to Hudde, III.129–32).

26. Letter 60 (to Tschirnhaus, III.200 [301]).

CHAPTER FIVE: POWER

1. Leibniz, Letter to Princess Elizabeth (1678): "It must be admitted that these arguments [the Cartesian proofs of God's existence] are somewhat suspect, as they proceed too quickly, and do us violence without enlightening us." The theme of "too fast" recurs constantly: Leibniz invokes against Descartes his own taste for a slow and weighty style, for a continuity that forbids "leaps," his taste for real definitions and polysyllogisms, for an *ars inveniendi* which takes time. When Leibniz reproaches Descartes for having thought that quantity of movement was conserved, one should see in this criticism a particular (and of

NOTES TO PAGES 83-90

course particularly important) case of a very general objection: Descartes, in all areas, mistakes the relative for the absolute, through proceeding too quickly.

2. D I.7s: "What he means by this I do not know. What does he call easy, and what difficult?... [note:] The spider...easily weaves a web that men could weave only with the greatest difficulty..." [248].

3. Descartes, *Third Meditation*, *Principles* I.17-18.

4. *Third Meditation*, *Principles* I.20-21 (but the text of the *Principles* avoids any explicit reference to the notions of easy and difficult).

5. *Arguments* [viz. Of the *Replies to the Second Objections*] *Drawn Up in Geometrical Fashion*, Axiom 8 (AT IX.128).

6. For all these objections made against Descartes by various correspondents, and for his replies, see the *Conversation with Burmann*, tr. J. Cottingham (Oxford, 1976), and also Letter 347 (to Mesland, AT IV.111).

7. ST I.i.3-9 [61-64].

8. ST II.xx.3n3 [Proposition 10: 136].

9. CU 76,n2: "Since...the origin of Nature cannot...be extended more widely in the understanding than it is in reality..., we need fear no confusion concerning its idea...."; "If such a thing did not exist, it could never be produced; and therefore the mind would be able to understand more things than Nature could bring about" [34].

10. Letter 40 (to Jelles, March 1667, III.142 [233]).

11. P I.7 Lemmata 1, 2; p.

12. E I.11s.

13. E I.11p3.

14. E I.11s [418].

15. Spinoza does of course often speak of an effort to persevere in being. But this *conatus* is itself a *potentia agendi*. Cf. E III.57p: *potentia seu conatus*; E III, General Definition of Affects: *agendi potentia sive existendi vis*; E.IV.29p: *hominis potentia qua existet et operatur*.

16. ST II.xx.3n3: "This idea then, considered alone, apart from all other ideas, can be no more than an idea of such a thing; it does not have an idea of such a thing. Because such an idea, so considered, *is only a part*, it cannot have

the clearest and most distinct concept of itself and its object; but the thinking thing, which alone is the whole of Nature, can. For a part, considered apart from its whole, cannot etc." [136].

17. E II.5p.

18. Letter 21 (to Blyenbergh, III.86).

19. P ii.2-3.

20. E IV.4p [549].

21. E IV.4p.

22. E IV.4p: "Man's power, insofar as it is explained through *his* actual essence, is part of God or Nature's infinite power, i.e., of *its* essence" [549].

23. E I.36p.

24. The identity of power and act, at least in the *Nous*, is a frequent theme of Neoplatonism, and is to be found in Christian as in Jewish thought. Nicholas of Cusa derives from it the notion of a *possest*, which he applies to God (*Oeuvres choisies*, ed. de Gandillac, Paris, 1942, pp. 543-46; de Gandillac, *La Philosophie de Nicolas de Cues*, pp. 298-306). This identity in God of act and power is extended by Bruno to the *Simulacrum*, that is, to the Universe or Nature (*On Cause, Principle, and Unity*, Third Dialogue).

25. This tradition is already taken to a logical conclusion by Hobbes (cf. *De Corpore*, Ch. 10).

26. Spinoza often speaks of an *aptitude* of body, corresponding to its power: a body is apt (*aptus*) to act and suffer action (E II.13s); it *can* be affected in a great number of ways (III, Postulate 1). Man's excellence derives from the fact that his body is "apt for the greatest number of things" (V.39). On the other hand, a *potestas* corresponds to a power of God (*potentia*); God can be affected in an infinity of ways, and necessarily produces all the affections that lie within his power (I.35).

27. On the variation of *vis existendi*, see E III, General Definition of Affects.

28. ST I.ii.22-25; E I.15s.

CHAPTER SIX: EXPRESSION IN PARALLELISM

1. ST I, Second Dialogue 5.

2. E II.3s.

3. E I.25s: "God must be called the cause of all things in the same sense in which he is called the cause of himself" [431]; II.3s: "It is as impossible for us to conceive that God does not act as it is to conceive that he does not exist" [449]; IV, Preface: "God or Nature acts from the same necessity from which he exists" [544].

4. E.II.7s.

5. E II.3s: "As everyone maintains anonymously" [449]; cf. also Letter 75 (to Oldenburg, III.228).

6. This already appears in the Proof of II.3, which appeals to I.16. And the Scholium itself emphasizes this reference ("*It follows from the necessity of the divine nature*... that God understands himself").

7. E I.16e,p.

8. E I.17s.

9. E I.17s, 33e2; ST I.iv.1-5.

10. E I.33p,s2; ST I.iv.7-9.

11. E I.17, 33e,p.

12. E II.7s. We saw above (Chapter Three) how Spinoza, in his theory of expression, came upon certain themes of a logic of propositions of Stoic origin, and taken up again by Ockham's school. But one should take other factors into account, the Hebrew language in particular. In his *Compendium grammatices linguae hebreae*, Spinoza brings out certain characteristics that constitute a real logic of expression based on the grammatical structures of Hebrew, and that lay the foundation of a theory of propositions. Without an annotated edition the reader who does not know the language cannot understand much of the book, so I can fasten only on certain elementary principles: (1) The atemporal character of the infinitive (Chs. 5, 33); (2) The participial character of modes (ibid.); (3) The determination of various kinds of infinitive, one of which expresses an action referred to a principal cause (the equivalent of *constituere aliquem regnantem* or *constitui ut regnaret*: cf. Ch. 12).

13. E I.21-23p.

14. E II.6p.

364

15. ST II.xix.7f., xx.4–5. Albert Léon showed in *Les Eléments cartésiens de la doctrine spinoziste sur les rapports de la pensée et de son objet* (Paris, 1907), that the passages of the *Short Treatise* do not necessarily imply any assumption of a real causality between attributes, or between soul and body (cf. p. 200).

16. ST II.xx.3n3: "The object cannot be changed unless the idea is also changed, and vice versa..." [136].

17. By "parallelism" Leibniz understands a conception of soul and body that makes them in a certain way inseparable, while excluding any real relation of causality between them. But it is his *own* conception he designates thus. Cf. "Reflections on the Doctrine of a Universal Spirit" (1702; Loemker 58), § 12.

18. E II.17s [451].

19. E II.7s [452].

CHAPTER SEVEN: THE TWO POWERS AND THE IDEA OF GOD

1. E II.7s: "I understand the same concerning the other attributes" [452].

2. Thus the soul is an idea that represents solely a certain mode of Extension: cf. E II.13e.

3. On this use of "individual" to signify the unity of an idea and its object, see E II.21s.

4. Letter 65 (from Tschirnhaus, III.207).

5. CU 85 [37].

6. E II.5,6.

7. ST II.xx.3n3 [136].

8. E I.30e.

9. Cf. E I.16p: *infinita absolute attributa.*

10. E II.3e,p.

11. Cf. E I.31p: *absoluta cogitatio*; Letter 64 (to Schuller, III.206): *intellectus absolute infinitus.*

12. Schelling, *Stuttgart Lectures* (1810): "The two unities or powers are again united in absolute Unity, and the joint positing of the first and second power is thus A^3.... The powers are henceforth posited equally as periods of God's

revelation" (French tr. Jankélevitch, in *Essais*, Paris, 1946, pp. 309–10).

13. ST I.viii.s4 [64; VVL I.7s3].

14. ST Appendix II.9: "All the infinite attributes, which have a soul just as much as those of extension do" [154].

15. E II.4e,p.

16. CU 99: We must "ask whether there is a certain being, and at the same time, what sort of being it is, which is the cause of all things, so that its objective essence may also be the cause of all our ideas" [41].

17. E I.31p: Understanding, being a mode of thinking "must be conceived through *absolute thought*, i.e., it must be so conceived through an *attribute* of God, which expresses the eternal and infinite essence of Thought that can neither be nor be conceived without that attribute" [43–45].

18. E II.1s: "A being that can think infinitely many things in infinitely many modes is necessarily infinite by virtue of thinking"[b] [448]. (That is: a being which has an *absolute* power of thinking has necessarily an *infinite* attribute which is Thought.) E II.5p: "We inferred that God can form the idea of his essence, and of all the things which follow necessarily from it, solely from the fact that God is a thinking thing" [450].

19. Cf. E II.5p: *Deum ideam suae essentiae...formare posse.*

20. It is infinite understanding, not the idea of God, that is called a mode: E I.31e,p; ST I.ix.3.

21. Commentators have often distinguished several aspects of the idea of God *or* infinite understanding. Georg Busolt has gone farthest, suggesting that infinite understanding belongs to *natura naturata* as the principle of finite intellectual modes, but to *natura naturans* as considered in itself (*Die Grundzüge der Erkenntnisstheorie und Metaphysik Spinozas*, Berlin, 1895, II.127ff.). The distinction seems to me, however, to be groundless, for, as principle of what follows objectively in God, the idea of God should, on the contrary, belong to *natura naturans*. This is why I believe a distinction between the idea of God, taken objectively, *and* infinite understanding, taken formally, to be more legitimate.

22. ST I.ix.3; Letter 73 (to Oldenburg, III.226).

23. Cf. ST II.xxii.4n1: "The infinite intellect, which we called the Son of

God, must exist in Nature from all eternity. For since God has existed from eternity, so also must his idea in the thinking thing, i.e., exist in itself from eternity; *this idea agrees* objectively with him" [139].

24. Victor Brochard expressed his doubts over this in "Le Dieu de Spinoza," *Etudes de philosophie ancienne et de philosophie moderne* (Paris, 1912), pp. 332-70.

25. To the two principles presented above – that God produces as he understands himself, and that he understands all that he produces – we must then add a third: God produces the form under which he understands himself and everything else. The three principles agree on a fundamental point: infinite understanding is not a locus of possibles.

26. Letter 70 (from Schuller, III.221 [338]).

27. Letter 66 (to Tschirnhaus, III.207).

28. Letter 66 (to Tschirnhaus, III.208 [310]).

29. Cf. E II.21s. Albert Léon summarizes the difficulty thus: "How can we escape this dilemma? Either an idea and the idea of the idea bear the same relation as an object foreign to Thought and the idea that represents it, and are then two expressions of the same content under different attributes; or their common content is expressed under one and the same attribute, and then the idea of the idea is absolutely identical to the idea in question, consciousness is absolutely identical to thought, and the latter cannot be defined independently of the former" (*Les Eléments cartésiens de la doctrine spinoziste sur les rapports de la pensée et de son objet*, p. 154).

30. CU 34-35: *altera idea* or *altera essentia objectiva* are used three times. The distinction between an idea and the idea of that idea is even classed with that between the idea of a triangle and the idea of a circle.

31. E II.21s (on there being a mere distinction of reason between an idea and the idea of that idea; cf. E IV.8p, V.3p).

32. *Critique of Judgment* §73.

33. The question is put by Schuller in Letter 63 (III.203 [305]).

CHAPTER EIGHT: EXPRESSION AND IDEA

1. Cf. CU 39: *Una methodi pars*; 106: *Praecipua nostra methodi pars*. Accord-

ing to Spinoza's comments, the exposition of this first part closes in 91-94.

2. CU 91: *Secundam partem*; and 94.

3. CU 37 (and 13: *Naturam aliquam humanam sua multo firmiorem*).

4. CU 106: *Vires et potentiam intellectus*; Letter 37 (to Bouwmeester, III.135): "It seems clear what the true method must be, and in what it especially consists, namely, only in the knowledge of the pure understanding, and of its nature and laws" [228].

5. CU 38 [19].

6. CU 105.

7. Cf. E II.33p.

8. E II.43e. (This passage is perfectly consistent with that at *Correction of the Understanding* 34-35, according to which, conversely, one does not need to know that one knows, in order to know.)

9. CU 33: "A true idea (for we have a true idea)..." [17]; 39: "Before all else there must be in us a true idea, as *an inborn tool*..." [19]. Such a true idea supposed by the Method poses no particular problem: we have, and recognize, it by the "inborn power of the understanding" (CU 31 [17]). Whence Spinoza can say that Method requires nothing but a "short account of the mind" (*mentis historiala*) of the sort taught by Bacon: cf. Letter 37 (to Bouwmeester, III.135 [228]).

10. E II.21s [468].

11. Cf. ST II.xv.2.

12. In his *Replies to the Second Objections*, Descartes presents a general principle: "One must distinguish between the *matter* or the thing to which we accord our belief, and the *formal reason* which moves our will to accord it" (AT IX.115). According to Descartes, this principle explains how, where the matter is obscure (in matters of religion), we may nonetheless have a clear ground of assent (the light of grace). But it applies also to the case of natural knowledge: the clear and distinct matter of our belief is not to be confused with its clear and distinct formal ground (in our natural light).

13. The definition (or concept) of a thing *explicates* its essence and *comprehends* its proximate cause: CU 95-96. It *expresses* the efficient cause: Letter 60

(to Tschirnhaus, III.200). The knowledge of the effect (idea) *involves* the knowledge of its cause: E I Axiom 4, II.7p.

14. CU 92: "Knowledge of the effect is nothing but acquiring a more perfect knowledge of its cause" [39].

15. Letter 37 (to Bouwmeester, III.135). This is the *concatenatio intellectus* (CU 95).

16. CU 19, 21 (on this insufficiency of clear and distinct ideas, see Chapter Nine below, "Inadequacy").

17. CU 72.

18. We have for example the idea of the circle as a figure, all of whose radii are equal: but this is only a clear idea of a "property" of the circle (CU 95). Similarly, in the closing search for a definition of the understanding, we have to set out from *clearly* known *properties* of the understanding: CU 106-10. Such is, as we have seen, the *requisite* of the Method.

19. Thus, *starting with* the circle as a figure with equal radii, we form the *fiction* of a cause, in this case a straight line revolving about one of its endpoints: *fingo ad libitum* (CU 72).

20. What interests Spinoza in mathematics is not at all Descartes's analytic geometry, but Euclid's synthetic method and Hobbes's genetic conceptions: cf. Robinson, *Kommentar zu Spinozas Ethik* pp. 270-73.

21. CU 110.

22. CU 94 [39].

23. Fichte, no less than Kant, starts from a "hypothesis." But unlike Kant he purports to reach an absolute principle that does away with the initial hypothesis: thus, once the principle is discovered, the given is replaced by a construction of the given, the "hypothetical judgment" by a "thetic judgment," analysis by genesis. Gueroult very well says, "At each stage [the *Wissenschaftslehre*] always asserts that, as a principle must depend only on itself, the analytic method should pursue no other goal than its own elimination; thus indeed it understands the constructive method as alone effective" (*L'Evolution et la structure de la doctrine de la science chez Fichte*, Paris, 1930, I.174).

24. Spinoza had invoked "due order" (*debito ordine*) at CU 44. At 46 he

adds: "If, by chance, someone should ask why I did not immediately, before anything else, display the truths of Nature in that order – for does not the truth make itself manifest? – I reply to him and at the same time warn him...he should first deign to consider the order in which we prove them" [21-22]. Most translators suppose there to be a gap in this last passage, and consider that Spinoza is making a "pertinent objection" to himself. They consider that later, in the *Ethics*, Spinoza found a way of setting out truths "in due order" (cf. Koyré's French translation of CU, p. 105). There seems to me to be not the slightest gap: Spinoza is saying that he cannot follow the due order *from the start*, because this order is only reached *at a certain stage* in the order of demonstration. And the *Ethics*, far from correcting this point, rigorously defends it, as we will see in Chapter Eighteen.

25. CU 49, 75, 99 [23, 33, 41]. (In this last passage many translators move *et ratio postulat* in order to make it apply to the whole sentence.)d

26. E I.26e.

27. CU 54 [16].

28. Cf. E V.30p: "to conceive things insofar as they are conceived through God's essence, as real beings" [610].

29. CU 42.

30. E II.45e: "Each idea of each body, or of each singular thing which actually exists, necessarily involves an eternal and infinite essence of God" [481]. (In the Scholium, and also in that to V.29, Spinoza adds that "actually existing things" here designates things as "true or real," as they follow from the divine nature, their ideas thus being adequate ones.)

31. CU 40-41.

32. Letter 37 (to Bouwmeester, III.135).

33. The "spiritual automaton" appears at CU 85. As for Leibniz, who doesn't use the expression earlier than the "New System" of 1695 (Loemker 47), he seems in fact to take it from Spinoza. And despite differences between their two interpretations, the spiritual automaton does have one aspect in common in both Leibniz and Spinoza: it indicates the new logical form of ideas, the new expressive content of ideas, and the unity of that form with that content.

34. Cf. CU 70–71.

35. CU 71 [32].

36. E V.31e.

37. On the distinction between infinity (understood negatively) and an infinite thing (conceived positively, but not in its entirety), see Descartes's *Replies to the First Objections*, AT IX.90. The Cartesian distinction in the *Fourth Replies*, between complete conception and entire conception is also in some ways applicable to the problem of the knowledge of God: the *Fourth Meditation* had characterized the idea of God as that of a "complete being" (AT IX.42), even though we do not have an entire knowledge of it.

38. Letter 64 (to Schuller, III.205) [307].

39. E II.46p: "*What gives* knowledge of an eternal and infinite essence of God is common to all things and is equally in the part and in the whole. And so this knowledge will be adequate" [482].

40. TP vi (II.159): "As God's existence is not self-evident, it must necessarily be inferred from ideas so firmly and incontrovertibly true..."; and TP, note 6 (II.315) reminds us that these ideas are common notions.

41. Cf. ST II.xxiv.9–13.

CHAPTER NINE: INADEQUACY

1. E II.9p [453]; and cf. II.11c: God "insofar as he also has the idea of another thing *conjointly* [Curley: "together" – TR] with the human mind..." [456]; III.1p: God "insofar as he also contains in himself, at the same time, the minds of other things" [493].

2. E II.36p [474].

3. E II.9c: "Whatever happens (*contingit*) in the singular object of any idea..." [454].

4. E II.12p: "For whatever happens in the object of the idea constituting the human mind, the knowledge of it is necessarily in God insofar as he constitutes the nature of the human mind, i.e., knowledge of this thing will necessarily be in the mind, or the mind will perceive it" [457].

5. E II.19, 23, 26.

6. On the part of chance (*fortuna*) in perceptions that are not yet adequate, see Letter 37 (to Bouwmeester, III.135).

7. *Indicare*: E II.16c2; IV.1s *Indicate* or *involve* are, then, opposed to *explicate*. Thus the idea of Peter as it is in Paul "indicates the state of Paul's body," while the idea of Peter in itself "directly explains the essence of Peter's body" (II.17s [465]). Similarly, ideas "that only involve the nature of things which are outside the human body" are opposed to ideas "that explain the nature of the same things" (II.18s [466]).

8. On the primary thing indicated: our ideas of affections indicate in the first place the constitution of our bodies, a *present*, and changeable, constitution (E II.16c2; III, General Definition of Affects; IV.1s). On the secondary or indirect thing indicated: our ideas of affections involve the nature of an external body, but indirectly, in such a way that we only believe in the *presence* of this body as long as our affection lasts (E II.16p; II.17e,p,c).

9. E II.35e,p.

10. E II.28p.

11. E II.24–25, 27–31.

12. E II.35s [473].

13. There is a concatenation (*ordo* and *concatenatio*) of inadequate ideas, as opposed to the order and concatenation of understanding. Inadequate ideas follow one another in the order in which they are impressed in us – the order of Memory: cf. E II.18s.

14. E II.33e,p; II.35s; IV.1e,p,s.

15. For an analogous example, see CU 21.

16. Cf E II.22–23.

17. E II.17s: "For if the mind, while it imagined nonexistent things as present to it, at the same time knew that those things did not exist, it would, of course, attribute this power of imagining to a virtue of its nature, not to a vice – especially if this faculty of imagining depended only on its own nature" [465] (that is: *if this faculty did not merely involve our power of thinking, but was also explained by it*).

18. See Letter 37 (to Bouwmeester), in which Spinoza uses the words

NOTES TO PAGES 152-156

"clear and distinct" to designate adequacy itself. Spinoza understands "clear and distinct" in a stricter sense to mean that which follows from what is adequate, that which must, then, have its ground in what is adequate: "We understand clearly and distinctly whatever follows from an idea which is adequate in us" (E V.4s [598]). But this passage is based on II.40, which stated that all that follows from an adequate idea is also adequate.

19. Leibniz, Letter to Arnauld: "Expression is common to all forms, and it is a genus of which natural perception, animal sensation and intellectual knowledge are species" (*The Leibniz–Arnauld Correspondence*, tr. Mason, Manchester, England and New York, 1967, p. 144).

20. Cf. Leibniz, "Meditations on Knowledge..."; "Discourse on Metaphysics" (Loemker 35) §24.

21. The criticism of the clear idea is pursued explicitly by Spinoza in CU 19,n; 21,n. Spinoza does not, it is true, say "clear and distinct." But this is because he reserves this phrase for his own use in a sense altogether different from Descartes's. We will see in the next chapter how Spinoza's criticism bears on the whole of the Cartesian conception.

CHAPTER TEN: SPINOZA AGAINST DESCARTES

1. Descartes, *Replies to the Second Objections*, AT IX.121. This passage, extant only in Clerselier's French translation, raises great difficulties: Alquié emphasizes these in his edition of Descartes (II.582). We will however consider in the following pages whether the passage may not be taken literally.

2. Descartes, *Rules*, Rule 12 (AT X.421). Again and again in Descartes a clear and distinct knowledge implies, as such, a confused perception of its cause or principle. J. Laporte gives all sorts of examples in *Le Rationalisme de Descartes* (Paris, 1945), pp. 98-99. When Descartes says "I *somehow* have in myself the notion of the infinite before that of the finite" (*Third Meditation*), we must understand by this that the idea of God is implied by that of myself, but confusedly or implicitly – rather as 4 and 3 are implied in 7.

3. For example, *Third Meditation*, AT IX.41: "I recognize that it would not be possible for my nature to be as it is, that is, that I should have in myself

the idea of God, did not God really exist."

4. CU 19 § 3; 21 (and its corresponding notes). All these passages describe a part of what Spinoza calls the third "mode of perception." *It is not here a question of a process of induction*: induction belongs to the second mode, and is described and criticized at CU 20. Here it is rather a question of a process of inference or implication of the Cartesian type.

5. CU 85 [37].

6. Cf. Aristotle, *Posterior Analytics* I.2 (71b30).

7. CU 92 [39].

8. Descartes, *Replies to the Second Objections*, AT IV.122 (once again, the passage is only extant in Clerselier's translation).

9. *Ibid.*

10. *Posterior Analytics* I.32 (88b25-30).

11. Descartes, *Replies to the Second Objections*, AT IX.122: "Synthesis, on the other hand, by a wholly different path, and by so to speak examining causes by their effects (although the proof it contains is often also from causes to their effects)...."

12. Alquié, in an oral contribution to a discussion of Descartes, brings out this point well: "I do not at all see that the synthetic order is the order of things.... A thing is the real unit; being is a confused unity; I am responsible for the order in what I know. And what must be established is that the order of my knowledge, which is always an order of knowing, *whether it be synthetic or analytic*, is true" (*Cahiers de Royaumont: Descartes*, p. 125).

13. CU 94: "The right way of *discovery* is to form thoughts from some given definition" [39].

14. CU 19 § 3.

15. CU 85.

16. CU 58: "The less the mind understands and the more things it perceives, the greater is its power of forming fictions; and the more things it understands, the more that power is diminished" [26-27]. Indeed, the more the mind imagines, the more its power of understanding remains *involved*, so the less it actually understands.

17. Cf. *First Objections*, AT IX.76; *Fourth Objections*, AT IX.162-66.

18. Descartes, *Replies to the First Objections*, AT IX.87-88: Those attached "to only the proper and strict meaning of efficient," "see here no other kind of cause which might have a *relation and analogy* to an efficient cause." They do not see that "it is quite permissible to consider that [God] *in a way* does the same thing in relation to himself, as an efficient cause in relation to its effect" (and cf. *Replies to the Fourth Objections*, AT IX.182-88: "All these forms of speech which have relation and analogy to the efficient cause...").

19. Descartes, *Principles* I.51 ("What substance is, and that it is a name which cannot be attributed to God and to creatures in the same sense").

20. E I.25s. It is odd that Lachièze-Rey, when citing this passage, inverts the order, as though Spinoza had said that God was cause of himself in the sense that he was cause of things. Such a transformation of the passage is not just an oversight, but amounts to the survival of an "analogical" perspective that *begins* with efficient causality (cf. *Les Origines cartésiennes*, pp. 33-34).

21. E I.20p.

22. ST I.ii.2n2 [66: Curley has a singular rather than plural subject. – TR].

23. ST I.ii.5n3 [67].

CHAPTER ELEVEN: IMMANENCE AND THE HISTORICAL
COMPONENTS OF EXPRESSION

1. *Enneads* VI.4.ii.27-32: "We [viz. Platonists] for our part posit being in sensible things, and then set *there* what must be everywhere; then, imagining the sensible as something vast, we ask how that nature *there* can come to extend into such a vast thing. But what one calls vast is in fact small; and what one thinks small is vast, because it comes as a whole, before all else, into each part of the sensible...." Plotinus here emphasizes the need to invert the Platonic problem, and start from the participated, or even from what grounds participation in the participated.

2. *Ibid.* VI.7.xvii.3-6. The theory of the Imparticipable, of giver and gift, is developed and deepened by Proclus and Damascius throughout their commentaries on the *Parmenides*.

3. On the Cause or Reason that produces while "remaining in itself," and on the importance of this theme in Plotinus, see René Arnou, *Praxis et theoria* (Paris, 1921), pp. 8-12.

4. The *Short Treatise* defines an immanent cause as acting *in itself* (I.ii.24). It is in this respect like an emanative cause, and Spinoza relates the two causes in his study of the categories of cause (ST I.iii.2). Even in the *Ethics* he uses *effluere* to indicate the way modes follow from substance (I.17s); and in Letter 43 (to Osten, III.161), we find *omnia necessario a Dei natura emanare*. Spinoza seems to be retreating from a familiar traditional distinction: an immanent cause was said to have a causality distinct from its existence, while emanative causality was not distinct from the existence of the cause (cf. Heereboord, *Meletemata philosophica* II.229). Spinoza could not, of course, accept such a differentiation.

5. V.2.i.5 [Armstrong V.59].

6. V.5.iv. There is of course in Plotinus a form common to all things; but this is a form of finality, the form of the Good, which must be understood in an analogical sense.

7. Cf. Gilson, *L'Etre et l'essence* (Paris, 1948), p. 42: "In a doctrine of Being, inferior things have being only by virtue of the being of superior things. In a doctrine of the One it is, on the contrary, a general principle that inferior things have being only by virtue of a higher thing not being; indeed the higher thing only ever gives what it does not have since, in order to give it, it must be above it."

8. De Gandillac has analyzed this theme in *La Philosophie de Nicolas de Cues* (Paris, 1942).

9. V.I.vii.30 [Armstrong V.37].

10. VI.6.xxix. The term *exelittein* (explicate, develop[e]) has a great importance in Plotinus and his successors, in relation to the theory of Being and Intelligence.

11. Cf. VI.2.xi.15: "One thing may have no less being than another, while yet having less unity."[f]

12. Boethius applies to eternal Being the terms *comprehendere* and *complectiri* (cf. *Consolation of Philosophy*, Prosa VI). The nominal couple *complicatio–explicatio*, or the adjectival *complicative–explicative*, take on great importance in

Boethius's commentators, notably in the twelfth-century School of Chartres. But it is above all in Nicholas of Cusa and in Bruno that the notions acquire a rigorous philosophical character: cf. de Gandillac, *La Philosophie de Nicolas de Cues*.

13. Nicholas of Cusa, *On Learned Ignorance*, II.3.g

14. On the category of expression in Eckhardt, cf. Lossky, *Théologie négative et connaissance de Dieu chez Maître Eckhart* (Paris, 1960).

15. III.8.viii; cf. V.3.x: "What explicates itself is multiple."[i]

16. VI.8.xviii.18: "The center is revealed as it is, as it is explicated, through its rays, but without explicating itself."[j]

17. Bonaventure develops a triad of expression, comprising the Truth that expresses itself, the thing expressed, and the expression itself: *In hac autem expressione est tria intelligere, scilicet ipsam veritatem, ipsam expressionem et ipsam rem. Veritas exprimens una sola est et re et ratione; ipsae autem res quae exprimuntur habent multiformitatem vel actualem vel possibilem; expressio vero, secundum id quod est, nihil aliud est quam ipsa veritas; sed secundum id ad quod est, tenet se ex parte rerum quae exprimuntur* (*De Scientia Christi, Opera omnia* V.14a). On the words "express" and "expression" in Augustine and Bonaventure, see Gilson, *The Philosophy of Saint Bonaventure*, tr. Trethowan and Sheed (London, 1958), pp. 124–25.

18. Thus Nicholas of Cusa remarks: "An image must indeed be contained in its model, for otherwise it would not really be an image.... The model is therefore in all its images, and all its images in it. Thus no image is either more or less than its model. Whence all images are images of a single model" (*The Game of Spheres*, tr. P. M. Watts, New York, 1986).

19. The word and notion, Participation (participation in the nature of God, or in his power), form a constant theme of the *Ethics* and the *Letters*.

20. Cf. E IV.4p.

21. Whenever Spinoza speaks of an "ultimate or remote cause" he makes it clear that the formulation is not to be taken literally: cf. ST I.iii.2; E I.28s.

CHAPTER TWELVE: MODAL ESSENCE

1. ST I.ii.19n [71].

2. The problem of intensity or degree plays an important role, especially in the thirteenth and fourteenth centuries: Can a quality, without changing its formal reason or essence, be affected by various degrees? And do these affections belong to the essence itself, or only to its existence? The theory of intrinsic modes or degrees is particularly developed in Scotism.

3. Cf. E II.15e,p.

4. Letter 12 (III.42 [Wolf, 121][b]).

5. E II.8e,c (and cf.I.8s2: We have true ideas of nonexistent modifications, because "their essences are comprehended in another in such a way that they can be conceived through it" [414]).

6. Leibniz, "On the Radical Origination of Things" (Loemker 51): "There is a certain urgency [*exigentia*] toward existence in possible things or in possibility or essence itself – a pretension to exist, so to speak – and, in a word, that essence in itself tends to exist" [487].

7. E I.25e [431].

8. At E I.24e,p Spinoza says that "The essence of things produced by God does not involve existence." That is to say: a thing's essence does not involve that thing's existence. But in the Corollary he adds "For – whether the things exist or not – so long as we attend to their essence, we shall find that it involves neither existence nor duration. So *their essence can be the cause neither of its own existence nor of its own duration* (*neque suae existentiae neque suae durationis*)." The [French] translators [and Curley, 431 – TR] seem to make a surprising blunder by having Spinoza say: "So their essence [viz. the essence of things] can be the cause neither of *their* existence nor *their* duration." Even were such a translation possible, which it is absolutely not, how would one understand what the Corollary added to the Proof? The blunder was no doubt suggested by Spinoza's allusion to duration. How can he speak of the "duration" of essence, since essence does not endure? But we do not yet know, at I.24, that essence does not endure. And even when Spinoza has said that it does not, he sometimes uses the term duration in a very general way, in a sense that is, literally, incorrect: cf. V.20s. The whole of I.24 appears, then, to me to be organized thus: 1. The essence of a thing produced is not a cause of the thing's existence (*Proof*);

2. But nor is it cause of its own existence as essence (Corollary); 3. *Whence* I.25, God is cause even of the essences of things.

9. In definitive pages devoted to Avicenna and Scotus, Gilson has shown how the distinction of essence and existence is not necessarily a real distinction (cf. *L'Etre et l'essence*, pp. 134, 159).

10. On the agreement of essences, cf. E I.17s.

11. ST Appendix II.11 (the first passage): "These modes, when considered as not really existing, are nevertheless equally contained in their attributes. And because there is no inequality at all in the attributes, nor in the essences of the modes, there can be no particularity in the idea, since it is not in Nature. But whenever any of these modes put on their particular existence, and by that are in some way distinguished from their attributes (because their particular existence, which they have in the attribute, is then the subject of their essence), then a particularity presents itself in the essences of the modes, and consequently in their objective essences, which are necessarily contained in the idea" [154-55]. ST II.xx.3n3 (the second): "Since the essence, without existence, is conceived as belonging to the meanings of things, the idea of the essence cannot be considered as something singular. That can only happen when the existence is there together with the essence, and that because then there is an object which did not exist before. E.g., when the whole wall is white, then one distinguishes no this or that in it" [136].

12. E II.8e,s.

13. E II.8c: "When singular things are said to exist, not only insofar as they are comprehended in God's attributes, but insofar also as they are said to have duration, their ideas also involve the existence through which they are said to have duration" [452]. (And cf. II.8s: When one actually draws some of the rectangles contained in a circle, "then their ideas also exist, not only insofar as they are only comprehended in the idea of the circle, but also insofar as they involve the existence of those rectangles. By this they are distinguished from the other ideas of the other rectangles" [453: where Spinoza's explanatory diagram is reproduced – TR].)

14. Cf. Duns Scotus, *Opus Oxoniense* I.3.i, ii.4n17. The comparison between

Spinoza and Scotus here bears only on the theme of intensive quantities or degrees. The theory of individuation attributed to Spinoza, as set out in the next paragraph, is altogether different from that of Scotus.

15. One may find in Fichte and Schelling an analogous problem of *quantitative difference and the form of quantifiability* in their relation to the *manifestation* of the absolute (cf. Fichte's letter to Schelling of October 1801, in *J. G. Fichtes Leben und litterarischen Briefwechsel*, ed. I. H. Fichte, Sulzbach, 1830–31, II.2.iv.28, p. 357).

16. An exaggeratedly Leibnizian interpretation has sometimes been given to Spinoza's conception of essences. Huan writes, for example, in *Le Dieu de Spinoza* (Paris, 1914) that "each embraces infinite reality from a particular point of view, and presents in its inner nature a microscopic image of the whole universe" (p. 277).

CHAPTER THIRTEEN: MODAL EXISTENCE

1. E I.28e,p.

2. The idea of a great number of external causes, and that of a great number of component parts form two linked themes: cf. E II.19p.

3. E II.15e,p. This point, among others, worries Blyenbergh (Letter 24, III.107): the soul, being composite, would no less than the body be dissolved after death. But this is to forget that the soul, and the body as well, have an intensive essence of a quite different nature from their extensive parts.

4. That is, imagination, memory, passion: cf. E V.21, 34; and V.40c: "But that *part* we have shown to perish..." [615].

5. Letter 12 (III.41–42 [201, 204]).

6. Letter 81 (to Tschirnhaus, III.241 [362]). On this example of the nonconcentric circles, and the sum of "unequal distances," see Gueroult, "La Lettre de Spinoza sur l'infini," *Revue de métaphysique et de morale* (October 1966).

7. Cf. Letter 12 (to Meyer, III.40–41).

8. Leibniz was acquainted with the greater part of the letter to Meyer. He criticizes various details, but on the subject of the infinity that may be greater or less, he comments: "This, of which most mathematicians, and Cardan in par-

ticular, are ignorant, is remarkably observed, and very carefully inculcated by our author" (PS I.137n21).

9. The geometric example in the letter to Meyer (the sum of unequal distances between two circles) is of a different nature to that given in the *Ethics* at II.8s (the totality of rectangles contained in a circle). In the first case it is a matter of illustrating *the status of existing modes*, whose parts amount to greater or lesser infinities, all these infinities taken together corresponding to the Face of the Universe. Thus the letter to Meyer likens the sum of unequal distances to the sum of changes in matter (III.42). But in the second case, in the *Ethics*, it is a matter of illustrating *the status of essences* of modes, as contained in their attribute.

10. Letter 12 (III.41 [204]). Similarly, in Letter 6 (to Oldenburg, III.22, the section "On Fluidity"), Spinoza refuses both an infinite progression and the existence of a void.

11. I do not understand why, in his study of Spinoza's physics, Rivaud saw here a contradiction: "How can one speak, in an extended space whose actual division is infinite, of completely simple bodies! Such bodies can be real only in relation to our perception" ("La Physique de Spinoza," *Chronicon Spinozanum* IV.32). 1. There would be contradiction only between the idea of simple bodies and the principle of infinite divisibility. 2. The reality of simple bodies lies beyond any possible perception. For perception belongs only to composite modes with an infinity of parts, and itself grasps only such composites. Simple parts are not perceived, but apprehended by reason: cf. Letter 6 (to Oldenburg, III.21).

12. Spinoza's exposition of physics comes in E II, after Proposition 13 (to avoid any confusion, references to this exposition are preceded by an asterisk). The theory of simple bodies takes up *Axioms 1, 2 and *Lemmata 1-3 (down to the second axiom of the last). Spinoza there insists on a purely extrinsic determination; he does, it is true, speak of the "nature" of bodies, on the level of simple bodies, but this "nature" refers only to such a body's previous state.

13. Rivaud, "La Physique de Spinoza," pp. 32-34.

14. ST II, Note to Preface § 7-14.

15. E II *Lemmata 4, 6, 7.

16. Letter 32 (to Oldenburg, III.120–21 [211]).

17. *Ibid.*

18. CU 101 [41].

19. Letter 30 (to Oldenburg, III.119): "I do not know how each of these parts is connected with the whole, and how with the other parts" [205].

20. M I.ii [304].

21. E II.8c: for the distinction between "existing with duration" and "existing *only* as being comprehended in their attribute" [452]; E V.29s: for the distinction between "existing in relation to a certain time and place" and "existing as contained in God and following from the necessity of his nature" [610].

22. Cf. E II.8c,s: *non tantum ... sed etiam....*

23. *Critique of Pure Reason*, tr. Kemp Smith (London, 1933), "Critique of the Fourth Paralogism," 1781 version: Matter "is a species of representations (intuition) which are called *external*, not as standing in relation to objects in themselves external, but because they relate perceptions to the space in which all things are external to one another, *while yet the space itself is in us....* Space itself, with all its appearances, as representations, is indeed only in me; but nevertheless the real, that is, the material of all objects of outer intuition, is actually given in this space independently of all imaginative invention" [A 370, 375].

24. Modal essences, insofar as they are comprised in the attribute, are already "explications." Thus Spinoza speaks of God's essence insofar as it "*explicates*" itself through the essence of this or that mode: E IV.4p. But there are two orders of explication, and the word *explicate* particularly suits the second.

Chapter Fourteen: What Can a Body Do?

1. Cf. E II.28p: "Affections are modes[a] with which the parts of the human body, and consequently the whole body, are affected" [470]. Cf. also II, *Postulate 3.

2. E III.51e,p, 57s.

3. E IV.39p [569].

4. E III.2s: "No one has yet determined *what the body can do*.... For no one has yet come to know the *structure* of the body" [495].

5. E III, Definitions 1-3.

6. ST II.xxvi.7-8.

7. E IV.4e,p,c.

8. E V.6s, 39s [614].

9. Cf. E V.20s.

10. An affect or feeling presupposes an idea from which it flows: ST Appendix II.7; E II, Axiom 3.

11. E III, General Definition of Affects: "I do not understand that the mind compares its body's present constitution with a past constitution, but that the idea which constitutes the form of the affect affirms of the body something which really involves more or less of reality than before" [542].

12. *Adequate* and *inadequate* initially qualify ideas. But they come, as a result, to qualify causes: we are the "adequate cause" of a feeling that follows from some adequate idea we have.

13. E III.1e,3e [493, 497].

14. The capacity to be affected is defined as the aptness of a body both for suffering and acting: cf. E II.13s ("the more a body is capable than others of doing many things at once, or being acted on in many ways at once..." [458]); IV.38e ("the more a body is rendered capable of being affected or of affecting other bodies in a great many ways..." [568]).

15. E IV.39s: "Sometimes a man undergoes such changes that I should hardly have said he was the same man. I have heard stories, for example, of a Spanish poet.... If this seems incredible, what shall we say of infants? A man of advanced years believes their nature to be so different from his own that he could not be persuaded that he was ever an infant, if he did not make this conjecture concerning himself from others" [569-70].

16. Leibniz's notes bear witness to a persistent interest in Spinoza's theory of action and passion: see, for example, *Textes inédits* (ed. Grua, Paris, 1948), II.667ff. for a discussion dating from after 1704. As Friedmann has well shown, Leibniz often expresses himself in terms analogous to those used by

Spinoza: *Leibniz et Spinoza*, p. 201.

17. Cf. Leibniz, "On Nature itself..." (1698; Loemker 53) § 11. This relation of active and passive force is analyzed by Gueroult in *Dynamique et métaphysique leibniziennes* (Paris, 1934), pp. 166-69.

18. ST II.xxvi.7 [147], I.ii.23 [72]; and cf. E III.3s: "The passions are not related to the mind except insofar as it has something which involves a negation" [498].

19. E II.17s.

20. Hence Spinoza, at E III, Definition of Desire, uses the words: "affection *of* the essence," *affectionem humanae essentiae.*

21. E III.3s: "They do not know what the body can do, or what can be deduced from the consideration of its nature alone" [496].

22. E V.42s [616].

23. E IV.4p.

24. Cf. Alquié, *Descartes, l'homme et l'oeuvre* (Paris, 1956), pp. 54-55. Descartes does, it is true, return to naturalist considerations in his last works, but these are negative rather than positive ones (cf. Alquié, *La Découverte métaphysique de l'homme chez Descartes* (Paris, 1950), pp. 271-72).

25. Leibniz, "On Nature Itself..." § 2; and cf. § 16: the construction of a philosophy "midway between the formal and the material" [507].

26. Cf. Leibniz's criticism of Boyle, "On Nature Itself..." § 3; and Spinoza's, in Letters 6, 13 (to Oldenburg: "I did not think, indeed I could not have persuaded myself, that this most learned gentleman had no other object in his *Treatise on Nitre* than to show the weak foundations of that childish and frivolous doctrine of substantial forms and qualities...." Letter 13, III.45 [208]).

27. Leibniz, "On Nature in Itself..." § 9 [502].

28. ST II.xix.8n: "two modes because rest is certainly not nothing" [131]. If one can speak of a "tendency" toward movement in Spinoza, one may do so only in the case where a body is inhibited from following the movement to which it determined from outside, by other bodies, no less external, which counter this determination. This is the sense in which Descartes had already spoken of a *conatus* (cf. *Principles* III.56-57).

29. E IV.38-39 (for the two expressions "whatever so disposes the human body that it can be affected in more ways" and "things which bring about the preservation of the proportion of motion and rest the human body's parts have to one another" [568]).

30. E III.9e,p.

31. On this determination of essence and *conatus* by any affection *whatever*, see E III.56p *ad fin.*; III, Definition of Desire. At III.9s Spinoza had defined desire simply as *conatus* or appetite "with consciousness of itself." That was a *nominal definition*. When, on the other hand, he shows that *conatus* is necessarily determined by an affection *of which we have an idea* (be it inadequate), he is giving a real definition, involving "the cause of consciousness."

32. E III.37p.

33. E III.54e.

34. E III.57p: *potentia seu conatus*; III, general definition of the affects, explanation: *agendi potentia sive existendi vis*; IV.24e: *Agere, vivere, suum esse conservare, haec tria idem significant.*

CHAPTER FIFTEEN: THE THREE ORDERS AND THE PROBLEM OF EVIL

1. E I.21-25.

2. Letter 64 (to Schuller, III.206).

3. ST Appendix I.4p: "All the essences of things we see which, when they did not previously exist, were contained in Extension, motion and rest..." [152].

4. ST I.ii.19n: "But, you say, if there is motion in matter, it must be in a part of matter, not in the whole, since the whole is infinite. For in what direction would it be moved, since there is nothing outside it? Then in a part. I reply: there is no motion by itself, but only motion and rest together; and this is, and must be, in the whole..." [71].

5. Letter 64 (to Schuller, III.206 [308]).

6. Parts that enter into some relation must formerly have existed in other relations. These initial relations have to combine if the parts subsumed in them are to enter into the new relation. The latter is thus in this sense *composite*.

Conversely, it *decomposes* when it loses its parts, which must then enter into other relations.

7. E II.29c: *ex communi Naturae ordine*; II.29s: *Quoties* [*mens*] *ex communi Naturae ordine res percipit, hoc est quoties externe, ex rerum nempe fortuito occursu, determinatur....* Alquié has emphasized the importance of this theme of the encounter (*occursus*) in Spinoza's theory of affections: cf. *Servitude et liberté chez Spinoza* (Sorbonne lectures), p. 42.

8. E IV d1, 31e; and above all 38,39e.

9. E IV.8.

10. Cf. E III.57p.

11. E IV.8e: "The knowledge of good and evil is nothing but a feeling of joy or sadness, insofar as we are conscious of it" [550].

12. E IV.5e: "The force and growth of any passion, and its perseverance in existing, are not defined by the power with which we strive to persevere in existing, but by the power of an external cause compared with our own" [549].

13. E IV.59p [579].

14. E IV.18p: "A desire that arises from joy is aided or increased by the feeling of joy itself.... And so the force of a desire that arises from joy must be defined both by human power and the power of the external cause" [555].

15. E III.37p.

16. Indeed love is itself a joy, added to the joy from which it proceeds... (cf. E III.37p).

17. Cf. E V.10e,p: "affects contrary to our nature" [601].

18. E V.37s.

19. E IV.8e,p.

20. E III.13e,28e; and 37p: "The power of acting with which the man will strive to remove the sadness" [515].

21. E IV.18p: "A desire that arises from sadness is diminished or restrained by the feeling of sadness" [555].

22. E III.15–16 "Accidental" is here no more opposed to "necessary" than was "fortuitous."

23. Cf. the "vacillation of mind" of E III.17 (there are two sorts of *vacilla-*

tion: one, defined in the Proof of this Proposition, is explained by extrinsic and accidental relations between objects; the other, defined in the Scholium, is explained by the different relations of which we are intrinsically composed.

24. E III.20e,23e [506, 507].

25. E IV.32-34.

26. E IV.37s2.

27. Cf. E IV.20s, Spinoza's interpretation of suicide: "or finally because hidden external causes so dispose his imagination and so affect his body, that it takes on another nature, contrary to the former, a nature of which there cannot be an idea in the mind" [557].

28. E IV.43.

29. E III.44p: "the sadness hate involves" [519]; 47e: "The joy which arises from our imagining that a thing we hate is destroyed, or affected with some other evil, does not occur without some sadness of mind" [520].

30. Cf. E III.47p.

31. Letter 19 (to Blyenbergh, III.65 [360]). The same argument is to be found in TP iv (II.139). The only difference between this divine revelation and our natural understanding is that God revealed to Adam the *consequence* of eating the fruit, the poisoning that would result, but did not reveal to him the *necessity* of this consequence; or Adam, at least, did not have an understanding powerful enough to understand this necessity.

32. Letter 22 (from Blyenbergh, III.96 [385]).

33. What Spinoza in his correspondence with Blyenbergh calls "works" are precisely the effects to whose production we are determined.

34. E III.8e: "The striving by which each thing strives to persevere in its being involves no finite time, but an indefinite time" [499]; E IV, Preface: "*No singular thing can be called more perfect for having persevered in existing for a longer time*" [546].

35. E IV.59s [580].

36. E IV.59s: "If a man moved by anger or hate is determined to close his fist or move his arm, that happens because one and the same action can be joined to any images of things whatever" [580].

37. Letter 23 (to Blyenbergh, III.99): *nihil horum aliquid essentiae exprimere*; it is here that Spinoza discusses the cases of Orestes and Nero.

38. Cf. Blyenbergh's objection (Letter 22, III.96): "Here again the question can be raised: if there were a mind to whose singular nature the pursuit of pleasures or crimes was not contrary, is there a reason for virtue which would necessarily move it to do good and avoid evil?" [385], and Spinoza's reply (Letter 23, III.101): "It is as if someone were to ask: if it agreed better with the nature of someone to hang himself, would there be reasons why he should not hang himself? But suppose it were possible that there should be such a nature. Then I say...that if anyone sees that he can live better on the gallows than at his table, he would act very foolishly if he did not go hang himself. One who saw clearly that in fact he would enjoy a better and more perfect life or essence by pursuing crimes than by following virtue would also be a fool if he did not pursue them. For crimes would be a virtue in relation to such a perverted human nature" [390].

39. Cf. E III, Definition of Sadness.

40. Letter 20 (from Blyenbergh, III.72).

41. Letter 21 (to Blyenbergh, III.87–88).

42. Letter 22 (from Blyenbergh, III.94 [383]).

43. E III, Definition of Sadness, Explanation: "Nor can we say that sadness consists in the privation of a greater perfection. For a privation is nothing, whereas the affect of sadness is an act, which can therefore be no other act than that of passing to a lesser perfection" [532].

44. E IV.68e [584].

45. These were Leibniz's criteria, and those of all who accused Spinoza of atheism.

46. E IV.68p.

47. *Genealogy of Morals*, in *Basic Writings*, tr. Kaufmann (New York, 1966), I.17.

CHAPTER SIXTEEN: THE ETHICAL VISION OF THE WORLD

1. E III.2s. This fundamental passage should not be considered apart from

II.13s which prepares it, and V, Preface, which develops its consequences.

2. Descartes, *Passions of the Soul* I.1-2.

3. Leibniz often explains that his theory of *ideal action* follows "established feelings" in preserving in its entirety the rule that apportions action and passion to soul and body in inverse proportion. For between two substances such as the soul and the body which "symbolize" one another, action must be attributed to that term whose *expression* is most distinct, and passion to the other. This is a constant theme of his correspondence with Arnauld.

4. E II.13s.

5. E III.2s [494].

6. E II.13s [458].

7. TP xvi (II.258 [200]).

8. On the identity of "naturally instituted law" and natural rights, see TP xvi; P ii,iv.

9. TP xiv (II.258-59); P ii,v.

10. These four theses, together with the four contrary theses outlined in the following paragraph, are well set out by Leo Strauss in his book *Natural Right and History* (Chicago, 1953). Strauss contrasts Hobbes's theory, whose novelty he emphasizes, with the conceptions of Antiquity.

11. P v.2: "For men are not born citizens [Elwes: "fit for citizenship"], but become such [Elwes "must be made so"]" [313].

12. TP xvi (II.266 [210]).

13. P ii.8 [294] (cf. E IV.37s2: "Everyone, by the highest right of nature, judges what is good and what is evil" [566]).

14. P ii.15: "So long as the natural right of man is determined by the power of every individual, and belongs to everyone, so long it is a nonentity, existing in opinion rather than fact, as there is no assurance of making it good" [296].

15. Cf. E IV.24e: *proprium utile.*b

16. Cf. E IV.35.

17. E IV.66s (free man and slave); 73s (strong man); V.42s (wise and ignorant).

18. Cf. E IV.67-73.

19. E IV.68.

20. _P ii.6 [293-94].

21. At E IV.69s Spinoza traces the Adamic tradition back to Moses: the myth of a reasonable and free Adam may be explained from the viewpoint of an abstract "hypothesis," by which one considers God "not insofar as he is infinite, but insofar only as he is the cause of man's existence" [584].

22. E IV.18s.

23. The idea of a becoming, or formative process, of reason had already been developed by Hobbes; cf. R. Polin's commentary, *Politique et philosophie chez Thomas Hobbes* (Paris, 1953), pp. 26-40. Both Hobbes and Spinoza conceive the activity of reason as a kind of addition, as the formation of a whole. But in Hobbes this is a matter of calculation, while in Spinoza it is a matter of combining relations, rooted, at least in principle, in intuition.

24. E IV.18s.

25. E IV.35.

26. E IV.32-34.

27. TP xvi (II.259 [201]).

28. P vi.1.

29. Cf. TP xvi (and E IV.37s2). Whatever the type of regime, contractual delegation always occurs, according to Spinoza, not to the gain of a third party (as in Hobbes), but to that of the Whole, that is, of the totality of contractors. Mme Francès is right in saying that Spinoza in this sense prepares the way for Rousseau (even though she minimizes the originality of Rousseau's conception of the way this whole is formed): cf. "Les Réminiscences spinozistes dans le Contrat Social de Rousseau," *Revue philosophique* (January 1951), pp. 66-67. But if it be true that the contract transfers power to the City as a whole, still the conditions of such a process, and its difference from a process of pure reason, require the presence of a second element through which the City as a whole in its turn transfers its power to a king or to an aristocratic or democratic assembly. Is this a *second* contract, genuinely distinct from the first, as is suggested at TP xvii? (Spinoza says in effect that the Hebrews formed a political whole by transferring their power to God, and *then* transferred the power of the whole

to Moses, taken as God's interpreter: cf. II.274.) Or does the first contract only exist abstractly, as the basis of the second? (In the *Political Treatise* the State seems never to exist in its *absolute* form, *absolutum imperium*, but always to be represented by monarchical, aristocratic or democratic forms, the last being the regime that comes closest to an absolute State.)

30. E IV.37s; P ii,xviii,xix,xxiii.

31. P iii.2 [301].

32. TP xvi (II.262-3), TP ii.21,iii.8,iv.4,v.1,,

33. The motive forces in the formation of the City are always fear and hope – fear of a greater evil and hope of a greater good. But these are essentially sad passions (cf. E IV.47p). The City, once established, must elicit *the love of freedom* rather than the fear of punishments or even the hope of rewards. "Rewards of virtue are granted to slaves, not freemen" (P x.8 [382]).

34. P iii.3,8.

35. In two important passages (Letter 50, to Jelles, III.172; and P iii.3) Spinoza says that his political theory is characterized by the maintainance of natural rights within the civil state itself. The principle must be differently understood in the case of the sovereign who is defined by his natural rights, these being equal to the sum of the rights relinquished by his subjects, and in the case of these subjects themselves who preserve their natural right of persevering in being, even though this right is now determined by common affections.

36. TP xx (II.306-7); P iii.10: "The mind, so far as it makes use of reason, is dependent, not on the sovereign [Elwes: "supreme authorities"], but on itself" [305].

37. E IV.35s; IV.73e,p.

38. On *pietas* and *religio*, again relative to our power of action, cf. E IV.37sl, V.41. On the "commands" (*dictamina*) of reason, cf. E IV.18s.

39. Reason, for example, denounces hatred and everything related: E IV.45-46. But this is solely because hatred is inseparable from the *sadness* it involves. Hope, pity, humility, repentance are no less denounced, since they also involve sadness: E IV.47,50,53-54.

40. Spinoza's analysis of superstition in the preface of the *Theologico-Political*

Treatise is very close to that of Lucretius: superstition is essentially defined by a mixture of greed and anxiety. And the cause of superstition is not a confused idea of God, but fear, sad passions and their concatenation (TP, Preface, II.85).

41. TP, Preface (II.87 [5]).

42. E IV.45s2 [572]; IV.50s [574]; IV.63s [582]; V.10s [602–3]; IV.67e [584].

43. P i.1 [287: indefinite articles supplied to accord with the French version – TR].

44. E IV Appendix 13 [590].

45. E IV.54s.

46. E IV.47s.

47. P x.8.

CHAPTER SEVENTEEN: COMMON NOTIONS

1. E IV.59p: "Insofar as joy is good, it agrees with reason (for it consists in this, that a man's power of acting is increased or aided)" [579].

2. E III.59e,p.

3. E III.58e,p; IV.59p.

4. E III.58e.

5. Active and passive feeling are distinguished in like manner to adequate and inadequate ideas. But between an inadequate and an adequate idea of an affection the distinction is one of reason only: E V.3p.

6. Cf. E IV.51p.

7. More or less useful, more or less easily discovered or formed: E II.40s1. More or less universal (*maxime universales, minime universalia*): TP vii (II.176).

8. Less universal common notions: E II.39e [474].

9. For this case of the most universal common notions: E II.37, 38e.

10. E II.29s: "So often as it is determined internally, from the fact that it regards a number of things at once, to understand their agreements, differences, and oppositions; so often as it is disposed internally, in this or another way, then it regards things distinctly, as I shall show below" [471].

11. E II.40s1.

12. Cf. E IV, Preface.

13. E II.40s1 [477].

14. E III.2s: "For no one has yet come to know the structure [*fabrica*] of the body so accurately that he could explain all its functions" [495].

15. Etienne Geoffroy Saint-Hilaire defines his "Philosophy of Nature" through the principle of compositional unity. He opposes his method to the classic method inaugurated by Aristotle, which considers forms and functions. Beyond these he proposes a determination of the variable relations between fixed anatomical components: different animals correspond to variations of relation, respective situation and dependence among these components, so that all are reduced to modifications of a single identical Animal as such. For resemblances of form and analogies of function, which must always remain external, Geoffroy thus substitutes the intrinsic viewpoint of compositional unity or the similarity of relations. He is fond of citing Leibniz, and a principle of unity in diversity. Yet I see him as even more of a Spinozist; for his philosophy of Nature is a monism, and radically excludes any principle of finality, whether external or internal. Cf. *Principes de philosophie zoologique* (1830), and *Etudes progressives d'un naturaliste* (1835).

16. E II.39e,p.

17. E II.38e,p.

18. E II.45e,s.

19. E II.46p: "So what gives knowledge of an eternal and infinite essence of God is common to all, and is equally in the part and in the whole" [482].

20. E II.40s1: By our method it would be established "which notions are common, which are clear and distinct only to those who have no prejudices..." [476].

21. Cf. E II.38–39, and similarly, TP vii, where Spinoza begins from the most universal notions (II.176–77).

22. Cf. E II.39p: From a common notion there follows the idea of an affection (and this is their practical function).

23. E IV.29e: "And, absolutely, no thing can be either good *or evil* for us, unless it has something in common with us" [560].

24. E IV.30e [560].

25. E V.10p [601].

26. E III.1p.

27. E V.3e [598]. And the following proposition specifies the way to form such a clear and distinct idea: by attaching the feeling to a common notion, as to its cause.

28. Cf. E V.2e,p; and V.4s: What is destroyed is not the passive joy itself, but the loves that proceed from it.

29. E IV.63cp: "A desire that arises from reason can arise solely from a feel-ing of joy which is not a passion" [582].

30. E V.4s [599].

31. E V.10e [601].

32. Cf. E V.20s.

33. E V.4e,c [598].

34. E IV.32e: "Insofar as men are subject to passions, they cannot be said to agree in nature." And the Scholium explains that "Things that agree only in a negation, or in what they do not have, really agree in nothing" [561].

35. E V.6s [600].

36. E V.18s [604].

37. This is the order given at E V.10. 1. To the extent that "we are not torn by feelings contrary to our nature," we have the power to form clear and distinct ideas (common notions), and to deduce from them affections linked one to another in accordance with reason. It is thus joyful passions (feelings agreeing with our nature) that provide the initial occasion to form common notions. We must *select* our passions, and even when we meet with something that doesn't agree with us, must try to reduce sadness to a minimum (cf. Scho-lium). 2. Having formed our first common notions, we are better able to avoid bad encounters and feelings opposed to us. And insofar as we necessar-ily still experience such feelings, we are able to form new common notions, which allow us to understand those disagreements and oppositions themselves (cf. Scholium).

CHAPTER EIGHTEEN: TOWARD THE THIRD KIND OF KNOWLEDGE

1. E II.41p.

2. CU 19.

3. On connection through memory or habit: E II.18s. On connection by resemblance, which characterizes knowledge by signs: E II.40ss1,2.

4. TP xvi (II.266 [210]).

5. E II.42e [478]; and cf. V.28e.

6. This religion of the second kind is not the same as what Spinoza, in the *Theologico-Political Treatise*, calls "the universal faith," "common to all men." As described in Chapter 14 (II.247–48), the universal faith still relates to obedience, and uses the moral concepts of fault, repentance and forgiveness in abundance: it mixes, in fact, ideas of the first kind and notions of the second kind. The true religion of the second kind, based solely on common notions, is given a systematic exposition only at E V.14–20. But the *Theologico-Political Treatise* gives valuable details: it is initially the religion of Solomon, who knew the guidance of natural light (iv, II.142–44). It is, in a different way, the religion of Christ: not that Christ had need of common notions in order to know God, but his teaching was in accordance with common notions, rather than based on signs (the Passion and Resurrection obviously belong to the first kind of religion: cf. iv, II.140–41,144). It is, lastly, the religion of the Apostles, but this only in a part of their teaching and activity (xi, *passim*).

7. Cf. Alquié, *Nature et vérité dans la philosophie de Spinoza*, pp. 30ff.

8. ST II.i.2–3.

9. CU 19–21 (cf. Chapter Ten above).

10. CU 101–2; and the *Correction of the Understanding* closes at the point (110) where Spinoza is seeking a common property (*aliquid commune*) on which all of the positive characteristics of understanding would depend.

11. Spinoza says, indeed, that "constant and eternal things" should give us knowledge of the "inner essence" of things; here we have the last kind of knowledge. But constant things must also, on the other hand, serve as "universals" in relation to changing existing modes: and here we have the second kind, and are in the domain of combining relations, rather than that of the

production of essences. The two orders are thus mixed together. Cf. CU 10.

12. E II.40s1: Speaking of the problem of notions, and their different kinds, Spinoza says that he had "thought about these matters at one time."[b] He is obviously speaking of the *Correction of the Understanding*. But he adds that he has "set these aside for another treatise": I take him to be referring to a reworking of the *Correction of the Understanding*, in terms of the closing considerations which forced him to begin all over again.

13. TP i: "Many more ideas can be constructed from words and figures than from the principles and notions on which the whole fabric of reasoned knowledge is reared" [25].

14. At E II.47s Spinoza expressly points out the similarity between common notions and things we can imagine, that is to say, bodies. This indeed is why the idea of God is there distinguished from common notions. Spinoza goes on to treat in the same way common properties which we "imagine" (V.7p), or "images related to things we understand clearly and distinctly" (V.12e [603]).

15. E IV.49; V.5.

16. E V.6e,p.

17. E V.7p: "A feeling that arises from reason is necessarily related to the common properties of things which we always regard as present (for there can be nothing which excludes their present existence) and which we always imagine in the same way" [600[c]].

18. E V.7e. (The passage relates only to feelings in the imagination about things "regarded as absent." But, taking time into account, imagination *always* comes to be determined to regard its object as absent.)

19. E V.8e,p.

20. E V.11–13.

21. Cf. E V.9,11.

22. TP vi (II.159 [84: with "ideas" rather than "notions" – TR]). See also the note relating to this passage (II.315).

23. E V.36s.

24. At E II.45–47 Spinoza passes from common notions to the idea of God (cf., above all, II.46p). At V.14–15 there is a similar transition: having shown

how a large number of images are easily joined to a common notion, Spinoza
concludes that we can join and relate all images to the idea of God.

25. E II.47s: "That men do not have so clear a knowledge of God as they
do of the common notions comes from the fact that they cannot imagine God,
as they can bodies" [482–83].

26. E II.46p (*id quod dat*).

27. E V.15p.

28. E IV.28p.

29. Cf. E V.17,19. Spinoza explicitly reminds us that God can experience
no increase in his power of action, and so no passive joy. And he here finds an
opportunity to deny that God can, in general, experience any joy at all: for the
only active joys known *at this point* in the *Ethics* are those of the second kind.
But such joys presuppose passions, and are excluded from God on the same
grounds as are passions.

30. E II.40s2.

31. E V.28e: "The striving, or desire, to know things by the third kind of
knowledge cannot arise from the first kind of knowledge, but can indeed arise
from the second" [609].

32. At E V.20s Spinoza speaks of the "basis" of the third kind of knowledge. This basis is "the knowledge of God" but is obviously not the knowledge
of God that will be provided by the third kind itself. As the context (V.15–16)
shows, it is here a question of the knowledge of God given by common notions.
Similarly at II.47s, Spinoza says we "form" the third kind of knowledge on the
basis of a knowledge of God. Once again the context (II.46p) shows that what
is in question is a knowledge of God belonging to the second kind of knowledge.

33. E II.40s2 [478] (and cf V.25p).

34. To what extent are ideas of the second and third kinds the same ideas?
Are they differentiated only by their function or use? The problem is a complex one. The most universal common notions do definitely coincide with ideas
of attributes. As common notions they are grasped in the general function they
exercise in relation to *existing modes*. As ideas of the third kind, they are considered in their objective essence, and insofar as they objectively contain *modal*

397

essences. The least universal common notions do not however, for their part, coincide with ideas of particular essences (relations are not the same as essences, even though essences express themselves in those relations).

35. P iv (II.140–41).

36. TP i (II.98–99).

Chapter Nineteen: Beatitude

1. At E V.36s Spinoza opposes the *general* proof of the second kind to the *singular* inference of the third.

2. E V.37s: Only existing modes can destroy one another, and no essence can destroy another.

3. Cf. E V.25–27.

4. E V.22p,36e.

5. Cf. E V.36s. (The general context here shows that what is in question is each person's own essence, the essence of his own body: cf. V.30.)

6. E V.29e.

7. E V.31e: "The third kind of knowledge depends on the mind, as on a formal cause, insofar as the mind itself is eternal" [610].

8. E V.27p: He who knows by the third kind of knowledge "is affected with the greatest joy [*summa laetitia*]" [609].

9. E V.32c.

10. Thus common notions do not as such constitute the essence of any singular thing: cf. E II.37e. And at V.41p, Spinoza reminds us that the second kind of knowledge gives us no idea of the eternal essence of the mind.

11. E V.29p. There are thus two kinds of eternity, one characterized by the *presence* of common notions, the other by the *existence* of singular essences.

12. On the affections of an essence in general, and on the adventitious and the innate, see E III, Explanation of the Definition of Desire.

13. According to E II.38,39p, common notions are indeed in God. But this only insofar as they are comprised in the ideas of singular things (ideas of ourselves and of other things) which are themselves in God. It is not so with us: common notions come first in the order of our knowledge. Thus they are in us

a source of special affections (joys of the second kind). God, on the other hand, experiences only affections of the third kind.

14. Cf. E V.14–20.

15. E V.31s: "Although we are already certain that the mind is eternal, insofar as it conceives things *sub specie aeternitatis*, nevertheless, for an easier explanation and better understanding of the things we wish to show, we shall consider it as if it were now beginning to be, and were now beginning to understand things *sub specie aeternitatis*..." [610–11].

16. E V.33s [611].

17. E V.33s.

18. Love toward God of the second kind: E V.14–20; the love of God of the third kind: E V.32–37.

19. E V.36e,c.

20. E V.36s.

21. Cf. E V.20s,38p.

22. On the parts of the soul, see E II.15. On the assimilation of faculties to parts, see E V.40cp.

23. E V.23s,29p. (This faculty of suffering, imagining or conceiving in time is indeed a *power*, because it "involves" the soul's essence or power of action.)

24. E V.22p.

25. E V.22p. This proof cites precisely that axiom of parallelism by which knowledge of an effect depends on and involves knowledge of its cause. Spinoza's formula *species aeternitatis* designates at once the *kind* of eternity that flows from a cause, and the intellectual *conception* that is inseparable from the cause.

26. E V.29e,p.

27. E V.23s. This experience necessarily belongs to the third kind of knowledge; for the second kind has no adequate idea of our body's essence, and does not yet give us the knowledge that our mind is eternal (cf. V.41p).

28. E V.21e: "The mind can neither imagine anything, nor recollect past things, except while the body endures" [607].

29. E V.40c: "The part of the mind that remains, however great it is, is more perfect than the rest" [615].

30. E V.34e: "Only while the body endures is the mind subject to feelings which are related to the passions" [611].

31. E V.40c: "The eternal part of the mind is the understanding, through which alone we are said to act. But what we have shown to perish is the imagination, through which alone we are said to suffer action" [615].

32. At E IV.39p,s Spinoza says that death destroys the body, and so "renders it completely incapable of being affected" [569]. But as the context makes clear, what are here in question are passive affections produced by other existing bodies.

33. Leibniz, Letter to the Landgrave of HesseRheinfels, August 14, 1683. Cf. Foucher de Careil, tr. O. Owen (Edinburgh, 1855). By taking the Spinozist eternity of the soul as similar to a mathematical truth, Leibniz overlooks all the differences between the third kind of knowledge and the second.

34. E V.38s [614]. While in existence we strive (V.39s) to train our body in such a way that it corresponds to a mind that is in the highest degree conscious of itself, of God, and of things. Then what relates to memory and imagination will be "of hardly any moment in relation to the understanding" [614].

35. E V.38p: "The more the mind understands things by the second and third kind of knowledge, the greater the part of it that remains unharmed" [613].

36. E V.38e,s.

CONCLUSION: THE THEORY OF EXPRESSION IN LEIBNIZ AND SPINOZA: EXPRESSIONISM IN PHILOSOPHY

1. On these two themes of mirror and seed (or branch), in their essential relation to the notion of expression, reference might be made, for example, to Eckhardt's trial. The themes are in fact among the principal heads under which he was accused (cf. *Edition critique des pièces rélatives au procès d'Eckhart*, ed. G. Théry, in *Archives d'Histoire doctrinale et littéraire du Moyen Age* (Paris, 1926–27).

2. On "simple forms taken absolutely," "the very attributes of God," and "the first causes and ultimate reason of things," see the Letter to Elizabeth

(1678), and the "Meditations on Knowledge" (1684). In the 1676 note, "Quod Ens perfectissimum existit," perfection is defined as an absolute positive quality or one *quae quicquid exprimit, sine ullis limitibus exprimit* (PS VII.261-62). Leibniz alludes, in the *New Essays*, to "original or distinctly knowable qualities" that can be carried to infinity.

3. Leibniz, *Discourse on Metaphysics* § 16 [314].f

4. Cf. the passage already cited (ch. 9, n. 19) from a letter to Arnauld: "Expression is common to all forms, and it is a genus of which natural perception, animal sensation and intellectual knowledge are species."

5. PS VII.263-64.

6. Letter to Arnauld (Janet I.594): "It is enough for what is divisible and material and dispersed into many entities to be expressed or represented in a single indivisible entity or substance which is endowed with a genuine unity" (Mason, p. 144). Cf. also *New Essays*, tr. A. G. Longley, New York, 1896, III.6 § 24 [p. 349]: Soul and machine "agree perfectly, and although having no immediate influence the one upon the other, they are mutually expressive, the one having concentrated into a perfect unity all that the other has dispersed in multiplicity" [Longley: "in the manifold."].

7. Draft of a letter to Arnauld (1686; Janet I.552-53, Mason, p. 84).

8. Letter to Arnauld (Janet I.596, Mason, p. 147).

9. Cf. *Textes inédits*, ed. Grua (Paris, 1948), p. 126: "As all minds are unities, one may say that God is the primitive unity, expressed by all the others according to their capacity.... Whence follows their operation in creatures, which varies according to the different combinations of unity with zero, or of positive with privative." These different types of unity *symbolize* one another: the relatively simple notions of our understanding, for example, symbolizing the absolute simples of the divine understanding (cf. "Elementa calculi" and "Introductio ad encyclopaedium arcanam"). A unity, of whatever type, is always the final cause in relation to the multiplicity it subsumes. And Leibniz uses the word "harmony," especially, to designate this referral of multiplicity to unity (cf. "Elementa verae pietatis" in Grua, p. 7).

10. Leibniz sometimes uses the word "emanation" to designate the crea-

tion and combination of unities: see, for example *Discourse on Metaphysics* § 14.

11. A recurrent theme in the correspondence with Arnauld is that God did not create Adam a sinner, but only created the world in which Adam sinned.

Translator's Notes

Deleuze has commented on a few points raised in these notes, and his comments are sometimes quoted or alluded to below. His reply to a general query relating to his use of capitalization may be given here: "My use of capitals is often somewhat arbitrary. I usually capitalize a word for one of two reasons: (1) When an important notion appears for the first time in some passage (subsequent uses being in lower-case), or (2) when some notion has a particular importance in a specific sentence (but not in adjacent sentences)."

INTRODUCTION

    a. *Dans son genre*: I take this phrase to echo Spinoza's *in suo genero* of Definition 2. A rather antiquated sense of "in its kind" corresponds to a colloquial sense of the French expression "in its way." And while attributes are no more Scholastic *genera* than modes are *species*, there is also something of this technical sense ("in its way" would directly correspond to *suo modo*, which would hardly do for an attribute). "Form" seems here to convey a similar interplay of two senses.

    b. Deleuze's gloss and note here underline the interplay in the Latin original of the two registers or instances – "technical" or Scholastic, and nontechnical or "informal" – of *modus*, each as it were illustrating the other (the same formula "*modi* qui...certo et determinato *modo* exprimunt" recurs in the next passage translated). The play carries over into the French *mode*, but then loses much of its force in the (or indeed *its*) less common English "mode."

403

c. "Epistemology," with its derivatives, may be taken as the English equivalent to the French *gnoséologie* (which Deleuze uses a few pages below as equivalent to "theory of knowledge"; his term here is *gnoséologique*). The term is sometimes contrasted with *épistémologie*, taken as the theory of that systematically organized and instituted knowledge we call "science." The current instability of this distinction is, however, reflected in Deleuze's use of *épistémologie* and its derivatives throughout Chapter 7 below, as equivalent to *gnoséologie* here.

d. *Sous l'espèce de l'éternité*: The Latin *species* has in Spinoza (like *genus, modus* and so on) both a "technical" and an "informal" usage; but to translate this key expression (with Curley and others) by taking only the technical sense of a logical "species" as subdivision of a genus (the latter, then, being eternity) seems to me both to contradict Spinoza's own generally derogatory "technical" use (cf. p. 36 below), and to miss the fundamental visual metaphor of the *aspect* or "viewpoint" of eternity (as opposed to that of duration). The Dutch equivalent used by Spinoza and his translators in this context is *gedaante*, and this itself retranslates variously into Latin as *species, forma* or *figura* (*species* is in turn sometimes rendered by *vertoning*, which is sometimes retranslated *repraesentamen* and so on). The "form of eternity" conveys some of the interplay of the various registers of *species aeternitatis*, but since the Latin formula is already so familiar I leave it (along with various other expressions such as *natura naturans* and *naturata, conatus* and so on) untranslated, and leave the interplay of "technical" and "nontechnical" (and of the various different "aspects," intentional, intelligible, sensible, logical . . . of the former) unresolved.

e. *S'exprimer*, being a reflexive verb – having the same thing as subject and object – can often be taken either as active or passive: here (as in many other cases) it may mean either what (actively) *expresses* itself, or what (passively) is *expressed*.

f. On the problem of how to render the interplay of senses among the Latin *implicare, involvere*, their French analogues (*impliquer, envelopper*, etc.), *explicare* and *its* French analogues, *complicare*, and so on (*multiple, complexe*, etc.), in the "differently folded" system of expression which is English, see the Translator's Preface.

g. The difficulties posed by using Elwes's versions, while we await the completion of Curley's translation of Spinoza's works, are illustrated by his translation here, from which I have departed toward the close: Elwes ends, "cannot be comprehended by any other means than proofs; if these are absent the object remains ungrasped." The Latin reads: "nullis aliis oculis videri possunt, quam per demonstrationes; qui itaque eas non habent, nihil harum rerum plane vident."

CHAPTER ONE

a. In Spinoza, the Dutch *vertoning* is both *repraesentamen* and *species*, "presentation" and "appearance"; the difficulty involved in translating Deleuze's *donnée de la représentation* is that both "representation" and "appearance" are more technically loaded in English than *représentation* in French, which corresponds rather to Spinoza's less technical *vertoning*.

b. "Attribute" nowhere occurs in the Scholium, although it is used as equivalent to "nature" in (the "equivalent") Proposition 5 (... *eiusdem naturae sive attributi*).

CHAPTER TWO

a. Curley takes the reference of this passage to be "Nature," rather than the attributes of Nature, and translates: "Existence belongs to its essence, so that outside it there is no essence or being" [152].

b. "They" are in this context hypothetical "corporeal and intellectual substances."

CHAPTER THREE

a. I have translated *affirmer* and its derivatives throughout this chapter as "affirm." While the more usual English term derives in several cases from "assert," this seems to involve no distortion of Deleuze's sense, and no great sacrifice of "natural" English, while allowing a uniformity coordinate with the French argument (using "assert" and its derivatives throughout would not work: *affirmative* could not, for example, be correctly translated as "assertive"). I have on the other hand alternated in my translation of the complementary *nier* (and

405

its derivatives) between "deny" and "negate" (and theirs), since to privilege either would lead to rather unnatural expressions, and the unity of the argument seems adequately maintained by affirmation. (The derivation of this group of French "negative" terms from the Latin *negare* is itself less uniform than the derivation of the complementary "affirmative" group.)

b. I have used the single term "word" to translate three French terms: *Parole*, *verbe* and *mot*. When rendering the first of these terms, "word" is capitalized (thus *Parole de Dieu* becomes "Word of God"). The second term is used by Deleuze both capitalized and (when implying a plurality of "Words") not, but is always capitalized in English to convey the scriptural resonance absent from the common French term for "word," *mot* (which appears throughout with lower-case initial in both French and English). The context in English generally allows the various different resonances of these three French renderings of Spinoza's (and Jerome's) single term *verbum* to be carried over. Sometimes, however, *Parole* has been rendered by "Speech" (*parole* without initial capital is always "speech") where this particular resonance is required and the context does not seem adequately to supply it.

c. Romans 1:20: The original Greek is somewhat ambiguous in two respects: Does "from the creation of the world" date the *visibility* or the *invisibility* of "the invisibles of God"? And are these invisible things known to understanding in or through created things (taking the Greek dative instrumentally) or known rather in or to the understandings of "creatures"? The King James translation used by Elwes, while itself remaining somewhat ambiguous, suggests (I think) the first interpretation in each case. The French translation given by Deleuze, on the other hand, appears to suggest the contrary interpretation in each case.

d. *Sens*: The normal English expression would be "theory of *meaning*," but here, as in similar contexts below, I have retained "sense" in order to convey the *sense* of the term more fully developed by Deleuze in his 1969 *Logic of Sense*, and to maintain that continuity with other instances of the same term which exemplifies just such a logic.

e. "Subject," "subjectively" and "objectively" have here, of course, their Scholastic senses of the logical subject of a proposition (or its ontological correlate), of what belongs to such a "subject" considered in itself ("subjectively"), and of what relates to the "objective" perception of the subject as *object* of an act of perception. After the shift from the primacy of ontology to that of epistemology typified by Descartes, "subjective" has come to designate that element in perception attributable to the psychological "subject" of the act, and "objective" the complementary component attributable to the "object" in itself, so that the Scholastic senses of the words have been effectively reversed (rather, perhaps, as light is now taken to travel from the object to the eye, whereas it had earlier been taken to travel from eye to object).

CHAPTER FOUR

a. ST I.ii.n2 [66].

b. "Confirmation of this scheme": *contre-épreuve* (cf. Chapter 9, note a).

c. *S'affirment*: The reflexive use of verbs in French often amounts to a "middle" voice, intermediate between active and passive, which cannot be directly rendered in English, for it has no such voice. Here, for example, *s'affirment* has a sense of both (or "between") "affirm" and "are affirmed." This does not usually cause much of a problem, but may do so when the discussion in which these middle-voice verbs occur turns on questions, precisely, of the subjects and objects of primary activities, the "categorical" articulation or constitution, say, of primary, "absolute" verbality or actuality.

CHAPTER FIVE

a. *Facile*: Modern English takes over only the derogatory sense from the Latin and French words for "easy."

b. "Can," *peut* ("is capable"), is in French cognate with "a capacity," *un pouvoir*, being the third person singular of the verb *pouvoir* (+ infinitive: "to be able to"), from which that substantive is taken. I reserve "power," the more common translation of *pouvoir*, to render *puissance*, which though generally synonymous in French is in the sequel systematically distinguished by Deleuze from *pouvoir*, as "actual" rather than merely "potential" power: power "in action," implemented. One should bear in mind that this distinction remains merely implicit in the Latin *potentia*, as in the English "power," and depends, "strictly speaking," on a metonymic transfer of the term that in Aristotle generally designates something "potential," to the "conditional" actuality that "fulfills" (French: *remplit*) or exercises such a capacity. Curley notes that "some French scholars" have thought to find in Spinoza a systematic distinction between *pouvoir* and *puissance*, illustrated by his use of *potestas* and *potentia* – but that "it is unclear that a systematic examination of Spinoza's usage would confirm even a prima facie distinction" [651], and he translates all occurences of both *potentia* and *potestas* by "power." One might, finally, reflect that Spinoza's solution of the thorny question of the actuality of potentiality in general, and of the potentiality involved in the distinction of actual and potential in particular – in effect that of the essence of existence, transmitted through Averroist theories of the Active Intellect – implies an ultimate convertibility between actual and potential power: "Gueroult...comments that Spinoza introduces the distinction in order to reduce it immediately to nothing" (Curley, *loc. cit.*); "To *potentia* there corresponds an *aptitudo* or *potestas*; but there is no aptitude or capacity that remains ineffective, and so no power that is not actual" (Deleuze, p. 93 below).

c. Curley uses "intellect" for *intellectus* (Spinoza uses the Dutch *verstand* for both this and *intelligentia*, which Curley translates "understanding"). In order to maintain consistency I have translated *entendement* whether it occurs in Deleuze or in his citations of Spinoza as "understanding" – thus retaining, in particular, the traditional English translation of "Treatise on the Correction of the Understanding" (Curley's "Treatise on the Emendation of the Intellect" – which title hardly has the straightforward connotations of Latin, Dutch, French or traditional English versions). Curley inclines to the view (the opposite is assumed by Deleuze, and material to his argument) that the *Correction of the Understanding* antedates the *Short Treatise*.

CHAPTER SIX

a. I have in this sentence rendered the same French word *science*, by the three words *scientia*, science and knowledge, as it seems here to be used as an equivalent to the Latin term, which has — combined — both of the latter senses. Or has, rather, a sense which has latterly become thus divided. (Deleuze points out that in Spinoza, *scientia* appears to comprise the second and third kinds of knowledge.)

b. "The object designated (which *s'exprime*)": An instance of the middle voice which I am not sure whether to construe as primarily active or passive, whether as object actively expressing itself "in" the sense of an expression designating it, or passively expressed (by a speaker) "through" that sense. The reflexive construction identifies the "object" as indeed object of the verb "express," but in general the matter of whether it or another "subject" is subject of the sentence has to be inferred from the context. Thus "comment ça se dit?" can only mean "how is that said, expressed?" or "how does one express that?"; and "il s'exprime bien" must just about always mean "he expresses himself well" — but the present context leaves the question open. (Deleuze has himself noted that in the case of the verb *exprimere* Latin — like English, but unlike French — always requires us to choose between active and passive.)

c. *S'exprimer* again: Scholastic philosophers insisted on the primacy of the *act* of expression or "intention," with the "active" and "passive" sides as complementary partial aspects of the act. The iteration of intention identified by Deleuze here was, for Scholasticism, the process of "reflection," in which the "intention" of an elementary act of intending an external object itself becomes "intended" in a second act. Thus the "reference" (in Fregean parlance) was called the "first intention" of an expression, and the "sense" the *intentio secunda*. The Fregean paradox that the sense of an expression can never be known qua sense, but only as a referent, never as a "concept," but only as transposed by reflection into the character of an "object" is well known, and has a long prehistory. The reliance on the complex of relations that arise when the activity of reflection or "thought" is itself considered as an object of thought constitutes of course a primary matrix, and associated dynamic, of correlation of subjects, objects, Thought and Extension, infinite and finite, from Plato and Aristotle on.

d. *Égalité de principe, isonomie*: "Equality" of principle seems rather odd in English, caught between a quantitative sense that is rather incongruous, and a more general sense that is in English (but not in French) more or less restricted to the moral order of rights, and *equally* incongruous. What is in question is that *congruence* of incongruities expressed here by "equally." Indeed the figure of "congruence," borrowed from geometry, fits fairly precisely, since what is in question is just two parallel "geometrically" developed structures (of "internal" Thought and "external" Extension) whose Spinozist "geometry" is identical, if terms in one "series" are exchanged throughout for corresponding terms in the other series.

e. The examples here all allude to the most fundamental "elements" of the Euclidean geometry that provides the form or frame of Spinoza's system. Thus the "straight line" is defined by Euclid precisely as a line all of whose parts have the same form as ("lie evenly with") the whole line: and this "straightness" is the simplest "link" that can obtain between the points of a line.

f. *Terrain d'affrontement* is both a military metaphor, and a physical image; to find an English equivalent, I have had to narrow the "area" or "field" of confrontation to a line, and temper somewhat the rather too adversarial "confrontation."

g. I take the quotation marks to signal an allusion to the basic (or rather "apical") Neoplatonic figure of the One "descending" into appearance or expression through the process of division and differentiation first expressed in the primary Triad or Trinity.

h. Curley has "infinite attributes," but it is not then clear whether "infinite" qualifies the attributes individually (as each infinite) or collectively (as an infinity).

i. *"Comprise"*: The quotation marks allude, according to Deleuze, to Spinoza's own terms at II.7, but they also perhaps underline the interplay of two senses of the French word: the inanimate sense of included, "comprised," and the "mental" sense of comprehension, usually translated as "understood." All languages appear to use the "extensional" figure of comprising as an image of "intensional" mental comprehension, and the duality of the image here underlines the "parallelism" of the intensional and extensional "series" of inclusion and exclusion.

CHAPTER SEVEN

a. To speak of "conditions" of the expression of substance might suggest that these are somehow actually, ontologically, prior to substance or (what is the same, being "necessary") its expression. We also speak of "conditions" for asserting certain things of substance and its expression. I have not always been quite sure where Deleuze's "conditions" are logical (or epistemological) conditions, ontological "conditions" in the sense of preconditions or ontological "conditions" in the Scholastic sense of the "postpredicament" of "habit" or "condition" that must always specify an activity and differentiate it from the range of other potential activities of which something is capable, if the power (potential, capacity) of the thing is to pass into act. I have construed several doubtful cases in this last sense. Spinoza's "attributes" are universal "conditions" of the sole substance which is Being itself, his "modes" variable "conditions" or "habits," different conditions of substance, different ways of it being actualized, "taking place." The Scholastics' "transcendentals" (one, good, true) were universal necessary "conditions" of actuality, of being, as such: "convertible" with being (and one another) in that each might be asserted of anything said to be. One might perhaps say that the complementary orders of ontological and epistemological "conditions," of "explication" and "implication," were "invertible" rather than convertible. Deleuze recognizes that "The whole question of conditions is very difficult and confusing," and adds that "Substance is of course unconditioned, but may still have internal conditions which relate to it in their totality (as the sum of all conditions)."

b. *Ergo ens, quod infinita infinitis modis cogitare potest, est necessario virtute cogitandi infinitum*: Curley takes *modi* "informally" here ("ways"), and *virtute cogitandi* as "in its power of thinking," rather than as an instrumental use of the ablative.

CHAPTER EIGHT

a. *Béatitude*: Curley follows earlier translators in rendering Spinoza's Latin term *beatitudo* as "blessedness," but the word sits rather uneasily with Deleuze's presentation of Spinoza (he remarks that "blessed" seems to me a very unfortunate translation of *beatus*"). The primary meaning of the term coined by Cicero (as of its Dutch equivalents *zaligheid*, *gelukzaligheid* – cf. German *seligkeit*, *glückseligkeit*) which marks the ultimate goal of Spinoza's philosophy, is simply "happiness," and that happiness is identified by Deleuze as the freeing of the mind from an essentially "passive" fixation in anthropomorphic religiosity. The passive participle "blessed" has a connotation of "arbitrary" dispensations of inscrutable grace, whereas Deleuze's final chapter presents Spinoza's vision of happiness as the leaving behind of "religious" fears of arbitrary divine judgment, along with all other "sad" passions. "Bless" is etymologically cognate with "blood" and has its roots in that "primitive" religion of fear and sacrifice which Spinoza takes as the lowest form of the anthropomorphism that is the greatest obstacle to happiness. "Happy" rather than "blessed" activity is the natural converse of "sad" passion, and I would happily render *beatitudo* simply by "happiness," had not Spinoza's French translators and Deleuze used *béatitude* rather than *bonheur*. Perhaps the latter term (a catchword of the French Enlightenment) is slightly anachronistic; Spinoza, after all, used the more "cosmic" *beatitudo* rather than *laetitia* or *felicitas* to designate "complete" felicity, or happiness "of the third kind." (Deleuze wondered if one could render *beatitudo* by White-head's "enjoyment": "for doesn't enjoyment sometimes rise to mystical heights?" But that would require an abandonment of the distinction between Spinozist "joy" in general and a beatific joy or *jouissance* – the full possession of joy in a sort of dispossession of oneself.)

b. For the dual sense of "reflect" here (as a sort of impersonal reflexivity of ideas as such, rather like the physical reflection of light, and as "our" reflection "on" the content), cf. Chapter 6, note c. The argument brought out here by Deleuze is, of course, against just this false dichotomy between the imaginary autonomy of our thinking "I," and the radical reflexivity of ideas "in themselves." We are "in" them as a "spiritual automaton" directed by their free process of "reflection," rather than they "in" us, as products of a reflection that we wrongly think of as a sort of arbitrary whim of the thinker.

c. *Expliquer l'essence, comprendre la chose par sa cause*: In translating the passages cited by Deleuze here, Curley uses "explain" for *explicare* and "include" for *comprehendere*: but this presents only the "intensional" side of the former term, and the "extensional" side of the latter, while Deleuze emphasizes the dual character of the first (by setting it within quotation marks), and the "intensional" or psychological character of the second (cf. Chapter 6, note i). I have tried to carry the characteristic duality of Spinoza's Latin terms over into "explicate" and "comprehend": it would, I think, be even more forced to follow Curley here, and render the second phrase above by "*include* the thing through its cause."

d. The translator's emendations rejected by Deleuze, here and in his previous note, are adopted by Curley, who provides argument and authority for the revisions in his notes at I.21–22, 41. (Deleuze, although rejecting Koyré's reading at CU 46, does in fact give the text as emended to conform with that reading; but I have restored the original order insisted on by Deleuze at CU 99: Curley has "it is required, and reason demands, that we ask as soon as possible").

CHAPTER NINE

a. *Contre-épreuve*: In its sole original sense an engraver's "counter-proof" taken to check against his plate by "offsetting" a fresh proof impression onto another sheet of paper (restoring the lateral inversion of the design as engraved on the plate). More recently it has also come to designate a scientist's verification of a result by the failure of an experiment designed to disprove it. Deleuze uses it in the figurative sense of a reverse or converse of a chain of consequences (as invoked for example in "indirect proof" which shows the absurdity of the negative of a proposition – proof *modus tollendo tollens* rather than *ponendo ponens* in Scholastic terminology).

b. The French "affection" normally has (like "modification" in both French and English) the sense both of a process (corresponding to the Scholastic *affectio*) and the result of that process (*affectus*). The latter sense is usually rendered in English by "affect," a correlate of "effect": an affect is "inwardly" directed toward an object as its final cause, an effect "outwardly" caused by an object as its efficient cause – for Spinoza they are merely two aspects of the same process. *Affect* was also the French equivalent of *affectus* until the sixteenth century, and has

413

recently been reintroduced in a related sense by French psychologists (borrowing from the German *Affekt*), followed by Deleuze himself in his study of cinema. Spinoza generally reserves *affectus* for our "second level" affection by an affection itself (although his usage is not altogether consistent: cf. Curley's note, p. 625), and Deleuze generally renders this as *sentiment*. (I in turn always translate *sentiment* as "feeling," and have changed Curley's "affects" to "feelings" to accord with Deleuze's terminology, except on the very few occasions where Deleuze himself retains *affect* [e.g., footnote 8 below]).

CHAPTER TEN

a. *Inventé*: Discovered or "invented" in the sense of an *ars inveniendi*, a way of generating new results which take one substantially beyond the information from which one begins – but in the Aristotelian tradition such *inventio*, precisely because it takes one beyond one's starting point, lacks the necessity guaranteed by deductive proof.

b. *Communauté*: Community in the literal sense of something common to all, but perhaps also community as the collective unity of the beings that share this common being. Deleuze notes that "formal" must here be understood "in the specific sense of 'considered in terms of form': it is being *qua* being that is common to all forms – a common being in various forms. The *formalis*, *formaliter* of Scotus."

CHAPTER ELEVEN

a. I have given here a literal translation of Bréhier's French version of the passage, since it cannot be reconciled with the English versions of MacKenna or Armstrong. Thus Bréhier translates *kai to pantachou ekei tithemetha* as *puis nous mettons* là-bas *ce qui devrait être partout*, taking *ekei* to be an instance of Plotinus's use of the word to indicate the One simply as *there* (a use which is elsewhere rendered "There" by MacKenna, "there" by Armstrong). Armstrong gives the whole passage as follows: "But since we put 'being' in the perceptible, we also put 'everywhere' there too, and since we think the perceptible is large we are puzzled about how that other nature spreads itself out in a largeness of this extent. But this which is called large is little, that is large, if, as we suppose, it reaches as a whole every part of this [perceptible All]" (*Enneads*, trans. Armstrong, London and Cambridge, Mass.: Loeb Classical Library, 1966–88, VI.279–281).

The unsuitability of MacKenna's idiosyncratic version as a substitute for Bréhier's French may be illustrated by his translation of the present passage: "It is our way to limit Being to the sense-known and therefore to think of omnipresence in terms of the concrete; in our overestimate of the sensible, we question how that other Nature can reach over such vastness; but our great is small, and this, small to us is great; it reaches integrally to every point of our universe" (3rd ed., revised. London: Page, 1959, p. 520).

b. *Conversion* (Latin *conversio*, Greek *epistrophē*): A conversion through "reversion" toward that from which it "proceeds" (*processio*, *proōdos*). A thing "remains" itself (*immanentia*, *monē*) only by the mirroring in it of these two complementary directions of "explication" and "implication" (cf., e.g., Proclus's *Elements of Theology*, with Dodds's introduction and commentary, 2nd ed., Oxford, 1963).

c. I.e., 137b–160c, *ei hen esti.* . . .

d. Armstrong has "Intellect" rather than "Intelligence," MacKenna has "Intellectual Principle."

e. Armstrong and MacKenna here use "unfold," but neither treats the verb *exelittein* and its cognates as having any systematic function in the *Enneads*, both translating it very variously in various other contexts.

f. *Esti mē hētton on huparchon hētton einai hen*: Armstrong's rendering is "It is possible to have no less real an existence, but to be less one" (VI.147); MacKenna's, "Less unity may not mean less Being."

g. "Deus ergo est omnia complicans in hoc, quod omnia in eo; est omnia explicans in hoc, quia ipse in omnibus" (ed. Gabriel, Vienna, 1964, I.332). Heron (*On Learned Ignorance*, London, 1954, p. 77) translates this crucial sentence "God . . . envelops all in the sense that all is found in Him; He is the development of all in the sense that He is found in all." Hopkins's version (Minneapolis 1981, p. 94) runs, "God is the enfolding of all things in that all things

415

are in Him; and he is the unfolding of all things in that He is in all things." I have
followed the French translation and Deleuze in remaining closer to Cusanus's
complicatio and *explicatio*, and the more "radical" complex of senses or dimensions embodied in this couple.

h. Armstrong here translates *exeilixen* as "unrolled" (III.387: I have added
the words "thereby" and "principle," which Bréhier's French translation takes
as implicit in the Greek). MacKenna's version runs, "Desiring universal possession, it flung itself outward, though it were better had it never known the desire
by which the Secondary came into being."

i. "What explicates itself [*ho d'exelittei heauto*] is multiple": Armstrong has
"That which explicates itself must be many" (V.109); MacKenna, "Anything capable of analyzing its content must be a manifold" [392].

j. Armstrong has "And what that centre is like is revealed through the lines;
it is as if it was spread out without having been spread out."

k. *Comprend*: "Comprises," once again, both in the inner "space" of Thought
and intellectual "comprehension," and the outward physical space of Extension
and physical "inclusion." I am not sure how far the comprehension here is one
of "understanding," and how far a vaguer figural sense with no specific implications for whether or not the idea of God itself "understands" anything.

CHAPTER TWELVE

a. Deleuze insists that not only *étendue* has what he calls in French *extension*. There is a difficulty here: whereas in French the Latin "processes" of
cogitatio and *extensio* are both usually rendered by the past participles (*pensée*
and *étendue*) of the corresponding French verbs, English follows the French
model in the first case (with the past participle "Thought," rather than "Cogi-
tation" or "Thinking"), but the Latin in the second: "Extension," rather than
"The Extended." The latter form would appear more appropriate in English to
the *result* of the process of "Extension": to the mediate infinite mode of Extension, rather than that prime activity or actuality itself, dynamically articulated
in its immediate infinite mode, the "laws of motion." In *Difference and Repetition*, Deleuze follows Bergson in opposing *étendue* as result (*extensum*), to

extension (*extensio*) as actuality, (and I think there is sometimes an echo of such *extensum* in the *étendue* of the present "complementary" study).

Deleuze goes on to find in Spinoza a rather Bergsonian intension or intensity of modal essence, and a corresponding "extensity" or extension of modal existence, prior to the traditional "intensional' or "intentional" composition of (inward) thoughts and "extensive" composition of (outer) bodies. This requires a variant reading (this chapter, notes 8, c) of a passage that Deleuze construes as referring to an *existence* of modal essences themselves, and (I think) a "numerical" interpretation of the "infinity" of the divine attributes as "infinitely many" (for a brief discussion of the latter question, see Wolf's note to Letter 64; Deleuze remarks that "There is, indeed, a difficulty. How can we speak of *two* powers on a level to which number does not apply? But the difficulty may perhaps be more a verbal than a real one."). The difficulty of finding a systematic distinction in Spinoza between an "ontological" axis of intensive essence and extensive existence, articulated as a scale of degrees of power, and an "epistemological" axis of intentional ideas and their embodiment in extended objects, seems to me to be reflected in rather odd mixtures of different orders of *inesse*, different ways of one thing "being in" another (cf. Chapter 13, notes a, d, f). That is to say, the "intensive" composition of essences seems sometimes to draw on the language of the "intensional" composition of forms in thought, and the "extensive" composition of existence seems to draw on the language of "outward" extension. Spinoza himself never speaks of "parts" as "intensive" or "extensive" (and it is not clear just what the Latin adjectives would be). He only qualifies different orders of composition contextually, by using the genitive of the particular "whole" in question: *pars extensionis, pars substantiae extensae, pars naturae, pars Dei...pars mentis, pars imaginationis, pars totius universi* and so on (and *extrinsecus* qualifies only *denominatio* and *notio*).

Deleuze notes that "It is quite true that one doesn't, strictly speaking, find *intensity* in Spinoza. But *potentia* and *vis* cannot be understood in terms of extension. And *potentia*, being essentially variable, showing increase and diminution, having degrees in relation to finite modes, is an intensity. If Spinoza doesn't use this word, current up to the time of Descartes, I imagine this is because he doesn't want to *appear* to be returning to a Precartesian physics. Leibniz is less concerned by such worries. And does one not find in Spinoza the expression '*pars potentiae* divinae'?"

If one is to systematize Spinoza's language of "composition" one might equally well, perhaps, equate the "intensive" composition of essences with the intentional composition of corresponding thoughts and definitions, and the "extensive" composition of existing modes with the extensional composition of their "embodiments," interpreting the "infinity" of attributes as just the "absolute" complementarity of intensional composition (one thought "being in" another logically) and extensional composition (one body "being in" another physically) — as the principle that the radical complementarity of these two "sides" ("inner" and "outer") of "being-in" is itself in no sense determined "from outside," but a correlate of the bare form of attribution (the initial complex, then, of "expression" itself). It is generally Spinoza's correspondents, rather than Spinoza, who take a "numerical" view of the "infinity" of attributes, and "the other attributes" serve no *practical* role in the system. Indeed it is the practical indifference of this question of the relation of Thought and Extension that no doubt explains why Spinoza himself did not systematically resolve it, beyond insisting on a general structural "parallellism" of the two orders of "internal" and "external" composition.

b. I have used Wolf's translation here, since his terminology is closer than Curley's [205] to that of the French version used by Deleuze, with its various echoes in Deleuze's own text (thus for "in virtue...depend": Curley has "by the force of the cause in which they inhere"). I have also rendered the two occurrences of *certae* as "certain things...certain others..." (rather than Wolf's "some...some...") to accord with Deleuze's version.

c. I think Deleuze is suggesting in his note here that the two instances of the feminine genitive (*suae*) of the (singular *or* plural) third person Latin possessive *suus* must refer to the grammatical subject of the sentence, *essentia sua*, since in general such a genitive can only be taken to refer to something different from the subject of a phrase when the reference is clearly *not* to the subject. Then, since the referent here *could* be construed as the (feminine) subject,

it *must* be. It might perhaps be argued by Curley and others, who adopt the traditional construal of the sentence, that "things" (also feminine) are already the
referent of the first genitive in the sentence ("their essence"), and are indeed the
"logical" (if not grammatical) subject of the whole proposition; and further,
that since Deleuze uses his own reading of this "mistranslated" sentence to introduce into Spinoza's argument in the *Ethics* the question of the modal essence's
own existence, and thereby to suggest that this might here (and so *must*) be what
Spinoza is talking about, his criticism is essentially circular. (They might perhaps also argue that although *we* do not know at this point that essence does
not endure, Spinoza presumably *did* know this, and would have little reason to
introduce a complication that would have no sense in the completed system.)

CHAPTER THIRTEEN

a. "In Extension" here seems to mean "in the order of extended bodies," for
to exist is elsewhere said to mean "to exist *outside* the attribute" (note c, below).

b. The sum of the unequal *orthogonal* distances between two given *nested*
nonconcentric circles.

c. "Relation" here translates the French *rapport*, which in turn translates
Spinoza's Latin *ratio* (*motus et quietus*), which Curley renders "ratio." Now
rapport has, among its many senses, that of a numerical ratio; the Latin *ratio*,
on the other hand, also has the general sense of the "reason" (essence, nature,
ground, cause, idea...) of some thing. While the characteristic relation between
the elementary parts of a simple body must be defined simply by some invariant "relation" (such as an equation of motion, a *ratio* or *lex cohaerantiae* or
unionis) between the variant external motions of those parts, since there are in
principle no "internal" differences between those incomposite parts – and while
bodies whose parts are themselves composite must of course ultimately be
"explicable" simply in terms of such elementary relations – it is not clear that
Spinoza's *ratio* is here quite as specific as a simple numerical "ratio" of component movements (one might note that, at the other end of the scale, the *idea
Dei* is called by Spinoza *infinita ratio*). Furthermore, the "relation" of the parts
of a highly composite body might be characterized, without a full' "explication,"

in terms of components (blood, bone and so on) that *were* "internally" (compositionally) different: this would in no sense be a mere quantitative "ratio." Deleuze uses *rapport* to cover all levels of constitutive "relations," as well as various other relations. There is sometimes a quantitative implication absent from the English "relation," but even were it possible to uniformly divide instances of *rapport* with such a resonance from those without it, and distinguish the first group as "ratios," this would quite disrupt the network of relations, the "reason" indeed, of the various different orders of *rapport*.

d. *Dans l'étendue*, "in" Extension: But is existing, then, the same as being "in," or "having," extension?

e. *Position* (Latin *positio*): It is difficult not to translate this and cognate terms as though what is being considered is a logical process of "positing" (here, "two ways of positing modes"), rather than the ontological "place" of essence and existence in Spinoza's scheme or Universe. But the same difficulty is *posed* by the French original, and I have tried simply to carry it over into English as it stands. Deleuze remarks that "modal *position* is at once ontological, logical, physical and psychological."

f. "Once they are posited outside their attribute": Here again, being "in" an attribute appears to be more or less the same as being conceived in, being formally in, having one's essence in, the attribute, and "attributes" appear rather like the mapping of Thought and Extension *into* Thought: being "in" them, then, is just being-in in the logical or conceptual sense. In the other sense of being-in, being "outside" the attributes seems rather like being (physically) "in" (the attribute of) Extension, *its* space (and time) – "extensively," that is, in the mode of being-in proper to that attribute (rather than to Thought and its logical or conceptual "inclusion"). Being "outside" "The Concept" then bears an interesting resemblance to Hegel's conception of the order of *contingency* – an order in principle excluded from Spinoza's deterministic system.

CHAPTER FOURTEEN

a. The French version has the "nontechnical" *façons*, "ways" (in which the body is affected).

b. *Pâtir*, to "suffer": A *passion* is something one suffers or undergoes *passively* (if not necessarily impassively, nor yet necessarily passionately). We suffer what is done to, or happens to, us; and our passions are opposed to our actions, what we "do" to something else, as agent rather than "patient." English does not have (as does French) a complex of cognate terms with which to render all the Latin cognates of *passio*, but the relations between these various aspects of "passive" suffering should be kept in mind.

c. Cf. Chapter 9, note b.

d. I have restored the traditional "patient" and "suffering," where Curley uses the circumlocutions "the one who is acted on" and "being acted on."

e. "Final" in the sense of being determined by ends, by "final causality."

CHAPTER FIFTEEN

a. Wolf has, "although it varies in infinite modes" but the French translation used by Deleuze takes this occurrence of *modus* as "nontechnical," rendering it by *manière*. The two senses here more or less coincide.

b. "Can be combined," presumably, in the sense that the destroying body and the decomposed parts of what it destroys can be together integrated without further conflict in the unitary "face of the whole universe." For it is hardly a characteristic of destruction in general (as opposed to assimilation – the "nutritional" decomposition of food, for example) that the results of destruction are incorporated with the destructive agent into a new "finite" individual unity, into a unitary "product" of the destruction. It might also be noted that the French use of the "middle" voice here, *se composant, se compose* is ambiguous between an indicative and a modal sense (between "is combined" and "can be combined").

c. It might be objected that *elastic* collision (of, say, billiard balls) has been defined above as an encounter in which there is no change of relations.

d. *Lignes*: "Lines" in a rather figurative sense.

e. In the French, extrinsic *relations*, as (implicitly) distinguished from the *rapports* (extrinsic and intrinsic), in which individual essences are expressed. A *rapport* on the level of finite individual bodies is, of course, in principle resoluble into a nested system of relations ultimately explicable simply in terms of the "purely extrinsic" relations of the body's infinitesimal elementary components. Yet the sense of "formula" or "ratio" of movement-and-rest, present as noted above (Chapter 13, note d) in *rapport*, but absent from mere *relation*, already on the elementary level introduces a distinction between "expressive" relations that define a certain invariance of physical structure, stable until disrupted "from outside," and the merely transient unstable "relation" exemplified in such disruptive interaction. The system of "expressive" relations "implicates" the whole unitary order of nested structures within the universal structure that is the invariant "face of the whole Universe" outwardly reflecting the "intensive" unity of the attribute of Extension. There is no alternative to rendering *rapport* by "relation," nor any other suitable English term for *relation*, but the sense of any particular "relation" is, I think, always conveyed by the context in which the word appears.

f. *Chatouillements*: As Curley notes [650–51], this is the term used by Descartes in the *Passions of the Soul* for the "excitement" which his Latin translator rendered by *titillatio*. Curley, in turn, renders Spinoza's use of the Latin term by "pleasure" – but this seems to me rather more general than either the French or Latin words, which both have strong connotations of inconsequential ephemeral distraction.

g. Here, and below, "full possession" translates *possession formelle*: strict, true, definitive possession.

h. "Natural understanding" has been taken from Wolf's version [150], being closer than Curley's "natural intellect" to the French *lumière naturelle*.

CHAPTER SIXTEEN

a. Natural "right" is here opposed to natural "law," very roughly as an internal or "subjective" principle to an external or "objective" one; but "natural law" is the traditional English translation of *jus naturale* (or *naturae*) and *droit naturel* (or *de la nature*). Indeed *jus* or *droit* (cf. German and Dutch *Recht*) is the normal term for "law" as a principle or system of principles (sometimes synonymous with *lex* or *loi*, sometimes perhaps with a sense of something derived from principles of "right," as against positive "laws" as "unnatural" constraints). Some senses of *droit* are naturally conveyed by "law," so I have sometimes used "rights" in the plural to convey the sense of a *system* of rights.

b. This is the sole occurence of the expression in the *Ethics*, and the familiar *suum utile* is substituted for the *proprium utile* of the enunciation in the closing statement of "what was to be proved" (*quod erat demonstrandum*). Curley simply translates both expressions "one's own advantage," presumably taking *proprium* as a mere variant of *suum*, introduced because *suum* had itself already appeared earlier in the same sentence (and departing – it seems to me unnecessarily – from the set of terms cognate with "useful"). The French (*Pléïade*) translator, on the other hand, departs here from the usual translation of *suum utile* (as *ce qui nous est utile*), to render both expressions by *l'utile qui nous est propre*, the utility "proper to us." Although *proprium* must here be considered *logically* equivalent to *suum* in the order of demonstrations, the resonance of "proper or true" (as opposed to apparent) utility, brought out by the French translation and emphasized here and below by Deleuze, may be taken to play a significant part in the network of sense later identified by Deleuze as constituting a second articulation of the *Ethics* parallel to or "beneath" the logical order of demonstration, and best seen in the system of scholia. Thus the resonance here of a man's "true" utility, his utility in the "proper sense" of the word, belonging to him properly or essentially, like the "proper motion" of a star – as opposed to an imaginary utility accidentally appearing to attach to some object or end in some particular configuration of his body in relation to surrounding bodies – echoes the *suum utile, quod revera utile est* ("his own advantage, what is really useful to him" [555]) of the Scholium to IV.18, a couple of pages above (and cf. TP i: *hominum verum utile*; iv: *nostrum utile revera*; v: *quod vere utile*).

c. The French *culture* has a sense of "cultivation," retained in our "agriculture," "apiculture" and so on, but largely lost in our "culture" itself.

d. *Civitas*: A term introduced into Latin philosophical vocabulary by analogy with the Greek *polis*, which of course meant both "city" and "state" when the two were (metonymically) equivalent, and "Athens" was both a town and the region (including other towns) administered from that town. Curley chooses

423

to translate the Latin throughout by "state," but since Deleuze maintains both terms, generally using *cité* rather than *état*, I have always translated the former "City" (capitalized to emphasize the character of a polity) and the latter "state," adapting Curley's translations where appropriate.

CHAPTER SEVENTEEN

a. The French *occasion* retains (as is seen in its common use to designate a shopping "bargain") the sense of (etymologically analogous) "chance" or "opportunity" present in the Latin *occasio*, but largely lost in the English homonym, and I have in a few constructions translated it by "chance" or "opportunity" rather than "occasion."

CHAPTER EIGHTEEN

a. Latin *experientia vaga*: The French translation used by Deleuze is *expérience vague*, and in order to accommodate Deleuze's etymological reflection here I have had to return to Boyle's "vague experience." Curley translates the expression "random experience," but this, while perhaps closer to the sense of "wandering" (*vagare*) is less close to the French, and has a dissimilar etymology.

b. The text as given by Deleuze adopts Joachim's variant reading "at one time," noted but rejected by Curley, who gives "from time to time."

c. To his translation of this passage Curley adds a note expressing his "surprise" at seeing " 'imagine' used in connection with knowledge which is necessarily adequate."

CONCLUSION

a. *Maudite*: The sense of an intrusion, repressed or exorcized, banished to the dark side of things, is reflected in the following sentences.

b. *Épaisseur*, most literally a "thickness": Here a density, opacity, "substantiality" or "substance" (not ontological – more a "physical" substance or materiality), a tangibility, a physical reality that is not a mere reflection of the way the word or theme "nature" is inscribed and articulated in some abstract logical pattern.

c. *Adéquat à*, makes man "adequate to" God. Etymologically this implies a certain *equality*: a "proportion" or equality of measure, ontologically or epistemologically, without any equality of finite and infinite essence (or, indeed, any formal "analogy" between finite and infinite): man and God become "commensurate" in the sense that the human and divine "spheres" are brought within a single "combinatorial" frame (rather as Galileo had *physically* integrated Heaven and Earth) whose *unity* is in principle accessible to "the spiritual automaton," to man's mind, even if its infinite *variety* is not. This echoes the extended discussion of the "adequacy" of ideas – and the possibility of our reaching an "adequate" idea of God, if not of all that is "implicated" in him – which runs through much of the earlier part of the book.

d. Or perhaps "involute," enfolded.

e. *Identité* must here, I think, be taken as marking the *unity* of form and content in ideas and their concatenation, without however eliding the fundamental distinction between the two aspects or components differently "identified" in that union (thus a couple of pages above Deleuze speaks in a similar context of the *unité* of these two elements in the "spiritual automaton"). In English "identity" does not seem to allow the retention of any fundamental distinction between the two terms here *referred* to an identical reality or modification of reality. (One might wonder, in passing, just how the Scholastic "metaphysical distinction" of form and content fits within the Spinozist system of distinctions as expounded by Deleuze.)

f. Loemker has "since *our substance* expresses..." but the text given by Gerhardt, and in Lestienne's critical edition (3rd ed., Paris, 1962, p. 54) runs: "On pourrait appeler notre essence [MS variant: *ou idée*], ce qui comprend tout ce que nous exprimons, et comme *elle* exprime notre union avec Dieu même, elle n'a point de limites et rien ne la passe." Deleuze has "rien ne l'excède," which seems equivalent to the standard text: Leibniz is identifying what we *call* "supernatural" as what lies in the "obscure background" beyond our clear knowledge of Nature, and insisting that although some things are *apparently* outside the order of Nature, nothing is *essentially* supernatural.

g. *La compréhension et...l'extension de la catégorie d'expression*: Roughly (I think) the "intension" and "extension" of the "category": what is "understood" as belonging to the concept (as its meaning), and what "falls under it" as a case of "expression," its application. Deleuze comments that "I call *expression* a 'category' because it applies to everything: substance, attribute, mode, thing, idea...."

h. *Pour le mieux*: I think there is an echo here of Voltaire's famous caricature of Leibniz and Wolff: "Tout est pour le mieux dans le meilleur des mondes possibles" ("All is *for the best* in the best of all possible worlds").

i. *Égal*: "Equal" does not in English bear quite the same sense of some *respect* in which, or viewpoint from which, the two terms are, or may be considered, equal (one of the terms here is of course the system of "points of view" on the other). "Equality," without some element of "valence" to suggest equality in some respect, seems to me rather too close to an identity.

j. The various registers of the terms used by Deleuze here, emphasized by his correlative appositions, *envelopper*, *impliquer*, *enrouler* and *développer*, *expliquer*, *dérouler* (involution–evolution, implication–explication and so on) cannot (as was noted in relation to a similar passage in the Introduction) be exactly transposed term-for-term into English equivalents. But the English appositions are I think equivalent, insofar as the device is, in each language, precisely an attempt to see in particular "centers" of sense or figural interplay, an "expressive" order of spatial metaphor that is taken to articulate each "system of expression," each language – an attempt to "express" expression itself.

k. Deleuze has confirmed that there is a suggestion here of these (knowing and being) being two "powers" of the absolute, rather in the sense that one speaks of the "square" and "cube" of a number as two of its "powers": cf. Chapter 7, note 12.

l. *Le sens*: The best commentary on this term is the next book written by Deleuze, his *Logic of Sense*. Since *sens* marks precisely the interplay of the different registers in a word – its various "senses" in the various "series" of terms whose intersection it constitutes, and whose interplay is mapped in the new "logic" of 1969 – I will not attempt any sketch of the various registers of the French word *sens* itself, and let this question mark the close of this book – and the "academic" phase of Deleuze's career – and mark the transition into the new phase which opens with his *Logic of Sense* and his move to Vincennes.

APPENDIX

a. "*Doubler*": The quotation marks presumably indicate that various senses of the word (to line a garment, fold a piece of paper, double ranks, double for someone, and so on) may be taken as suggestions as to what Deleuze intends by it, but that its sense here is dependent on its context.

b. *Goûts*.

Final Note. I would like, finally, to note the angelic patience of my editor, Rennie Childress, and the heroically indulgent collaboration of my friend Hugh Tomlinson, and to thank both for their faith that I would eventually get to this last full stop.

Index

Species, 36, 42, 45, 64, 65, 67, 152,
161, 182, 199, 257, 277, 327.
Spiritual automaton, 115, 132, 140,
152–53, 160, 322, 324, 326, 335.
State, 265–66; civil, 259ff., 266–67,
289–90, 294.
Stoicism, 62, 174, 258.
Structure (anatomical), 278.
Suarez, 29, 65.
Sufficient reason, 72, 73–74, 81, 85,
99, 119, 134, 135, 139, 152, 228,
321–22, 323.
summum bonum, 51.
Sun, 148, 149–50.
Superstition, 270–71.
Symbolization, 232, 233, 234, 331,
332; symbolism, 54, 57, 79, 178,
328, 329.

TETRAGRAMMATON, 58.
Theism, 101, 253.
Theology, 55ff., 63, 66, 93, 259,
322–23; negative, 53–54, 165, 172,
173, 178.
Thomism, 63, 163.
Thought, 14, 30, 46, 50, 55, 59, 81,
87, 90, 106, 113, 114, 115, 118–21,
122ff., 127, 130, 131, 133, 136,
142–43, 145, 153, 177, 192, 257.
Transcendence, 53, 109, 172, 176,
177–78, 232, 256, 269, 277, 322.
Triads, first (modal), 19, 27ff., 43–44,
82, 111; second (absolute), 81–82;
third (power), 95.
Truth, 130ff., 140ff., 149, 151–52,
161, 321; *see also* Adequacy.
Tschirnhaus, Ehrenfried Walther von,
20–21, 114.
Tyranny, 270.

UNITY, 16, 173, 182, 329, 331.
Universals, 161, 277, 279, 281–82,
286–87, 289, 292–93, 298–99;
negative, 34.
Univocity, 48–49, 59, 63–64, 66–67,

70, 72, 81, 102–03, 104, 142, 165–
66, 167, 180–81, 182, 196–97,
300, 330, 332–33.
Utility, 239, 240–41, 243, 248, 261,
263–64.
uytdrukken, uytbeelden, 15.

VACUUM, 33, 204.
vertoonen, 15.
Violence, 169–70, 249–50, 268.
vis, 88–89.
Voice of God, 44–45, 123.

WISDOM, 123.
Word, 44, 45, 49, 50, 56, 57, 123,
176, 177, 179, 185, 323.

Index of Textual References

437

*All numbers in parentheses refer to
the page number of vol. II of the
Van Vloten and Land edition.

441

*All numbers in brackets refer to
the page number of vol. II of the
Van Vloten and Land edition.

Universal Spirit," 365n17

Zone Books series design by Bruce Mau
Type composed by Archetype
Printed and bound by Maple Press